*New Beacon Bible Commentary

JOSHUA
A Commentary in the Wesleyan Tradition

Stephen J. Lennox

BEACON HILL PRESS
OF KANSAS CITY

Copyright 2015
by Beacon Hill Press of Kansas City

ISBN 978-0-8341-3492-8

Cover Design: J.R. Caines
Interior Design: Sharon Page

Unless otherwise indicated all Scripture quotations are from the *Holy Bible, New International Version*® (NIV®). Copyright © 1973, 1978, 1984, 2011 by Biblica, Inc.™ Used by permission. All rights reserved worldwide.

The following versions of Scripture are in the public domain:

American Standard Version (ASV).

King James Version (KJV).

The following copyrighted versions of the Bible are used by permission:

The Holy Bible, English Standard Version (ESV), copyright © 2001 by Crossway Bibles, a division of Good News Publishers. All rights reserved.

Good News Translation® (*Today's English Version*, Second Edition) (GNT). Copyright © 1992 American Bible Society. All rights reserved.

The *New American Bible, revised edition* (NABRE), © 2010, 1991, 1986, 1970 Confraternity of Christian Doctrine, Washington, D.C. Used by permission of the copyright owner. All Rights Reserved. No part of the New American Bible may be reproduced in any form without permission in writing from the copyright owner.

The *New American Standard Bible*® (NASB®), © copyright The Lockman Foundation 1960, 1962, 1963, 1968, 1971, 1972, 1973, 1975, 1977, 1995.

The *New English Bible* (NEB), © the Delegates of the Oxford University Press and the Syndics of the Cambridge University Press 1961, 1970.

The *New Jerusalem Bible* (NJB), copyright © 1985 by Darton, Longman & Todd, Ltd., and Doubleday, a division of Bantam Doubleday Dell Publishing Group, Inc. Reprinted by permission.

Hebrew-English Tanakh (NJPS), © 2000 by The Jewish Publication Society. All rights reserved.

The *Holy Bible, New Living Translation* (NLT), copyright © 1996, 2004, 2007, 2013 by Tyndale House Foundation. Used by permission of Tyndale House Publishers, Inc., Carol Stream, IL 60188. All rights reserved.

The *New Revised Standard Version* (NRSV) of the Bible, copyright 1989 by the Division of Christian Education of the National Council of the Churches of Christ in the USA. All rights reserved.

Library of Congress Cataloging-in-Publication Data

Lennox, Stephen J.
   New Beacon Bible commentary, Joshua / Stephen J. Lennox.
     pages cm
   Includes bibliographical references.
   ISBN 978-0-8341-3492-8 (pbk.)
  1. Bible. Joshua—Commentaries. I. Title. II. Title: Joshua.
  BS1295.53.L46 2015
  222'.207—dc23

2014047079

DEDICATION

As I was finishing this book I learned of the death of my beloved mentor
and professor, David A. Dorsey (1949-2014). More than anyone else,
Dave taught me to love God with both my heart and my mind.
He modeled an excellence in scholarship and teaching that I strive to attain.
I dedicate this book to his memory.

COMMENTARY EDITORS

General Editors

Alex Varughese
    Ph.D., Drew University
    Professor of Biblical Literature
    Mount Vernon Nazarene University
    Mount Vernon, Ohio

Roger Hahn
    Ph.D., Duke University
    Dean of the Faculty
    Professor of New Testament
    Nazarene Theological Seminary
    Kansas City, Missouri

George Lyons
    Ph.D., Emory University
    Professor of New Testament
    Northwest Nazarene University
    Nampa, Idaho

Section Editors

Joseph Coleson
    Ph.D., Brandeis University
    Professor of Old Testament
    Nazarene Theological Seminary
    Kansas City, Missouri

Robert Branson
    Ph.D., Boston University
    Professor of Biblical Literature
        Emeritus
    Olivet Nazarene University
    Bourbonnais, Illinois

Alex Varughese
    Ph.D., Drew University
    Professor of Biblical Literature
    Mount Vernon Nazarene University
    Mount Vernon, Ohio

Jim Edlin
    Ph.D., Southern Baptist Theological
        Seminary
    Professor of Biblical Literature and
        Languages
    Chair, Division of Religion and
        Philosophy
    MidAmerica Nazarene University
    Olathe, Kansas

Kent Brower
    Ph.D., The University of Manchester
    Vice Principal
    Senior Lecturer in Biblical Studies
    Nazarene Theological College
    Manchester, England

George Lyons
    Ph.D., Emory University
    Professor of New Testament
    Northwest Nazarene University
    Nampa, Idaho

CONTENTS

General Editors' Preface	13
Acknowledgments	15
Abbreviations	16
Bibliography	19
INTRODUCTION	29
A. History of Interpretation	30
1. Inner-Biblical and Intertestamental Readings	30
2. Joshua in the New Testament and Early Church	31
3. Joshua in Rabbinic Thought	31
4. Joshua in the Modern Period	31
a. Source Criticism	32
b. History and Archaeology	35
c. Literary Approaches	37
d. Cultural Factors Shaping the Interpretation of Joshua	38
e. Joshua as Christian Scripture	40
5. Conclusion	40
B. Interpreting Joshua Today	41
1. Introduction	41
2. Joshua as Ancient History	41
3. The Evidence for a Historical Conquest	42
4. Authorship and Dating of the Book of Joshua	45
5. Reading Joshua as Christian Scripture	47
C. Theology of the Book of Joshua	47
1. God Keeps His Promises	47
2. God Fights for His People	49
3. God Works through Humans	50
D. Excursus on the Violence in the Book of Joshua	53
1. Read This Book in Its Historical Context	55
2. Read This Book in Light of God's Revealed Character	57
3. Read This Book in Light of God's Revealed Plan	60
E. Overview	63
F. Purpose	65
G. Outline for Joshua	65
COMMENTARY	67
I. Joshua 1	67
A. God's Marching Orders for Invasion (1:1-9)	68
1. Command to Invade and Promise of Victory (1:1-5)	68
2. Counsels Courage and Obedience to Law (1:6-9)	70

	B. Joshua's Marching Orders for Invasion (1:10-18)	72
	1. Command to Leaders of People (1:10-11)	72
	2. Command to Transjordan Tribes (1:12-15)	73
	3. People's Response (1:16-18)	74
II.	Joshua 2	77
	A. Joshua Instructs Spies to Explore the Land (2:1)	78
	B. Discovery Avoided by Deception (2:2-7)	80
	C. Rooftop Confession of Yahweh's Sovereignty (2:8-14)	81
	D. Escape—with an Oath of Honesty (2:15-23)	85
	E. Report to Joshua: YHWH Has Given Whole Land to Us (2:24)	86
III.	Joshua 3	89
	A. In Camp on East Side of the Jordan (3:1-5)	91
	B. Joshua Instructs Priests to Carry Ark Down to Jordan (3:6-8)	93
	C. Yahweh Stops Jordan and People Begin to Cross (3:9-17)	93
IV.	Joshua 4	97
	A. Erection of Memorial Stones (4:1-9)	99
	B. People Finish Crossing While Jordan Is Stopped (4:10-13)	100
	C. Joshua Instructs Priests to Carry Ark Up Out of Jordan (4:14-18)	101
	D. Encamped West of the Jordan (4:19-24)	102
V.	Joshua 5	107
	A. Introduction (5:1)	108
	B. Circumcision (5:2-9)	108
	C. Passover (5:10-12)	112
	D. Encounter with Commander of Yahweh's Army (5:13-15)	114
VI.	Joshua 6	119
	A. God's Instructions to Joshua (6:1-5)	120
	B. Joshua Delivers Instructions to Priests and People (6:6-7)	123
	C. Day One (6:8-11)	123
	D. Days Two through Six (6:12-14)	124
	E. Day Seven (6:15-21)	124
	F. Aftermath (6:22-27)	125
VII.	Joshua 7	129
	A. Sin and Its Consequences (7:1-5)	129
	1. Achan's Sin (7:1)	129
	2. First Attack on Ai (7:2-5)	130
	B. Removal of Sin (7:6-26)	131
	1. Israel's Response to Military Defeat (7:6-9)	131
	2. God's Explanation and Instructions (7:10-15)	132
	3. Israel Follows God's Instructions (7:16-26)	134

VIII.	Joshua 8	139
	A. Second Battle with Ai (8:1-29)	139
	1. Preparations for the Battle (8:1-13)	139
	2. The Battle (8:14-23)	142
	3. Destruction of Ai (8:24-29)	143
	B. Covenant Renewal at Mount Ebal (8:30-35)	145
IX.	Joshua 9	149
	A. Gibeon's Response to Israel's Victories (9:1-15)	150
	1. Coalition of Kings Responds to Ai (9:1-2)	150
	2. Gibeonites' Response (9:3-15)	151
	B. Punishment of Gibeonites for Their Deceit (9:16-27)	153
	1. Israel's Response (9:16-23)	153
	2. Gibeonites' Submission (9:24-25)	155
	3. Summary (9:26-27)	155
X.	Joshua 10	159
	A. Central Campaign (10:1-27)	160
	1. Coalition against Gibeon (10:1-5)	160
	2. Israel's Defense of Gibeon (10:6-15)	162
	3. Ceremony at Makkedah (10:16-27)	167
	B. Southern Campaign (10:28-39)	169
	C. Summary of Both Campaigns (10:40-43)	171
XI.	Joshua 11	175
	A. Northern Campaign (11:1-15)	177
	1. Very Large Coalition against Israel (11:1-5)	177
	2. Joshua's Response (11:6-15)	179
	B. Summary of Conquest (11:16-23)	181
	1. Conquest of Entire Land (11:16-20)	181
	2. Defeat of the Anakites (11:21-22)	182
	3. Summary of Conquest and Rest from War (11:23)	183
XII.	Joshua 12	185
	A. Conquest of the Transjordan (12:1-6)	186
	1. Introduction (12:1)	186
	2. King Sihon of the Amorites and King Og of the Bashanites (12:2-5)	187
	3. Moses Conquered and Gave to Transjordan Tribes (12:6)	188
	B. Conquest of Canaan (12:7-24)	188
	1. Introduction (12:7-8)	188
	2. List of Kings (12:9-24)	189
XIII.	Joshua 13	197
	A. Introduction to Land Remaining (13:1-7)	199
	B. Land Remaining East of Jordan (13:8-33)	201
	1. Boundaries (13:8-14)	201
	2. Inheritance of Reubenites (13:15-23)	202

	3. Inheritance of the Gadites (13:24-28)	203
	4. Inheritance of the Half-tribe of Manasseh (13:29-31)	203
	5. Summary of Transjordan Allotment (13:32-33)	204
XIV.	Joshua 14	207
	A. Introduction to the Division of the Land West of the Jordan (14:1-5)	208
	1. Introduction (14:1)	208
	2. Assignment by Lot to Nine and a Half Tribes (14:2)	209
	3. Previous Allotment to Two and a Half Tribes and Explanation of How There Came to Be Twelve Tribes (14:3-4)	210
	4. Allotment of Land as Commanded to Moses (14:5)	210
	B. Hebron Given to Caleb (14:6-15)	210
	1. Caleb Requests Land from Joshua (14:6-12)	210
	2. Joshua Grants Caleb's Request (14:13-15)	213
XV.	Joshua 15	217
	A. Boundaries around Judah (15:1-12)	219
	1. Introduction and Southern Boundary (15:1-4)	219
	2. Eastern Boundary and Northern Boundary (15:5-11)	219
	3. Western Boundary (15:12)	220
	B. Caleb's Inheritance (15:13-20)	220
	1. Expulsion of Anakites from Vicinity of Hebron (15:13-17)	220
	2. Land Grant Narrative for Aksah (15:18-19)	221
	3. Summary (15:20)	222
	C. Towns within Judah (15:21-63)	222
	1. Negev Region (15:21-32)	222
	2. Western Foothills (15:33-47)	223
	3. Hill Country (15:48-60)	224
	4. Desert (15:61-62)	225
	5. Unable to Dislodge the Jebusites (15:63)	225
XVI.	Joshua 16—17	229
	A. Overview of Allotment for Cisjordan Josephite Tribes (16:1-4)	230
	1. Southern Boundary (16:1-3)	230
	2. Summary (16:4)	231
	B. Allotment for Ephraim (16:5-10)	231
	1. Boundary for Ephraim's Territory (16:5-9)	231
	2. Boundary Lacunae (16:10)	232
	C. Allotment for Manasseh (17:1-13)	233
	1. Introduction (17:1-2)	233
	2. Daughters of Zelophehad (17:3-6)	233
	3. Boundary for Manasseh's Territory (17:7-10)	234
	4. Manasseh's Cities within Other Tribes (17:11)	235
	5. Boundary Lacunae (17:12-13)	236
	D. Josephite Desire for More Land (17:14-18)	236
	1. Appeal (17:14)	236

	2. Joshua's Response (17:15)	237
	3. Further Protest (17:16)	237
	4. Joshua's Second Response (17:17-18)	237
XVII.	Joshua 18—19	239
	A. Survey and Allotment of the Land (18:1-10)	243
	1. Introduction (18:1-2)	243
	2. Joshua's Instructions to All Israelites (18:3-7)	244
	3. Joshua's Instructions to Surveyors (18:8-9)	245
	4. Land Distributed (18:10)	245
	B. Allotment to Benjamin (18:11-28)	245
	1. Introduction (18:11-20)	245
	2. Town List (18:21-28)	246
	C. Allotment for Simeon (19:1-9)	246
	1. Introduction (19:1)	246
	2. Towns in Simeon (19:2-8a)	247
	3. Summary (19:8b-9)	247
	D. Allotment for Zebulun (19:10-16)	247
	1. Introduction and Boundary List (19:10-14)	247
	2. Town List and Summary (19:15-16)	248
	E. Allotment for Issachar (19:17-23)	248
	F. Allotment for Asher (19:24-31)	248
	G. Allotment for Naphtali (19:32-39)	249
	H. Allotment for Dan (19:40-48)	250
	1. Introduction and Town List (19:40-46)	250
	2. Explanation for Relocation and Summary (19:47-48)	250
	I. Allotment for Joshua (19:49-50)	251
	1. Land Grant to Joshua as Yahweh Commanded (19:49-50a)	251
	2. Grant of Timnath Serah in Ephraim (19:50b)	251
	J. Summary of Final Allotment (19:51)	251
XVIII.	Joshua 20	253
	A. God's Command to Joshua (20:1-6)	254
	1. Introduction (20:1)	254
	2. Command to Joshua (20:2)	254
	3. Purpose of Cities (20:3)	254
	4. Procedure (20:4-6)	256
	B. Designation of Cities of Refuge (20:7-9)	257
	1. Cities in Cisjordan (20:7)	257
	2. Cities in Transjordan (20:8)	258
	3. Purpose of Cities Summarized (20:9)	258
XIX.	Joshua 21	259
	A. Introduction (21:1-3)	261
	B. Summary of Allocation (21:4-8)	262
	1. Lot for the Kohathites (21:4-5)	262

        2. Lot for the Gershonites (21:6) — 263
        3. Lot for the Merarites (21:7) — 263
        4. Summary (21:8) — 263
    C. Towns Allotted by Clan (21:9-42) — 263
        1. Kohathites (21:9-26) — 263
        2. Gershonites (21:27-33) — 265
        3. Merarites (21:34-40) — 266
        4. Summary (21:41-42) — 266
    D. Section Summary (21:43-45) — 266

XX. Joshua 22 — 271
    A. Dismissal (22:1-8) — 273
        1. Joshua Dismisses the Transjordan Tribes with a Call to Remain Faithful (22:1-5) — 273
        2. Joshua's Blessing on the Transjordan Tribes (22:6-8) — 274
    B. Transjordan Tribes Build an Altar (22:9-10) — 275
    C. Israel's Reaction to the Altar (22:11-20) — 277
        1. Israelites Learn of Altar and Muster Army (22:11-12) — 277
        2. Israelites Send Delegation to Inquire (22:13-20) — 277
    D. Transjordan Tribes Defend Their Actions (22:21-29) — 279
        1. Altar Not Built in Rebellion (22:21-23) — 279
        2. Altar Built in Fear of Future Alienation (22:24-29) — 279
    E. Israel Accepts Explanation (22:30-33) — 280
        1. Phinehas and Others Respond (22:30-31) — 280
        2. Phinehas and Others Report Back to Israelites (22:32-33) — 281
    F. Naming of Altar (22:34) — 281

XXI. Joshua 23 — 283
    A. Past Successes and Future Victories (23:1-5) — 284
        1. Introduction (23:1-2a) — 284
        2. Past Successes (23:2b-4) — 285
        3. Future Victories (23:5) — 287
    B. Call to Remain Loyal to Yahweh (23:6-8) — 287
    C. Past Success Should Lead to Future Loyalty (23:9-11) — 288
    D. Warning against Disloyalty to Yahweh (23:12-13) — 289
    E. Past Successes Ensure Future Justice (23:14-16) — 289

XXII. Joshua 24 — 293
    A. Joshua's Farewell Speech (24:1-15) — 294
        1. Preamble (24:1) — 294
        2. Historical Prologue (24:2-13) — 295
        3. Fear Yahweh (24:14-15) — 298
    B. Response (24:16-24) — 299
        1. People: We Will Serve Him (24:16-18) — 299
        2. Joshua: You Are Not Able to Serve Him (24:19-20) — 299
        3. People: Yes, We Will (24:21) — 299

	4. Joshua: Are You Sure? (24:22*a*)	300
	5. People: We Are Sure (24:22*b*)	300
	6. Joshua: Reject Idolatry and Serve Yahweh (24:23)	300
	7. People: We Will Serve Yahweh (24:24)	300
C.	Renewal of Covenant (24:25-28)	300
D.	Final Matters (24:29-33)	302
	1. Death and Burial of Joshua (24:29-30)	302
	2. Israel's Obedience (24:31)	302
	3. Joseph's Burial (24:32)	302
	4. Eleazar's Death (24:33)	303

GENERAL EDITORS' PREFACE

The purpose of the New Beacon Bible Commentary is to make available to pastors and students in the twenty-first century a biblical commentary that reflects the best scholarship in the Wesleyan theological tradition. The commentary project aims to make this scholarship accessible to a wider audience to assist them in their understanding and proclamation of Scripture as God's Word.

Writers of the volumes in this series not only are scholars within the Wesleyan theological tradition and experts in their field but also have special interest in the books assigned to them. Their task is to communicate clearly the critical consensus and the full range of other credible voices who have commented on the Scriptures. Though scholarship and scholarly contribution to the understanding of the Scriptures are key concerns of this series, it is not intended as an academic dialogue within the scholarly community. Commentators of this series constantly aim to demonstrate in their work the significance of the Bible as the church's book and the contemporary relevance and application of the biblical message. The project's overall goal is to make available to the church and for her service the fruits of the labors of scholars who are committed to their Christian faith.

The *New International Version* (NIV) is the reference version of the Bible used in this series; however, the focus of exegetical study and comments is the biblical text in its original language. When the commentary uses the NIV, it is printed in bold. The text printed in bold italics is the translation of the author. Commentators also refer to other translations where the text may be difficult or ambiguous.

The structure and organization of the commentaries in this series seeks to facilitate the study of the biblical text in a systematic and methodical way. Study of each biblical book begins with an ***Introduction*** section that gives an overview of authorship, date, provenance, audience, occasion, purpose, sociological/cultural issues, textual history, literary features, hermeneutical issues, and theological themes necessary to understand the book. This section also includes a brief outline of the book and a list of general works and standard commentaries.

The commentary section for each biblical book follows the outline of the book presented in the introduction. In some volumes, readers will find section ***overviews*** of large portions of scripture with general comments on their overall literary structure and other literary features. A consistent feature of the commentary is the paragraph-by-paragraph study of biblical texts. This section has three parts: ***Behind the Text***, ***In the Text***, and ***From the Text***.

The goal of the ***Behind the Text*** section is to provide the reader with all the relevant information necessary to understand the text. This includes specific historical situations reflected in the text, the literary context of the text, sociological and cultural issues, and literary features of the text.

In the Text explores what the text says, following its verse-by-verse structure. This section includes a discussion of grammatical details, word studies, and the connectedness of the text to other biblical books/passages or other parts of the book being studied (the canonical relationship). This section provides transliterations of key words in Hebrew and Greek and their literal meanings. The goal here is to explain what the author would have meant and/or what the audience would have understood as the meaning of the text. This is the largest section of the commentary.

The ***From the Text*** section examines the text in relation to the following areas: theological significance, intertextuality, the history of interpretation, use of the Old Testament scriptures in the New Testament, interpretation in later church history, actualization, and application.

The commentary provides ***sidebars*** on topics of interest that are important but not necessarily part of an explanation of the biblical text. These topics are informational items and may cover archaeological, historical, literary, cultural, and theological matters that have relevance to the biblical text. Occasionally, longer detailed discussions of special topics are included as ***excurses.***

We offer this series with our hope and prayer that readers will find it a valuable resource for their understanding of God's Word and an indispensable tool for their critical engagement with the biblical texts.

Roger Hahn, Centennial Initiative General Editor
Alex Varughese, General Editor (Old Testament)
George Lyons, General Editor (New Testament)

ACKNOWLEDGMENTS

I am very grateful to the editors of this series, particularly Alex Varughese, for the privilege of contributing. I also appreciate the helpful suggestions of Robert Branson, my section editor, and those at Beacon Hill Press.

I'm thankful for my wife, Eileen. She has always been a patient and loyal supporter of my writing efforts. Our son, Ethan, was also a great help in editing and proofreading the finished product.

No commentary stands on its own but benefits from previous efforts. I am tremendously thankful to all those who have preceded me in an effort to mine the riches of this wonderful biblical book. Especially deserving of my gratitude are Richard S. Hess, David M. Howard Jr., and K. Lawson Younger Jr. for taking seriously the nature of this book as both ancient artifact and divinely inspired Scripture. I also want to express particular thanks for the life and teaching of the late David A. Dorsey, whose influence on my understanding of Joshua will be abundantly evident to those who read this book.

Being able to devote so much time and attention to God's Word is a rich blessing, made possible, in part by the wonderful institution where I've been privileged to teach for over twenty years. Special thanks go to President David Wright, Dean Darlene Bressler, and my associate dean, Dave Ward. I'm also grateful for the wonderful questions of many classes of OT Survey students through the years and to the secretarial staff of the School of Theology and Ministry, who assisted in many ways large and small.

I am most grateful to God for calling me to the preaching and teaching of his Word.

—Stephen J. Lennox

ABBREVIATIONS

With a few exceptions, these abbreviations follow those in *The SBL Handbook of Style* (Alexander 1999).

General

→	see the commentary at
ANE	ancient Near East
B.C.	before Christ (follows date)
bk.	book
ch	chapter
chs	chapters
DH	Deuteronomic History
EA	El-Amarna tablets
e.g.	for example
exp.	expanded
f(f).	and the following one(s)
ibid.	*ibidem*, in the same place
i.e.	that is
lit.	literally
LXX	Septuagint
mg.	marginal reading
MT	Masoretic Text (of the OT)
n.	note
NT	New Testament
OT	Old Testament
pl.	plural
Q	Qumran
repr.	reprint(ed)
rev.	revised
sec.	section
sg.	singular
sic	thus was it written
v	verse
vv	verses

Modern English Versions

ASV	American Standard Version
ESV	English Standard Version
GNT	Good News Translation (Today's English Version)
KJV	King James Version
NABRE	New American Bible, Revised Edition
NASB	New American Standard Bible
NEB	New English Bible
NIV	New International Version
NJB	New Jerusalem Bible
NJPS	Tanakh (The Hebrew Bible)
NLT	New Living Translation
NRSV	New Revised Standard Version

Print Conventions for Translations

Bold font	NIV (bold without quotation marks in the text under study; elsewhere in the regular font, with quotation marks and no further identification)
Bold italic font	Author's translation (without quotation marks)

Behind the Text: Literary or historical background information average readers might not know from reading the biblical text alone

In the Text: Comments on the biblical text, words, phrases, grammar, and so forth

From the Text: The use of the text by later interpreters, contemporary relevance, theological and ethical implications of the text, with particular emphasis on Wesleyan concerns

Old Testament

Gen	Genesis
Exod	Exodus
Lev	Leviticus
Num	Numbers
Deut	Deuteronomy
Josh	Joshua
Judg	Judges
Ruth	Ruth
1—2 Sam	1—2 Samuel
1—2 Kgs	1—2 Kings
1—2 Chr	1—2 Chronicles
Ezra	Ezra
Neh	Nehemiah
Esth	Esther
Job	Job
Ps/Pss	Psalm/Psalms
Prov	Proverbs
Eccl	Ecclesiastes
Song	Song of Songs/ Song of Solomon
Isa	Isaiah
Jer	Jeremiah
Lam	Lamentations
Ezek	Ezekiel
Dan	Daniel
Hos	Hosea
Joel	Joel
Amos	Amos
Obad	Obadiah
Jonah	Jonah
Mic	Micah
Nah	Nahum
Hab	Habakkuk
Zeph	Zephaniah
Hag	Haggai
Zech	Zechariah
Mal	Malachi

(Note: Chapter and verse numbering in the MT and LXX often differ compared to those in English Bibles. To avoid confusion, all biblical references follow the chapter and verse numbering in English translations, even when the text in the MT and LXX is under discussion.)

New Testament

Matt	Matthew
Mark	Mark
Luke	Luke
John	John
Acts	Acts
Rom	Romans
1—2 Cor	1—2 Corinthians
Gal	Galatians
Eph	Ephesians
Phil	Philippians
Col	Colossians
1—2 Thess	1—2 Thessalonians
1—2 Tim	1—2 Timothy
Titus	Titus
Phlm	Philemon
Heb	Hebrews
Jas	James
1—2 Pet	1—2 Peter
1—2—3 John	1—2—3 John
Jude	Jude
Rev	Revelation

Apocrypha

Bar	Baruch
Add Dan	Additions to Daniel
Pr Azar	Prayer of Azariah
Bel	Bel and the Dragon
Sg Three	Song of the Three Young Men
Sus	Susanna
1—2 Esd	1—2 Esdras
Add Esth	Additions to Esther
Ep Jer	Epistle of Jeremiah
Jdt	Judith
1—2 Macc	1—2 Maccabees
3—4 Macc	3—4 Maccabees
Pr Man	Prayer of Manasseh
Ps 151	Psalm 151
Sir	Sirach/Ecclesiasticus
Tob	Tobit
Wis	Wisdom of Solomon

Dead Sea Scrolls

1QS	*Serek Hayakad* or *Rule of the Community*

Greek Transliteration

Greek	Letter	English
α	alpha	a
β	bēta	b
γ	gamma	g
γ	gamma nasal	n (before γ, κ, ξ, χ)
δ	delta	d
ε	epsilon	e
ζ	zēta	z
η	ēta	ē
θ	thēta	th
ι	iōta	i
κ	kappa	k
λ	lambda	l
μ	mu	m
ν	nu	n
ξ	xi	x
ο	omicron	o
π	pi	p
ρ	rhō	r
ρ	initial rhō	rh
σ/ς	sigma	s
τ	tau	t
υ	upsilon	y
υ	upsilon	u (in diphthongs: au, eu, ēu, ou, ui)
φ	phi	ph
χ	chi	ch
ψ	psi	ps
ω	ōmega	ō
ʼ	rough breathing	h (before initial vowels or diphthongs)

Hebrew Consonant Transliteration

Hebrew/Aramaic	Letter	English
א	alef	ʼ
ב	bet	b
ג	gimel	g
ד	dalet	d
ה	he	h
ו	vav	v or w
ז	zayin	z
ח	khet	ḥ
ט	tet	ṭ
י	yod	y
כ/ך	kaf	k
ל	lamed	l
מ/ם	mem	m
נ/ן	nun	n
ס	samek	ṣ
ע	ayin	ʿ
פ/ף	pe	p; f (spirant)
צ/ץ	tsade	ṣ
ק	qof	q
ר	resh	r
שׂ	sin	ś
שׁ	shin	š
ת	tav	t; th (spirant)

BIBLIOGRAPHY

Commentaries

Auld, A. Graeme. 1984. *Joshua, Judges, and Ruth*. Old Testament Daily Study Bible Series. Louisville, Ky.: Westminster John Knox Press.

Boling, Robert G., and G. Ernest Wright. 1982. *Joshua: A New Translation with Introduction and Commentary*. Vol. 6 of the Anchor Bible. New Haven, Conn.: Yale University Press.

Bratcher, Robert G., and Barclay M. Newman. 1992. *A Handbook on the Book of Joshua*. New York: United Bible Societies.

Butler, Trent C. 1983. *Joshua*. Vol. 7 of *Word Biblical Commentary*. Edited by David A. Hubbard, Glenn W. Barker, John D. W. Watts, and Ralph P. Martin. Waco, Tex.: Word Books.

Calvin, John. N.d. *Commentaries on the Book of Joshua*. Translated from the Original Latin, and Collated with the French Edition by Henry Beveridge. Grand Rapids: Christian Classics Ethereal Library. Online: http://www.ccel.org.

Coote, Robert B. 1994. The Book of Joshua. Vol. 2 of *The New Interpreter's Bible*. Nashville: Abingdon Press.

Creach, Jerome F. D. 2003. *Joshua. Interpretation: A Bible Commentary for Teaching and Preaching*. Edited by James Luther Mays, Patrick D. Miller, and Paul J. Achtemeier. Louisville, Ky.: John Knox Press.

Garstang, John. 1931. *Joshua, Judges. The Foundations of Bible History*. New York: Richard R. Smith.

Hamlin, E. John. 1983. *Inheriting the Land: A Commentary on the Book of Joshua. International Theological Commentary*. Edited by George A. F. Knight and Fredrick Carlson Holmgren. Grand Rapids: Eerdmans.

Harris, J. Gordon, Cheryl A. Brown, and Michael S. Moore. 2000. *Joshua, Judges, Ruth. New International Biblical Commentary*. Peabody, Mass.: Hendrickson Publishers.

Hawk, L. Daniel. 2000. *Joshua. Berit Olam: Studies in Hebrew Narrative and Poetry*. Edited by David W. Cotter. Collegeville, Minn.: Liturgical Press.

Hess, Richard S. 1996a. *Joshua: An Introduction and Commentary. Tyndale Old Testament Commentaries*. Edited by D. J. Wiseman. Downers Grove, Ill.: IVP Academic.

Howard, David M., Jr. 1998a. *Joshua*. Vol. 5 of *The New American Commentary*. Edited by E. Ray Clendenen, Kenneth A. Mathews, David S. Dockery. Nashville: Broadman and Holman.

Keil, C. F., and F. Delitzsch. 1978. *Joshua, Judges, Ruth, I & II Samuel*. Vol. 2 of *Commentary on the Old Testament in Ten Volumes*. Translated by James Martin. Grand Rapids: Eerdmans.

McConville, J. Gordon, and Stephen N. Williams. 2010. *Joshua. The Two Horizons Old Testament Commentary*. Edited by J. Gordon McConville and Craig Bartholomew. Grand Rapids: Eerdmans.

Miller, J. Maxwell, and Gene M. Tucker. 1974. *The Book of Joshua. The Cambridge Bible Commentary*. Edited by P. R. Ackroyd, A. R. C. Leaney, and J. W. Packer. New York: Cambridge University Press.

Nelson, Richard D. 1997. *Joshua: A Commentary. The Old Testament Library*. Edited by James L. Mays, Carol A. Newsom, and David L. Peterson. Louisville, Ky.: Westminster John Knox Press.

Pitkänen, Pekka M. A. 2010. *Joshua*. Vol. 6 of *Apollos Old Testament Commentary*. Edited by David W. Baker and Gordon J. Wenham. Downers Grove, Ill.: IVP Academic.

Soggin, J. Alberto. 1972. *Joshua: A Commentary. The Old Testament Library*. Edited by Peter Ackroyd, James Barr, John Bright, and G. Ernest Wright. Translated by R. A. Wilson. Philadelphia: Westminster Press.

Steele, Daniel. 1873. *The Book of Joshua*. Repr., Salem, Ohio: Schmul Publishing, 2000.

Woudstra, Marten H. 1981. *The Book of Joshua. The New International Commentary on the Old Testament*. Edited by R. K. Harrison. Grand Rapids: Eerdmans.

Monographs and References

Aharoni, Yohanan, and Michael Avi-Yonah. 1977. *Macmillan Bible Atlas*. New York: Macmillan.
Aquinas, Thomas. 1948. *Summa Theologica*. South Bend, Ind.: Christian Classics.
Auld, A. Graeme. 1998. *Joshua Retold: Synoptic Perspectives*. Edinburgh: T&T Clark.
Beitzel, Barry J. 1985. *The Moody Atlas of Bible Lands*. Chicago: Moody Press.
Berman, Joshua. 2004. *Narrative Analogy in the Hebrew Bible: Battle Stories and Their Equivalent Non-battle Narratives*. Leiden: Brill.
Bienkowski, Piotr. 1986. *Jericho in the Late Bronze Age*. Warminster, U.K.: Aris and Phillips.
Blevins, Dean G., Charles D. Cros, David E. Downs, Paul W. Thornhill, and David P. Wilson, eds. 2009. *Manual of the Church of the Nazarene, 2009-2013*. Kansas City: Nazarene Publishing House.
Boling, Robert G. 1975. *Judges. The Anchor Bible*. Garden City, N.Y.: Doubleday and Co.
Branson, Robert D. 2009. *Judges: A Commentary in the Wesleyan Tradition*. Kansas City: Beacon Hill Press of Kansas City.
Brueggemann, Walter. 2009. *Divine Presence Amid Violence: Contextualizing the Book of Joshua*. Eugene, Ore.: Cascade.
Calvin, John. N.d. *Institutes of the Christian Religion*. Translated by Henry Beveridge. Christian Classics Ethereal Library. Online: http://www.ccel.org.
Cleave, Richard. 1999. *The Holy Land Satellite Atlas*. Nicosia, Cyprus: Rohr Productions.
Collins, John J. 2004. *Does the Bible Justify Violence?* Minneapolis: Fortress Press.
Collins, Kenneth. 2007. *The Theology of John Wesley: Holy Love and the Shape of Grace*. Nashville: Abingdon Press.
Cowles, C. S., Eugene H. Merrill, Daniel L. Gard, and Tremper Longman III. 2003. *Four Views on God and Canaanite Genocide: Show Them No Mercy*. Counterpoints Series. Edited by Stanley Gundry. Grand Rapids: Zondervan.
Craigie, P. C. 1976. *The Book of Deuteronomy. The New International Commentary on the Old Testament*. Grand Rapids: Eerdmans.
_____. 1978. *The Problem of War in the Old Testament*. Grand Rapids: Eerdmans.
Curtis, Adrian H. W. 1994. *Joshua*. Old Testament Guides. Edited by R. N. Whybray. Sheffield: Sheffield Academic Press.
Dever, William G. 2003. *Who Were the Early Israelites and Where Did They Come From?* Grand Rapids: Eerdmans.
Dorsey, David. 1999. *The Literary Structure of the Old Testament*. Grand Rapids: Baker. Boldface and underlining within quotes from this source are that of the author.
Earl, Douglas S. 2010a. *The Joshua Delusion? Rethinking Genocide in the Bible*. Eugene, Ore.: Cascade Books.
_____. 2010b. *Reading Joshua as Christian Scripture*. Journal of Theological Interpretation Supplements. Edited by Murray Rae. Winona Lake, Ind.: Eisenbrauns.
Eichrodt, Walther. 1961. *Theology of the Old Testament*. Vol. 1 of *The Old Testament Library*. Translated by J. A. Baker. Philadelphia: Westminster Press.
Ellul, Jacques. 1969. *Violence: Reflections from a Christian Perspective*. Translated by Cecelia Gaul Kings. New York: Seabury Press.
Freedman, D. N., ed. 1992. *The Anchor Bible Dictionary*. 6 vols. New York: Doubleday.
Ginzberg, Louis. 1968. *Legends of the Jews*. Philadelphia: Jewish Publication Society.
Hall, Sarah Lebhar. 2010. *Conquering Character: The Characterization of Joshua in Joshua 1-11*. New York: T&T Clark.
Harrington, Daniel J., and Anthony J. Saldarini. 1987. *Targum Jonathan of the Former Prophets: Introduction, Translation, and Notes*. Wilmington, Del.: Michael Glazier.
Hawk, L. Daniel. 1991. *Every Promise Fulfilled*. Louisville, Ky.: Westminster/John Knox Press.
Hawkins, Ralph K. 2012. *The Iron Age I Structure on Mt. Ebal: Excavation and Interpretation. Bulletin for Biblical Research Supplement 6*. Winona Lake, Ind.: Eisenbrauns.
Hoffmeier, James K. 1996. *Israel in Egypt: The Evidence for the Authenticity of the Exodus Tradition*. New York: Oxford University Press.
_____. 2005. *Ancient Israel in Sinai*. New York: Oxford University Press.
Holladay, William L. 1971. *A Concise Hebrew and Aramaic Lexicon of the Old Testament, Based upon the Lexical Work of Ludwig Koehler and Walter Baumgartner*. Grand Rapids: Eerdmans.
Jenkins, Philip. 2011. *Laying Down the Sword: Why We Can't Ignore the Bible's Violent Verses*. New York: HarperCollins.

Josephus. 1979. *Antiquities of the Jews*. Translated by William Whiston. Grand Rapids: Baker Book House.
Kaufmann, Yehezkel. 1953. *The Biblical Account of the Conquest of Palestine*. Jerusalem: Magnes Press, Hebrew University.
Latvus, Kari. 1998. *Anger and Ideology: The Anger of God in Joshua and Judges in Relation to Deuteronomy and the Priestly Writings*. Sheffield: Sheffield Academic Press.
Lawrence, Paul. 2006. *The IVP Atlas of Bible History*. Downers Grove, Ill.: IVP Academic.
Lewis, C. S. 1950. *The Lion, the Witch, and the Wardrobe*. New York: Collier Books.
Liverani, Mario. 1990. *Prestige and Interest: International Relations in the Near East c1600-1100 BC*. Padua: Sargon.
Long, Burke O. 1968. *The Problem of Etiological Narrative in the Old Testament*. Beihefte zur Zeitschrift für die alttestamentliche Wissenschaft 108. Edited by Georg Fohrer. Berlin: Verlag Alfred Töpelmann.
Longman, Tremper. 2013. *The Baker Illustrated Bible Dictionary*. Grand Rapids: Baker Books.
Maimonides, Moses. 1964. *The Guide of the Perplexed*. Translated by Shlomo Pines. Chicago: University of Chicago Press.
Miller, Patrick D. 1973. *The Divine Warrior in Early Israel*. Cambridge, Mass.: Harvard University Press.
Moran, William L. 1992. *The Amarna Letters*. Baltimore: Johns Hopkins University Press.
Murray, Andrew. 1984. *The Holiest of All: An Exposition of the Epistle to the Hebrews*. New York: Fleming H. Revell.
Noll, K. L., and Brooks Schramm. 2010. *Raising Up a Faithful Exegete: Essays in Honor of Richard D. Nelson*. Winona Lake, Ind.: Eisenbrauns.
Noth, Martin. 1991. *The Deuteronomistic History*. 2nd ed. Translated by Jane Doull and John Barton. Journal for the Study of the Old Testament 15. Edited by David J. A. Clines and Philip R. Davies. Sheffield: JSOT Press.
Oden, Thomas C. 1989. *The Word of Life*. Vol. 2 of *Systematic Theology*. San Francisco: Harper.
Origen. 2002. *Homilies on Joshua. The Fathers of the Church*. Translated by Barbara J. Bruce. Edited by Cynthia White. Washington, D.C.: Catholic University of America Press.
Pardee, Dennis. 2002. *Ritual and Cult at Ugarit*. Edited by Theodore J. Lewis. Atlanta: Society of Biblical Literature.
Parker, Simon B. 1997. *Stories in Scripture and Inscriptions: Comparative Studies on Narratives in Northwest Semitic Inscriptions and the Hebrew Bible*. New York: Oxford University Press.
Parkinson, R. B., trans. 1997. *The Tale of Sinuhe and Other Ancient Egyptian Poems 1940-1640 BC*. New York: Oxford University Press.
Pinker, Steven. 2011. *The Better Angels of Our Nature: Why Violence Has Declined*. New York: Viking.
Polzin, Robert. 1980. *Moses and the Deuteronomist*. New York: Seabury Press.
Rad, Gerhard von, Ben C. Ollenburger, and Judith E. Sanderson. 2000. *Holy War in Ancient Israel*. Eugene, Ore.: Wipf and Stock.
Roberts, Alexander, and James Donaldson, eds. 1950. *Ante-Nicene Fathers*. Grand Rapids: Eerdmans.
Römer, Thomas C., ed. 2000. *The Future of the Deuteronomistic History*. Bibliotheca Ephemeridum Theologicarum Lovaniensium CXLVII. Leuven: Leuven University Press/Peeters.
Rowlett, Lori L. 1996. *Joshua and the Rhetoric of Violence: A New Historicist Analysis*. Journal of the Study of the Old Testament Sup. 226. Sheffield: Sheffield Academic Press.
Schwartz, Regina M. 1997. *The Curse of Cain: The Violent Legacy of Monotheism*. Chicago: University of Chicago Press.
Shanks, Hershel, ed. 1999. *Ancient Israel: From Abraham to the Roman Destruction of the Temple*, rev. and exp. ed. Washington, D.C.: Biblical Archaeology Society/Upper Saddle River, N.J.: Prentice Hall.
Sing to the Lord. 1993. Kansas City: Lillenas Publishing Company.
Stern, Philip D. 1991. *The Biblical ḤEREM: A Window on Israel's Religious Experience*. Edited by Ernest S. Frerichs, Wendell S. Dietrich, Calvin Goldscheider, David Hirsch, and Alan Zuckerman. Atlanta: Brown Judaic Studies [211].
Thomas, Heath A., Jeremy Evans, and Paul Copan, eds. 2013. *Holy War in the Bible: Christian Morality and an Old Testament Problem*. Downers Grove, Ill.: IVP Academic.
Treier, Daniel J. 2008. *Introducing Theological Interpretation of Scripture: Recovering a Christian Practice*. Grand Rapids: Baker Academic.

van der Meer, Michaël N. 2004. *Formulation and Reformulation: The Redaction of the Book of Joshua in the Light of the Oldest Textual Witnesses.* Supplements to Vetus Testamentum (102). Edited by H. M. Barstad et al. Leiden: Brill.

Weinfeld, Moshe. 1995. *Social Justice in Ancient Israel and in the Ancient Near East.* Jerusalem: Magnes Press.

Wright, Christopher J. H. 2008. *The God I Don't Understand: Reflections on Tough Questions of Faith.* Grand Rapids: Zondervan.

Younger, K. Lawson, Jr. 1990. *Ancient Conquest Accounts: A Study in Ancient Near East and Biblical History Writing.* Journal for the Study of the Old Testament Supp. 98. Edited by David J. A. Clines and Philip R. Davies. Sheffield: JSOT Press.

Articles

Aharoni, Miriam. 1993. Arad: The Israelite Citadels. Pages 82-87 in vol. 1 of *The New Encyclopedia of Archaeological Excavations in the Holy Land.* Edited by Ephraim Stern. 4 vols. Israel Exploration Society and Carta, Jerusalem/New York: Simon and Schuster.

Aharoni, Yohanan. 1969. Rubute and Ginti-Kirmil. *Vetus Testamentum* 19(2):137-45.

_____. 1971. Khirbet Raddana and Its Inscription. *Israel Exploration Journal* 21(2):130-35.

_____. 1974. Three Hebrew Seals. *Tel Aviv* 1(4):157-58.

_____. 1993a. Arad. Page 75 in vol. 1 of *The New Encyclopedia of Archaeological Excavations in the Holy Land.* Edited by Ephraim Stern. 4 vols. Israel Exploration Society and Carta, Jerusalem/New York: Simon and Schuster.

_____. 1993b. Kedesh (in Upper Galilee). Pages 855-56 in vol. 3 of *The New Encyclopedia of Archaeological Excavations in the Holy Land.* Edited by Ephraim Stern. 4 vols. Israel Exploration Society and Carta, Jerusalem/New York: Simon and Schuster.

_____. 1993c. Megiddo. Pages 1003-12 in vol. 3 of *The New Encyclopedia of Archaeological Excavations in the Holy Land.* Edited by Ephraim Stern. 4 vols. Israel Exploration Society and Carta, Jerusalem/New York: Simon and Schuster.

Alden, Robert L. 1980. `ôt, *Theological Wordbook of the Old Testament.* Vol. 1. Edited by R. Laird Harris, Gleason L. Archer, Jr., Bruce K. Waltke. Chicago: Moody Press.

Alt, Albrecht. 1967. The Settlement of the Israelites in Palestine. Pages 173-221 in *Essays on Old Testament History and Religion.* Translated by R. A. Wilson. Garden City, N.Y.: Doubleday and Company.

Amiran, Ruth, and Ornit Ilan. 1993. Arad: The Canaanite City. Pages 75-82 in vol. 1 of *The New Encyclopedia of Archaeological Excavations in the Holy Land.* Edited by Ephraim Stern. 4 vols. Israel Exploration Society and Carta, Jerusalem/New York: Simon and Schuster.

Angel, Hayyim. 2008. "There Is No Chronological Order in the Torah": An Axiom for Understanding the Book of Joshua. *Jewish Bible Quarterly* 36(1):4-11.

Assis, Elie. 2003. "How Long Are You Slack to Go to Possess the Land" (Jos. XVIII 3): Ideal and Reality in the Distribution Descriptions in Joshua XIII-XIX. *Vetus Testamentum* 53(1):1-25.

Auld, A. Graeme. 1978. Cities of Refuge in Israelite Tradition. *Journal for the Study of the Old Testament* 10:26-40.

Barr, James. 1984. *Migras* in the Old Testament. *Journal of Semitic Studies* 29(1):15-31.

_____. 1990. Mythical Monarch Unmasked? Mysterious Doings of Debir King of Eglon. *Journal for the Study of the Old Testament* 48:55-68.

Beck, Pirhiya, and Moshe Kochavi. 1993. Aphek (in Sharon): Excavations in the 1970s and 1980s. Pages 64-72 in vol. 1 of *The New Encyclopedia of Archaeological Excavations in the Holy Land.* Edited by Ephraim Stern. 4 vols. Israel Exploration Society and Carta, Jerusalem/New York: Simon and Schuster.

Ben-Arieh, Sarah. 1993. Gedor, Tel. Page 468 in vol. 2 of *The New Encyclopedia of Archaeological Excavations in the Holy Land.* Edited by Ephraim Stern. 4 vols. Israel Exploration Society and Carta, Jerusalem/New York: Simon and Schuster.

Ben-Barak, Zafrira. 1978. The Case of the Daughters of Zelophehad in Light of a New Document from Nuzi. *Shnaton* 3:116-23.

Benjamin, Paul. 1992. Anab. Page 219 in vol. 1 of *The Anchor Bible Dictionary.* Edited by D. N. Freedman. 6 vols. New York: Doubleday.

Ben-Tor, Amnon. 1993. Jokneam. Pages 805-11 in vol. 3 of *The New Encyclopedia of Archaeological Excavations in the Holy Land.* Edited by Ephraim Stern. 4 vols. Israel Exploration Society and Carta, Jerusalem/New York: Simon and Schuster.

_____. 2008. Hazor. Pages 1769-76 in (Supplementary Vol. 5) of *The New Encyclopedia of Archaeological Excavations in the Holy Land*. Edited by Ephraim Stern. Jerusalem: Israel Exploration Society.
Ben Zvi, Ehud. 2010. On the Term "Deuteronomistic" in Relation to Joshua-Kings in the Persian Period. Pages 61-71 in *Raising Up a Faithful Exegete*. Winona Lake, Ind.: Eisenbrauns.
Betz, Arnold. 1992. Shihor. Page 1212 in vol. 5 of *The Anchor Bible Dictionary*. Edited by D. N. Freedman. 6 vols. New York: Doubleday.
Block, Daniel I. 2013. Review of Ralph K. Hawkins, *The Iron Age I Structure on Mt. Ebal: Excavation and Interpretation. Bulletin for Biblical Research Supplement 6.* Winona Lake, Ind.: Eisenbrauns, 2012. *Bulletin for Biblical Research* 23(1):94-96.
Braulik, Georg. 2011. Gott kämpft für Israel. *Biblische Zeitschrift* 55(2):209-23.
Callaway, Joseph A. 1968. New Evidence on the Conquest of `Ai. *Journal of Biblical Literature* 87(3):312-20.
_____. 1993. Ai. Pages 39-45 in vol. 1 of *The New Encyclopedia of Archaeological Excavations in the Holy Land*. Edited by Ephraim Stern. 4 vols. Israel Exploration Society and Carta, Jerusalem/New York: Simon and Schuster.
_____. 1999. The Settlement in Canaan: The Period of the Judges. Revised by J. Maxwell Miller. Pages 55-89 in *Ancient Israel: From Abraham to the Roman Destruction of the Temple*. Edited by Hershel Shanks. Washington, D.C.: Biblical Archaeology Society.
Campbell, K. M. 1972. Rahab's Covenant: A Short Note on Joshua ii 9-21. *Vetus Testamentum* 22:243-44.
Cassuto, Umberto. 1975a. Biblical and Canaanite Literature. Pages 16-59 in vol. 2 of *Biblical and Oriental Studies*. Jerusalem: Magnes Press.
_____. 1975b. The Lachish Ostraca. Pages 229-39 in vol. 2 *Biblical and Oriental Studies*. Jerusalem: Magnes Press.
Childs, Brevard Springs. 1974. Etiological Tale Re-examined. *Vetus Testamentum* 24(4):387-97.
Clarke, T. A. 2010. Complete v. Incomplete Conquest: A Re-examination of Three Passages in Joshua. *Tyndale Bulletin* 61(1):89-104.
Coats, George W. 1985. The Ark of the Covenant in Joshua: A Probe in the History of a Tradition. *Hebrew Annual Review* 9:137-57.
Cohen, Jeffrey M. 2003. When Did We Become a Nation? *Jewish Bible Quarterly* 31(4):260-62.
Cohen, S. 1962. Archite. Page 209 in vol. 1 of *Interpreter's Dictionary of the Bible*. Edited by George Arthur Buttrick. Nashville: Abingdon Press.
Combet-Gallard, Corina. 2005. L`expulsion du mal: un acte de naissance de l`Eglise. *Foi et Vie* 104(1):43-61.
Copan, Paul. 2009. Yahweh Wars and the Canaanites: Divinely Mandated Genocide or Corporate Capital Punishment? Responses to Critics. *Philosophia Christi*, Series 2 11(1):73-90.
Crawford, John. 2004. Caleb the Dog: How a Biblical Good Guy Got a Bad Name. *Bible Review* 20(2):20-27.
Creangă, Ovidiu. 2010. Variations on the Theme of Masculinity: Joshua's Gender In/stability in the Conquest Narrative (Josh. 1-12). Pages 83-109 in *Men and Masculinity in the Hebrew Bible and Beyond*. Sheffield: Sheffield Phoenix Press.
Crown, Alan D. 1973. An Alternative to Yadin's Interpretation of Joshua XI 10-13 and Judges IV. *Milla wa-Milla* 13:29-32.
Davies, Philip R. 2010. The Deuteronomistic History and "Double Redaction." Pages 51-59 in *Raising Up a Faithful Exegete*. Winona Lake, Ind.: Eisenbrauns.
de Vaux, Roland. 1993. Far`ah, Tell el- (North). Page 433 in vol. 2 of *The New Encyclopedia of Archaeological Excavations in the Holy Land*. Edited by Ephraim Stern. 4 vols. Israel Exploration Society and Carta, Jerusalem/New York: Simon and Schuster.
Dever, William G. 1993. Gezer. Pages 496-506 in vol. 3 of *The New Encyclopedia of Archaeological Excavations in the Holy Land*. Edited by Ephraim Stern. 4 vols. Israel Exploration Society and Carta, Jerusalem/New York: Simon and Schuster.
Dickerson, Ben, and Derrel R. Watkins. 2003. The Caleb Affect: The Oldest-Old in Church and Society. *Journal of Religious Gerontology* 15(1):201-13.
Dieterle, Christiane. 1998. Le monceau de pierres de Josue 7:26, ou que faire du Dieu cruel? *Foi et Vie* 97(4):41-54.
Dorsey, David A. 1980. The Location of Biblical Makkedah. *Tel Aviv* 7(3):185-93.
Dozeman, Thomas B. 2010. Joshua in the Book of Joshua. Pages 103-16 of *Raising Up a Faithful Exegete*. Winona Lake, Ind.: Eisenbrauns.

Dyck, Elmer H. 1992. Michmethath. Page 815 in vol. 4 of *The Anchor Bible Dictionary*. Edited by D. N. Freedman. 6 vols. New York: Doubleday.

Earl, Douglas S. 2013. Joshua and the Crusades. Pages 19-43 of *Holy War in the Bible: Christian Morality and an Old Testament Problem*. Edited by Heath A. Thomas, Jeremy Evans, and Paul Copan. Downers Grove, Ill.: IVP Academic.

Edelman, Diana. 1991. Are the Kings of the Amorites "Swept Away" in Joshua XXIV 12? *Vetus Testamentum* 41(3):279-86.

Eitan, Abraham. 1993. Aphek (in Sharon). Pages 62-64 in vol. 1 of *The New Encyclopedia of Archaeological Excavations in the Holy Land*. Edited by Ephraim Stern. 4 vols. Israel Exploration Society and Carta, Jerusalem/New York: Simon and Schuster.

Elitzur, Yoel. 1994. Rumah in Judah. *Israel Exploration Journal* 44(1):123-28.

_____. 2004. Mul: "Near, Below, on the Same Side As." *Lesonenu* 67(1):7-19.

Eshel, Hanan. 1995. A Note on Joshua 15:61-62 and the Identification of the City of Salt. *Israel Exploration Journal* 45(1):37-40.

Fensham, F. Charles. 1963. Clauses of Protection in Hittite Vassal-Treaties and the Old Testament. *Vetus Testamentum* 13(2):133-43.

_____. 1964. Treaty between Israel and the Gibeonites. *Biblical Archaeologist* 27(3):96-100.

Finkelstein, Israel. 1981. The Shephelah of Israel. *Tel Aviv* 8(1):84-94.

Finkelstein, Israel, David Ussishkin, and Baruch Halpern. 2008. Meggido. Pages 1944-50 in vol. 5 (Supplementary) of *The New Encyclopedia of Archaeological Excavations in the Holy Land*. Edited by Ephraim Stern. Jerusalem: Israel Exploration Society.

Fleishman, Joseph. 2006. A Daughter's Demand and a Father's Compliance. *Zeitschrift für die Alttestamentliche Wissenschaft* 118(3):354-73.

Fleming, Daniel E. 1999. The Seven-day Siege of Jericho in Holy War. Pages 211-28 in *Ki Baruch Hu*. Winona Lake, Ind.: Eisenbrauns.

Frankel, Rafael. 1992. Ziddim. Pages 1089-90 in vol. 6 of *The Anchor Bible Dictionary*. Edited by D. N. Freedman. 6 vols. New York: Doubleday, 1992.

Frendo, Anthony J. 2013. Was Rahab Really a Harlot? *Biblical Archaeology Review* 39(5):62-65, 74-76.

Fretheim, Terence E. 2004. God and Violence in the Old Testament. *Word and World* 24(1):18-28.

_____. 2010. The Self-limiting God of the Old Testament and Issues of Violence. Pages 179-91 in *Raising Up a Faithful Exegete*. Winona Lake, Ind.: Eisenbrauns.

Garfinkel, Yosef, and Saar Ganor. 2008. Khirbet Qeiyafa: Sha'arayim. *Journal of Hebrew Scriptures* 8 (electronic).

Gelb, I. J. 1973. Prisoners of War in Early Mesopotamia. *Journal of Near Eastern Studies* 32(1/2):70-98.

Geraty, Lawrence T. 1993. Heshbon. Pages 626-30 in vol. 2 of *The New Encyclopedia of Archaeological Excavations in the Holy Land*. Edited by Ephraim Stern. 4 vols. Israel Exploration Society and Carta, Jerusalem/New York: Simon and Schuster.

Girard, René. 1999. Violence in Biblical Narrative. *Philosophy and Literature* 23(2):387-92.

Glock, Albert E. 1993. Taanach. Pages 1428-33 in vol. 4 of *The New Encyclopedia of Archaeological Excavations in the Holy Land*. Edited by Ephraim Stern. 4 vols. Israel Exploration Society and Carta, Jerusalem/New York: Simon and Schuster.

Goetze, A. 1975. The Struggle for the Domination of Syria (1400-1300 B.C.). Pages 1-20 of vol. 2, part 2 of *The Cambridge Ancient History*. 3rd ed. Cambridge: Cambridge University Press.

Good, Robert M. 1985. The Just War in Ancient Israel. *Journal of Biblical Literature* 104(3):385-400.

Gorg, Manfred. 1975. Saron als Politische Einheit. *Biblische Zeitschrift* 19(1):98-99.

Greenberg, Moshe. 1959. The Biblical Conception of Asylum. *Journal of Biblical Literature* 78(2):125-32.

Greenhut, Zvi. 1993. The City of Salt. *Biblical Archaeology Review* 19(4):32-43.

Halpern, Baruch. 1975. Gibeon: Israelite Diplomacy in the Conquest Era. *Catholic Biblical Quarterly* 37:303-16.

Hasel, Michael G. 2008. Merenptah's Reference to Israel: Critical Issues for the Origin of Israel. Pages 47-59 in *Critical Issues in Early Israelite History*. Edited by Richard S. Hess, Gerald A. Klingbeil, and Paul J. Ray Jr. Winona Lake, Ind.: Eisenbrauns.

Hawk, L. Daniel. 2005. Joshua, Book of. Pages 564-75 in *Dictionary of the Old Testament Historical Books*. Downers Grove, Ill.: IVP Academic.

_____. 2008. Conquest Reconfigured: Recasting Warfare in the Redaction of Joshua. Pages 145-60 in *Writing and Reading War*. Atlanta: Society of Biblical Literature.

Heller, Jan. 1966. Die Schweigende Sonne. *Communio Viatorium* 9(1):73-78.

Hess, Richard S. 1994a. Asking Historical Questions of Joshua 13-19: Recent Discussion Concerning the Date of the Boundary Lists. Pages 191-205 in *Faith, Tradition, and History*. Winona Lake, Ind.: Eisenbrauns.
———. 1994b. Fallacies in the Study of Early Israel: An Onomastic Perspective. *Tyndale Bulletin* 45(2):339-54.
———. 1996b. Non-Israelite Personal Names in the Book of Joshua. *Catholic Bible Quarterly* 58:205-14.
———. 1997. West Semitic Texts and the Book of Joshua. *Bulletin for Biblical Research* 7:63-76.
———. 2002. Literacy in Iron Age Israel. Pages 82-102 in *Windows into Old Testament History*. Grand Rapids: Eerdmans.
———. 2008. The Jericho and Ai of the Book of Joshua. Pages 33-46 in *Critical Issues in Early Israelite History*. Edited by Richard S. Hess, Gerald A. Klingbeil, and Paul J. Ray Jr. Winona Lake, Ind.: Eisenbrauns.
Holladay, John S. 1968. The Day(s) the Moon Stood Still. *Journal of Biblical Literature* 87(2):166-78.
Horn, S. H. 1962. Heshbon. Pages 410-11 in Supplemental Volume of *Interpreter's Dictionary of the Bible*. Edited by Keith Crim. Nashville: Abingdon.
Howard, David M., Jr. 1998b. "Three Days" in Joshua 1-3: Resolving a Chronological Conundrum. *Journal of the Evangelical Theological Society* 41:539-50.
Hubbard, Robert L., Jr. 1991. The Go'el in Ancient Israel: Theological Reflections on an Israelite Institution. *Bulletin for Biblical Research* 1:3-19.
Huffmon, Herbert B. 1985. Amorites. Page 27 in *Harper's Bible Dictionary*. Edited by Paul J. Achtemeier. San Francisco: Harper San Francisco.
Hunt, Melvin. 1992. Ibleam. Page 355 in vol. 3 of *The Anchor Bible Dictionary*. Edited by D. N. Freedman. 6 vols. New York: Doubleday.
Johnson, Siegfried S. 1992. Archite. Page 369 in vol. 1 of *The Anchor Bible Dictionary*. Edited by D. N. Freedman. 6 vols. New York: Doubleday.
Jones, Clay. 2009. We Don't Hate Sin So We Don't Understand What Happened to the Canaanites: An Addendum to "Divine Genocide" Arguments. *Philosophia Christi*, Series 2 11(1):53-72.
Jones, Gwilym H. 1989. The Concept of Holy War. Pages 299-321 in *World of Ancient Israel*. Cambridge: Cambridge University Press.
Kasten, Douglas L. 2000. Narrator Devices in Joshua's Ruse: Translating Joshua 8:15. *Journal of Translation and Textlinguistics* 13:1-13.
Kaufman, Ivan T. 1992. Samaria Ostraca. Page 921 in vol. 5 of *The Anchor Bible Dictionary*. Edited by D. N. Freedman. 6 vols. New York: Doubleday.
Kelso, James Leon. 1993. Bethel. Pages 192-94 in vol. 1 of *The New Encyclopedia of Archaeological Excavations in the Holy Land*. Edited by Ephraim Stern. 4 vols. Israel Exploration Society and Carta, Jerusalem/New York: Simon and Schuster.
Kenyon, Kathleen M. 1993. Jericho. Pages 674-81 in vol. 2 of *The New Encyclopedia of Archaeological Excavations in the Holy Land*. Edited by Ephraim Stern. 4 vols. Israel Exploration Society and Carta, Jerusalem/New York: Simon and Schuster.
Kitchen, K. A. 2002. Hazor and Egypt: An Egyptological and Ancient Neareastern Perspective. *Scandinavian Journal of the Old Testament* 16(2):309-13.
Knauf, Ernst A. 1984. Beth Aven. *Biblica* 65(2):251-53.
Knoppers, Gary N. 2000. Is There a Future for the Deuteronomistic History? Pages 119-34 in *The Future of the Deuteronomistic History*. Leuven: Leuven University Press.
Kruger, Hennie. 2000. Sun and Moon Marking Time: A Cursory Survey of Exegetical Possibilities in Joshua 10:9-14. *Journal of Northwest Semitic Languages* 26(1):137-52.
Kuan, Jeffrey K. 2009. Biblical Interpretation and the Rhetoric of Violence and War. *Asia Journal of Theology* 23(2):189-203.
Lerner, Berel Dov. 2000. Rahab the Harlot and Other Philosophers of Religion. *Jewish Bible Quarterly* 28(1):52-55.
Lewis, Arthur. 1985. Joshua. *NIV Study Bible*. Edited by Kenneth Barker. Grand Rapids: Zondervan.
Lichtheim, Miriam, ed. 2006. The Report of Wenamun. Pages 224-30 in vol. 2 of *Ancient Egyptian Literature: The New Kingdom*. Berkeley: University of California Press. First published in 1976.
Liid, Dale C. 1992. Waters of Merom. Page 705 in vol. 4 of *The Anchor Bible Dictionary*. Edited by D. N. Freedman. 6 vols. New York: Doubleday.
Lockwood, Peter F. 2010. Rahab: Multi-faceted Heroine of the Book of Joshua. *Lutheran Theological Journal* 44(1):39-50.
Luria, Ben-Zion. 1989. The Location of Ai. *Dor Le Dor* 17(3):153-58.

Malamat, Abraham. 1960. Hazor "The Head of All Those Kingdoms." *Journal of Biblical Literature* 79:12-19.

———. 1982. How Inferior Israelite Forces Conquered Fortified Canaanite Cities. *Biblical Archaeology Review* 8(2):24-35.

Mazar, A., and George L. Kelm. 1980. Canaanites, Philistines and Israelites at Timna/Tel Batash. *Qadminot* 13(3):89-97.

McAffee, Matthew. 2010. The Heart of Pharaoh in Exodus 4-15. *Bulletin for Biblical Research* 20(3):331-53.

McGarry, Susan E. 1992. Avvim. Pages 531-32 in vol. 1 of *The Anchor Bible Dictionary*. Edited by D. N. Freedman. 6 vols. New York: Doubleday.

McGovern, Patrick E. 1992. Beth-Shan. Pages 693-96 in vol. 1 of *The Anchor Bible Dictionary*. Edited by D. N. Freedman. 6 vols. New York: Doubleday.

Millard, Alan R. 2008. Were the Israelites Really Canaanites? Pages 156-68 in *Israel: Ancient Kingdom or Late Invention?* Edited by Daniel I. Block. Nashville: B&H Academic.

Miller, Patrick D. 1965. God the Warrior: A Problem in Biblical Interpretation and Apologetics. *Interpretation* 19(1):39-46.

Miroschedji, Pierre de. 1993. Jarmuth, Tel. Pages 661-65 in vol. 2 of *The New Encyclopedia of Archaeological Excavations in the Holy Land*. Edited by Ephraim Stern. Israel Exploration Society and Carta, Jerusalem/New York: Simon and Schuster.

———. 2008. Jarmuth, Tel. Pages 1792-97 in vol. 5 (Supplementary) of *The New Encyclopedia of Archaeological Excavations in the Holy Land*. Edited by Ephraim Stern. Jerusalem: Israel Exploration Society.

Mosca, Paul G. 1984. Who Seduced Whom? A Note on Joshua 15:18//Judges 1:14. *Catholic Biblical Quarterly* 46(1):18-22.

Na'aman, Nadav. 1980. The Shihor of Egypt and Shur that Is before Egypt. *Tel Aviv* 7(1):95-109.

Nelson, Richard D. 1995. The Day the Sun Stood Frozen in Amazement. *Lutheran Theological Seminary Bulletin* 76(4):3-10.

———. 2005. Joshua. Pages 559-62 of *Dictionary of the Old Testament Historical Books*. Downers Grove, Ill.: IVP Academic.

Neufeld, Edward. 1980. Insects as Warfare Agents in the Ancient Near East: Ex. 23:28; Deut. 7:20; Josh. 24:12; Isa. 7:18-20. *Orientalia* 49:30-57.

Nicholson, E. W. 1997. The Problem of SNH. *Zeitschrift für die Alttestamentliche Wissenschaft* 89(2):259-65.

Niehaus, Jeffrey. 1980. Pa'am ehat and the Israelite Conquest. *Vetus Testamentum* 30(2):236-39.

Noort, Edward. 1998. 4QJosh. *Journal of Northwest Semitic Literature* 24(2):127-44.

Oded, Bustanay. 1991. "The Command of the God" as a Reason for Going to War in the Assyrian Inscriptions. Pages 223-30 in *Ah, Assyria—Studies in Assyrian History and Ancient Near Eastern Historiography Presented to Hayim Tadmor*. Jerusalem: Magnes Press.

Ofer, Avi. 1993. Hebron. Pages 606-9 in vol. 2 of *The New Encyclopedia of Archaeological Excavations in the Holy Land*. Edited by Ephraim Stern. 4 vols. Israel Exploration Society and Carta, Jerusalem/New York: Simon and Schuster.

Olávarri-Goicoechea, Emilio. 1993. Aroer (in Moab). Pages 92-93 in vol. 1 of *The New Encyclopedia of Archaeological Excavations in the Holy Land*. Edited by Ephraim Stern. 4 vols. Israel Exploration Society and Carta, Jerusalem/New York: Simon and Schuster.

Oren, Eliezer. 1982. Ziklag—A Biblical City on the Edge of the Negev. *Biblical Archaeologist* 45(3):155-66.

Pakkala, Juha. 2008. The Nomistic Roots of Judaism. Pages 251-68 in *Houses Full of All Good Things: Essays in Memory of Timo Veijola*. Edited by Juha Pakkala and Martti Nissinen. Helsinki; Göttingen: Finnish Exegetical Society; Vandenhoeck and Ruprecht.

Paley, Samuel M., and Yosef Porath. 1993. Ḥefer, Tel. Pages 609-14 in vol. 2 of *The New Encyclopedia of Archaeological Excavations in the Holy Land*. Edited by Ephraim Stern. 4 vols. Israel Exploration Society and Carta, Jerusalem/New York: Simon and Schuster.

Petrovich, Douglas. 2008. The Dating of Hazor's Destruction in Joshua 11 by Way of Biblical, Archaeological, and Epigraphical Evidence. *Journal of the Evangelical Theological Society* 51(3):489-512.

Rainey, Anson F. 1980. The Administrative Division of the Shephelah. *Tel Aviv* 7(3):194-202.

———. 1983. The Biblical Shephelah of Judah. *Bulletin of the American Schools of Oriental Research* 251:1-22.

Richter, Sandra L. 2005. Deuteronomistic History. Pages 219-30 in *Dictionary of the Old Testament Historical Books*. Downers Grove, Ill.: IVP Academic.

Ring, Yitskhak. 1977. The Biblical List of 31 Kings in the Book of Joshua against Parallels in Mycenaen Greek Tablets. *Tarbiz* 46(1):141-44.

Römer, Thomas. 2010. Book-endings in Joshua and the Question of the So-called Deuteronomistic History. Pages 87-101 in *Raising Up a Faithful Exegete*. Winona Lake, Ind.: Eisenbrauns.

Rosel, Hartmut N. 1980. Die Überleitungen vom Josua—Ins Richterbuch. *Vetus Testamentum* 30(3):342-50.

Rowlett, Lori L. 1992. Inclusion, Exclusion, and Marginality in the Book of Joshua. *Journal for the Study of the Old Testament* 55:15-23.

Sarna, Nahum M. 1999. Israel in Egypt: The Egyptian Sojourn and the Exodus. Pages 33-54 in *Ancient Israel: From Abraham to the Roman Destruction of the Temple*, rev. and exp. ed. Revised and edited by Hershel Shanks. Washington, D.C.: Biblical Archaeology Society/Upper Saddle River, N.J.: Prentice Hall.

Sasson, Jack M. 1966. Circumcision in the Ancient Near East. *Journal of Biblical Literature* 85(4):473-76.

Sawyer, John F. A. 1972. Joshua 10:12-14 and the Solar Eclipse of 30 September 1131 BC. *Palestine Exploration Quarterly* 104:139-46.

Schäfer-Lichtenberger, Christa. 2001. Hazor—A City State Between the Major Powers. *Scandinavian Journal of the Old Testament* 15(1):104-22.

Schatz, Elihu A. 2013. The Length of the Rule of Joshua and the Periods of Subjugation in the Book of Judges. *Jewish Bible Quarterly* 41(1):32-34.

Scott, R. B. Y. 1952. Meteorological Phenomena and Terminology in the Old Testament. *Zeitschrift für Die Alttestamentliche Wissenschaft* 64(1):11-25.

Sensenig, Peter M. 2012. Chariots on Fire: Military Dominance in the Old Testament. *Horizons in Biblical Theology* 34(1):73-80.

Shanks, Hershel. 2012. When Did Ancient Israel Begin? New Hieroglyphic Inscription May Date Israel's Ethnogenesis 200 Years Earlier than You Thought. *Biblical Archaeology Review* 38(1):59-62, 67.

Sherwood, Aaron. 2006. A Leader's Misleading and a Prostitute's Profession: A Re-examination of Joshua 2. *Journal for the Study of the Old Testament* 31(2):43-61.

Shiloh, Yigal. 1993. Megiddo: The Iron Age. Pages 1012-24 in vol. 3 of *The New Encyclopedia of Archaeological Excavations in the Holy Land*. Edited by Ephraim Stern. 4 vols. Israel Exploration Society and Carta, Jerusalem/New York: Simon and Schuster.

Sipilä, Seppo. 2008. On the Concept of God in the Masoretic Text of Joshua. Pages 477-87 in *Houses Full of All Good Things*. Helsinki: Finnish Exegetical Society.

Smelik, William F. 1999. The Use of *hzkir bsm* in Classical Hebrew: Josh 23:7; Isa 48:1; Amos 6:10; Ps 20:8; 4Q504 iii 4; 1QS 6:27. *Journal of Biblical Literature* 118(2):321-32.

Smith-Christopher, Daniel L. 2008. Gideon at Thermopylae? On the Militarization of Miracle in Biblical Narrative and "Battle Maps." Pages 197-212 in *Writing and Reading War*. Atlanta: Society of Biblical Literature.

Snaith, Norman H. 1978. The Altar at Gilgal: Joshua 22:23-29. *Vetus Testamentum* 28(3):330-35.

Spina, Frank. 2001. Reversal of Fortune: Rahab the Israelite and Achan the Canaanite. *Bible Review* 17(4):24-30, 53-54.

Stander, H. F. 2006. The Greek Church Fathers and Rahab. *Acta Patristica et Byzantina* 17:37-49.

Stern, Ephraim. 1993a. Dor. Pages 357-68 in vol. 1 of *The New Encyclopedia of Archaeological Excavations in the Holy Land*. Edited by Ephraim Stern. 4 vols. Israel Exploration Society and Carta, Jerusalem/New York: Simon and Schuster.

———. 1993b. Kedesh, Tel (in Jezreel Valley). Page 860 in vol. 3 of *The New Encyclopedia of Archaeological Excavations in the Holy Land*. Edited by Ephraim Stern. 4 vols. Israel Exploration Society and Carta, Jerusalem/New York: Simon and Schuster.

———. 2008. Dor. Pages 1695-1703 in vol. 5 (Supplementary) of *The New Encyclopedia of Archaeological Excavations in the Holy Land*. Edited by Ephraim Stern. 4 vols. Jerusalem: Israel Exploration Society.

Stone, Lawson G. 1991. Ethical and Apologetic Tendencies in the Redaction of the Book of Joshua. *Catholic Biblical Quarterly* 53(1):25-35.

Thigpen, J. Michael. 2006. Lord of All the Earth: Yahweh and Baal in Joshua 3. *Trinity Journal* 27(2):345-54.

Trebolle Barrera, Julio C. 2008. A Combined Textual and Literary Criticism Analysis: Editorial Traces in Joshua and Judges. Pages 437-63 in *Florilegium Lovaniense*. Leuven: Peeters.

Tur-Sinai, N. H. 1959. The Extent of the Battle of the Waters of Merom. *Bulletin of the Israel Exploration Society* 24:33-35.

Ussishkin, David. 1983. Excavations at Tel Lachish 1978-1983: Second Preliminary Report. *Tel Aviv* 10(2):97-185.

_____. 1993. Lachish. Pages 897-911 in vol. 3 of *The New Encyclopedia of Archaeological Excavations in the Holy Land*. Edited by Ephraim Stern. 4 vols. Israel Exploration Society and Carta, Jerusalem/New York: Simon and Schuster.

_____. 1995. The Destruction of Megiddo at the End of the Late Bronze Age and Its Historical Significance. *Tel Aviv* 22(2):240-67.

Walton, John H. 1994. Joshua 10:12-15 and Mesopotamian Celestial Omen Texts. Pages 181-90 in *Faith, Tradition, and History*. Winona Lake, Ind.: Eisenbrauns.

Ward, William A. 1997. Summary and Conclusions. Pages 105-12 in *Exodus: The Egyptian Evidence*. Winona Lake, Ind.: Eisenbrauns.

Weinstein, James. 1997. Exodus and Archaeological Reality. Pages 87-103 in *Exodus: The Egyptian Evidence*. Winona Lake, Ind.: Eisenbrauns.

Wesley, John. 1984a. God's Love to Fallen Man. Pages 231-40 in vol. 6 of *The Works of John Wesley*. 3rd ed. 1872. Repr. Peabody, Mass.: Hendrickson Publishers.

_____. 1984b. Plain Account of Christian Perfection. Pages 366-446 in vol. 11 of *The Works of John Wesley*. 3rd ed. 1872. Repr. Peabody, Mass.: Hendrickson Publishers.

Wiseman, D. J. 1964. Rahab of Jericho. *Tyndale Bulletin* 14:8-11.

Wolf, Herbert Martin. 1994. The Historical Reliability of the Hittite Annals. Pages 159-64 in *Faith, Tradition, and History*. Winona Lake, Ind.: Eisenbrauns.

Wood, Bryant G. 1990. Dating Jericho's Destruction: Bienkowski Is Wrong on All Counts. *Biblical Archaeology Review* 16(5):45-49, 68.

_____. 2000a. Khirbet el-Maqatir, 1995-1998. *Israel Exploration Journal* 50(1-2):123-30.

_____. 2000b. Khirbet el-Maqatir, 1999. *Israel Exploration Journal* 50(3-4):249-54.

_____. 2001. Khirbet el-Maqatir, 2000. *Israel Exploration Journal* 51(2):246-52.

_____. 2008. The Search for Joshua's Ai. Pages 205-40 in *Critical Issues in Early Israelite History*. Edited by Richard S. Hess, Gerald A. Klingbeil, and Paul J. Ray Jr. Winona Lake, Ind.: Eisenbrauns.

Yamauchi, Edwin M. 1994. The Current State of Old Testament Historiography. Pages 1-36 in *Faith, Tradition, and History*. Winona Lake, Ind.: Eisenbrauns.

Younger, K. Lawson. 1994. Judges 1 in Its Near Eastern Literary Context. Pages 207-27 in *Faith, Tradition, and History*. Winona Lake, Ind.: Eisenbrauns.

_____. 1995. The Configuring of Judicial Preliminaries: Judges 1.1-2.5 and Its Dependence on the Book of Joshua. *Journal for the Study of the Old Testament* 68:75-92.

_____. 2008. The Rhetorical Structuring of the Joshua Conquest Narratives. Pages 3-32 in *Critical Issues in Early Israelite History*. Edited by Richard S. Hess, Gerald A. Klingbeil, and Paul J. Ray Jr. Winona Lake, Ind.: Eisenbrauns.

Yurco, Frank J. 1997. Merenptah's Canaanite Campaign and Israel's Origins. Pages 27-55 in *Exodus: The Egyptian Evidence*. Winona Lake, Ind.: Eisenbrauns.

Zertal, Adam. 1986. An Early Iron Age Cultic Site on Mount Ebal, Excavation Seasons 1982-1987. *Tel Aviv* 13:105-65.

Ziv, Yehudah. 1985. Neqeb—An Incline. *Beth Mikra* 101:269-73.

Zorn, Jeffrey. 1992. Hazar-Susah. Page 84 in vol. 3 of *The Anchor Bible Dictionary*. Edited by D. N. Freedman. 6 vols. New York: Doubleday.

INTRODUCTION

The book of Joshua is central to the message of the Bible. It describes a crucial moment in the fulfillment of God's promise to establish his people in a land of their own. In it we see the completion of what God began in the exodus. It clarifies how God works with his people; its stories illustrate how God brings salvation. For these reasons and more, Joshua has for centuries occupied an important place within Judaism and Christianity.

Lately, however, Joshua has fallen on hard times. Archaeologists have raised questions about its historicity. Scholars have criticized its literary quality, labeling it a hodgepodge of propaganda stitched clumsily to a few old legends. The book certainly appears to be less valued than in the past.

Even those who relish the victories of the book's opening chapters tend to lose interest in its tedious allotment of the land. We quote God's command to Joshua at the opening of the book: "be strong and very courageous" (1:7) and Joshua's declaration at its conclusion: "as for me and my household, we will serve the LORD" (24:15), but few of us can identify favorite passages from in between. Many readers, even those committed to the book's divine inspiration, cringe at its violence. This book is embarrassing, like learning your great-grandfather was in the Ku Klux Klan.

Such may have been on the mind of commentators Robert G. Boling and G. Ernest Wright. They began their commentary on Joshua admitting that anyone "who would write a commentary on this book has a difficult task ahead" (1982, 4). They determined, however, that such a commentary was necessary, for "the traditions of the Book of Joshua must stand in the very center of any consideration of biblical religion" (ibid., 34).

Boling and Wright are correct on both counts. Significant challenges do face the interpreter of Joshua, yet now more than ever, God's people must understand and embrace this book. "The contemporary community of faith is impoverished theologically," writes another commentator, "when it fails to attend to Joshua" (Creach 2003, 3). This book is my attempt to help restore Joshua's riches to the church. By addressing the book's historical, literary, and theological challenges, I hope to allow its timeless message to be heard.

Since all biblical interpretation occurs in a particular context, shaped in part by previous interpretations, I begin with a survey of how this book has been interpreted from ancient times to the present, dwelling on how this book is read today. I then describe my interpretive approach, which seeks to read this book as an example of ancient rather than modern history. Although it contains historical details, it conveys them according to ancient rules for writing history. As nearly as we can tell, the unknown author prepared this account of the conquest at some point between the period of the judges and the beginning of the monarchy, drawing on earlier material, yet crafting a unified and coherent story. We attempt to give careful attention to the latest scholarly views of Joshua, whether archaeological, historical, or literary, yet our real interpretive goal is to read each passage as Christian Scripture, explaining its message in light of God's character and redemptive plan.

A. History of Interpretation

I. Inner-Biblical and Intertestamental Readings

Joshua's importance was realized evidently even while the rest of the OT was being written. It set a pattern followed by later historical works. For example, the transition phrase, "after the death of X" (Josh 1:1) appears again in Judg 1:1; 2 Sam 1:1; and 2 Kgs 1:1. Several psalms display an awareness of the conquest of Canaan (Pss 44; 74:15; 78; 80; 105; 106; 114; 135; 136), one presumably gained from the book of Joshua. The portrayal of Joshua in this book seems to have shaped the portrayal of King Josiah, particularly in the description of their similar attitudes toward the law of Moses (see Josh 1:8; 8:30-35; 24:26 with 2 Kgs 23:1-3; Josh 1:7; 23:6 with 2 Kgs 22:2; Josh 5:10-12 with 2 Kgs 23:21-23) (see Nelson 1997, 21-22, though Nelson postulates a different reason for these similarities). Postexilic Jews remembered Joshua's days as the golden era of obedience (Neh 8:13-18).

The book of Joshua also inspired many during the intertestamental period, including the Maccabeans (1 Macc 2:55; 2 Macc 12:15), and the authors of Sirach (46:1, 4, 7-8) and 4 Esdras (7:107). We find several references to Joshua among the Qumran literature (e.g., Psalms of Joshua [4Q378-379]). Josephus considered Joshua a military hero and wonder worker (*Antiquities of the Jews* 4.165, 5.61).

2. Joshua in the New Testament and Early Church

The NT contains several references to events in the book of Joshua. Rahab appears in the genealogy of Jesus (Matt 1:5) and Stephen speaks of Joshua in his sermon (Acts 7:45). Twice the book of Hebrews mentions events in Joshua, once to contrast the rest enjoyed by the Israelites with that experienced through the gospel (4:8-9) and once in celebration of faith (11:30-31). The last NT reference to this book, like the first, celebrates Rahab (Jas 2:25).

Early Christian interpreters made much of the comparison between the first and second Joshua. This was due largely because the early church read the OT in Greek (LXX) rather than in Hebrew; in Greek, the names Joshua and Jesus are identical. The Epistle of Barnabas, an early Christian work, treated Joshua's name change by Moses as a foreshadowing of Jesus (12:8-9). For the early church father Irenaeus, Joshua succeeding Moses and leading the Israelites into Canaan prefigured how Jesus surpassed the Law and brought eternal blessing to his followers (Fragment 19, Roberts and Donaldson 1950, I:571-72). Justin Martyr, another early church father, made a similar point in his *Dialogue with Trypho* (Roberts and Donaldson 1950, I:255-56, 265-66). The book of Joshua also received attention because of Marcion and others who criticized its violent portrayal of God, criticisms answered by other church fathers, such as Origen (2002, 123).

3. Joshua in Rabbinic Thought

The rabbis also celebrated the book of Joshua, honoring Joshua as a giant (Ginzberg 1968, IV:14), an ideal disciple of the law of Moses (ibid., 4; VI:170), and one of three for whom the sun stood still (*b. Ta'an.* 20a, as cited in Nelson 2005, 562). They believed Joshua married Rahab (Ginzberg 1968, IV:5), herself an ideal proselyte whose profession of faith was linked with those of Moses, Jethro, and Naaman. An ancestress to eight prophets (including Jeremiah and Ezekiel), she is also considered one of the four most beautiful women (with Sarah, Abigail, and Esther) and one of the four most seductive (with Ruth, Jael, and Michal) (Auld 1998, 131).

4. Joshua in the Modern Period

In the early modern era, increasing attention was directed toward the literary and historical nature of the book of Joshua. Focus turned to the sources of the book (e.g., Alt, Noth) and to how the archaeological evidence supported (e.g., Garstang) or contradicted (e.g., Kenyon) the written record. More recently, the book has been examined through a literary lens (e.g., Hawk) and sharply criticized for its violence.

a. Source Criticism

Some have challenged the traditional view that the book of Joshua provides a historical account of the Israelites during the years between the deaths of Moses and Joshua. They argue that the book of Joshua is actually a much later work that, though utilizing earlier sources, presents a largely fictionalized account that served the concerns of a much later audience. Notable in the formation of this understanding were Albrecht Alt (1883-1956) and Martin Noth (1902-68). They argued the book of Joshua was only part of a lengthy narrative that began with Deuteronomy and continued to the end of 2 Kings.

According to Alt and Noth, this story was written by an anonymous author (or authors), known to scholars as the Deuteronomist(s), who lived during the late monarchy and/or exilic period. This story was written to emphasize the importance of a single nation under a single God worshiping at a single site and carrying out the law of Moses with a single mind. Those who obeyed would prosper; those who disobeyed would be destroyed. This sweeping narrative, known as the Deuteronomic History (DH), was intended to explain Israel's failure (Noth 1991, 122, 134). (Branson provides a very helpful summary of this hypothesis [2009, 26-33].) The book of Joshua thus serves as an introduction to this saga, the Deuteronomist primarily focusing on Israel's history as found in Judges through Kings (Noth 1991, 136).

Scholars who embrace the DH hypothesis point to evidence suggesting that Joshua was the work of several authors using multiple sources. For example, Joshua touts a complete triumph by a unified nation, while Judges presents the conquest as partial and the Israelites divided. Scholars point to internal contradictions, such as with the conquest of Hebron. Joshua 14:13-15 describes it as given to Caleb, while later it is given to the Levites with Caleb receiving only fields and pastureland (21:11-12). Editorial activity seems especially obvious in chs 3—4, where there appear to be two crossings of the Jordan (3:17; 4:10-13) and two piles of stones (4:8, 9), awkwardly joined into one.

Multiple hands would explain the many duplications, such as the two references to Joshua's age (13:1 and 23:1), the land allotment inserted awkwardly between them. Another apparent duplication, the book's multiple endings (21:43-45; 22:1-6; 23:1-16; 24:1-28; 24:29-33), prompted one scholar to assert "that these two testaments of Joshua cannot be the work of one author (otherwise one should definitively give up the historical investigation of the Hebrew Bible!)" (Römer 2010, 93; see pp. 88, 99; for other examples cited as editorial activity, see Hawk 2005, 566-70; Curtis 1994, 30; Nelson 1997, 8; Auld 1998, 110; Barrera 2008, 460).

Scholars point out various sources used by the Deuteronomist. Because Josh 1—12 appears to focus on the tribe of Benjamin and the location of Gilgal, some scholars believe an ancient source lies behind these chapters, a collection of traditions about Benjamin and preserved at the sanctuary at Gilgal (Soggin 1972, 9; Miller and Tucker 1974, 8; Butler 1983, xxx; Hawk 2005, 569). The phrase "to this day," which appears several times in Joshua (4:9; 5:9; 6:25; 7:26; 8:29; 9:27; 10:27; 15:63; 16:10), is taken to indicate another cluster of sources, known as etiological narratives. These are stories that originated to explain why something is the way it is (e.g., how a certain cairn of stones originated). Yet another source, an ancient itinerary, is thought to lie behind the account of Israel's battles in ch 10. The land allotments of chs 13—21 are thought to be based on still another set of sources: administrative documents from the time of the monarchy.

Many scholars consider the portrait of Joshua to be too stereotypical to be historical. They argue that this portrayal, though possibly based on a real person, is now just a fictional character in a story, like King Arthur or Robin Hood. This explains why he "sits very light to much of the material" in the first part and why he sometimes disappears altogether (Curtis 1994, 70-71; Latvus notes that Joshua seems almost invisible in chs 9 and 22 [1998, 54-55, 65]).

Also taken as support for the DH hypothesis are the textual variants between the Masoretic Text (MT) and the Septuagint (LXX). The LXX is shorter than the MT by 4 to 5 percent. The two differ particularly in chs 5, 6, 20, and 24, but, as Butler notes, the LXX "shows numerous divergences from the Hebrew text in every chapter, at times in every verse of a chapter" (1983, xviii). More than one version of the book seems to indicate a "certain instability and history of development within the text" (Knoppers 2000, 126), rather than an eyewitness account.

Although the scholarly consensus for the DH has been quite strong, it appears to be weakening. It is becoming increasingly evident that Deuteronomy and Joshua arose during the second millennium (before 1000 B.C.) rather than the first. "Where they can be recognized in comparative ancient Near Eastern texts," writes Hess,

> individual names and objects and territory descriptions attest to a second millennium BC date. In many cases, such as the non-Israelite Hurrian names, there would be no reason to preserve these names and edit them into a later text. They are not famous or otherwise known. The simplest explanation remains that the texts that preserve these names also preserve a similar antiquity, dating from the late second millennium BC. With this evidence, the boundary descriptions and town lists from the second half of the book suggest that all of Joshua was intended as the application of a covenant document such as Deuteronomy or Joshua 24.

The book of Joshua describes the acquisition of the land and expresses these blessings in detail in chapters 13-21 just as Deuteronomy had specified the obligations of the law in chapters 12-26. Both on levels of literary form and of individual lexical items, this document reflects an authentic West Semitic scribal tradition whose antiquity reaches back into the second millennium BC. (1997, 76)

As Hess implies, the covenant agreements described in Deuteronomy and Joshua more closely reflect the type of covenants from the earlier period (for Deuteronomy, see Craigie 1976, 24-29; for Joshua, see Hess 1996a, 50). Nothing in the book of Deuteronomy, including its characteristic emphases—a single nation under a single God worshiping at a single site and single-mindedly carrying out the law of Moses with blessings to those who obey and disaster to those who disobey—requires a date past the time of Moses, except of course, the account of Moses' death (Hess 1996a, 33).

Growing appreciation for the literary skill of the ancient author has allowed us to recognize as artistry what earlier critics dismissed as duplications and careless editing (e.g., Younger's study of Josh 9—12 revealing "sophisticated rhetorical structuring" and "complex macrostructures" in these chapters [2008, 32]). This point will be illustrated in the commentary to follow.

On closer examination, some of the supposed contradictions between Joshua and Judges are more apparent than real (see Clarke 2010, 89-104). As Younger explains, "While the conquest account in Joshua narrates in a partial and selective manner the initial victory that 'softened up' the land, the partial selective account of Judges 1 narrates the failure to subjugate that land later" (1994, 227). These two accounts written according to the standards of ancient history differ, says Younger, because they were written for different purposes (ibid.). Far from contradictory, Judg 1 may be dependent on Josh 13—19 for "many of its macro-structures" (Younger 1995, 76). Kaufmann considers Judg 1 "the perfect continuation of Joshua" (1953, 86).

There are other problems with the DH hypothesis. Although it suggests the portrayal of Joshua is stereotypical, Hall has demonstrated that "there are too many distinctive features of Joshua's characterization to read it as exclusively paradigmatic or idealized" (2010, 9). He is "a full-fledged character," she argues, "one whose authority is established largely in relation to that of his predecessor, but whose leadership exhibits several distinctive features" (ibid.). Nor does he disappear from the book. Instead, the author periodically de-emphasizes Joshua to place additional emphasis elsewhere. Moreover, it is itself surprising that Joshua, an Ephraimite, would appear at all in a book supposedly focused on traditions relating to the tribes of Benjamin or Judah.

Recent scholarship has weakened the arguments based on the presence of etiological narratives. Childs and others have demonstrated that etiologies do not necessarily produce narratives (Childs 1974, 387-97; Long 1968), and Stern questions how much can be made of the presence of specific narrative forms (1991, 21). Younger points out that references to "to this day" are found in the Annals of Thutmose III (1990, 225).

Nor do the numerous textual divergences between the MT and the LXX prove textual fluidity over a long process of development. After a thorough study, van der Meer concludes, "By far the majority of the MT-LXX variants can be ascribed to literary initiatives introduced by the Greek translator" rather than a text that predates both the MT and the LXX (2004, 534). Earl contends the differences between the textual witnesses are mostly "changes in emphasis rather than gist" (2010b, 119).

To speak of a DH hypothesis is, itself, misleading. For some supporters, "the systematic and unified character of the work suggests a single hand" (Soggin 1972, 5), and "offers the reader a reasonably coherent plot" (Nelson 1997, 13). For others, DH is "a collection of books that are multivocal, complex, and do not show a tightly written, univocal, coherent unity" but is instead "a 'mental shelf' that includes different, though related books, not a single composition" (Ben Zvi 2010, 65 n. 10; see Pakkala 2008, 262; Latvus 1998, 67; Davies 2010, 57; Kaufmann 1953, 6). According to Knoppers, recent scholarship postulates "so many narrative complexes and deuteronomistic editions . . . that one wonders whether it makes sense to speak any longer of a unified work" or "deliberate plan" (2000, 124). As debate continues on how many hands were at work, how to tell them apart (Richter 2005, 227), who they were, and when they finished their work, one scholar describes the situation as "chaotic" (Auld 1998, 136-37).

b. History and Archaeology

Because modern interpreters are particularly interested in historical questions, scholars have given increased attention to the veracity of the Bible's historical accounts. Archaeology, one of the most helpful tools for answering such questions, began to be aggressively employed in the mid-nineteenth century. Although the archaeological evidence occasionally matches the account given in Joshua, even conservative scholars confess that the current evidence is "mixed and inconclusive" at best (Yamauchi 1994, 17). Other scholars are more adamant. According to one, "the empirical evidence of archaeology and language does not remotely resemble the biblical narrative of the Exodus and the Conquest" (Ward 1997, 111).

Currently, scholars propose three different versions for how the Israelites came to possess the land of Canaan. Some continue to argue for the traditional view, that there was a violent invasion and occupation, much like what is described in Joshua. As noted above, this view faces significant obstacles from the archaeological evidence for the Late Bronze Age period. Cities that Joshua supposedly conquered do not appear to have been occupied. Jericho does not appear to have been conquered in the Late Bronze Age as described by Joshua. The evidence is inconclusive for other sites as well, such as Ai. Garstang wrote in 1931 that he found "a considerable proportion" of Late Bronze Age I (ending around 1400 B.C.) pottery in Ai, but the material has since been lost (as cited in Callaway 1999, 67). Those sites that were destroyed during this time, such as Hazor and Lachish, offer no evidence conclusively identifying the conquerors as Israelites (Nelson 1997, 3). "Of the more than forty sites that the biblical texts claim were conquered," writes William Dever, "no more than two or three of those that have been archaeologically investigated are even potential candidates for such an Israelite destruction in the entire period from *ca.* 1250-1150 B.C." (2003, 71). For many, the obstacles faced by the traditional view are insurmountable.

Recent archaeological surveys demonstrate significant population growth in the foothills, central highlands, and Galilee during the Late Bronze Age. One estimate puts the number minimally at 21,000. These inhabitants terraced hillsides, plastered cisterns, and built homes with a layout different from their neighbors. All of these features might point to an Israelite presence, but not conclusively. For Hawk, the

> archaeological analysis of settlement patterns and material remains strongly suggests that the central areas of what would become the land of Israel were settled mainly by people within the land, rather than from culturally distinct groups from outside the land. (2005, 571)

Those who dismiss the traditional view fall into one of two camps. One proposes that the Israelites were originally desert nomads who gradually infiltrated Israel's highlands, eventually unifying into the nation of Israel under one God, Yahweh. The other postulates a revolt of Canaanite peasants. The former, known as the infiltration model, fits easily with the DH hypothesis, which allows the book of Joshua some historical basis. Perhaps, it is argued, the DH was composed to develop a sense of cohesion among these nomads that became Israel. This view agrees at several points with the traditional view: the settlers in Canaan left a nomadic existence for a more sedentary mode of life and came into conflict with urban Canaanites. The infiltration model contends, however, that this took place over centuries, not years and was much less violent than the traditional view. The infiltration model fits the archaeological survey evidence of a "general deurbanization of Canaan" and increased population in the highlands at the close of the Late Bronze Age and the beginning of the Iron Age (Harris 2000, 6). This view does not explain, however, how former nomads learned to farm in the steep and rocky highlands (Hawk 2005, 572).

The peasant revolt model, associated with George Mendenhall and Norman Gottwald, argues that Israel emerged from within Canaan. They were originally Canaanite peasants who threw off their rulers in the Canaanite city-states and organized along with an assortment of escaped slaves, mercenaries, those seeking a better economic life, pastoral nomads, and bandits (Dever 2003, 181-82). These peasants may have been motivated to leave the lowlands for the hills of Canaan for agrarian freedom (Dever) or for religious reasons (Mendenhall). As with the infiltration model, the peasant revolt model fits nicely with the DH, which presents the violent conflict as between "Israel" and the cities of Canaan (Hawk 2005, 572). The peasant revolt model also fits the situation described in the Amarna letters. These letters, numbering around three hundred, were written in the fourteenth century B.C. between Canaanite leaders and their Egyptian overlords. These leaders sought Egyptian help from international and domestic enemies. Many of the letters speak of the 'Apiru (or Habiru), "displaced people who were considered foreigners and/or outsiders of lower class" (Longman 2013, 715) who troubled this region and the entire Near East. Although the name sounds like the word "Hebrew," the scholarly consensus leans heavily against associating the Israelites with the 'Apiru. Nevertheless, the letters do show how concerned the Canaanite rulers were about a revolting underclass (Moran 1992, 148 [EA 77], 188 [EA 114], 212 [EA 130]).

The peasant revolt hypothesis also explains how the settlers in the highland region had the time and expertise to develop the needed agricultural innovations (Dever 2003, 178). Dever contends that the "recent archaeological evidence for indigenous origins of some sort is overwhelming" (ibid., 167). Although he also believes the more recent archaeological evidence indicates some military conflicts (ibid., 72, 82).

Beyond conservative evangelical interpreters who continue to hold to the traditional view, the prevailing scholarly consensus is for the infiltration or peasant revolt models. Most modern scholars believe Canaan was occupied not violently, but peacefully and piecemeal, more like what we find in Judges.

c. Literary Approaches

More recently, scholars have begun to employ a literary approach that focuses, not on the sources behind the book (as in source criticism), but on the text as we have it. This approach has showcased the book's literary artistry and theological complexity. Here again, however, there is not complete agreement. One scholar points out how the book of Joshua reveals a tension between "authoritarian dogmatism," that is, inflexible application of Mosaic law, and "critical traditionalism," which recognizes the need to be flexible in application, depending on the circumstances (Polzin 1980, 84). Another contends that the book of Joshua was meant to encourage Israel not to identify itself by its land, religion, or ethnicity but by the covenant whereby God has chosen them and they were to choose God (Hawk 2000, xxxii).

d. Cultural Factors Shaping the Interpretation of Joshua

Culture always shapes how people read the Bible. Not surprisingly, the particular questions and concerns of modernity and postmodernity have exposed aspects of the book of Joshua to greater scrutiny. For example, modernity has not been particularly accepting of accounts of the miraculous. Some deny the possibility that miracles can occur. Many others, however, resist miracle accounts because, as moderns, they insist on discovering and emphasizing the simplest natural cause behind a given effect. The ancients, by contrast, were more interested in supernatural causes than natural ones. Even where natural causes were involved, ancient writers were more inclined to emphasize the divine hand at work.

We can be glad for modernism's interest in natural causes, since it has led to wonderful benefits in science, medicine, and other fields. It has also sensitized us to how often in the Bible God accomplished miracles using nature. He used "a strong east wind" to part the Red (Reed) Sea (Exod 14:21) and likely stopped the Jordan with a landslide (→ Josh 3). For those who go further and rule out the possibility of divine intervention, there can be no miracles, God cannot have revealed himself to humans such as Moses or Joshua, and Israel's claims to having been divinely chosen are invalid. Obviously, adopting this point of view prevents the book of Joshua from being read as its author presumed it would be.

While modernists struggle with the miraculous, those influenced by postmodernism react against claims of absolute Truth. This reaction is not entirely unwelcome. Even those who do not agree with the philosopher Foucault that "all history-writing is fiction" (as quoted in Dever 2003, 142) should welcome the insight that each of us comes to a particular subject from a particular perspective. We can appreciate the recognition that science is not the infallible arbiter of truth and that past claims of absolute Truth have been proven wrong. For example, we now know the earth rotates around the sun rather than the sun rotating around the earth. To have any credibility in the marketplace of ideas, we need to acknowledge and confess that claims of absolute Truth have been used as weapons to justify wrong behavior, such as invoking biblical warrant to justify violence against another group. That contemporary culture is less dogmatic in asserting what we think is true is not entirely bad.

This aversion to absolute Truth can go too far, such as when it denies the possibility of a metanarrative, those big stories that seek to explain much, most, or everything. Metanarratives cannot exist, we are told, since everyone comes from a particular perspective and no one can get up high enough to see the whole terrain. Nor can they come to us from the outside, since this presumes the miracle of revelation. Furthermore, we are reminded, those who made such claims left the world in shambles (e.g., the Crusades, sixteenth- and seventeenth-century European wars of religion).

Illustrative is Regina M. Schwartz's critique of the metanarrative of monotheism, the belief in one God. She blasts this grand story for fostering an exclusivism that has left a trail of violent devastation (1997, 39). Its danger lies in its assertion that "its truth is *the* Truth" (ibid., 33, emphasis original). Schwartz thinks it would be much better for truth to become "truths, or better, stories, that illuminate and enrich each other with their variety and multiplicity rather than being partial installments on the one true story" (ibid., 173). For Schwartz, the Bible is "far too dangerous to continue authorizing. The old 'monotheistic' Book must be closed so that the new books may be fruitful and multiply" (ibid., 176). Her view illustrates the suspicion toward powerful grand stories and demonstrates why a traditional reading of the book of Joshua, with monotheism driving its exclusivist plot, seems out of bounds.

Yet another cultural emphasis, egalitarianism, shapes our reading of Joshua. Founded on the principle that all are created equal, Americans are working hard as a society to achieve racial and gender equality. In this atmosphere, Joshua's story of a chosen nation violently displacing Canaan's inhabitants seems barbaric (Brueggemann 2009, 13). If Israel's claims to have been divinely chosen are rejected, we have only one nation exalting itself at the expense of another.

An aversion to violence may be one of the most powerful cultural factors in lowering the credibility of the book of Joshua. We hear far too much of war, genocide, the evil effects of colonization, and violence inspired by religion. We cannot read the book of Joshua as we did before. For many,

> Much of the book of Joshua is repulsive, starting with ethnic cleansing, the savage dispossession and genocide of native peoples, and the massacre of women and children—all not simply condoned but ordered by God. These features are worse than abhorrent; they are far beyond the pale. Excoriable deeds and many others of at least questionable justifiability have been committed with the sanction of the book of Joshua, such as the decimation of the Native American peoples. People who regard themselves as peaceable Christians tend to shun the book of Joshua as not simply unedifying but irreconcilable with their faith, or to justify a tacit Marcionism by equating the worst parts of the book of Joshua with the entire OT. (Coote 1994, 578; see Kuan 2009, 189-203)

(For more on violence in Joshua, see the excursus later in this introduction).

The Bible cannot be read in a cultural vacuum. Even if possible, a reading that ignores the major questions facing any culture (e.g., how can God be good if he employs violence?) would be shirking its responsibilities. This commentary will attempt to take seriously these responsibilities when interpreting the book of Joshua.

e. Joshua as Christian Scripture

Some biblical scholars are once again asking what it means to read the OT as Christian Scripture (see Earl 2010b). This means interpreting a given text more like how it was interpreted in the early church and Middle Ages, in the context of the whole Bible and Christian doctrine. For some, this includes reading the Bible in a more than literal sense, even allegorically.

Practitioners of what is called theological interpretation consider the Bible to be a historical artifact, but much more. It can and should be studied objectively, like *The Iliad* or Shakespeare's plays, employing the historical-critical method. Questions should be asked about how we received the text, the meaning of its words and sentences, and the historical context that lies behind them (Treier 2008, 199). The Bible is much more than an object of history, however, representing an infallible and authoritative intersection where God meets with believers in Christian community by his Spirit.

History and the historical-critical approach to the Bible, once thought able to provide an objective, unbiased record of the facts, are now understood to be influenced by the perspective of the historian. If the interpreter's perspective cannot help but shape the outcome, what should that perspective be? Those who employ theological interpretation opt for the centuries old practice of reading Scripture through the perspective of Christian doctrine, the rule of faith.

Theological interpretation, while in some ways a return to a premodern approach, never completely disappeared in the modern era. A form of theological interpretation continued as the primary approach among some, including the late-nineteenth-century American Holiness Movement. From within this movement Martin Wells Knapp produced his heavily allegorical reading of Israel's history, *Out of Egypt, Into Canaan: or, Lessons in Spiritual Geography* (1887).

5. Conclusion

As this survey has demonstrated, the book of Joshua has moved from a central place in the biblical message to a neglected corner, disregarded as a source of historical information, challenged as a source of truth, and associated by many with the worst of humanity. I hope to show that the book of Joshua, when understood in its ancient and biblical context, can once again speak to contemporary culture with a message as timely and important as ever.

B. Interpreting Joshua Today

1. Introduction

For those who consider the book of Joshua to be divinely inspired, the challenges described above can be cause for alarm. "How can this be God's Word," we ask, "if it doesn't tell the truth about Israel's origins?" Actually, from earliest days the church refused to base the inspiration of this book on its being read as literal history. There is plenty of history here, but it must be read according to its ancient context. We must employ the guidelines by which ancient—not modern—history was written. As well as reading Joshua in its ancient context, we must read it in its biblical and theological context. Reading the book as both ancient and timeless, we can hear God speaking to us through its words.

2. Joshua as Ancient History

I find no compelling reasons to dismiss the essential historicity of the conquest so long as we read Joshua's description through the lens of ancient rather than modern history. The latter perspective insists on a historical account being written from an objective and impartial point of view; ancient history was assumed to be biased. No one in the ancient world thought the book of Joshua presented a straightforward account of the bare facts. Everyone assumed the book's author was a faithful follower of Yahweh and was writing, in part, to persuade others to be faithful followers themselves. As Sarna explains, the concern of an ancient historian "was with the didactic use of selected historical traditions for a theological purpose" (1999, 35; Younger 1995, 262).

We like our history in chronological order, but ancient historians felt free to jump forward and backward without warning. The ancient writer placed a lengthy speech in the mouths of the spies as they dangled from Rahab's window, not because the conversation took place at that moment, but because by placing it there he was able to better make his point.

We assume our historians are exact in their details. If Lindbergh's flight across the Atlantic took thirty-three and a half hours, that is what we expect to be told, and not a half-hour more or less. Ancient historians, by contrast, employed hyperbole, or intentional exaggeration (Wolf 1994, 164; Yamauchi 1994, 29). Ancient historians often described military exploits using hyperbole, as when the Egyptian pharaoh single-handedly defeated the Hittites. This is not dishonest; the authors knew their readers expected such descriptions rather than bare facts. Such "broad sweeping statements of victory . . . create an image of complete conquest for ideological reasons" (Younger 1995, 261). Both ancient historians and their readers knew that since the purpose of the writing was to persuade, facts would be employed creatively. Ancient historical accounts were less like newspaper reports and more like what is now called creative nonfiction, true information but creatively presented to persuade.

Although some ancient historical accounts originally circulated in writing, Israel's low literacy rate meant its histories likely first circulated orally. Even after being written down, an account like that found in the book of Joshua likely continued to circulate orally as well. This provided more fluidity to the historical accounts than what we are accustomed to today (Parker 1997, 9-10; see Hess 2002).

Since the purpose of ancient history was more to persuade than to describe, the Israelite historians responsible for books like Joshua wanted their readers to recognize God's hand at work in the nation of Israel and to respond by submitting to his Law. This explains why most of the historical books came to be known as Former Prophets. Like the Latter Prophets (e.g., Isaiah, Hosea), the Former Prophets, though historians, were also God's spokesmen, conveying God's message through the ancient standards of history writing.

That it was God's message is fundamentally important. To say the biblical authors expressed truth creatively under the inspiration of the Holy Spirit is very different from saying that the biblical authors invented Israel's history as propaganda in order to persuade Israel to believe invented details to shape their national identity. The purpose of this history was God's before it was any author's.

The book of Joshua, wrote Hamlin, is "remembered, condensed, and structured history" (1983, xiv). Its arrangement "does not necessarily reflect the actual course of events, which were doubtless much more complex, extended in time, and without the simple order found in the story as we have it" (ibid., xiv-xv). Beginning with such assumptions helps make greater sense of how the biblical and archaeological evidence fit together.

3. The Evidence for a Historical Conquest

Something resembling the exodus and conquest appears to have been known to the Israelites early in their history as a nation. Egyptian captivity hardly seems the kind of heritage a nation would "be likely to invent for itself, and faithfully transmit century after century and millennium after millennium" (Sarna 1999, 38). Most scholars agree that the Song of the Sea (Exod 15), which celebrates how Israel was delivered from the Egyptians and planted in Canaan, can be dated to the twelfth or thirteenth century B.C. (Yurco 1997, 45). The exodus from Egypt and the conquest of Canaan are referenced throughout the historical books (Josh 2:10; Judg 3:1; 5:1-5; Neh 9), psalms (see Pss 44, 65, 74, 78, 80, 105, 106, 114, 135, 136), and prophets (Isa 51:9-11; Hos 4:15; 9:15; 12:13; Amos 4:4; 5:5; Mic 6:4-5). The abundance of such references, their appearance in a wide variety of literature from early to late in Israel's history, and the ways they are employed suggests these events were already well known to the Israelites. This does not prove that the conquest occurred precisely as related in the book of Joshua, only that some type of conquest likely happened. As Butler puts it, "The experience of conquest of the land under divine leadership pervades Israel's entire tradition and must be accounted for by any specific theory" (1983, xli). The biblical account may be a literary product that is presented in a "highly telescoped" fashion (Malamat 1982, 26-27). "But at the core," says Malamat,

> a military conquest remains. Despite poetic embellishment and distortion, this ancient tradition reflects an intimate and authentic knowledge of the land, and a knowledge of its topography and demography—all as they relate to military strategy—which strongly support the conclusion that the settlement of the Israelites in Canaan was accompanied by substantial military operations. (Ibid., 27)

Many elements in the book of Joshua appear to be quite old. We have already mentioned how the covenants in Joshua more closely resemble those from the second millennium B.C. than from a later time. Another archaic element is how the book of Joshua refers to the land of Canaan. Joshua speaks of the boundaries of the land in ways that resemble how this same land was described by Egypt at the end of the second millennium (Hess 1996a, 26). According to Kaufmann, the OT presents five different conceptions of the land of Israel, each corresponding to different circumstances within Israelite history. He argues that in Joshua, the land "is a conception *peculiar to its own time*. We do not find it in the Pentateuch, and by the time of the Judges it is already out-of-date" (1953, 56-57, emphasis original).

The book of Joshua describes the city of Hazor in ways that seem quite old. It seems to know of a Jabin dynasty (11:1), of the city's status as "head" of all the kingdoms in that area (11:10), and of its destruction in the Late Bronze Age, all facts supported by archaeology. We see the book's archaic character in how one of its central elements—the completion of the conquest—is forgotten later in the books identified as part of the DH. "Neither David nor Solomon, nor anyone after them," says Kaufmann, "aspires to carry out Joshua's national testament. No prophet, no patriot, no dreamer of dreams demands the 'completion' of the Conquest" (1953, 62).

Even the boundary lists of Josh 13—21, considered by some to reflect monarchic administrative records, are likely much older. Kaufmann observes that for records to be useful to a government, they must be "clear and unambiguous," a description that does not fit these lists (ibid., 14-15). In fact, these descriptions are similar to boundary descriptions found in treaties from Ugarit and the Hittite capital in the Late Bronze Age (Hess 1996a, 58). Hess points out that like the lists in these treaties, Joshua's boundary lists contain introductions and conclusions indicating the land or lands on behalf of which the boundary is concerned, what he calls "brief historical notes that intersperse the boundary descriptions." Where there are duplicate descriptions, Hess notes, both sets of lists contain "slight variations in the spellings, sequence and selection of the place names as well as in the appearance of prepositions and notes that occur between the place names" (ibid., 59). In both sets "the parties involved and present at the point of decision represent the lands on both sides of the boundary" (ibid.). As well, these descriptions share a common purpose: "to define a legal relationship between the political groups involved" (ibid.). The boundary descriptions, it seems, are much more at home in the Late Bronze Age than in later periods.

If the book of Joshua contains a version of historical events and archaic elements, how do we account for the relative absence of corroborating archaeological evidence and the presence of conflicting evidence? First, we ought to give sufficient attention to the corroborating evidence we do have. For example, the book of Exodus and archaeology agree that the Israelites labored in the Goshen region of Egypt (Hoffmeier 1996, 122) and the cities of Rameses and Pithom, cities that had vanished into oblivion by the time of the DH (Yurco 1997, 44). The Merenptah Stele, dated to around 1210 B.C., identifies an ethnic group known to the Egyptians as Israel living in Canaan, perhaps in the highlands. That the inscription identifies Israel as a people group rather than a nation fits the Israelites as we meet them in Joshua and Judges (Dever 2003, 206; Hasel 2008, 47-59). An even earlier Egyptian inscription, perhaps dating to 1400 B.C., is said to mention the Israelites, although this identification is still contested (Shanks 2012, 59-62, 67).

Several sites that can be identified with some certainty on both sides of the Jordan attest occupation in the Late Bronze and Early Iron Age (Pitkänen 2010, 55). Archaeology and the Bible agree that Hazor and Lachish were destroyed during this period. While we do not know who did the destroying, Israel is certainly a prime suspect. Evidence for a burgeoning settlement in the highlands, as described earlier, fits the description of the conquest found in Joshua (Hess 1996a, 40). This area experienced a "population explosion" in the twelfth century by settlers whose material remains are strongly connected with the Israelites (Dever 2003, 98).

That the archaeological evidence for the Israelites is not convincing may have something to do with their having been nomads for a generation. This would likely make their archaeological footprint too subtle to detect (Yamauchi 1994, 33). Millard notes that "the biblical texts make it plain that the Israelites did not have a distinctive material culture of their own" (2008, 168). The situation is not unlike that of earlier Hyksos, a highly Egyptianized group of Semites who left Egypt in the sixteenth century (Weinstein 1997, 94). Although we do not know where the Hyksos went after leaving Egypt, a likely destination would have been Canaan. Yet archaeological evidence for their presence there is all but absent, raising questions about what archaeologists might be expected to discover about a migration of slaves.

It is also worth noting that the absence of evidence is not evidence of absence. Many sites have yet to be positively identified or even located; even when a site is confidently identified, only a fraction of that site is actually excavated (Yamauchi 1994, 34). Hess cautions against giving material culture "a logical and necessary priority over the written evidence" (1994b, 345). Archaeologists have located the city of Dibon in the Transjordan but have found no material evidence for Late Bronze Age settlement, in spite of solid extrabiblical inscriptional evidence that a city by that name existed at that time (Sarna 1999, 50; Hess 1994b, 342-44).

Some have sought to resolve the incompatibility between archaeology and Joshua by dating the exodus and conquest of Canaan prior to the Late Bronze Age, perhaps in the mid-1400s B.C. at the end of the Middle Bronze period. While some biblical evidence could be marshaled to support this date and some archaeological problems could be resolved, very few scholars argue for this early date, in part because of the lack of evidence for a large population settling in Canaan at this time (Weinstein 1997, 95).

This commentary is written from the perspective that the book of Joshua preserves at least a core of historical truth. During the Late Bronze Age, Israelites left captivity in Egypt (Sarna 1999, 45) and encountered the Canaanites, likely resulting in violent conflict. Since we are reading an ancient rather than a modern account, the details, sequence, chronology, and scope of the actual conquest may have actually been different from what we read here. What we have are the historical events as interpreted by the author in order to convey his overall purpose, to portray the conquest as the keeping of God's covenant promise to give Canaan to his people.

4. Authorship and Dating of the Book of Joshua

As noted earlier, some have proposed that the book of Joshua was composed in the late preexilic or postexilic period after a long period of development involving several authors utilizing multiple sources, some of them possibly ancient. In my estimation, this hypothesis does not adequately account for the data. Evidence suggests instead that the book was written no earlier than a generation after the latest events described and no later than the early decades of the monarchy. Although Joshua is the book's central human figure and is credited with writing some things during his lifetime (Josh 24:26), he probably did not write this book. This is not claimed anywhere in the book and, as we will see, several aspects suggest a later hand. Others traditionally suggested as authors include Aaron's sons, Eleazar and Phinehas.

It appears the book of Joshua was written no earlier than a generation after the events it describes. Little in the book indicates an eyewitness account; only once in the Hebrew does the author refer to "we" (5:1). Instead, it contains an account of Joshua's death and the deaths of those who outlived him (24:31). The author quotes Joshua's words from the Book of Jashar (10:12-13), something Joshua would not do if he were the author, nor would the anonymous author need to do if Joshua had been alive. One argument for an earlier date is that Rahab is described as still living among the Israelites (6:25). This more likely refers to Rahab's descendants remaining among the Israelites for generations. Even hundreds of years after David's death, people could still use his name when they meant his descendants (see Hos 3:5).

Additional evidence for dating the book of Joshua comes from what it has to say about the Phoenicians. Joshua 13:4-6 speaks of their destruction, yet by David's reign Israel was once again on good terms with the Phoenicians (2 Sam 5:11; 1 Kgs 5:1). During Joshua's time, Sidon appears to have been the chief city of the Phoenicians (Josh 11:8; 19:28), but by David's day Tyre had outstripped Sidon in significance. This evidence suggests a date for the book of Joshua prior to David's reign.

At several points the author repeats the Hebrew phrase rendered "to this day" (4:9; 5:9; 6:25; 7:26 [twice]; 8:28, 29; 9:27; 10:27; 13:13; 14:14; 15:63; 16:10), suggesting some time has elapsed between the events described and the writing of this book. The latest event recorded, according to Kaufmann, is the conquest of Leshem (Laish) by the tribe of Dan (Josh 19:47) (1953, 7). By leaving us at this point, the author of Joshua "reflects the situation created by the movement of Dan northwards, at the very moment of the migration" (ibid., 22), probably sometime during the twelfth century B.C. The earliest date for the writing of the book of Joshua seems to be in the several decades after this point, during the time of the Judges (ibid., 79).

As to latest date when the book could have been written, the Canaanites were still dwelling in Gezer (Josh 16:10). They were likely removed from this town at the close of David's reign or the beginning of Solomon's (see 1 Kgs 9:16). According to Josh 15:63, the Jebusites remain in control of the city of Jerusalem. Early in his reign David defeated the Jebusites and established his capital in Jerusalem (2 Sam 5:3, 6-9). When the book of Joshua was written, the location for the permanent central sanctuary had not yet been established (Josh 9:27), although Jerusalem was chosen during David's reign (see 2 Sam 6; 24:18). The latest date for the writing of this book appears to be early in David's reign.

Since the author of Joshua was not an eyewitness, he would have composed this work from oral and written sources. These sources included the Book of Jashar, and likely also semiofficial lists of territorial allotments, cities of refuge, and Levitical towns, among others. We cannot rule out the possibility that the book underwent some revision after this point.

5. Reading Joshua as Christian Scripture

This commentary seeks to interpret Joshua theologically. This means employing the best in historical-critical scholarship, fully investigating all we can know of the world behind and beneath the text and attempting to comprehend the author's intended meaning. I seek to pay careful attention to the book as an example of the genre of ancient history. Hebrew terms will be studied in light of their use through the OT. Ancient Near Eastern culture and history will be examined to shed light on the text as we have it.

Having taken pains to understand the literal meaning, I especially want to understand this meaning in light of God's work as revealed throughout the rest of Scripture and the Christian theological tradition. I want to read the human author's meaning in light of the meanings intended by the divine author. Although I do not employ the full-blown allegorical approach of Origen or Martin Wells Knapp, I share their assumption that the book of Joshua contains meanings not fully apparent to the original audience, but only clear in light of subsequent events in God's redemptive plan. I conclude each chapter with an extended theological reflection.

C. Theology of the Book of Joshua

Among the many theological truths in the book of Joshua, three portraits of God predominate: One who keeps his promises, who fights for his people, and who allows humans to partner with him in his work.

1. God Keeps His Promises

From its opening verses to its closing chapter, the book of Joshua presents the conquest of Canaan primarily as God keeping the promises he made to the patriarchs, to Moses, and to Israel. Hess considers that "each part of Joshua emphasizes the gracious and redemptive work of God on behalf of Israel and of Joshua" (1996a, 51). This helps to explain the "air of joyful optimism" (Woudstra 1981, 32) that shines through the book in spite of the contrasting "dark frames" of militarism and violence (Sipilä 2008, 478).

Centuries before Joshua's day, God swore an oath to Abram to give the land of Canaan to his descendants (Gen 15:7, 16, 18-21). God repeated this promise to Isaac (26:3) and again to Jacob (28:13). This promise pervades Jacob's final blessing to his sons and explains his insistence that he be buried in Canaan (ch 49). It was because of the promise of the land that Joseph commanded his bones be carried to Canaan when, as he said, "God will surely come to your aid and take you up out of this land to the land he promised on oath to Abraham, Isaac and Jacob" (50:24).

Although memory of the promise likely dimmed during the centuries in Egypt, Moses fanned it into flame when he returned to Egypt under divine commission (Exod 6:8). Even in the wilderness, Israel knew they were heading for this promised land. The laws of Leviticus presume a settled, not nomadic existence. Numbers describes the sending of the spies to explore Canaan (ch 13) as well as other passages that anticipate the conquest (27:12; 33:53). Deuteronomy is filled with promises and warnings about proper behavior in this promised land (e.g., Deut 6:10-11; 7:1 ff.; 9:3-5; 11:25; 12:10; 13:2-12; 25:19).

God made and kept this promise because of the covenant he "cut" with Israel. Genesis 15 describes a covenant "cutting" ceremony, with God himself passing between the pieces to seal his promise to Abram. It was because of this covenant that God rescued his people from Egypt and gave them the Law on Mount Sinai. This was the Law Joshua was instructed to keep (Josh 1:7-8), the Law he followed in the circumcision ceremony at Gilgal (ch 5), the Law that was reaffirmed in the ceremony in 8:30-35 and then again in chs 23—24. The centrality of the covenant is also evident in the prominent role assigned by the author of Joshua to the ark of the covenant (see chs 3—4, 6—8). Israel possessed the land because of the covenant and would keep that land only as they kept the covenant.

Keeping the covenant meant loving God and others wholeheartedly (Deut 6:4-5) but remaining separate from whatever defiles. Howard contends that avoiding defilement is one of the main themes of the book of Joshua (1998a, 60). Before they crossed the Jordan, the Israelites were to consecrate themselves (Josh 3:5); just after they entered, all Israelite males were circumcised, breaking free from past reproach (5:9). The people were to separate themselves from the spoils of Jericho (6:18) and the inhabitants of Canaan. They were even to keep themselves separate from Yahweh, maintaining a distance of a thousand yards between themselves and the ark while crossing the Jordan. Even Joshua was reminded of the importance of separation when instructed by the commander of Yahweh's army to remove his sandals (5:15). In his Law, God had made clear that Israel must be holy as he was holy. Not surprisingly, separation appears prominently in a book that takes Israel from the relative isolation of the wilderness into the settled and spiritually inhospitable land of Canaan.

The book of Joshua focuses on this land. This can be seen in many ways, including the great attention given to the crossing of the Jordan (chs 3—4), the conquest accounts (chs 6, 10—11), the list of conquered kings (ch 12), and most noticeably in the extended description of the land's allotment (chs 13—21). This may be the least interesting part of the book to the modern reader, but one can easily imagine generations of ancient Israelites lingering over these highly detailed verses, reading them as tangible evidence of God's faithfulness to keep his promise. This emphasis can even be seen in the account of Joshua's burial. Like the tombs of the other patriarchs, says Nelson, Joshua's grave "points to Israel's assured ownership of the land" (2005, 561-62).

Aside from its physical beauty, the land was special to Israel because it represented God's gift of rest (see Exod 33:14; Josh 1:13; 21:44; 23:1) (Earl 2010b, 26). This included rest from wandering in the wilderness. It probably also suggested something even more significant (→ 1:12-15). In this land they could experience God's blessings and become a source of blessing to others. The author of Ps 95 and the author of the book of Hebrews (Heb 3—4) took up this theme of rest in the land, although they emphasize "the 'not yet' of the complete fulfillment of these promises" (Woudstra 1981, 33). According to Butler (1983, 236), Josh 21:43-45 can be the summary of the book of Joshua:

> So the LORD gave Israel all the land he had sworn to give their ancestors, and they took possession of it and settled there. The LORD gave them rest on every side, just as he had sworn to their ancestors. Not one of their enemies withstood them; the LORD gave all their enemies into their hands. Not one of all the LORD's good promises to Israel failed; every one was fulfilled.

2. God Fights for His People

The idea of God as warrior can be traced back to the earliest days of Israel's history (Miller 1973, 63; von Rad 2000; Craigie 1978). It appears, for example, in some of Israel's earliest poetry, such as Exod 15 (Miller 1973, 168). One often encounters the divine name Lord of Hosts, rendered more clearly as "LORD of Heaven's Armies" (NLT). Frequent references to God as king imply he is also warrior; the two roles were inseparable in the ancient Near East (ANE) (ibid., 174).

In many ways, the book of Joshua makes clear that the battle for Canaan will be won, not by Israel, but by Yahweh, the Heavenly Warrior. God waited until the Israelites had crossed into enemy territory to have them be circumcised (Josh 5). What better way to remind them that victory depended on his power, not theirs? The curious military strategy of marching around Jericho was intended to make the same point. Their defeat at Ai came because of their disobedience, not military weakness. The author of Joshua explicitly credits Yahweh, not the Israelite army, with Israel's victory against the central coalition: "More of them died from the hail than were killed by the swords of the Israelites. . . . Surely the LORD was fighting for Israel!" (10:11, 14). Similar assertions are made concerning the victories over the southern (v 42) and northern coalitions (11:6, 20). Not just individual campaigns but the conquest of the whole land was said to be Yahweh's doing (23:3, 9-10; 24:18).

3. God Works through Humans

Although God fights for his people, he also requires them to join in the fight. There is no contradiction here; throughout the Bible God demonstrates that being his people requires this same synergy. According to Hall, the "relationship between divine and human agency is a fundamental component" of the ideology of the book of Joshua (2010, 167). The power is God's, but he graciously allows his people to participate with him and reap the benefits. They must participate with gratitude for what God has done, not with pride for what they have accomplished. This explains why the pace of the first half of the book is so "stop and go." Israel was to stop and mark each accomplishment with a memorial of what God had done before going on (Josh 4:1-24; 5:2-12; 7:6-26; 8:30-35; 10:16-27) (Kaufmann 1953, 92-93). For Hall, the halting pace conveys God's desire that Israel retain the connection between conquest and covenant (2010, 139).

This divine-human synergy can be seen in the author's portrayal of Joshua. The author provides few biographical details about Joshua. We know nothing of his appearance, his wife, or his children. Instead, the portrait of Joshua focuses largely on how God could use a faithful man. In Num 13:16 we see Moses changing Hoshea's name to Joshua, making Joshua the first person in the Bible to be given a name that explicitly includes the divine name, Yahweh. In this name change, Moses asserted something about Yahweh, about Israel, and about Joshua. Joshua's new name, "Yahweh is salvation," expressed Moses' faith in God's care for the oppressed, care he had powerfully manifested in deliverance from Egyptian bondage. Joshua's new name reminded the Israelites that even as they had been delivered from Egypt, God would finish that work by settling them in a land of their own. By changing Joshua's name, Moses was also saying something about Joshua: deliverance would come through him. Joshua would deliver as army commander—"as a mediating presence between God and the nation" (Hawk 2000, xix)—but most of all as a living example of how deliverance would be accomplished by faithful obedience to the Law.

Joshua is called the "son of Nun" thirty-one times in the OT, ten of these in the book of Joshua (Exod 33:11; Num 11:28; 13:8, 16; 14:6, 30, 38; 26:65; 27:18; 32:12, 28; 34:17; Deut 1:38; 31:23; 32:44; 34:9; Josh 1:1; 2:1, 23; 6:6; 14:1; 17:4; 19:49, 51; 21:1; 24:29; Judg 2:8; 1 Kgs 16:34; 1 Chr 7:27; Neh 8:17). Even King David is only called "son of Jesse" nineteen times. This frequency is significant for at least two reasons. First, it clarifies that the Joshua we meet in the book that bears his name is the same Joshua we met in the Pentateuch (Hall 2010, 19). More importantly, it reinforces Joshua's humanness. He through whom deliverance would come was only human, one who could stumble, as when failing to seek God regarding the Gibeonites (Josh 9:14). By presenting Joshua as a human like us, the author demonstrates how an ordinary person could be used in extraordinary ways by God.

The author's emphasis on Joshua as a man mightily used by God is evident in what is said—or rather, not said—about Joshua's physical appearance. He was not said to have Saul's height (1 Sam 9:2), Moses' vigor (Deut 34:7), or the good looks of Joseph (Gen 39:6) or David (1 Sam 16:12). All we are told about Joshua's body involves his mouth and hands. With his mouth he speaks for God (Josh 3:7-13; 4:15-17) and to God (10:12); with his hands he builds memorials of God's actions (4:5-8, 20-24), circumcises the Israelites (5:3), and exacts God's justice (6:2; 8:1-2, 18, 26; 10:8, 26) (Creangă 2010, 90). Silence regarding Joshua's appearance, apart from mention of his mouth and hands, emphasizes God's extraordinary employment of an ordinary human.

The author may intend the reader to see Joshua as the last patriarch. Like Jacob he built an altar at Shechem and demanded obedience to Yahweh (Gen 33:20; 35:2-4; Josh 8:30-31; 24:23). Like Sarah, Abraham, Rachel, Leah, Isaac, Jacob, and Joseph (Gen 23:19-20; 25:9-10; 35:19, 29; 49:29-32; Josh 24:32), but unlike Moses, his place of burial was identifiable.

With more confidence we can say that the author presents Joshua's character in such a way as to prompt a comparison with Moses (Hall 2010, 196). The book opens with a clear statement that asserts Mosaic primacy: Moses is the servant of Yahweh but Joshua is only Moses' aide (1:1-2). Yet even from this opening account we see Joshua as almost a new Moses. He too receives a personal commission by Yahweh (1:1-9), speaks directly with God (e.g., 3:7-8), is exalted in the eyes of Israel (3:7; 4:14), succeeds by Yahweh's presence (1:5, 9, 17; 3:7; 7:12), cooperates with God in producing miracles (3:7-17; 6:1-20; 10:8-15), and receives divine encouragement on the eve of battle (6:2; 8:1-2; 10:8; 11:6) (Hall 2010, 196). Like Moses, Joshua faithfully carries out God's commands (4:15-17; 11:6, 9, 15) and conveys God's words (3:9). Like those made by Moses, Joshua's decisions have lasting consequences. Like Moses, Joshua delivers a farewell speech with promises and warnings (Hawk 2005, 565).

While a comparison can easily be made between the two, Hall is right to note that Joshua is not actually presented as a second Moses: "Some features of his character are presented as a deliberate departure from the leadership of his predecessor. Joshua is shown to excel in the very areas in which Moses proves weakest" (2010, 197-98). Unlike Moses, Joshua always eagerly obeys precisely as instructed, leads the people without provoking their objections, and plays an active role in Israel's battles. "Joshua's freedom to propose a miraculous strategy for the battle at Gibeon," notes Hall, "is depicted as both unprecedented and unparalleled (10:12-14)" (2010, 198). The difference between the two men may be most stark when one compares Moses' experience at the burning bush (Exod 3) with Joshua's encounter with the commander of the Lord's armies (Josh 5:13-15). Unlike Moses, Joshua offers no excuses, but instead inquires after the Lord's instruction.

The author's comparison of Joshua with Moses, therefore, is nuanced. Joshua is like Moses in many ways but unlike him in others. This is clear in Joshua's relationship with the law of Moses. He does not become Moses' successor as the next lawgiver in Israel. Instead Joshua submits to the Law and promotes it among the people (see Nelson 2005, 561, who cites Josh 1:7-8, 13; 4:10; 8:30-35; 11:12-15; 22:2; 23:6). He is as much teacher of the Law as general, the latter role largely dependent on the former (Hall 2010, 22). Nor is Joshua merely a lifelong deputy. Not only with the battle at Gibeon, but throughout the book, "Joshua responds to Yahweh's general commission by exercising his own initiative and thoughtful leadership. The dynamic of Joshua's ingenuity will characterize the whole of the conquest narrative" (ibid.). Although subordinated to Moses at the beginning, by the end of the book, Joshua is called the **servant of Yahweh** (24:29), the same title given to Moses in 1:1 (Hawk 2005, 565).

Some have proposed that the author of Joshua believed that the promise of a prophet like Moses (Deut 18:15-19) was fulfilled in Joshua (Harris 2000, 4). In the ancient Near East, there would have been a prophet who divined the will of the gods (perhaps by examining the liver of a sacrificial animal), and the king who would carry out that will. Read against that context, Joshua is seen to fulfill both roles (Hall 2010, 93). He speaks prophetically—both "forth-telling" or preaching, and foretelling, as in predicting the future (Josh 6:26; 23:5)—and also serves "as a messenger for the direct communication of Yahweh ('thus says Yahweh' [Josh 7:13; 24:2-13])" (Nelson 2005, 562). Little wonder later writers spoke of him as a prophet (Sir 46:1). Whether or not he was the prophet promised in Deut 18, Joshua does fulfill a prophetic role in this book.

A more challenging question is whether the author meant to portray Joshua as a model for future kings. Many have assumed that the Deuteronomist presented Joshua as a model for King Josiah. Others have suggested the book of Joshua is anti-monarchy, pointing out that the only kings mentioned in the book oppose Israel and are destroyed. Joshua is here presented as one who "kills kings; he does not model them" (Dozeman 2010, 115; see Brueggemann 2009).

Unlike the book of Judges, which repeatedly anticipates the monarchy, the book of Joshua says nothing about a king or even who would govern after Joshua. Perhaps we are meant to understand this as Joshua's mistake; by failing to appoint a successor, he doomed Israel to the anarchy that followed. Perhaps it is a veiled statement of support for a king, anticipating the more explicit support in Judges (see 19:1; 21:25). Or perhaps silence on succession was not intended as a statement about the best way to govern Israel but was meant to highlight the responsibility of each Israelite, particularly each elder, to follow

Yahweh as Joshua had. Or possibly a de-emphasis on human kingship was meant as a subtle affirmation of divine sovereignty in a synergistic relationship with faithful humanity.

D. Excursus on the Violence in the Book of Joshua

The book of Joshua presents God as a warrior, a disturbing picture of a God who not only employs violence but instructs his people to carry it out on his behalf. Jenkins identifies "The Most Disturbing Conquest Texts": Exod 17:8-16; 23:23; 34:11-17; Num 21; 25:1-18; 31:1-24; 33:50-56; Deut 2:24-37; 3:1-7; 7:1-2, 16; 13; 20; 25; Josh 6; 8; 10; 11:20; 1 Sam 15, although this list is not exhaustive (2011, 36-39). No commentary on the book of Joshua intended to address cultural concerns can ignore the violent God we meet here.

Interpreters have understood this violent material in a variety of ways. Some have embraced it, either gladly or reluctantly. The former represent those Christians who have taken these passages as license to kill. Although accepted scholarly opinion tends to promote the truism that the book of Joshua was widely used to justify the Crusades, evidence for such use is scarce (Earl 2013, 19-43).

A much larger group, not personally supportive of violence, believes it must be justified since God commanded it of his people in the Bible. Though they do not know how it is justified and are not sure it should be, they do not want to question God's justice. Hence they fail to fashion a fully Christian position on violence and remain blind to the power of biblical texts to "not only *say*, but *do*" (Brueggemann 2009, 9, emphasis original).

Many believers ignore these passages, either by turning a blind eye or actually excising them. An example of the latter is seen in the Revised Common Lectionary, which eliminated such texts from its public Bible readings, leaving us with what Jenkins called "an acceptable Bible Lite" (2011, 15). Others ignore these passages by what Steven Pinker calls "benevolent hypocrisy," paying no attention to what these texts assert while taking our ethics from gentler sources (2011, 11-12, 17).

Others have gone still further by denying that such violent texts are inspired. Marcion is our best-known example of such a position, but he is not alone. Kuan concludes, "Ultimately, we must say no to such [violent] constructions of the divine, even if it means that we are forced to confront our own notions of what we mean by the sacred text" (2009, 201). Another modern Marcionite avers, "The God of the crucified and powerless Jesus cannot be the same as the deuteronomistic God of anger" (Latvus 1998, 91). For Latvus, "The God that deuteronomistic theologians created in their own image was thus the God of strict dogmatism, intolerance and fundamentalism—and of course: the God of anger" (ibid.).

Some affirm the divine inspiration of these passages out of one side of their mouths but deny it out of the other, because they supposedly contradict the words of Christ (see C. S. Cowles in Cowles et al. 2003, 11-60). Cowles and others who take this approach must ignore the violent passages in the NT as well, many of which are spoken by or involve Jesus.

Some deny such passages are God's words but are only human words about God. Israelite assertions of Canaanite sinfulness or claims to follow God's commands to destroy others are only hollow self-justifications (Collins 2004, 13). We cannot be as sure of God's will as the Israelites claimed to be, something Collins considers a good thing:

> The Bible has contributed to violence in the world precisely because it has been taken to confer a degree of certitude that transcends human discussion and argumentation. Perhaps the most constructive thing a biblical critic can do toward lessening the contribution of the Bible to violence in the world is to show that such certitude is an allusion. (Ibid., 32-33)

Still others have sought to prove these violent texts are both inspired and safe to use, but by questionable means. Origen, for example, sought to spiritualize violent passages. In one of his homilies on Joshua, he encouraged his listeners to "manage wars of this type spiritually" (2002, 123). While I agree that such passages have implications for spiritual warfare, we cannot so easily dismiss the historical basis for these accounts.

Another questionable approach reads between the lines of the passage what is not there. The rabbis sought to resolve the problem by contending that Joshua gave the Canaanites a chance to leave Canaan voluntarily (Auld 1998, 132). Brueggemann contends God cannot be blamed for what happened to the northern coalition in Josh 11. The passage does not tell us, Brueggemann writes, what God did to "hand over" the enemy coalition to Israel. He contends that "a close reading shows Yahweh really does nothing in this verse and indeed does not promise to do anything beyond a general commitment of solidarity and legitimation. The action is left to Joshua and to Israel" (2009, 23).

Yet another questionable approach of maintaining both the inspiration and safety of these verses is to treat it *only* as a literary product and not actual history (see Earl 2010a). A story about violence is thought to be less problematic than a historical account describing violence. Centuries after Israel settled in the land, at a time when they were incapable of such military feats, Israel is said to have invented these stories about a violent conquest (Smith-Christopher 2008, 211). In this way, says Hawk, the author of Joshua actually "undercuts claims of divine sanction for such agendas" (2005, 573; see Rowlett 1996, 183; Rowlett 1992, 15-23). Reading the violent passages as only literary creations from a later date does not solve the problem, however, since it still regards violence positively (Collins 2004, 14-15). A positive view of violence, even violence that did not really happen, can fuel acts of violence in God's name. Further, this explanation fails to take these passages seriously as ancient history.

How then are we to read the book of Joshua, including these violent texts, as God's inspired Word, yet still of use for Christians today? How can we read this book as it seeks to be read? How can we maintain that the God we meet here is, like Aslan, not tame, but good (Lewis 1950, 76)? God has said and done some very harsh things and has instructed his people to do the same. But he had his reasons, reasons that render such passages both inspired and usable. Their use can never be to sanction violence, since God's reasons for the conquest were unique and unrepeatable.

Even as we seek to make sense of how these passages can be both inspired and safe to employ, we must remember that some pain goes beyond the reach of words. As Job discovered, even helpful explanations can be misunderstood as attempts to minimize past pain or excuse past abuses. With this qualification, let me suggest that a helpful approach to addressing this question requires that Joshua be read in its historical context, in light of God's revealed character, and in light of God's redemptive plan.

I. Read This Book in Its Historical Context

With any other literature, this point would be too obvious to mention, but the nature of the Bible as inspired sometimes leaves the mistaken impression that God spoke these words only to us today. The Bible records timeless truth, but it does so in ways that are historically conditioned. To hear what God is saying through the Bible today, we must begin by listening to its passages over the shoulder of the Bible's original audience. When we do, we discover that God revealed the truth at a level and in ways that his people could understand. Calvin compared it to a parent speaking baby talk to a child (*Institutes*, Bk. 1, ch 13, sec. 1). God allowed himself to be described as a warrior, wrote Miller, in ways "quite similar to the ideas expressed in the language, mythology, and imagery of other nations in the ancient Near East" (1965, 42). God stooped to describe himself to ancient Israel as a warrior, not because he is essentially violent, but because he wished to portray his mighty kingship. That particular analogy came with violent connotations. In time, God would shed those connotations until Israel's king arrived gently, on a donkey, as the Prince of Peace (Isa 11:1).

Reading Joshua in light of its historical context requires us to recognize the significant differences that exist between that time and this. Even the definition of violence is different. We tend to use the term, according to Creach, "rather broadly to mean something like exertion of physical force that injures or abuses." The OT opts for a more narrow definition, one that "refers principally to actions that tear at the fabric of Israelite society by defying the sovereignty of God" (2003, 15). Good argues that the Israelites understood their involvement in warfare as a judicial activity. Divinely commanded warfare was "the expression of a *legal* judgment of Yahweh made for the purpose of resolving a dispute between Israel and the neighboring states" (1985, 387). This may help to explain why the conquest does not appear to raise ethical problems for the Israelites.

Nor would the conquest have raised ethical issues for Israel's neighbors. In that day, warfare was widely seen as a religious act, begun by seeking the will of a god and carried out with the help of that god, divine symbols prominently displayed. If victorious, one celebrated to the glory of one's god. According to Jones, "The main groups of people in the area interpreted national warfare as holy or religious wars," even viewing the battlefields as temples (1989, 299, see 300-301; see Oded 1991, 223-30). Because religion was closely associated with nationality, warfare in a god's name meant bad news for the enemy. As Liverani cogently expressed it, "The best foreigner is a dead one, next comes a submitted one" (1990, 144).

Although not all warfare implied the total annihilation and desolation of the enemy as an act of consecration to the deity, this practice was common enough to have a name: *ḥerem*, known both to Israel and her neighbors. The term appears in the line at the exact center of the inscription on the Mesha Stele. This monument commemorates Moab's victories over Israel (Stern 1991, 43). The concept of *ḥerem* is known by different names throughout the ANE (see ibid., 2, which identifies a similar concept in Sumerian, Hittite, and Old Babylonian literature, contra Jenkins 2011, 43). While the discovery of destroyed precious objects found by Sir Flinders Petrie cannot be proven to be an example of *ḥerem*, such artifacts do "illustrate the fact that unusual acts of destruction on the scale of the חרם [*ḥerem*] were not strange to the inhabitants of Canaan, at least at the beginning of the 2nd millennium" (Stern 1991, 66). Even without extrabiblical evidence, we could deduce the idea of *ḥerem* from the close association of warfare, religion, and nationality across the region at that time.

According to Stern, *ḥerem* meant more than consecration through destruction; it meant the restoration of cosmic order out of chaos (ibid., 3). This can be seen in the cosmic nature of the exodus and the conquest as described in passages such as Exod 15 and Pss 78, 114. The Canaanites had poisoned the land through idolatry. When the Israelites forcefully removed them, the land was once again allowed to experience what it was intended for (ibid., 50, 110, 222). According to Boling and Wright:

> The epic events of Egypt and Canaan are of universal significance and the whole can be spoken in terms which remind one of Canaanite cosmogony, while the battles are generalized, so that Israel may understand

the whole history of earth's warfare as the divine battle for justice. (1982, 25)

The *ḥerem* was meant to prevent the unthinkable: God's people permitting the destruction of God's creation.

How the ancients waged war is an important part of the historical context; how they wrote about war is another. The book of Joshua provides an inspired version of an ancient battle account and should be read accordingly. As noted earlier, we should assume that absolute statements, such as "the entire land had been taken" or "the total city destroyed," were never intended to be understood literally, but as hyperbole. "The claims to conquest have been overstated," says Younger. "This is a very similar situation in the vast majority of ancient Near Eastern conquest accounts" (1990, 244). No doubt there was some bloodshed involved in the conquest, but reading these as literary expressions rather than newspaper accounts diminishes the violence to some extent.

2. Read This Book in Light of God's Revealed Character

While no amount of explanation can make pleasant reading of the conquest, the Bible does provide a rationale for God's actions. God is sovereign; this much is made abundantly clear in the material leading up to the book of Joshua. God rules over everything, having created everything. As Creator, he established an orderly realm characterized by justice and righteousness (see Pss 89:2[3]; 96:10). As Creator of all, he owns all: every person, every place, everything. As the psalmist writes, "To Yahweh belong the earth and all it contains, the world and all who live there" (Ps 24:1 NJB). Specifically, he rules the nation of Israel because he miraculously created it from an elderly childless couple and because he rescued this nation from slavery in Egypt. At Mount Sinai he made a covenant with the Israelites in which they swore to be his subjects and he to be their sovereign.

The relationship between king and subject was well known in the ancient world. Subjects were required to love their king, that is, to demonstrate loyalty through sacrifice and service on the king's behalf. The king, considered the shepherd of his people, was required to protect and provide for his subjects, especially the neediest among them, widows and orphans in particular. This he did through his policies and by ensuring justice in the courts. Across the ancient Near East, the measure of a king's reign was more than his wealth and power, but how well he looked after the weak. "The establishment of a just society," wrote Weinfeld, "is the responsibility of the king" (1995, 45; see pp. 45-56 for numerous examples from the ANE).

Not surprisingly then, the Pentateuch is filled with examples of God's concern for his people, especially the weak. A large proportion of the Mosaic law is devoted to ensuring that people treat each other fairly. For example, they are not to move boundary stones (e.g., Deut 19:14; 27:17) or harvest the edges of their fields (e.g., Lev 19:9). They should only punish in ways that fit the crime, also known as the *lex talionis* or "eye for eye, tooth for tooth" (e.g., Exod 21:24). The Heavenly King protected not only his subjects but also the foreigners living among them (e.g., 22:21). We have not properly understood the God who commanded the destruction of the Canaanites until we also take note of his equally binding commands to show compassion to the foreigner.

King Yahweh led his people through the wilderness to the land of Canaan, a portion of his territory currently occupied by squatters. As far back as Genesis, God had indicated his intention to displace these inhabitants. The time for eviction had now come. Weinfeld sees here a parallel to the (ANE) practice of settling freed servants in holy territory (1995, 233). Israel was not given land that had belonged to the Canaanites; Israel was given land that belonged to God but was occupied by the Canaanites. Actually, the Israelites are not given this land at all. They are merely permitted to live on God's property as tenants (see Exod 15:17; Lev 25:23; Ps 78:54) (Weinfeld 1995, 234-35, 242; Earl 2010b, 143).

Why did God not locate Israel elsewhere in some uninhabited place, avoiding a bloody conquest? God chose Canaan for its location, strategically situated on the land bridge between three continents. What Goetze said about nearby Syria was also true for Canaan: "In antiquity possession of this key position assured supremacy in the world as it then existed" (1975, 1). On this land bridge, where Israel could have maximal impact on the world, God would accomplish his purposes in and through his people: not world supremacy, but world redemption.

God's purposes were best accomplished in the land of Canaan but could not be accomplished if the Canaanites remained. The problem with the Canaanites was not their race; in fact, they did not represent a single race but a conglomeration of ethnic groups. Ethnicity was not the issue at all. If this was simply a matter of a good race eliminating an evil one, the stories of Rahab and Achan make no sense. Hence, the term "genocide," with its implications of ethnic cleansing, cannot properly be applied to the conquest. As Christopher J. H. Wright notes, "The conquest of Canaan is *never* justified on ethnic grounds in the Bible, and any notions of ethnic superiority—moral or numerical—are resoundingly squashed in Deuteronomy" (2008, 92, emphasis original).

The problem with the Canaanites was their morality, or lack of it. The Canaanites were being removed from the land, not because of Israel's superiority, but "on account of the wickedness of these nations" (Deut 9:5). The text accuses the Canaanites of sexual improprieties, divination, and child sacrifice (Lev 18; 20; Deut 18:9-12), but especially of idolatry (Deut 12:1-7, 29-31) (Jones 2009, 53-72). Nor was the issue that the Canaanites were more wicked than others living at that time, only that Israel could not live alongside them and thrive (see Deut 20:16-18). If Israel needed to be in Canaan but could not dwell there among the Canaanites, King Yahweh had to protect his subjects by removing the Canaanites. Those who consider the Bible authoritative cannot escape the conclusion that the God we meet in this book, "the Giver of all life, has certainly the right to withdraw life or to command that it be withdrawn" (Craigie 1978, 60).

God is no rage-aholic, furiously condemning the Canaanites to die. The few references to God's anger found in the book of Joshua refer to his anger at Israel, never at Canaan. By contrast, Assyrian accounts describe attacks prompted by the gods' wrath against their enemies (Oded 1991, 226-27). Nor is God bloodthirsty. "If there is a distinctive feature of Israel's attitude towards war," writes Hess, "it is that God did not approve of all wars" (1996a, 43). What he commands the Israelites to do to the Canaanites is unique in the Bible. At no other time and in no other location is Israel instructed to conduct aggressive military action. When the Israelites do engage in battle on their own authority, they are defeated (see Num 14:39-45).

According to the book of Joshua, God actually limited the warfare against the Canaanites. The *ḥerem* was generally directed against select Canaanite cities. Stern notes, "The urban nature of the phenomenon is certain. Practically every instance of the חרם [*ḥerem*] is directed at a city with the exception of the Amalekites, who were a menace to Israelite cities, such as Ziklag (1 Samuel 30)" (1991, 225). In Joshua, the only places under the *ḥerem* were southern Canaan (Num 21:2-3; Josh 10:28-39), Jericho (6:21), Ai (8:26), and Hazor (11:11). Perhaps these locations were targeted to serve as examples, prompting those in other cities and the countryside to flee to safety. The *ḥerem* may have been intended to be more instructive than destructive.

The Canaanites knew Israel was planning to invade. They heard how Yahweh had delivered the Israelites from Egypt and had given them victories over more powerful enemies (see 2:9-11). The Canaanites faced a choice: surrender, flee from their homes, or defend what they thought was theirs. Rahab took the first choice. No mention is made in Joshua of specific Canaanites taking flight, but there is considerable textual support for the Canaanites choosing the second option and abandoning their homes (Exod 23:27-31; 33:2; Lev 18:24; Num 33:51-52; Deut 6:19; 7:1; 9:4; 18:12; Josh 24:12, 18; 1 Chr 17:21; Pss 78:55; 80:8). According to Copan, the language of expelling the Canaanites occurs three times more often than the language of destruction (2009, 83). "When a foreign army might pose a threat in the ANE," writes Copan, "women and children would be the first to remove themselves from harm's way—not to mention the population at large: 'When a city is in danger of falling,' observes Goldingay, 'people do not simply wait there to be killed; they get out. . . . Only people who do not get out, such as the city's defenders, get killed'" (ibid., 83).

With the exception of Rahab and the Gibeonites, the book of Joshua focuses only on the Canaanites who chose not to run for their lives but to remain and fight. God did not force these to remain, in spite of how some interpret the reference to God hardening their hearts (Josh 11:20; see Jenkins 2011, 46). The verb "hardened" can have this meaning, but here it likely means that God allowed these Canaanites to harden their own hearts (see McAffee 2010, 331-53). These who did not surrender or flee were so determined to hold on to this land that they behaved in ways that defied common sense (as did Pharaoh in the face of Moses' demands). God gets the credit (according to the author of Joshua) or blame (according to Jenkins and others) because he brought about the circumstances that led to the Canaanites' self-hardening.

The author of Joshua does not point to Canaanite depravity or even idolatry as the cause of the conquest. He focuses on how the Canaanites had become "increasingly resistant to the actions of Yahweh. The Israelites are depicted not as a savage, unstoppable war machine blazing over Canaan, but as reacting to the Canaanite kings' opposition to Yahweh" (Stone 1991, 34).

Only at Jericho and Ai do the Israelites appear on the offensive, although neither instance involves an actual attack. Every campaign past this point "is portrayed as a *defensive* reaction to Canaanite aggression" (Earl 2010b, 166; Stone 1991, 33). The Canaanites knew this invasion was for all the marbles, as Rahab's confession (Josh 2:9-11) makes clear. The Canaanite leaders knew that Israel's previous battles had involved *ḥerem*, the complete destruction of all they encountered (see 2:10). These leaders also knew the Israelites would not be able to take captives. Societies in the ANE without sufficient economic organization to use POWs or the civic power to control them "would kill them" (Stern 1991, 38; see Gelb 1973, 71). Any uncertainty about Israel's intentions in the minds of the Canaanites should have been removed by reports of what happened to Jericho. The destruction and cursing of that city was meant to send a message to both the Canaanites and the Israelites that Yahweh, Creator and King, was now laying claim to his land.

3. Read This Book in Light of God's Revealed Plan

The conquest must be understood, not only in light of God's character as Creator and King, but also in light of his redemptive plan. Although this plan reached its climax on Calvary, the OT reveals much about God's intermediate and ultimate solutions for the problem of sin.

God chose to engage this fallen world, rather than destroy it (see Gen 8:21). According to his plan of engagement, God permitted the disease of sin to remain for the time being. To enable his people to cope with sin's effects, he provided intermediate measures, what one might call "work-arounds." Temporary antidotes such as conscience, government, and family were given to allow humanity to flourish even in a fallen world. Meanwhile God was preparing humanity to understand and participate in his ultimate solution for the problem of sin, accomplished on the cross of Christ (see Fretheim 2010, 179-90). Much of the Mosaic law was part of the curriculum that prepared the Israelites to recognize and understand God's ultimate solution when Christ arrived.

Choosing to deal with sin by combining short-term solutions with preparation for the ultimate reconciling work of Christ meant that the effects of sin continued to be experienced, even in the "work-arounds" themselves. Human governments provide an example. God directed people to form governments to help them live in a fallen world. Yet any government existing in a fallen world will, of necessity, be required to employ violence to deal with inevitable threats. Threats from within require police, and threats from without require an army engaged in warfare (Craigie 1978, 71). As Ellul explains, violence is "the order of Necessity." It is not that violence is a necessity,

> but rather that a man (or a group) subject to the *order* of *Necessity* follows the given trends, be these emotional, structural, sociological, or economic. He ceases to be an independent, initiating agent; he is part of a system in which nothing has weight or meaning; and (this is important) so far as he obeys these inescapable compulsions he is no longer a moral being. (1969, 91, author's emphasis and capitalization)

God limited himself to work in a fallen world where even the solutions, such as government, were not without negative consequences. Even violence is in "the order of Necessity." This scenario, while not ideal, is the best possible option under the circumstances.

An essential component of God's redemptive plan was to create the nation of Israel from which to bring the Messiah. This required Israel to participate in violence against internal and external threat. As a nation, Israel was bound to its divine King; subservience to any other king meant rebellion. Craigie spells out the implications for Israel:

> The continuing independence of the Hebrew kingdoms was not simply a matter of survival, but it was also a matter of vital religious importance. And military strength and the potential of war were contingent necessities of national survival and independence. (1978, 70)

Not only did Israel's existence as an independent nation necessitate violence, but God's plan required Israel to carry out that violence. There were times when God responded to a violent world with violent actions (e.g., the Flood), but always in response to human sin. "God's use of violence, inevitable in a violent world," writes Fretheim, "is intended to subvert human violence in order to bring the creation along to a point where violence is no more" (2004, 25). God could have brought about the conquest through natural disasters like what occurred in Sodom and Gomorrah or through plagues like those that devastated Egypt. Instead, God had Israel take up the sword, no doubt to further prepare his people to carry out his plan.

One of the lessons learned from wielding the sword was the great importance of loyalty and obedience. They also learned more about the nature of their God. They learned of his faithfulness to them, as made clear in Mic 6:5: "And remember your journey from Acacia Grove to Gilgal, when I, the LORD, did everything I could to teach you about my faithfulness" (NLT). The Israelites learned about God's jealousy by recognizing the lengths necessary to preserve their relationship with him (Josh 6:21; 7:25). They learned about his power to bring victory against a superior and established enemy (6:20), and they learned about his compassion as he welcomed a family of Canaanites into their midst (v 25).

God also intended the Israelites to learn about themselves. They needed to discover that no human—not a chosen man like Joshua nor a blessed nation like Israel—can solve the problem of sin. The book of Joshua bears sober testimony to this truth. Achan's disobedience, Israel's failure to inquire of God concerning the Gibeonites, and Israel's inability to conquer the allotted land signal troubles ahead for the nation of Israel. Indeed, the book of Joshua can only be understood in light of the fall of the northern kingdom in 722 B.C. and that of the southern kingdom in 586 B.C. As Craigie observes, "The history of the nation of Israel functions as a parable of warning: political institutions may be essential to the existence of human society, but they cannot be equated with the Kingdom of God" (1978, 81). Although a sobering discovery, it is a necessary one. Israel's failure makes clear that the problem of sin will not be solved by humans, but only by divine intervention (ibid., 99).

Even more, the conquest of Canaan can only be understood when read in light of the cross of Christ. The cross makes clear that while God permits violence, his ultimate purpose has always been to remove violence by taking it on himself. "God the Warrior becomes the Crucified God," writes Craigie, "the one who receives in himself the full force of human violence" (ibid., 99-100). The cross is not a celebration of violence but an essential part of its removal. By submitting to violence, God insured its eventual destruction. Admittedly, God's people have too often taken up violence on his behalf, but this does not negate the gospel's clear implications: the removal of sin removes the need for violence. This is true on a personal level, for as a person experiences God's grace, he or she increasingly turns the other cheek. Living in a fallen world means that systemic violence continues. It may be necessary for governments to take up the sword to prevent greater violence. Nevertheless, the gospel promises a kingdom without sin, and thus a world without violence.

Beyond personal transformation and eventual peace, the truth of the gospel unfolds as society is transformed. Over the millennia humanity has become more humane. According to Steven Pinker, contemporary society is arguably the least violent in the history of humanity (2011, 692). He contends that the causes of violence, namely predation, dominance, revenge, sadism, and ideology have been overpowered by self-control, empathy, morality, and reason (ibid., 672). Although Pinker considers religion part of the problem and not the solution, all four of these antidotes can be shown to flow essentially from God's redemptive plan as revealed in the Bible. Because of the work of the gospel in the world, we have come to increasingly recognize the essential dignity and equality of humans, regardless of race or gender. We are constantly learning what this means for how we treat one another and govern ourselves. Much of this transformation can be traced to an increasing comprehension of the Bible's message. Apparently, when it comes to God's curriculum, class is still in session.

That we would eventually find the conquest morally offensive has always been part of God's plan. "The Bible is the first text to represent victimization from the standpoint of the victim," says Girard,

> and it is this representation which is responsible, ultimately, for our own superior sensibility to violence. It is not our superior intelligence or sensitivity. The fact that today we can sit in judgment over these texts for their violence is a mystery. No one else has ever done that in the past. It is for biblical reasons, paradoxically, that we criticize the Bible. (1999, 392)

By submitting to violence through our identification with Christ, God assured the eventual disappearance of violence. Analogously, by submitting to these violent texts as divinely inspired and authoritative, they can be transformed into a source of hope and peace. By recognizing that only a virulent disease would call forth such a drastic remedy, we come to a deeper understanding of the seriousness of sin. By submitting to these texts as God's Word, we learn to read them in a way that honors God, through the ears of the weak and helpless. Reminders of the inevitability of violence in a fallen world help us live more responsibly as citizens of two kingdoms, seeking the transformation of this one while reserving our ultimate loyalty for the kingdom of God (Craigie 1978, 110-11).

E. Overview

The book of Joshua has been aptly described as both the pivot and threshold for the rest of the Bible (McConville and Williams 2010, 1). The Pentateuch pivots into the historical books on the hinge that is the book of Joshua. According to Keil and Delitzsch, the book of Joshua is "more closely related to the Pentateuch, both in its form and contents, than any other book of the Old Testament" (1978, 2; see Stern 1991, 138; Dozeman 2010, 109-10; Pitkänen 2010, 66). The action in Joshua picks up where Numbers ends; Deuteronomy functions as one long pause in the action. Of course, Deuteronomy is more than a pause, but "clearly provides both the framework and point of view by which the events of Joshua are rendered" (Hawk 2005, 567).

Joshua explicitly fulfills the commands given by Moses (see Josh 8:30-35 with Deut 11:29-30; 27:1-8), and many of Deuteronomy's motifs are repeated in Joshua. One such motif is the principle of retribution, found throughout the Pentateuch but most prominently in Deuteronomy. This principle, which contends that obedience leads to blessing and disobedience leads to disaster, is a major theme in Joshua. For example, one sees the first phrase illustrated by Jericho's defeat (Josh 6) and the second by the disasters associated with Achan's sin (ch 7). Another of the Pentateuch's themes is the promise of the land, a theme that resounds in Joshua (→ Theology of the Book of Joshua). As noted earlier, the closing verses of this pivotal book portray the Israelites burying Joseph's bones in the promised land, in fulfillment of Joseph's command (24:32).

While the book of Joshua continues the story of the Pentateuch, it also looks back on the Pentateuch as a unique and settled authority. As Creach notes, "We see here in Joshua one of the first signs of an awareness of Scripture, a holy text that serves as the primary authority for a community of faith" (2003, 7). Israel must obey the precepts of the Pentateuch to the letter; their very success depends upon it.

Hamlin suggests reading the covenant at Mount Ebal (8:30-35) as the "centerpiece of the entire narrative," looking back to the first mention of God's teaching (1:7-8), the celebration of the Passover (5:11), and the sin of Achan (7:11), and looking ahead to the Levitical towns (ch 21) and final summaries (23:6-11; 24:14, 23). He points out the Mosaic law is also restated at the covenant ceremony at Shechem (24:25), and that the book contains a symmetry of festivals at beginning (5:11), middle (8:30-35), and end (24:1-18) (1983, xv-xvi).

By distinguishing itself from the Pentateuch in this way, the book of Joshua serves as the threshold for the books that follow. The books of Joshua through Kings are known as the Former Prophets because they retell the history of Israel through a theological lens. Israel's history was evaluated not by its power or prestige, but by how faithfully they observed the laws of Moses. The land they gained through obedience, as described in Joshua, they would sadly forfeit through disobedience. The last of the writing prophets, in almost his last words, recalled the threshold of the book of Joshua when he instructed Israel to "remember the law of my servant Moses" (Mal 4:4; see Josh 1:7-8).

F. Purpose

Although the book of Joshua describes how Joshua led Israel to obtain the promised land, the focus is not on Israel or Joshua. The book's hero is God, and its purpose is to demonstrate how Yahweh kept his promise to give the Israelites the land of Canaan. Because this promise was made in the context of the covenant between God and his people, its fulfillment confirmed the identity of Israel as his people and God's commitment to bless them in response to their obedience. Joshua's opening and closing chapters frame the book's common theme: God's fulfillment of his promise (Woudstra 1981, 15-16).

G. Outline for Joshua

I. Conquering the Land (1:1—12:24)
  A. Invasion (1:1—5:12)
    1. Preparation for Invasion (1:1—2:24)
    2. Crossing the Jordan (3:1—4:24)
    3. Circumcision at Gilgal (5:1-12)
  B. Initial Conquest (5:13—8:35)
    1. Conquest of Jericho (5:13—6:27)
    2. Achan and Ai (7:1—8:29)
    3. Covenant Renewal (8:30-35)
  C. Coalitions against Israel (9:1—11:15)
    1. Gibeonite Deception (9:1-27)
    2. Central and Southern Coalition (10:1-43)
    3. Northern Coalition (11:1-15)
  D. Summary of Conquest (11:16—12:24)
    1. Summary Description of Conquest (11:16-23)
    2. Conquered Kings (12:1-24)
II. Allotting the Land (13:1—21:45)
  A. Overview of Allotment (13:1—14:5)
    1. God's Assessment (13:1-7)
    2. Allotment of Transjordan (13:8-33)
    3. Summary of Cisjordan Allotment (14:1-5)
  B. Allotment for Judah, Ephraim, and Manasseh (14:6—17:18)
    1. Caleb's Allotment—Part 1 (14:6-15)
    2. Allotment for Judah—Part 1 (15:1-12)
    3. Caleb's Allotment—Part 2 (15:13-19)
    4. Allotment for Judah—Part 2 (15:20-63)
    5. Allotment for Tribes of Joseph in Cisjordan (16:1—17:18)
  C. Allotment for Remaining Tribes and Joshua (18:1—19:51)
    1. Introduction (18:1-10)
    2. Allotment for Benjamin (18:11-28)

   3. Allotment for Simeon (19:1-9)
   4. Allotment for Zebulun (19:10-16)
   5. Allotment for Issachar (19:17-23)
   6. Allotment for Asher (19:24-31)
   7. Allotment for Naphtali (19:32-39)
   8. Allotment for Dan (19:40-48)
   9. Allotment for Joshua (19:49-50)
   10. Summary (19:51)
  D. Allotment for Cities of Refuge and Levites (20:1—21:45)
   1. Allotment for Cities of Refuge (20:1-9)
   2. Allotment for Levites (21:1-45)
III. Covenant Obedience: Key to Maintaining the Land (22:1—24:33)
  A. Crisis Concerning Obedience (22:1-34)
  B. Joshua's Call to Obedience (23:1-16)
  C. Covenant Renewal (24:1-27)
  D. Joshua's Burial in Canaan (24:28-33)

COMMENTARY

I. JOSHUA 1

BEHIND THE TEXT

The book of Joshua begins by looking back, as an epilogue to the Pentateuch, and by looking forward, as a prologue to the history of Israel's conquest of Canaan (Hall 2010, 10). This is apparent even in the grammar of the chapter. Hall notes that of the twenty relative clauses with the Hebrew word *'ašer*, half look back (vv 3, 5, 6, 7, 13, 14, 15, 16, 17 [twice]) and half look ahead (vv 2, 3, 7, 9, 11, 15 [twice], 16, 18 [twice]) (ibid.). The story picks up where Deuteronomy leaves off, the author presuming we know what has happened in that book. Given that much of Josh 1 paraphrases passages from Deuteronomy (see chart below), one commentator calls this chapter "a thematic reprise of the Book of Deuteronomy" (Polzin 1980, 74).

Joshua 1	Deuteronomy
v 3	11:24
v 4	11:24
v 5	7:24; 11:25
v 6	1:21; 31:6
v 7	5:32-33; 29:9; 31:6-8
v 8	29:9
v 9	1:21; 31:6-8
vv 12-15	3:18-20
v 18	1:21; 31:6

Deuteronomy stresses the unity of Israel, a theme emphasized in Josh 1 by specifically referring to the Transjordan tribes as an important part of the nation. Auld points out how Josh 1 reflects Deuteronomy in reverse order. It begins where Deuteronomy ends (ch 34), with the death of Moses, then makes reference to the book of the law (chs 4—31), and then mentions the Transjordan tribes (chs 1—3) (1984, 15). Joshua 1 even copies the literary style of Deuteronomy with speeches (four of them) in the second person.

The link is not just with Deuteronomy but with the whole of the Pentateuch. The major figure in the Pentateuch, Moses, is referred to so often in Josh 1 he nearly eclipses Joshua himself. The main theme of Joshua, the conquest of Canaan, is the fulfillment of a promise made early and often to the patriarchs (Gen 12:1-3, 7; 15:18-21; 22:17-18; 24:7; 26:3; 50:24) and to Moses and the Israelites (Num 11:12; 14:16, 23; Deut 1:8, 35; 6:10). Throughout the Pentateuch, God clearly showed that his gracious gifts were conditioned on Israel's obedience, a lesson repeated in the opening chapter of the book of Joshua. Joshua 1 emphasizes not only God's gift ("to give," *ntn*, is used eight times) but also his demand for obedience to the Law (vv 7, 8).

Joshua 1 also serves as a prologue to the book of Joshua. The chain of command pattern—God to Joshua (vv 1-9), Joshua to the people (vv 10-15)—introduced in Josh 1 is repeated several times throughout the book (chs 4, 6, 8) (Nelson 1997, 32). Elements introduced in the first chapter are revisited in later chapters: the crossing of the Jordan (1:2; chs 3—4, 22), the conquest (1:3-6, 9; chs 2, 6, 8, 10—12), the allotment of the land (1:6; 11:23; 12:1-6; chs 13—21) and the importance of obeying the Law (1:7-8; 8:30-35; chs 5, 7, 9, 23—24) (ibid., 30). God's message to Joshua (1:1-9) encapsulates the rest of the book: Israel would occupy this land if they faithfully obeyed. More specifically, Josh 1 describes the initial preparation for the invasion, demonstrates that the conquest results from God's orders, and reminds the reader that all of this is in fulfillment of God's promise.

IN THE TEXT

A. God's Marching Orders for Invasion (1:1-9)

After a brief introductory phrase, the opening speech belongs to God. He commands Joshua to prepare to cross the Jordan, guarantees success in accordance with his promises to Moses, and emphasizes the importance of keeping the law of Moses.

1. Command to Invade and Promise of Victory (1:1-5)

■ 1 The chapter opens with a reference to Moses' death. Since several other OT books begin by describing the death of Israel's leader (see Judg 1:1; 2 Sam

1:1; 2 Kgs 1:1), one might consider the phrase to be merely stylistic, how one ought to begin an account of Israel's history. At least in this passage there seems to be more to it, for Moses' death is mentioned a second time only one verse later. The narrator of the book of Joshua clearly wants to emphasize Moses, perhaps for three reasons. First, this emphasis connects the book of Joshua with Israel's story up to this point. We are meant to hear what follows in light of what has gone before, from creation to the patriarchs, from the exodus to Mount Sinai, from the plains of Moab to Mount Nebo, and now to the edge of the Jordan River.

A second reason to emphasize Moses concerns his close association with the Israelites. He had been their George Washington, their Martin Luther King, their Nelson Mandela, guiding them to freedom. It was Moses who provided them with food, water, and guidance. It was Moses who interceded for them. But now Moses is dead. His death brought uncertainty for the Israelites, especially now as they stood on the brink of a significant but perilous new venture.

By connecting Moses' death with God's command to Joshua to lead the Israelites into Canaan, the narrator signals that Joshua was Moses' duly appointed successor. This smooth and divinely sanctioned leadership transition stands in stark contrast to the end of Joshua and the beginning of Judges, which omit any mention of the passing of the torch of leadership. Third, by mentioning Moses' death, the narrator illustrates how disobedience robbed one leader of the chance to do what another is now being commanded to do. By drawing this connection, the narrator inserts a warning to the reader: Israel's success depends on their obedience to God.

Joshua is the perfect successor, for he has been **Moses' aide**. The word **aide** can imply either priestly service (see Aaron in Exod 28:35) or personal service (e.g., Joseph to Potiphar in Gen 39:4). Although never having served in a priestly role, the first is possible since Joshua was connected more than once with holy sites (see Exod 24:13; 33:11). Here the reference to Joshua as Moses' aide likely emphasizes his role as Moses' lieutenant. While Joshua is described as Moses' aide, Moses is twice referred to as God's **servant** (vv 1, 2), a word that denotes a closer and more significant relationship to a superior than does **aide**.

■ **2** Although we have been told of Joshua's commission to leadership twice before (Num 27:12-23; Deut 31:1-8), we might have expected God's first word to Israel's new commander to be a reaffirmation of that commission, but that is not what we find. Nor do we have a general command to obey, or even a promise of God's presence. Instead, God commands Joshua to "go now and cross this Jordan" (NJB). The abruptness of the command not only emphasizes both the nature of the conquest of Canaan, however challenging, as God's will but also stresses that Israel must respond with immediate obedience. By referring to "this Jordan" (**the Jordan**), God draws special attention to the river, which at that moment rushed nearby at uncrossable flood stage. This will not be the last time in the conquest account that Joshua and the Israelites were called upon to trust God's power and wisdom in the face of an impossible situation.

Twice God emphasized that the conquest was to be the work of all Israel; this once disobedient and rebellious people would now obey as a single nation. The focus later in this chapter on the Transjordan tribes serves the same purpose. What God had promised to Moses would be fulfilled for Joshua and Israel.

■ **3** Everywhere Joshua steps (**where you** [sg.] **set your** [sg.] **foot**), God will give that land to Israel (**I will give you** [pl.]). As noted in the commentary introduction, the book of Joshua presents God as one who keeps his promise to give this land to the Israelites. We also see that God is a promise-maker, assuring his faithful servant of victory (v 5a), his presence (vv 5b, 9), and success (vv 7, 8).

■ **4** God provides a survey of Israel's future boundaries, using language quite similar to Deut 11:24. The two verses are identical, apart from minor stylistic variations, with two exceptions: Josh 1:4 adds the demonstrative pronoun "this" (not included in the NIV) to Lebanon and also adds the phrase, **all the Hittite country**. Both modifications appear to serve the same purpose: to accentuate the miraculous nature of the conquest. As Howard points out, because Lebanon was not visible from where Israel stood, identifying it as "this Lebanon" meant Israel would even occupy what they could not then see (1998a, 82). The land of the Hittites could refer to the area north of Lebanon or, more likely, the land west of the Jordan River that was currently occupied by other nations. Not only would they possess what they could not yet see, but they would occupy land now possessed by others. If Israel ever extended to the full measure of these boundaries, it was during the glory days of Solomon's reign.

■ **5** Hearing God reaffirm the promises he had made to Moses (vv 2-4) must have been incredibly encouraging to Joshua. Even this encouragement is surpassed, however, by God's promise to be with Joshua as he had been with Moses. The phrase **stand against you** could refer both to opposition from within Israel or to enemy resistance. Joshua would be unshakable because God would neither **leave** nor **forsake** him. Using both terms when only one was necessary may have been God's way of emphasizing his intent to remain present with Joshua.

2. Counsels Courage and Obedience to Law (1:6-9)

■ **6** Absolutely crucial to the success of this invasion would be Joshua's courage and obedience to the law of Moses. The phrase that opens this section, **be strong and courageous**, appears three more times in the chapter. By emphasizing this phrase, the narrator accomplishes at least three things. First, he has alerted the reader to the impossible challenge facing Joshua. God has already spoken of "this Jordan," emphasizing the watery barrier. He has referred to "this Lebanon" and the Hittites, emphasizing land still unseen and still occupied. As if these were not terrifying enough, God repeatedly commands Joshua to be courageous. Joshua and the Israelites are facing very real challenges, making fear a constant temptation.

A second reason to emphasize this call to courage is to contrast Israel's mind-set with their enemies, often described as trembling with fear (2:9, 24; 5:1; 10:2). Third, by repeating this phrase three times, the narrator has connected this scene with an earlier one, recorded in Deut 31. There Moses repeats this same phrase three times, once to all Israel and twice to Joshua (vv 7, 23). Linking these scenes allows the narrator to remind his readers that God is now fulfilling the promises he made earlier. The link also provides a subtle warning, since the context of the scene in Deuteronomy was God's sobering announcement of Israel's eventual rebellion.

■ **7-9** Hawk (2000, 10-11) has observed that verses 7-9 are arranged chiastically:

A Be strong and very courageous. Be careful to obey all the law my servant Moses gave you (v 7*ab*);

  B do not turn from it to the right or to the left, that you may be successful wherever you go (v 7*c*).

    C Keep this Book of the Law always on your lips (v 8*a*);

    C' meditate on it day and night (v 8*b*),

  B' so that you may be careful to do everything written in it. Then you will be prosperous and successful (v 8*cd*).

A' Have I not commanded you? Be strong and courageous. Do not be afraid; do not be discouraged, for the LORD your God will be with you wherever you go (v 9).

This type of chiastic arrangement, quite common in the OT, allows a narrator to subtly make several important points. By placing A parallel to A', we are shown that the command (A) is balanced by the promise (A'). We are also shown that while Joshua must obey the Law given him by Moses, God's servant, God promises to be especially near to Joshua. The Hebrew literally reads **with you is the Lord your God** to emphasize God's nearness. What it means to obey the Law is described in B and B', first negatively (B), then positively (B'), with success as the result. The central element in a chiastic structure is most important; here there are two, both focusing on **this Book of the Law**, for therein lay the secret to success.

Comparing the Law to a path, Joshua must not turn from it (see Josh 23:6; Deut 5:32; 17:20; 31:29). Should he remain on that path, he and all Israel will arrive safely at their proper destination; should he deviate from that path, disaster will follow. Such warnings remind me of the wooden boardwalks in Yellowstone National Park where the ground is unstable due to the abundance of hot springs. What appears to be solid may be nothing more than a thin shell of mineral deposits. Staying on the boardwalk is the only safe route; stepping off invites disaster.

God told Joshua to **Keep this Book of the Law always on your lips** (v 8*a*) and **meditate on it** constantly (v 8*b*). Some see these commands as suggesting that Joshua was to have a teaching role. More likely, God was commanding him to incorporate the Law into his daily life and leadership. The verb for **meditate** is elsewhere likened to the sound of doves (Isa 38:14) and the growling of a lion (Isa 31:4). God called on Joshua to speak the Law to himself, so that its tenets would take root in his mind and thus, in his behavior. Here lies the path to success and prosperity.

B. Joshua's Marching Orders for Invasion (1:10-18)

1. Command to Leaders of People (1:10-11)

Immediately after the mantle of leadership was placed on his shoulders (vv 1-9), Joshua responded, first by commanding the leaders of Israel (vv 10-11), then the Transjordan tribes (vv 12-15). His prompt and ready response reveals his intention to faithfully follow the directions he had been given both by Yahweh and by Moses. At the same time that we see Joshua the obedient follower, we also see Joshua the innovator. God commanded him to "get ready to cross the Jordan River" (v 2), but Joshua determines when the crossing will occur and what needs to happen in preparation (vv 10-15). We will see this initiative again as he sends out the spies (2:1) and determines how the crossing will occur (3:1-6). God values obedience but also welcomes the innovation and initiative that arise from our having been created in his image.

■ **10-11** In these verses, Joshua addressed those responsible to carry out his instructions. The term **officers** elsewhere describes elders and judges (Deut 1:15; 16:18), but later passages in Joshua (8:33; 23:2; 24:1) distinguish officers from both elders and judges. This being a military expedition, it makes sense that Joshua would turn at this moment to military commanders; those prepared to lead Israel's soldiers (see similar use in Deut 20:5-9).

Joshua commanded the people: **get your provisions ready** in preparation for crossing the Jordan. This indicates that a change is about to take place in how Israel receives its food. Until now, they had depended on the manna, but that supply will cease on their arrival in the land (see 5:12). God would continue to provide, but in a different way, a way that would require Israel to take a more active role. The second notable thing about this command is that it is not what one might expect. A command to prepare their supplies rather than a command to arm themselves indicates that the principal combatant in the battle will be God, not Israel.

It is unclear how to understand the reference to **three days**. Taken literally, three days would not be long enough for the spies to reach Jericho and return (ch 2). Keil and Delitzsch suggest as many as eight days would be needed for that trip (1978, 31), although Howard considers that estimate too high (1998b, 539-50). Three days may be an idiom for a short time (see Exod 19:11; Esth 4:16; Hos 6:2) (Pitkänen 2010, 117), or the journeys of the spies and the Israelites could be described as happening simultaneously over the course of three days (Hall 2010, 35). Perhaps three days refers only to the amount of time given to the Israelites to prepare to move and does not refer to when they actually set out (Harris 2000, 24; see Keil and Delitzsch 1978, 31, citing Gen 40:13, 19, 20). It is also possible that the spies had been sent prior to the events of Josh 1.

2. Command to Transjordan Tribes (1:12-15)

■ **12** Joshua turns next to the tribes who had already been allotted land east of the Jordan. They are called Transjordan tribes because they would settle across the Jordan, to the east, as opposed to those that settle on the western side, known as the Cisjordan tribes.

■ **13** Joshua begins by calling them to remember what Moses had commanded them (see Deut 3:18-20). God was giving them **rest**, an important term denoting security (Deut 12:10; 25:19) and settledness, the awareness that one has reached one's proper place. **Rest** is the Sabbath's chief occupation, as modeled by God himself (Exod 20:8-11). **Rest** was to characterize the Israelites when they had taken full possession of the land (Josh 21:44; 22:4; 23:1). For the OT believer, rest came to represent the reward of obedience (see 2 Sam 7:1, 11; 1 Kgs 5:4; 1 Chr 22:9, 18; 23:25; 2 Chr 14:6-7; 15:15; 20:30). Micah described God's coming kingdom as a time when all could rest peacefully beneath "their own vine and under their own fig tree, and no one will make them afraid" (Mic 4:4; see vv 1-4; Isa 2:2-4).

Little wonder that the writer of Hebrews chose this term to describe God's salvation (Heb 4). The rest promised by Joshua in ch 1 anticipates this more complete rest, as pulling into a rest area on the highway anticipates and is surpassed by pulling into one's home driveway. God intended more for his people than a place to live; even their entry into Canaan was part of his larger plan to remove the curse of sin from our lives and from this world. This is the ultimate rest, to be fully reconciled to God, freed from the guilt and the power of sin, and to be fully reconciled to our neighbor, ourselves, and the natural world.

■ **14-15** Joshua instructed the Transjordan tribes to lead in the invasion, leaving behind all their possessions except what they would need for war. **Ready for battle** in Hebrew is literally the number **50**. This term could refer to military formation (i.e., each unit having fifty soldiers or arranged in five squadrons), as in the NJB's translation: "you fighting men must cross in battle formation." Or it could be an idiom describing preparations for battle (as NIV). By leading Israel into battle, the Transjordan tribes would illustrate how Israel is one nation, a unity that will be tested later in the book (see Josh 22).

3. People's Response (1:16-18)

■ **16-18** Although the author presents the response as coming from the Transjordan tribes, he likely meant the reader to understand the response of these tribes as the response of all Israel. This would explain the silence of the Israelite officials after Joshua gave them their instructions in vv 10-11. It would also support the "all Israel" theme, which is pervasive throughout the book of Joshua. By putting the response in the mouth of the Transjordan tribes, the author has portrayed the eager obedience of all Israel. The Transjordan tribes have less of an obligation to enter into battle, having already attained their land. If these who had already received their land were willing to fight, how much more the rest of the Israelites.

They begin their response with enthusiastic obedience, specifically promising to do whatever Joshua commanded and go wherever they were sent (vv 16-17*a*). They then offer a word of counsel to Joshua (v 17*b*). Some see in their counsel a veiled threat or nagging doubt (Nelson 1997, 36), but Hess is likely correct to understand their words as a "confession and prayer that the LORD may abide with Joshua just as he did with Moses" (1996a, 79). If any doubt did remain within the people at this point, Yahweh removes it in 3:7 (Woudstra 1981, 66). The people then swear a strong oath (1:18). This is the only place in the OT where rebellion against words refers to the words of a human leader rather than God. This oath anticipates the punishment of Achan (ch 7) but also confirms that leadership has been fully transferred to Joshua from Moses.

FROM THE TEXT

In God's commands to Joshua, especially 1:6-9, we can discern several important truths. First is God's change of strategy. For decades he spoke through an individual, Moses, but now it was the words of Moses as recorded in the book of the law that were to guide his people. This strategic change helped establish the written law of Moses as normative for all future generations of Israel. The written Law provided an important benchmark for God's people in a way that even divinely inspired leadership alone never could. Though we serve an unchanging God whose ways are always perfect, his ways may change without diminishing his perfection.

The written Law also facilitated the development of Israel as God's chosen nation. By inspiring Scripture, God provided yet another demonstration of his willingness to reside with his people. He had already done so through the tabernacle; the gift of the written Word demonstrates even further his desire to be known and loved. Israel's awareness of the Law as a source of blessing is abundantly displayed in the psalms that celebrate the Law, such as the beautiful Ps 19 and the exhaustive litany of Ps 119. By increasingly revealing himself to his people, God was preparing them for that time when the Word would become flesh and tabernacle among them (see John 1:14).

We also see in these verses a clarification of the connection between obedience and God's blessing. The opening verses of Joshua seem to support the "prosperity gospel" so prominent in some Christian circles. Those opposed to this message have reacted by reinterpreting OT promises like these, omitting any reference to material blessings and confining them only to spiritual blessings. This reaction, while well-intentioned and partly true, has obscured an important truth. No, God is not a heavenly vending machine dispensing health and wealth to the faithful. But we must not miss the truth that our best hope of experiencing the goodness of God's creation is by living according to God's eternal Law.

These verses also challenge the erroneous view that claims that the purpose of the Mosaic law was only to show the Israelites that they could not keep it and needed a different way to be reconciled to God. Clearly, the Mosaic law was not impossible to keep or how could Joshua be expected "to obey all the law" (v 7) and "do everything written in it" (v 8)? Only by keeping the Law could he know success (v 8), and success is precisely what he knew. If the Mosaic law was impossible to keep, what are we to do with passages like Deut 30:11-14, which claim that keeping God's command is within Israel's reach? How are we to read the psalmists' claim to be blameless before God (see 18:23, 25 and many other passages)? What are we to say to Paul, who claims to have kept the Law blamelessly (see Phil 3:6)? How are we to make sense of psalms like 19 and 119 (and others) that celebrate the Law as God's good gift to his people?

In his new covenant, God changes the specific provisions of the Mosaic law but not its essence. He removes the necessity for sacrifices by offering once for all the spotless Lamb of God, and he removes the necessity to observe those provisions of the Law that were culturally conditioned. The essence, however, remains obligatory for every believer, whether during the OT period, the NT period, or today. What is that essence? According to Jesus, the whole Law is fulfilled by loving God and loving one's neighbor (Matt 22:34-40). To live by love fulfills the Law. We may not always be happy, healthy, and wealthy, but God has designed this world so that our greatest hope for happiness and our surest defense against self-destructive and self-impoverishing behavior is a life of love. He has also placed within us his Holy Spirit so that we can know and do what love requires. We see the perfect example in Jesus, the greater Joshua.

II. JOSHUA 2

2:1-24

BEHIND THE TEXT

Having heard God's promises, Joshua takes action to prepare for the coming invasion of Canaan (Sherwood 2006, 43-61). He sends two spies to "look over the land, . . . especially Jericho" (2:1). Joshua was not likely motivated by fear, since he had already been promised success (see 1:3-9). God's promise had been short on details, and Joshua understood that promised success did not mitigate his responsibility to provide informed leadership. This is likely why he sent the spies. This chapter demonstrates that God had already defeated the enemy, who, as the spies quickly discovered, were cowering in fear at Yahweh's power. As Campbell points out, one either responds to this power with "obedience and submission of faith" or, as the Canaanites did, reject Yahweh's claims and experience defeat and destruction (1972, 244). Israel's occupation of the promised land was as good as accomplished, in fulfillment of God's promise.

The chapter appears to be chiastically arranged:
A Joshua instructs spies to explore the land (v 1)
  B Discovery avoided by deception (vv 2-7)
    C Rooftop confession of Yahweh's sovereignty (vv 8-14)
  B' Escape—with an oath of honesty (vv 15-23)
A' Report to Joshua: YHWH has given whole land to us (v 24)

The central element in a chiastic structure is the focal point; it is here we find Rahab's confession of faith in Yahweh. The author also emphasized Rahab's confession by slowing down the dramatic time and presenting her words as direct speech (see Hall 2010, 43, citing Robert Alter).

The author put so much stress on Rahab's words because she alone responded in the right way. All the Canaanites knew that God had miraculously delivered Israel from Egypt and defeated the Amorites. Rahab's neighbors heard and became terrified, but she responded in faith. She believed that Yahweh, not any of the gods of her ancestors, was indeed Lord of heaven and earth. What is more, she immediately put her faith into action by protecting the spies in return for their protection for her and her family when Yahweh gives Israel the land.

IN THE TEXT

A. Joshua Instructs Spies to Explore the Land (2:1)

■ 1 The chapter opens by referring to Joshua as **son of Nun**. Some suggest this descriptive phrase may appear at the beginning and end of this chapter to mark the boundaries of the episode (see Howard 1998a, 97 n. 96; Boling and Wright 1982, 143) although the phrase can also occur at places other than boundaries (see Josh 6:6). The author may employ this more formal way of referring to Joshua to draw attention to his role at that moment. Some contend the sending of the spies was an act of faithlessness on Joshua's part. God has already promised victory and the text contains no divine command to send spies. By doing so, Joshua put Israel in the awkward position of having to violate God's command by sparing Canaanites. "By sending the spies," writes Harris, "Joshua risked the success of the mission" (2000, 27).

Others see no problem with Joshua's decision. He could have acted on a divine command about which we are not told, or he could have been employing his initiative as he does elsewhere (→ 1:10-18). Woudstra sees in Joshua's strategy "evidence of his foresight as a general" (1981, 68). This ambiguity may be intentional on the part of the author, prompting the reader to wonder if Joshua has already stumbled.

The term **secretly** could be translated ***skillfully*** (Hess 1996a, 83). If we read **secretly**, it would mean the mission of the spies was kept secret from the Canaanites, but likely also from the Israelites. The negative report of an earlier spy expedition had brought disastrous repercussions (see Num 13), and Joshua may want to avoid any possibility of a repeat. **Secretly** is missing from the LXX and Syriac versions.

The author mentions that the spies were sent **from Shittim**. A place descriptor, though not totally out of place here, would fit better at the opening of ch 1. Its placement here may be intended to bring to mind an earlier unpleasant event that took place at Shittim during Israel's wilderness wanderings. It was here that the Israelite men were tempted to sexual immorality by Moabite women (Num 25). By alluding to past unpleasantness, the author has raised a sobering question: At this crucial moment, will the Israelites disobey as they did in the past?

The spies' specific assignment remains somewhat unclear. The word **spies** suggests espionage. It is used this way by Joseph when he accused his brothers (Gen 42:9) and to indicate those sent by Moses to reconnoiter Jazer (Num 21:32). A different term is used to describe the twelve men, including Caleb and Joshua, who explored Canaan (Num 13). Although Joshua told these men to **look over the land**, they seem to do very little spying and go only to Jericho, located about two hours by foot from the Jordan. Hess believes the men were sent to inform those Canaanites willing to convert how they might do so (1996a, 82). This seems unlikely since Joshua says nothing of such an assignment and the spies are mostly passive, even when faced with a real Canaanite convert. Joshua may have instructed them to explore the land of Canaan with particular focus on Jericho (KJV, NIV, NLT, NRSV), to explore "the region of Jericho" (NJPS), or specifically, to scope out the city of Jericho (ibid., 82 n. 1). Most likely they were meant to go further and spy more extensively since the king of Jericho identifies these as men who had come to explore "the whole land" (v 3). If so, the men aborted their mission after having visited only Jericho, probably because they found there something more important than anything else they were to look for.

They made this discovery at **the house of a prostitute named Rahab**. By identifying her by name the author marks this prostitute as someone significant. We are told her name while the king and spies go unnamed. Many find it problematic that Israelite spies visit a prostitute. Josephus and other early Jewish interpreters seek to avoid impropriety by identifying her as an innkeeper. This is possible, since the consonants in this Hebrew word are those used for a female person who feeds another (Frendo 2013, 62). Wiseman argues that the term rendered **prostitute** could be used to describe someone who conducts business with foreigners, not necessarily business of a sexual nature

(1964, 8-11). The traditional rendering as **prostitute**, while awkward, is most likely. This is how the NT describes her (Heb 11:31), and no mention is made of Rahab's husband (see Josh 2:13). Sacred prostitution was commonplace in Canaan, but there seems no evidence to assume Rahab's line of work was so dignified. Because she was likely occupied in the world's oldest profession, Rahab stood on the margins of her society. She also lived on the margins of Jericho, right on or in the wall (v 15), so a visit to her home was less noticeable.

B. Discovery Avoided by Deception (2:2-7)

■ **2-3** The Canaanites' fear made them especially vigilant, allowing them to learn of the spies' arrival in Jericho before the gates closed at twilight. When the king, that is, the ruler of this small city-state, was informed, he promptly sent officials to Rahab's house. Perhaps the spies had been seen entering there, or perhaps Rahab was already known for her pro-Israelite views, or her house may have been one of the most likely places where spies would try to hide. The consequences of shielding the enemy are dire. The Code of Hammurabi threatens with death any tavern keeper who fails to hand over conspirators to the authorities (No. 109).

■ **4** Our familiarity with this story may insulate us from the shock of what follows. Rahab, a Canaanite prostitute, hid the spies and lied about it to the king's messengers. No explanation is provided; the author even modifies the usual word order in these verses to make the narrative more vivid and suspenseful (Woudstra 1981, 70). Watching her hide the spies and face down the messengers leaves us full of respect for Rahab's courage. What must the spies have thought when they realized that God had sent a Canaanite woman prostitute to save their lives!

As with her occupation, Rahab's deceitful answer raises ethical questions. Some believe she should have told the truth and trusted God to provide another way to rescue the spies. Others consider her lie the lesser of two evils; her words, while understandable, still require repentance. Keil and Delitzsch call it "a sin of weakness, which was forgiven her in mercy because of her faith" (1978, 35). Others do not consider her deception sinful, citing her noble motives. Chrysostom, when discussing this passage, referred to her words this way: "O good lie! O good guile!" (Stander 2006, 46). Harris may be right that her sacred obligation to show hospitality to her guests outweighed the need to tell the truth; he is likely wrong when he excuses her actions as those of someone "marginal and helpless" (2000, 28).

Perhaps telling the truth meant something different then than it does now. Not only Rahab, but Tamar (Gen 38:13-26), Joseph (Gen 42), the Hebrew midwives (Exod 1:19), Moses (Exod 10:9), Jonathan (1 Sam 20:28), David (1 Sam 27:10), and Jeremiah (Jer 38:24-27) misled others by words, actions, or both, for the glory of God and another's good. If these notables did the same thing and were not punished, perhaps Rahab's words were not wrong when judged by the standards of her own day. It is also worth noting that Rahab spoke in the context of war. Most would agree that at such times, the enemy has forfeited its right to know the truth.

■ **5-7** Meanwhile, the two men hid on the flat roof of the house. Twice the author tells of their being hidden (vv 4, 6), drawing attention to Rahab's courage and cunning. Literally, we are told that Rahab *hid him* (i.e., rather than "them"), perhaps to emphasize her concern for each of the two men. She concealed them under **stalks of flax** (v 6). The stalks had been placed on the roof either to dry in the sun (before obtaining seeds used to make linseed oil) or to absorb the nighttime dew in preparation for extracting the fibers from which to make linen (Creach 2003, 33).

Rahab's ruse succeeded. Whatever God thought of her words, he demonstrated that he is a God who protects his people, including a prostitute newly joined to Israel. The king's messengers set off toward the river in hot pursuit. Rahab had said nothing about heading toward the river, but this was the logical direction given that the Israelites were camped on the opposite shore. The closing of the gate after the pursuers (v 7) indicates not only the insecurity of the Canaanites but also the vulnerability of the spies.

C. Rooftop Confession of Yahweh's Sovereignty (2:8-14)

2:5-10

■ **8** The reference to **night** implies that all of the events of the chapter thus far likely took place in a single day. On the darkened rooftop, Rahab reveals why she spared their lives and endangered her own. In what is "one of the longest uninterrupted statements by a woman in a biblical narrative" (Hess 1996a, 88), Rahab confesses her faith in Yahweh. Several times in her answer to the king's messengers she referred to what she did not know (vv 4-5); in striking contrast are her confident assertions in vv 9-13 of what she does know.

■ **9-10** In the first part of her confession, Rahab testifies to her belief that Yahweh has given Canaan to Israel. What he did to Egypt and the Amorites east of the Jordan River convinced her that no one can stand against him. Even the Jordan in flood stage is no barrier to the God who **dried up the water of the Red Sea** (v 10). The keynote of the whole book—Yahweh's ability to fulfill his promise to give this land to Israel—is sounded here by a Canaanite prostitute. As Creach observes, "The author of Joshua used Rahab's voice to remind the reader of God's earlier promises about life in the promised land (Deut. 1:21; Josh. 1:2) and to offer proof that those earlier promises were in effect" (2003, 37).

Rahab is also the first character in the book of Joshua to mention the *ḥerem* (Hawk 2000, 45 n. 10). She relates that the Israelites did not simply defeat **Sihon and Og,** they **completely destroyed** them (v 10) (see Deut 2:34; 3:6). We are not told how Rahab knew this, but her mention of it implies not only that the Canaanites were aware of this practice but also that they were doomed to suffer the same fate if Israel was victorious. Knowing that her only choice was either surrender or annihilation, Rahab chose to save herself and her family.

■ **11** In the second part of her confession (vv 11-13), Rahab affirms that Yahweh is the Lord of heaven and earth. Howard points out that this phrase is only used three times earlier (Exod 20:4; Deut 4:39; 5:8). In each passage it affirms God's "exclusive claims to sovereignty" (1998a, 103). Butler considers Rahab to have uttered a "monotheistic confession" (1983, 33; see Howard 1998a, 103), though this seems to claim too much. Even a culture as polytheistic as Egypt could assert that Amun was "the one, the only one" (http://www.sacred-texts.com/pag/ppr/ppr16.htm, accessed 8/20/13). More likely Rahab was asserting henotheism, the superiority of Yahweh to all other gods. She refers to Yahweh's deeds, but seems unaware of God's uniqueness (Lerner 2000, 52-55). What Rahab does affirm is still a remarkable statement of faith, earning her reputation as a model believer (Heb 11:31; Jas 2:25).

■ **12-13** Acting on her belief in Yahweh's supremacy, Rahab appeals to the spies to spare her family when the Israelites invade. Not only is she the first person in the book to use the word *herem*, but she is also the first to use *hesed* (v 12), kindness borne of loyalty to a common cause (Boling and Wright 1982, 147). As she has shown them *hesed*, she asks them to reciprocate, and confirms this by an oath in Yahweh's name. What this kindness should look like she makes abundantly clear in v 13: **spare the lives** of her family and **save us from death**. Rahab asks for a **sure sign** (v 12), that is, a "true token" (KJV), "reliable sign" (NJPS), "sign of good faith" (NRSV), or "some guarantee" (NLT). Some take this to refer to the scarlet cord that will hang in her window (Bratcher and Newman 1992, 30); more likely the sign she seeks is their oath in Yahweh's name. Requesting such a pledge is yet another demonstration of her newfound yet remarkable faith in the God of the Israelites.

K. M. Campbell has noted the six-part covenant formula in Rahab's response: (1) Preamble (v 11): "For the LORD your God is God in heaven above and on the earth below"; (2) Prologue (vv 9-11): what the Canaanites had heard about what God had done for Israel; (3) Stipulations (by Rahab, vv 12-13; by the spies, vv 18-20): protection promised to Rahab and family on condition of obedience; (4) Sanctions (vv 18-20): salvation for Rahab's family if they keep the covenant; death of anyone who breaks it; (5) Oath (vv 14, 17); (6) Sign of the Covenant (vv 18-21): the scarlet cord (1972, 243). She was entering into a covenant with the spies, as Israel's representatives, entrusting herself to Israel's care.

Both parts of her confession assert that God has terrified the Canaanites, just as he promised:

> I will send my terror ["great fear" in Josh 2:9] ahead of you and throw into confusion every nation you encounter. I will make all your enemies turn their backs and run. (Exod 23:27)

> This very day I will begin to put the terror and fear of you on all the nations under heaven. They will hear reports of you and will tremble and be in anguish because of you. (Deut 2:25)

> No one will be able to stand against you. The LORD your God, as he promised you, will put the terror and fear of you on the whole land, wherever you go. (Deut 11:25)

Rahab's words resemble even more closely those sung by the Israelites in Exod 15:15-16 after the crossing of the Red Sea:

> The chiefs of Edom will be terrified, the leaders of Moab will be seized with trembling, the people of Canaan will melt away ["melting in fear" in Josh 2:9, 24]; terror ["great fear" in Josh 2:9] and dread will fall on them. By the power of your arm they will be as still as a stone—until your people pass by, LORD, until the people you bought pass by.

Rahab employs several terms to describe the Canaanites' terror. It was a "great fear" (v 9), a term elsewhere translated as terror like the fear of death (Ps 55:4[5]). Also according to Josh 2:9, the Canaanites were "melting in fear" (see v 24). "Melt" elsewhere describes the effects of an earthquake (Ps 75:3[4]; Amos 9:5; Nah 1:5) or that of a building collapsing in a flood (Nah 2:6). A different term for "melted" is used in Josh 2:11, one which elsewhere describes what happened to the manna in the heat of the sun (Exod 16:21), what happens to a candle in the flame (Pss 68:2[3]; 97:5; Mic 1:4), and what happens to water "cascading down a slope" (Mic 1:4 NJPS). It is also the same word used to describe the demoralizing effect of the report of the ten spies (Deut 1:28). Twice more this term will be used to describe the fear of the Canaanites (Josh 5:1; 7:5). The phrase, "everyone's courage failed" (v 11) could be more literally translated, *one's spirit could not yet stand before you.*

■ **14** For the first time in this chapter the spies speak. Confident of the coming victory (**when the LORD gives us the land**), they promise to preserve the lives of Rahab and her family, as she has preserved theirs. She has asked for *ḥesed* and a "sure [*ĕmet*] sign" (v 12) and they promise to treat Rahab and her family **kindly [***ḥesed***] and faithfully** (*ĕmet*). She must, however, maintain strict secrecy **on this matter of ours.** This **matter** could refer to their promise to Rahab, their espionage, the larger Israelite mission, or all three. Rahab's secrecy not only would allow the spies to escape and report back to Joshua but also would protect Rahab from mistreatment and prevent the Canaanites from complicating matters by holding Rahab hostage.

To some interpreters, the spies' response was a disastrous mistake, the first step toward Israelite apostasy: "With the commands to show courage and maintain unswerving loyalty ringing in their ears, the spies, of all people, should have been intent on total compliance. Yet from start to finish they are cowardly, self-serving and disloyal" (Lockwood 2010, 40). Hawk concurs: "The spies' response jangles with the calls for wholehearted obedience to the commands of Moses with which the book begins" (2000, 46; see similar sentiments in Hawk [1991, 59-71], Harris [2000, 27], and Polzin [1980, 86]). After all, allowing the Canaanites any quarter was expressly forbidden by God who had commanded, "Make no treaty with them, and show them no mercy" (Deut 7:2; see Exod 23:32-33). Some commentators even suggest sexual impropriety, asserting the likelihood that the spies entered Rahab's house not just to hide, but for sexual favors (Spina 2001, 26). Rahab has a provocative name for a prostitute ("broad") and the same consonants (r-h-b) in Ugaritic, a language similar to Hebrew, do refer to a woman's sexual organs (ibid.). Are we meant to understand something ominous in the spies' departure from Shittim (v 1), site of an earlier Israelite rebellion involving sexual immorality? Even the term used to describe Rahab, prostitute (*zônāh*) (v 1), is related to the word that describes Israel's lascivious behavior (*liznôt*) in Shittim (Num 25:1) (Hall 2010, 37).

What he does and does not say strongly suggests the author intended us to see the behavior of the spies as above reproach. He more likely alluded to the earlier disaster in Shittim to create dramatic tension (what will the Israelites do this time?) and to show that this time the spies pass this test with flying colors, even when hiding in a brothel (ibid., 41-42). Had it been otherwise, we would have expected some word of condemnation. Nor does the text raise any question about the treaty they made with Rahab. Given the furor made over Achan's sin (ch 7), the author's silence at this point speaks volumes.

That Rahab truly converted is clear. Her confession echoes the sentiments of Deuteronomy, she is able to recognize how God was fulfilling his promises to Israel, and her confession occupies the most prominent place in this chapter. If any question remains, note how her faithfulness shines in contrast to Achan's faithlessness (ch 7). After Jericho's destruction, Rahab is permitted a place among the Israelites (6:25), and no ordinary place at that. She becomes ancestress to King David and to Jesus. According to the rabbis, she became Joshua's wife. The early church fathers considered Rahab as a symbol of the church (Stander 2006, 42).

The spies did not violate God's command; they recognized within that command God's compassionate heart. They realized that the ban need not be enforced where there is a genuine conversion, such as the one they witnessed in Rahab. "The only way, apparently," say Boling and Wright, "to avoid the ban is to make a covenant. Here it is done openly" (1982, 147).

Far from being a harbinger of Israelite apostasy, this story echoes other stories of divine deliverance. Her clever deception of a wicked king brings to mind the brave Hebrew midwives in Exod 1. As Lot protected the angels from the wicked Sodomites at his door (Gen 19), so Rahab shielded the spies. The blood on the doorposts at Passover (Exod 12) resembles, both in color and purpose, the scarlet cord in Rahab's window (Hall 2010, 38-39).

D. Escape—with an Oath of Honesty (2:15-23)

According to the structure outlined in the introduction to this chapter, vv 2-7 (B Discovery avoided by deception) correspond with vv 15-23 (B' Escape—with an oath of honesty). In vv 2-7, discovery by the king of Jericho is avoided by Rahab's deception. In the latter verses, the spies escape, but only after an oath of honesty. The author reports how they left the city (v 15), then provides Rahab's instructions for how the men can escape capture by their pursuers (v 16). Then follows a long and important conversation between the spies and Rahab (vv 17-21), followed by another account of their escape (vv 22-23). This lengthy interchange did not occur while the spies dangled by a rope, or else all hope for secrecy would be gone. Instead it took place prior to exiting Rahab's window. Such is the nature of Hebrew narrative: action is arranged purposefully, though not always sequentially. We see a similar chronological disjunction in the conquest of Jericho where the author inserts a long speech by Joshua just when we are expecting a battle cry (6:16-19).

■ **15** The wall around the city was probably of casemate construction, that is, two parallel walls joined by small walls at intervals. The space in between could be filled by rubble or could be built into dwellings (Longman 2013, 1700). This would account for how Rahab's house could be "within the wall itself" but also "on the outer side of the city wall" allowing her to "let them down by a rope through the window" (NRSV).

■ **16** The spies, hiding on the roof, had not seen which way the pursuers had gone, but Rahab did. Knowing they had gone east, she instructed the spies to head west into the mountains, away from the Jordan. They were to remain hidden there for **three days** (v 16). As noted in the commentary on Josh 1, this appears to contradict the chronology implied in 1:10. Some have tried to alleviate this problem by suggesting that Rahab instructed the spies to stay in the hills until the third day (Ralbag, as cited by Angel 2008, 4) or by suggesting this chapter is out of chronological sequence (Angel 2008, 3).

■ **17-20** Verses 17-20 provide the conditions of the oath of v 14. Although spoken earlier, the author may have placed them here to emphasize the conditions of the vow: her home must be marked with a scarlet thread (v 18*a*), all her family must be with her in the house (vv 18*b*-19), and strict secrecy must be maintained (v 20). Having agreed to these terms, Rahab "let them down by a rope through the window" (v 15). More precisely, she likely secured the rope so they could lower themselves to safety outside the wall under cover of darkness. The spies followed her advice, hiding in the mountains to the west. We do not know when Rahab tied the cord in the window, although it was probably closer to the time of the invasion. By mentioning it here the author lets us know of Rahab's intention to keep all the terms of the agreement.

Some contend that the **scarlet cord** (v 18) is the same rope used to lower the spies to safety. This seems unlikely for at least two reasons. First, the author uses two different words to describe them, and second, a "cord of thread" seems too slender to lower the spies (Creach 2003, 38). Ecclesiastes 4:12 uses this same term (*ḥûṭ*); only when it is at triple strength is it "not quickly broken." Samson broke the ropes tied around his wrists as easily as if they were threads (*ḥûṭ*) (Judg 16:12). We are not told where this scarlet "cord of thread" came from, but it seems more likely that it came from Rahab's house rather than having the spies bring it with them. If it was in Rahab's house, it may have been material for a fine garment (see Exod 35:35). The author may have had other reasons for speaking of this scarlet cord. The term rendered **scarlet** is elsewhere translated ***two*** (as in two spies) while **cord** can also be translated ***hope***. He likely intended us to see the **scarlet cord** in connection with Passover given the similarity in color and purpose to the blood God instructed the Israelites to place on their doorframes.

■ **21-23** Meanwhile, the pursuers sought the spies **all along the road** (v 22), literally, ***in all the way,*** that is, "all over the countryside" (GNT) that lay between Jericho and the fords of the Jordan. Finding no one, the pursuers returned to Jericho. After the coast was clear, the spies made their way to the Jordan River, likely to the ford where the river was most passable.

The NIV says they **forded the river** (v 23), suggesting an easy, shallow crossing. Since the river was at flood stage (3:15), getting across would not have been that easy. The Hebrew only says ***they crossed over*** so perhaps they swam, no easy feat given the strong current and the river's breadth.

E. Report to Joshua: YHWH Has Given Whole Land to Us (2:24)

■ **24** In v 23, the author provides a summary of their report ("everything that had happened to them"). We hear the spies' own words in v 24; direct speech is employed for emphasis. They tell Joshua what Rahab had told them, almost word for word: **The LORD has surely given the whole land into our hands; all the people are melting in fear because of us.** We hear nothing of military importance: the size of the wall, how many soldiers are in Jericho, any alliances among the kings. The spies may have gone for this information and may have intended to travel further to secure it, but no sooner had they arrived at their first stop than they learned something more important than any other information: God had already been at work ahead of them and the Canaanites were paralyzed with fear. There was no need to go further, for they knew that "a nation palsied with despair is already conquered" (Steele 1873 [2000], 24).

FROM THE TEXT

The spies were taught this lesson by a Canaanite prostitute who, in faith, chose to become part of Israel. Commentators who see this chapter as a step toward apostasy criticize the spies as passive and weak, unable to do more than "parrot" Rahab (Hawk 2000, 51). A better way to read this story is as a celebration of Rahab's faith and a miniature of God's larger story of redemption (see Heb 11:31). Rahab reveals this plan in who she is and what she does. A condemned Canaanite woman prostitute; at that moment one could hardly describe a more hopeless situation. But with God, there are no hopeless situations. He has never been willing for any to perish, but for all to come to repentance. He reached Rahab and used her to accomplish his purposes, illustrating that "whosoever will" may come (Rev 22:17). No wonder the early church fathers considered Rahab a great example of faith, repentance, a model of the church, patroness of salvation, and proof of God's love for humanity (Stander 2006, 47).

Nor has God ever authorized any other way to be reconciled to him than the way of faith. Without faith it is impossible to please God, but with it, even someone as hopeless as Rahab could find and please him. The scarlet cord, like the blood on the doorposts, is the sign of faith at work. So too is the spies' response. We hear their faith in the confident assertion that God would give the land to Israel (Josh 2:14, 18) and in their claim to Joshua that the transfer had already occurred (v 24). God was on the move, and victory belonged to those who would put their faith in him, no matter who they might be.

III. JOSHUA 3

BEHIND THE TEXT

Joshua 3 and 4 describe how Israel entered Canaan by crossing the Jordan. Some commentators see in these chapters the combination of many sources. This explains, they say, the chronological discrepancies ("three days" [v 2], "tomorrow" [v 5]); the delayed fulfillment (v 12) or lack of fulfillment (v 5) of certain commands; why priests are described as standing at the edge (vv 8, 13, 15) and then at the middle of the river (v 17); the very long, complex sentence in vv 14-16; and the variety of names given to the ark of the covenant (Nelson 1997, 55). According to Nelson, "the logical digressions and persistent reiterations" in these chapters are "undoubtedly the result of a complicated history of composition and redaction," though Nelson admits "no hypothesis to unravel the history of their formation has met with general acceptance" (ibid.).

It seems more likely that these chapters are the work of a single author, in part because of their unifying elements. Several verbs appear repeatedly: the term for "cross over" appears twenty-two times in these two chapters; the verbs for "stand" and "finish" occur five times each. Note as well the prominence of certain themes, such as the exaltation of Joshua and stoppage of the water. Whatever disjunctions exist in the passage are the result of the author's deliberate intention and characteristic of Hebrew narrative style (Woudstra 1981, 78).

Keil and Delitzsch propose one option: the author described the crossing in three stages (3:7-17; 4:1-14; 4:15-24), preceded by a time of preparation (3:1-6) (1978, 39). Howard offers another: the author described the crossing using "a slow, deliberate buildup (3:1-13) to a deliberate and repetitive climax (3:14-17), followed by a satisfying and drawn-out reflection on its significance (4:1-5:1)" (1998a, 118).

A still more convincing explanation of how these chapters reflect the work of one author yet possess "logical digressions and persistent reiterations" comes from Dorsey (1999, 94):

  a in camp on east side of Jordan (3:1-5)
  - Joshua promises that Yahweh will do great deed
    b **Joshua instructs priests to carry ark down to Jordan** (3:6-8)
    - Joshua instructs priests to carry ark before people (3:6)
    - Yahweh instructs Joshua that priests should carry ark down to Jordan, promises to <u>magnify</u> Joshua (3:7-8)
      c **Yahweh stops Jordan and people begin to cross** (3:9-17)
      - <u>Levites</u>, with ark, remain <u>in middle of Jordan</u>
        d CENTER: erection of memorial stones (4:1-9)
      c' **people finish crossing while Jordan is stopped** (4:10-13)
      - <u>Levites</u>, with ark, remain <u>in middle of Jordan</u>
    b' **Joshua instructs priests to carry ark up out of Jordan** (4:14-18)
    - Yahweh <u>magnifies</u> Joshua; instructs him to command priests to carry ark up out of Jordan (4:14-16)
    - Joshua instructs priests to carry ark out of Jordan (4:17-18)
  a' in camp on west side of Jordan (4:19-24)
  - Joshua recounts mighty acts that Yahweh has done, memorialized by stones

Dorsey's outline explains how these chapters hang together and where the author intended to put the emphasis: upon the memorial stones (4:1-9). The action proceeds slowly, ritual-like, to demonstrate the significance of this event. The stately cadence allows the reader to "savor this wonderful event" (Howard 1998a, 118) and mark its true significance. Israel's procession to and across the Jordan is marked by frequent pauses and speeches. Events are arranged more to make a theological point than to maintain chronological order. Everything about these two chapters—their emphatic vocabulary, elaborate structure, and stately cadence—suggests that crossing the Jordan was a moment of great consequence. More than just a great miracle, this marks a moment of great consequence, as God further fulfills his promise in response to Israel's obedience.

IN THE TEXT

A. In Camp on East Side of the Jordan (3:1-5)

■ 1 The chapter opens with the Israelites breaking camp near **Shittim** and traveling **to the Jordan**, a journey of probably no more than ten miles (Howard 1998a, 119). Nowhere in chs 3 and 4 does the author refer to the Jordan as a river. Of course he knew it was a river (see 1:2) but does not describe it that way. He may have avoided the term to more clearly connect this crossing with that of the Red Sea, a connection he alludes to several times before making it explicitly in 4:23.

The author describes this trek as beginning **early in the morning**. This phrase could be only a time indicator (i.e., they left shortly after the sun rose), but given the significance of the moment, we might consider another possibility. Elsewhere this phrase is used idiomatically to express prompt obedience (Gen 19:27; 20:8), something similar to what we mean when we say, "I'll get to that first thing" (Boling and Wright 1982, 158-59). Having heard the spies' report (Josh 2:23-24), Israel promptly demonstrated their ready obedience by breaking camp and traveling to the Jordan. There they paused before **crossing over**, the first of twenty-two times the verb *'br* will appear in chs 3 and 4.

■ 2 It is not clear how the author intended **three days** to be understood. These may refer to the same three days mentioned in Joshua's command to his officials in 1:11. If so, its fulfillment is described in 3:2. Howard disagrees, noting that the instructions in 1:11 were that the crossing would occur within three days, while, according to 3:2, the instructions came at the end of the three days. He argues for a second three-day period, with the actual crossing occurring on the seventh day (1998a, 120).

■ 3 The three-day period, whenever it occurred, would have given the Israelites plenty of time to observe the Jordan at flood stage and realize the impossibility of crossing without divine assistance. This may have been why the officers emphasize the pronoun **you** in **you are to move out**; who would not need an extra nudge to move in the direction of a swollen and rushing river?

This command of the officers also contains the first of several references to **the ark of the covenant**. As the following chart makes clear, the ark goes by many names in these two chapters:

The ark of the covenant of Yahweh your God (3:3)

The ark of the covenant (3:6 [twice], 8, 14; 4:9)
The ark of the covenant of the Lord of all the earth (3:11)
The ark of Yahweh, the Lord of all the earth (3:13)
The ark (3:15 [twice]; 4:10)
The ark of the covenant of Yahweh (3:17; 4:7, 18)
The ark of Yahweh your God (4:5)
The ark of Yahweh (4:11)
The ark of the *Testimony* (4:16)

I contend that the variety of terms is not the result of multiple sources, but the author's way of emphasizing a variety of points.

In 3:3 it is called **the ark of the covenant of the Lord your God**, a title emphasizing Israel's past and present relationship with Yahweh. The officers announce to the Israelites that the God who willingly entered into covenant relationship with them, rescued them from Egypt, confirmed his covenant with them at Sinai and daily reaffirmed it by his presence in the cloud, at the tabernacle, and through the manna—this God is **your God**. He will go before them into the Jordan, borne as he instructed them, on the shoulders of the Levitical priests. Israel must **follow** in obedience; this was their covenant responsibility. Only those who know themselves to be in covenant with God would be so daring as to enter a flooded river.

■ **4** They must follow, but not too closely. Although many modern translations wait until later to render the word of caution, in the original it opens the verse, as seen in the KJV:

Yet there shall be a space between you and it, about two thousand cubits by measure: come not near unto it, that ye may know the way by which ye must go: for ye have not passed this way heretofore.

Clearly it is very important that some distance be preserved to protect Israel from the ark's sanctity. Why must it be **about two thousand cubits**, or one thousand yards? This is the same amount of pasture land to be provided around each Levitical city (Num 35:5), so perhaps divine property requires this much of a buffer. One thousand yards is about half a mile, meaning that although the ark was at a safe distance from the Israelites, it was still within sight. Throughout their wilderness wanderings, they had been able to look to the pillar of cloud by day and of fire by night for assurance of God's presence and guidance. Now the ark would testify "that the living God is among" them (v 10), close enough to guide but still far enough away to avoid any careless contact. The tension between closeness and distance can be seen in v 4, which begins with a warning but quickly moves to comfort: "for ye have not passed this way heretofore" (KJV). God knew the Israelites were on unfamiliar ground and needed a reliable guide. He would fill this role.

It does seem strange that the reason for the distance was "so that you may know by what route to march" (v 4 NJPS). If you are leading people on a new route, you are more likely to tell them to stay close, not keep their distance. Keil and Delitzsch explain that "the ark was carried in front of the people, not so much to show the road as to a make a road by dividing the waters of the Jordan" (1978, 41).

■ **5** Verse 5 contains another puzzling time reference. Joshua informs the people God will do great things in their midst **tomorrow**, but the crossing seems to commence immediately. Perhaps this comment was made earlier or was meant to refer to the fact that the crossing would take place more quickly than anyone could image.

As noted earlier, the chronological references in the passage do not necessarily play a chronological role in the development of the plot. As Howard reminds us, "The author's primary concern is not chronology but theological reflection" (1998a, 118). The people must **consecrate** themselves, likely by ceremonial washing and abstaining from sexual relations (see Exod 19:10, 15) so that they may fully participate in the **amazing things** God has in store. The same phrase was used to describe events in Egypt, including the parting of the Red Sea (Exod 3:20; 15:11; Ps 106:22; Mic 7:15).

B. Joshua Instructs Priests to Carry Ark Down to Jordan (3:6-8)

■ **6-8** The ceremonial procession now begins, with the priests following Joshua's instructions to take up the ark and **pass on ahead of the people** (v 6). God, symbolized by the ark, was on the move; the priests, representing Israel, immediately obeyed in spite of the apparent impossibility of success. The focus then shifts to Joshua, who is given a word of encouragement and direction from God (v 7). The exaltation promised in Josh 1:1-9 will begin today, God says. **All Israel** (v 7) will know that God is with Joshua as he had been with Moses. As noted in Josh 1, being likened to Moses is a two-edged sword. It implies not only great authority but also great responsibility and significant challenge. Joshua's exaltation comes, though not by his great deeds; he does not even extend a staff over the Jordan. The Hebrew emphasizes the pronoun "you" at the beginning of v 8—"You are the one who shall command the priests" (NRSV). God's presence is what makes Joshua great; all he must do is be obedient.

C. Yahweh Stops Jordan and People Begin to Cross (3:9-17)

■ **9-13** Before continuing with his description of the procession (vv 14-17), the author includes these words of Joshua (vv 9-13). He explains that the coming miracle is God's assurance of a victorious conquest. By stopping the Jordan's flow, God not only reveals his intention that Israel would cross into the land but also proves his power over the land's inhabitants. He proves he is **the living God** (v 10), actively keeping his promises for Israel's benefit.

Thigpen argues that the parting of the Jordan is meant as a "blatant polemic" against Baal, the Canaanite storm god (2006, 345). He points out that the divine names **living God** (v 10) and **Lord of all the earth** (v 11) are similar to names given to Baal. The crossing occurs when "the Jordan is at flood stage" (v 15), heightening the similarities between this event and those described in the Baal Epic where that god defeats Yamm, god of sea and river (ibid., 345-54). Much as the plagues surrounding Israel's departure from slavery marked Yahweh's defeat over the Egyptian gods (Exod 12:12), Israel's entrance into Canaan is presented in such a way as to highlight Yahweh's defeat over Baal, his chief rival in the land.

For the first time in Joshua, the enemies are named (v 10). **Canaanites** can be used to describe all inhabitants of Canaan, but here probably refers to those living by the Mediterranean Sea (see 5:1 and 11:3; Num 13:29). Although the Hittite kingdom was principally located in the territory we now know as Turkey, **Hittites** migrated to this area and exercised considerable influence (see Gen 23; Amarna letters). The **Hivites** lived primarily in the central and northern parts of the land, including Gibeon (Josh 9; 11:19) and Shechem (see Gen 34:2, 13) (Freedman 1992, 3:234). We know little about the **Perizzites**, except that they lived with other groups in the hills of Canaan (see Josh 11:3; 17:15). Joshua 12:8 suggests the Israelites displaced them, but some still remained in the time of the Judges (Judg 3:5) (ibid., 5:231). We are also uninformed about the **Girgashites**, beyond their ancestry among the sons of Ham (Gen 10:15-16).

The term **Amorites** could describe all inhabitants of Canaan (see Josh 24:15; Gen 15:16), as well as those in the kingdoms of Sihon and Og, encountered by the Israelites before crossing the Jordan. Here **Amorites** likely refers to a more specific group, perhaps those living in the territory extending west from the Dead Sea to the Mediterranean (Josh 10:5; Judg 1:34-35) (Huffmon 1985, 27). The **Jebusites** were those living in and around Jerusalem (earlier known as Jebus) (Josh 11:3; Num 13:29; Judg 1:21; 19:10-11; 2 Sam 5:6).

In v 11, Joshua explains what will take place very soon. As the author describes the scene, we are meant to see Joshua extending his arm and pointing to the priests standing with the ark at the edge of the Jordan (**See** or **Behold**). These men will carry **the ark of the covenant of the Lord of all the earth . . . into the Jordan ahead of** the Israelites. As noted above, Joshua may have chosen this way of describing the ark to emphasize Yahweh's defeat over Baal. With this phrase he also asserts that it was Yahweh, not the peoples just mentioned, who is the rightful owner of the land they were about to enter. As owner, Yahweh had the right to reclaim possession from these squatters and give this land to Israel, with whom he was in a covenant relationship. Joshua will emphasize this important truth again in v 13. Joshua next instructs the people to choose one man from each tribe, although we must wait until 4:2-3 to learn why they are needed. Like Joshua's instructions to the priests (3:6, 8, 13), here is another example of the author's technique of beginning something, then setting it down and taking it up later.

To this point, the people are not told how they will get across the Jordan. In v 3, the officers tell the people to follow the ark, but at a safe distance. Two verses later, Joshua informs the people that Yahweh is about to do something incredible, but he does not say what it will be (v 5). Then the priests are told to take the ark (v 6) and stand in the river (v 8). Only in v 13 do the people learn that when the ark enters the river, its flow will be cut off, allowing the people to pass through. By revealing the plan incrementally, the author has increased the reader's anticipation of a marvelous miracle. As soon as the priests step into the river, the water will cease to flow from upstream and **stand up in a heap** (v 13). The same Hebrew word (*nēd,* **heap**) was used in Exod 15:8 and Ps 78:13 to describe how the waters of the Red Sea piled up when the Israelites crossed; one more way the author connects this crossing with the earlier one.

■ **14-17** With v 14, the procession resumes. As before, the crossing is described slowly and in great detail, a narrative technique that emphasizes the significance of this moment. This slow and detailed pace becomes more apparent when vv 14-16 are rendered literally, as in Howard's translation that follows. The italicized words actually tell the story, while the other words provide background information.

> *And it happened*—when the people set out from their tents to cross the Jordan, with the priests carrying the ark of the covenant before them, and when those carrying the ark came as far as the Jordan, and [when] the feet of the priests carrying the ark were dipped into the edge of the waters (now the Jordan overflows all its banks all the days of the harvest)—*that the waters coming down from above stood! They rose up [in] one heap,* a very far distance away, at Adam, the city that is opposite Zarethan, *and the [waters] coming down upon the Sea of the Arabah, the Salt Sea, were completely cut off.* And the people crossed opposite Jericho. (1998a, 130)

This literal translation also reveals how abruptly the parenthetical mention of the river being at flood stage interrupts the narrative, an abruptness smoothed over in many English translations (see NIV, NLT, NRSV). The harvest referred to is that of the barley crop, which occurs in April (see 2 Sam 21:9-10;

Isa 18:4-5). Note too how this parenthetical insertion heightens the miraculous nature of what happens: **the water from upstream stopped flowing** (v 16).

God stopped the river at Adam, a town about twenty miles upstream. Presumably, he could have staunched the flow anywhere, but he did so at a location where landslides are known to occur, slides that can temporarily dam the river. According to Pitkänen, such landslides have occurred many times throughout history, as recently as 1927 (2010, 137). The stopping of the Jordan is no less a miracle if God used a landslide to bring it about since it then becomes a miracle of timing. The same thing is true in the parting of the Red Sea. It took place as the result of an all-night wind, but at precisely the moment when needed. By having the waters stop so far away, Israel was given a wide stretch of dry riverbed, allowing the crossing to occur more quickly. Twice in v 17 the author points out that the ground was dry, probably yet another allusion to the crossing of the Red Sea (see Exod 14:21 and Josh 2:10). The author also notes the crossing of the Jordan took place **opposite Jericho** (v 16), anticipating the conquest of that city.

FROM THE TEXT

No closer than half a mile from God's presence. As with so many other passages in Scripture, this tiny detail reveals much. By requiring this distance between the ark and the Israelites, God reinforced the truth that while he is wholly Other, even dangerously so, he willingly comes near for the good of his people. The Israelites were able to be close—within one thousand yards—but not too close for their own good. God reveals himself even while he conceals himself.

This is the paradox of knowing God, both then and now. Although too holy to approach, we can experience his blessed presence if we faithfully obey. We can know him, but only "through a glass, darkly" (1 Cor 13:12 KJV). As Thomas Aquinas put it, "the more perfectly do we know God in this life, the more we understand that He surpasses all that the mind comprehends" (1948, 3:1203).

We could not come closer to God, but he came closer to us, in the person of his Son. While we cannot know him in his totality, we can know his love through Christ. As Paul writes, "God demonstrates his own love for us in this: While we were still sinners, Christ died for us" (Rom 5:8). We can have God's Spirit dwelling within us, making God's mind known to us (1 Cor 2:6-16). We "have not come to a [flaming] mountain," says the writer of Hebrews, but "to Mount Zion, . . . to God, the Judge of all," and "to Jesus the mediator of a new covenant" (Heb 12:18, 22-23, 24). While this bespeaks a tremendous privilege, it also contains a great danger, as the writer goes on to warn us: "See to it that you do not refuse him who speaks" (v 25). The demand for a holy life is no less promising and compelling for the believer today than it was when Israel stepped into the Jordan River, with the ark half a mile ahead.

IV. JOSHUA 4

4:1-24

BEHIND THE TEXT

As noted earlier, chs 3 and 4 were meant to be read as a single story whose highlight is the erection of the memorial stones (4:1-9). These verses occupy the central place in the narrative of the crossing; their position is made more significant by a slower pace and abundant repetition. Even Keil and Delitzsch, who do not argue for a chiastic structure, consider the stone memorial the main point of the crossing narrative (1978, 47).

Why might the author have made the erection of memorial stones the central element of this story? Because this was a moment to remember! When the Israelites crossed the Jordan, they did more than move from one location to another. As Nelson put it,

> The Jordan is not just an item of geography, but part of a symbolic system. It represents the boundary between being a landless people and being a nation that possesses a homeland. . . . To cross the Jordan boundary meant a transformation into nationhood. (1997, 68)

Not only had they become a nation possessing a homeland, but they were doing so in unity. Throughout the account of the crossing and the entire book, the author will emphasize Israel as one people, all twelve tribes united for a common purpose (see 3:12, 17; 4:1, 2, 3, 4, 5, 8, 9, 11, 14, 20). This point is made in both obvious and subtle ways. More obviously, we see the two and a half tribes leaving their homes and families east of the Jordan and crossing over with the others (4:12). More subtly, note the play on words between "stood firm [$hākēn$] on dry ground" (3:17 NJB) and "appointed" ($hēkîn$) in 4:4. As Hess notes, this wordplay "associates the action of the priests that initiates the 'amazing things' and that of the memorial that remembers the 'amazing things'" (1996a, 106 n. 1).

By emphasizing these memorial stones, the author highlights the importance of reminders. God's nature as promise-maker and promise-keeper made it important for Israel to have a good memory. Yet Israel, composed of human beings like us, seemed likely to forget. By commanding the construction of this memorial, God recognizes that humans are only "dust" (Ps 103:14) with short memories. With such reminders of how God keeps his promises, the Israelites would more likely remain faithful to their part in God's redemptive plan.

After describing the erection of the memorial stones (Josh 4:1-9), the author relates how the people finished crossing on dry ground (vv 10-13). The flow of water resumes once the ark has left the Jordan (vv 14-18) and the Israelites reach the camp of Gilgal where the memorial is erected (vv 19-24). Yet, as in ch 3, the account does not proceed in chronological order. The whole nation was said to have "finished crossing" in v 1 but does not actually finish crossing until v 11. Before the crossing, Joshua commanded the people to choose men to pick up stones (3:12), but not until after the crossing does God give this command to Joshua (4:2). We generally tell stories in chronological order, but the ancient Hebrews were comfortable sacrificing chronology to serve a larger purpose. So each time we hear about the twelve men (3:12; 4:2-3, 4-7, 8-9, and 20-24), the author supplies new information, building the story of the stones gradually, as if stone by stone. We heard in 3:12 that twelve men were to be chosen, one from each tribe. In 4:2-3 we learn why they were chosen: so that each would take up a stone from where the priests were standing and carry it to the place where the Israelites would spend the night. Verses 4-7 add the command that these men should carry their stone on their shoulder in order to build a memorial for the future while vv 8-9 explain that it was Joshua who built this memorial and that it remains until the time the book of Joshua was written. The last reference to the men in these chapters (vv 20-24) tells where the stones were erected—Gilgal—and provides more detail about what these stones mean.

IN THE TEXT

A. Erection of Memorial Stones (4:1-9)

■ **1-5** The men who take up the stones are told to **put them down** where they will lodge for the night (v 3). This particular verb appears elsewhere in the book of Joshua with the meaning of rest (see 1:13, 15; 21:44; 22:4). This suggests that in addition to serving as a memorial of the miraculous crossing, the stones also visibly represent the land's new owners, not unlike the planting of a flag on conquered territory. Abraham appears to have followed a similar practice in building altars during his travels through Canaan. The men were chosen by their respective tribes (see 3:12; 4:2), but v 4 refers to those appointed by Joshua. These are the same men; the difference reflects another characteristic of Hebrew narrative, where the same result can be ascribed to different causes. The Hebrew of v 5 leaves it unclear whether these men are to cross over **before the ark** (i.e., ahead of it) or "in the presence of" the ark (i.e., they are to go closer to the ark than anyone else) (Nelson 1997, 63); the latter seems more likely. Everyone is to go ahead of the ark since the priests who hold it will remain in the middle of the river until all cross. These men are specifically instructed to pick up stones that lie at the priests' feet, that is, in their presence.

■ **6-8** Verses 6-7 explain the purpose for this pile of stones: to be a **sign among you** (v 6) and **a memorial to the people of Israel forever** (v 7). The Hebrew word for **sign** is often used to describe God's miracles, particularly those done during the exodus (see Exod 7:3; Deut 6:22; Josh 24:17; Ps 78:43). Here it indicates that the stones signify something more than just stones, as the scarlet cord hanging in Rahab's window was more than a cord (Josh 2:12) (Alden 1980, 18).

The stones are also called a **memorial**. This need not be anything monumental, like the Lincoln Memorial in Washington, D.C. After all, this was made of only twelve stones, each stone no larger than a man could carry on his shoulder for several miles. Yet, invested with an explanation, these stones would remind future Israelites of God's miraculous intervention. Apart from this explanation, the memorial was only a pile of stones. While signs and memorials are crucial to reminding us of God's work in our lives, their efficacy depends on the living witness of believers.

■ **9** Verse 9 has traditionally been read to indicate that there were two piles of stones, one at their lodging place (Gilgal) and one in the middle of the river (see NIV mg.). Joshua may have erected a pile of stones in the river to mark the spot where the priests stood, but this seems unlikely. Mention of such a pile occurs abruptly and without any command from God (though Joshua sometimes does things without us hearing a divine command [1:10 ff.]).

There seems to be no purpose, however, in erecting a pile of stones where no one would see them. Nor would this pile likely remain a pile once struck by the powerful surge of water that would follow the release of the river from behind its temporary dam upstream (see 3:16). The reference to the pile remaining for years (4:9) seems to better fit the pile on land than any pile in the middle of the river. Coats correctly notes the significance of these stones being taken from the riverbed, precisely where the priests stood, those whose shoulders bore the symbol of God's presence (1985, 141, 145).

B. People Finish Crossing While Jordan Is Stopped (4:10-13)

■ **10** According to Dorsey's chiastic outline (1999, 94), 3:9-17 (c Yahweh stops Jordan and people begin to cross) correspond to 4:10-13 (c' People finish crossing while Jordan is stopped). Both passages describe the completion of the crossing while the Jordan is stopped. Some even contend the opening verse of the latter passage (v 10) echoes the closing verse of the earlier section (3:17).

> The priests who carried the ark of the covenant of the LORD stopped in the middle of the Jordan and stood on dry ground, while all Israel passed by until the whole nation had completed the crossing on dry ground. (3:17)
>
> Now the priests who carried the ark remained standing in the middle of the Jordan until everything the LORD had commanded Joshua was done by the people, just as Moses had directed Joshua. The people hurried over. (4:10)

Read in this light, the priests recede into the background and the people "take center stage as the subject of the main verb ['was finished']" (Nelson 1997, 70). The people are completely obedient, not only choosing men to carry the stones (v 8), but doing *all* that Joshua, Moses, and Yahweh had commanded. The Hebrew word for "all" appears twice in v 10, though the NIV renders the first appearance as **everything** and leaves the second untranslated. We also note the people's obedience in their eager and orderly crossing (**hurried**, v 10).

Mention of **Moses** is surprising, in part because he has not been mentioned for several chapters and in part because we know nothing about him giving this instruction. Moses did command Joshua that the Transjordan tribes should cross the Jordan ahead of the Israelites (Num 32:28-30). He also spoke about Joshua crossing the Jordan ahead of the Israelites (Deut 31:3), though he does not state this as a command. The same Hebrew term appears twice in Josh 4:10, rendered the first time as **commanded** and the second as **directed**. Most likely, the author is drawing attention to Joshua's faithful obedience to the Lord and Moses, following in the footsteps of his predecessor.

■ **11-12** Verse 11 describes the priests stepping out of the Jordan while v 12 speaks of the crossing of the Transjordan tribes, implying that the Transjordan tribes crossed last of all. This would contradict the statement that this group **crossed over, ready for battle, in front of the Israelites, as Moses had directed them** (v 12). There is no contradiction so long as we remember that Hebrew narrative often "expresses simply the order of thought, and not of time" (Keil and Delitzsch 1978, 51).

■ **13** Interpreters are divided how we should understand the forty thousand troops crossing into Canaan. Some connect this with the preceding verse and take this number to refer to the size of the Transjordan battalion. Forty thousand seems too few, however, according to the census of Num 26. This prompts Woudstra to argue that contrary to the impression given in Josh 1:14 that all the Transjordan men would be crossing, only forty thousand actually crossed (Woudstra 1981, 93). Others have argued that this number does not refer to the Transjordan soldiers, but to all the Israelites or to all the soldiers of the twelve tribes. Both of these interpretations opt for a much smaller number of Israelites than the two to three million suggested by a literal reading of the earlier censuses (see Hoffmeier 2005, 153-59, for a helpful treatment of the number of Israelites who left Egypt). Treating the forty thousand as all the Israelites seems problematic since the passage describes them as **armed for battle**, when not every Israelite was supposed to fight (see Deut 20). Pitkänen estimates that if this number refers to only Israelite soldiers, the total number of Israelites would be between 150,000 to 175,000 (2010, 138-39). Still another interpretation translates the Hebrew term '*eleph*, usually rendered thousand, in a less common way, as groups, troops, or "contingents" (see Boling and Wright 1982, 176; Hess 1996a, 113).

C. Joshua Instructs Priests to Carry Ark Up Out of Jordan (4:14-18)

■ **14** In 3:7-8, Yahweh had promised to magnify Joshua to the stature of Moses in the eyes of all Israel. That promised magnification took place on the day Israel crossed the Jordan. It would continue for all Joshua's life, just as Moses had been revered all his life (4:14). Why, specifically, did God exalt Joshua at this moment? What he did took great courage: choosing to obey God in spite of the obvious impossibility of the situation. As Moses had courageously stretched his rod over the Red Sea, so Joshua bravely marched his people to the swollen Jordan and commanded the priests to step in. God wants humble obedience that gives no thought to personal honor but seeks only to obey (see Luke 17:7-10). George Coats contends that what the staff was to Moses, the ark was to Joshua, both symbolizing divine power employed by a human leader (1985, 140, 145).

■ **15-17** As noted earlier, the ark of the covenant goes by several names in this story. In v 16 it is called the **ark of the covenant law**, the only time it receives this name in the book. The Hebrew rendered **covenant law** is used to describe the tablets of stone on which were carved the Ten Commandments (see Exod 31:18) but can also be used to describe the commands of the Mosaic law more generally (see Ps 122:4). The term is so closely associated with the ark that it sometimes appears by itself to refer to the ark, **ark of the covenant law** (see Exod 27:21; 30:36; the NIV supplies "ark" in these two passages although it is missing in the original). Perhaps the author employed this term in Josh 4:16 and 18 to emphasize how the crossing displayed God keeping his promise to his covenant partner.

The author has chosen several ways to emphasize the moment the ark left the Jordan. Yahweh himself commands it to **come up** (v 17) out of the riverbed. A vivid verb describes the lifting of the priests' feet from the floor of the river. This word is used elsewhere to describe something torn or pulled (Lev 22:24), an army enticed from its secure location (Josh 8:16), and the snapping of a string (Judg 16:9; Eccl 4:12), sandal thong (Isa 5:27), or tent rope (Isa 33:20; Jer 10:20). It is also used to describe forcible removal from one's tent (Job 18:14), and the process of heating metal to remove impurities (Jer 6:29). Some have suggested this verb was used because the priests would have to pull themselves free of the mud in which they had been standing (see Nelson 1997, 64 n. j), but 3:17 speaks of the riverbed as dry. The author appears to have chosen this term to emphasize the moment the priests left the Jordan. He also explicitly mentions the soles of the priests' feet. This emphasis is clearer in the more literal ASV: "the soles of the priests' feet were lifted up unto the dry ground" (4:18). Mentioning the soles of the feet brings to mind the promise that Israel would possess every plot of land trod by the soles of their feet (1:3).

■ **18** Finally, the author emphasizes the significance of stepping out of the Jordan by pointing out how the river rushed back to **flood stage** just as soon as the priests stood on the shore. Boling and Wright capture the significance of this moment: "The gates are closed. The divine king and his subjects have entered into the royal estate" (1982, 177).

D. Encamped West of the Jordan (4:19-24)

■ **19-20** The crossing that began in the Israelite camp east of the Jordan (3:1-5) ends in their camp on the western bank. What Yahweh had promised, he has fulfilled. What Israel was commanded to do, they faithfully obeyed. All of this took place **on the tenth day of the first month**, that is, the month of Abib (4:19). The author includes this detail to connect this event with the commemoration of Passover. Some forty years earlier, while still in Egypt, God had told the Israelites they were to begin their calendar with the date they had departed from Egypt (Exod 12:3; 13:4). That year and each year thereafter, on the tenth day of the first month, they were to select the Passover lamb. On this same date forty years and many miles later, the Israelites had miraculously entered the promised land. The author is pointing out that the crossing marked the end of one era, characterized by exodus and wandering, and the beginning of a new era, one of conquest and rest (Nelson 1997, 70). The crossing of the Jordan marks the beginning of the Passover to be celebrated at Gilgal (Josh 5:10-12). The crossing also corresponds to the miraculous night in Egypt. The same Hebrew term *'br*, "cross over," which appears so prominently in chs 3 and 4, is also used to describe God passing through Egypt to claim each firstborn son (Exod 12:12, 23). Earlier God delivered the Israelites by passing over them as he passed through Egypt; here he delivers Israel by enabling them to pass through a flood-swollen river. There he exempted the Israelites from disaster because of the blood of the Passover lamb on the doorframe, a mark of the covenant; here he spared the Israelites by his own presence, symbolized in the ark of the covenant.

The Israelites camped that night at Gilgal, perhaps two miles west of the Jordan. It seems likely this site was unoccupied and became known as Gilgal due to events that took place there (see Josh 5:9). Gilgal is mentioned several times throughout this book (5:1-9, 10-12; 9; 10:6-7) and elsewhere in the OT. A site known as Gilgal is also one of the stops on Samuel's circuit (1 Sam 7:16), where Saul was crowned king (1 Sam 11:15), the location of an altar to Yahweh (1 Sam 15:21, 33) and possibly to other gods (Hos 4:15; 9:15; 12:11; Amos 4:4; 5:5), and the headquarters for a group of prophets (2 Kgs 4:38). We cannot be sure these all refer to the same place, since there appear to be at least two other towns by this name (see Freedman 1992, 2:1022).

■ **21-23** Throughout these two chapters, the author has emphasized this event by repeatedly describing the erection of the stone memorial. In v 21 we are told where the memorial is located (Gilgal) and that it will be for present and future generations of Israelites. We have noted that the author wants us to connect the crossing of the Jordan with the earlier crossing of the Red Sea. This is why he does not refer to the Jordan as a river in chs 3 or 4 and why he used terms associated with the Red Sea to describe this event: "heap" (3:13), "amazing things" (3:5), and **dry ground** (4:22; 3:17). Phrases appear here ("the hand of the LORD is powerful" [4:24]) that are also associated with the earlier crossing, such as the "mighty hand" of the Lord (see Exod 3:19; 6:1; 13:9, 14, 16; 14:31; Deut 6:21; 7:8; 9:26) (Woudstra 1981, 96). Joshua explains that the miracle of the crossing of the Jordan memorialized by these stones will demonstrate Yahweh's mighty power (Josh 4:24). Something very similar appears twice in reference to the Red Sea crossing (Exod 14:4, 18). Finally, in

Josh 4:23, the two crossings are explicitly connected: **The Lord your God did to the Jordan what he had done to the Red Sea when he dried it up before us until we had crossed over.**

Linking the Red Sea and Jordan miracles strengthens the connections between Moses and Joshua. Perhaps this connection is what helped Joshua lead the Israelites so faithfully and courageously. Connecting the miracles of the Red Sea and Jordan benefited the Israelites by reminding them they were God's people. They had been promised this land by the same God who had released them from bondage in Egypt, that God with whom they were in a covenant relationship. Later Israelites remembered the connection between the miracles, as when the psalmist rejoiced in God who "turned the sea into dry land; they crossed the river on foot" (Ps 66:6 NJPS).

Attentive readers will note the pronouns in Joshua's words in vv 22-23: Yahweh **dried up the Jordan before you** and the Red Sea **before us**. Possibly Joshua was reminding the Israelites that only he and Caleb remain from the generation that crossed the Red Sea. If so, he provided a subtle warning to this new generation. It is also possible that by **you** and **us**, Joshua was referring to all the Israelites before him, not just to himself and Caleb. If so, the Israelites were being reminded that what one generation of God's people experiences, all experience (for another example, see Deut 1:26, 34-35; Josh 24:5-7).

■ **24** Joshua informed the Israelites why God wrought this mighty miracle: **so that all the peoples of the earth might know that the hand of the Lord is powerful and so that you might always fear the Lord your God**. When Rahab became aware of God's mighty power, she changed her allegiance from other gods to Yahweh (2:9-13). God intended to produce the same sense of awe among others, perhaps to the same end. The awesome impact of this miracle caused Canaanite rulers as far away as the Mediterranean to melt in fear (5:1). God also intended this miracle to bring about reverent obedience on Israel's part, not only among those who personally experienced this miracle, but among God's people from then forward (***forever***).

FROM THE TEXT

Christians have long viewed Israel's crossing of the Jordan as having significance beyond the historical event. Many saw in this a foreshadowing of Jesus' baptism (see Matt 3:13-17; Mark 1:9-11; Luke 3:21-23; John 1:29-39), which occurred in the same river; some place it relatively near this spot. As Israel crossed the Jordan to begin the conquest, Jesus came up from the water to begin his earthly ministry. The obedient faithfulness that characterized Joshua and the Israelites characterized Jesus. God magnified Joshua for his faithfulness (4:14); Jesus emerged from the baptismal waters of the Jordan to hear his heavenly Father's blessing.

One can also observe a connection between the crossing of the Jordan and our own baptism as believers. We too enter the waters by faith, having first consecrated ourselves to the Lord (3:5). As this crossing was to produce reverent Israelites, we rise from our baptism to "obey God's holy will and keep His commandments" (*Manual* 2009, 239). As this miracle at the Jordan demonstrated God's power, the commitment of the baptized believer can reveal God's transforming power. The Israelites who crossed the Jordan on the tenth day of the first month of that year demonstrated their identification with the nation of Israel. Just so, in baptism we mark our identification with the community of believers. The early church encouraged believers to take every opportunity to "remember your baptism," continuing the example of the Israelites, who constructed this stone memorial to always remind them what God had done for them.

Crossing the Jordan has also been seen as a metaphor for death, as in William Williams' (1717-91) well-known hymn, "Guide Me, O Thou Great Jehovah":

> When I tread the verge of Jordan,
> Bid my anxious fears subside.
> Death of death, and hell's destruction,
> Land me safe on Canaan's side.
> Songs of praises, songs of praises
> I will ever give to Thee;
> I will ever give to Thee.
> *Sing to the Lord*, No. 96

The instinct to see in this miracle an image of death is not without basis. In many ways, Israel's crossing of the Jordan represented that nation's transition from death to life. Although liberated from Egypt to enjoy the promised land, their rebellion left them wandering in the wilderness. In those forty years they had been able to experience a measure of fellowship with God and with each other, but it was overshadowed by the death of a generation. Now they stood with their backs to the wilderness, to death, facing the land of promise and of rest, a land where their true potential could be realized.

> On Jordan's stormy banks I stand,
> And cast a wishful eye
> To Canaan's fair and happy land,
> Where my possessions lie.
> —Samuel Stennett, 1727-95
> *Sing to the Lord*, No. 651

Between their unfulfilled past and their bright future lay the Jordan, able to be crossed only by faith in God's gracious presence.

> And when my task on earth is done,
> When by Thy grace the vict'ry's won,
> E'en death's cold wave I will not flee,
> Since God through Jordan leadeth me.
> —Joseph H. Gilmore, 1834-1918
> *Sing to the Lord*, No. 99

This scene at the Jordan is not only a picture of death but a picture of death's death. In it we catch a glimpse of that day when, through the power of the cross, God overcomes the curse against the natural world (see Rom 8:18-27). Because of that curse, implemented as a result of humanity's fall in the garden (Gen 3), nature now represents an obstacle, not an ally. As Origen wrote, "To a sinner, all creation is an enemy" (2002, 51). Now we make our living through the sweat of our brow, wrestling with nature to yield up its bounties. This will not be the case when God cancels the curse. Then the harvest will be so abundant that the reaper will not finish before it is time for the sower to sow (Amos 9:13).

Israel's crossing of the Jordan allows a brief glimpse of what it looks like when the chaos of the curse is momentarily tamed, when nature works in harmony with humanity. Instead of sweeping them to their death, the Jordan politely stands aside, allowing God's people to cross. Many years later another Joshua would come to tame unruly nature, even destroy death, as a foretaste of a curse-free world.

V. JOSHUA 5

BEHIND THE TEXT

Chapter 5 serves a key transitional role in the book of Joshua. It looks all the way back to the exodus from Egypt and marks the decisive concluding moment to that decades-long journey. It also looks forward to the coming conquest by describing the Israelites' elaborate process of consecrating themselves to that end. More than most chapters, here we see the real purpose of the book, to demonstrate how God kept his promise to give Israel the land of Canaan.

IN THE TEXT

A. Introduction (5:1)

■ 1 The opening verse of this chapter could just as easily have been the closing verse of ch 4. It describes the outcome of the miracle of crossing the Jordan and what was anticipated in 4:24. It also fits at the opening of the new chapter since it demonstrates how the Israelites are able to engage, unhindered, in the important ceremonies that follow. Those ceremonies, including mass circumcisions and the observance of Passover, appear to have taken place within the week following the crossing and were intended to consecrate the Israelites for the task ahead.

The author describes the Amorite kings as **west of the Jordan**, though the Israelites are, by now, also west of the Jordan. Woudstra believes this was to distinguish these kings from the Amorites east of the Jordan whom the Israelites had already dispatched (see 2:10) (1981, 99). Mentioning the defeat and demoralization of Amorites both east and west contributes to an overall picture of Israelite victory.

The Amorite kings in view are those ruling the city-states of the central highlands, such as Jerusalem. Not just those nearby, but even the Canaanite kings as far away as the Mediterranean Sea had heard of the miracle at the Jordan and were "paralyzed with fear" (NLT). By saying **their hearts melted and they no longer had the courage**, the author reuses Rahab's language (see 2:11). He may have done this to emphasize the connection between the Red Sea and Jordan crossings or to reaffirm Rahab's truthfulness, but most certainly he wanted to demonstrate how Yahweh was preparing the way for his people. Heart-melting terror appears to be the normal response on encountering the living God, as evidenced by the Israelites at Mount Sinai (Exod 19—20), Isaiah in the temple (see Isa 6), and the guards on Easter Sunday morning. Only once in the book does the author speak of events in which "we" (Josh 5:1 NIV mg.) took part. This may mean he, himself, was present at the crossing, although then one must wonder what he means when he speaks of things being present "to this day" (4:9; 5:9). Possibly, this reflects an earlier source, but more likely the author, though not himself among the generation that crossed over, identifies with those who did (→ 4:22-23; 24:5-7).

B. Circumcision (5:2-9)

■ 2 The first of the two ceremonies involved the circumcision of all the Israelite males who had not been circumcised—or at least not properly circumcised—during the wilderness wanderings. The author mentions this ceremony took place **at that time**, explicitly connecting the circumcision with the crossing of the Jordan. There are at least three reasons for linking these events. First, it clarifies why the enemies did not attack during the time Israel camped in Gilgal: they are melting in fear at the miracle of the Jordan. Second, it clarifies that the circumcision was a precursor to the second ceremony, the observance of Passover.

The third reason to link the crossing and circumcision was to make clear that the command came *after* the Israelites had crossed the Jordan. Emphasizing this sequence allows one to recognize something about God's character. He could easily have commanded these circumcisions while they waited on the eastern bank of the Jordan, safely protected from the Canaanites by the flooded Jordan. At the time the Israelites were recovering, they were likely unaware that their enemies were at that moment frozen in fear. For all they knew, their enemies were marching toward their camp, even while they lay in agony. Incapacitating the Israelite army in enemy territory was God's way of reminding them to trust him.

God wanted them to learn a second lesson about his character, particularly about his grace. Before the crossing, he required a consecrated people (3:5), but not until after he had worked this great miracle, so rich in covenant significance, did he require from them the sign of the covenant. As observed by Keil and Delitzsch, "It is the rule of divine grace first to give and then to ask" (1978, 57). Abram followed God for twenty-four years before the command came to be circumcised. Moses encountered God at the burning bush before his abrupt reminder to circumcise his own son (see Exod 4:25).

Only after God redeemed the Israelites from Egypt did he lay upon them the responsibilities of the Mosaic law at Sinai. Grace gives first, then asks. Paul expressed this truth in these words: "But God demonstrates his own love for us in this: While we were still sinners, Christ died for us" (Rom 5:8). John put the same truth more simply: "We love because he first loved us" (1 John 4:19).

In camp at Gilgal, Joshua was told to **make flint knives and circumcise the Israelites again**. Metal knives were available but were probably not as sharp as knives made from flint. Although no further mention is made of these knives in the MT, the LXX of Josh 24:30 says they were buried with Joshua. God told Joshua to make the knives *for yourself* (sg.). From this one could infer that Joshua was to perform all the circumcisions, but that seems unlikely given the number of men involved. More likely, use of the singular is meant to emphasize Joshua's obedience in seeing to this enormous undertaking.

More perplexing, why does God command him to **circumcise the Israelites again**, or more literally, *a second time*? Perhaps the first time took place in Egypt when the earlier generation had been circumcised. If the younger generation had not been circumcised while wandering in the wilderness, this occasion in Gilgal would be the second time. The reason for not circumcising earlier is unclear, though Keil and Delitzsch suggest it was because the younger generation was intended to bear the "whoredom" of their fathers (1978, 55). A second possibility is suggested by the LXX, which translates 5:5 to say that not all who left Egypt had been circumcised.

Yet a third possibility is to see both the first and second circumcisions in reference to this younger generation. While wandering in the wilderness, the older generation had circumcised these young boys, but in the Egyptian fashion, where the foreskin is slit but not removed. The "second time" would then refer to a proper job, slicing around the penis and "rolling off" the foreskin entirely (Sasson 1966, 473-76). This interpretation avoids the conclusion that the Israelites and Moses had completely neglected this essential sign for an entire generation.

■ 3 Some have understood **Gibeath Haaraloth** as a location already important to the inhabitants of Canaan as a place of circumcision. According to this view, Joshua chose this spot to demonstrate Yahweh's superiority over the gods of Canaan (Boling and Wright 1982, 189). Abram did something similar when he built altars at locations used for pagan worship (see Gen 12:6-7; 13:18). More likely **Gibeath Haaraloth** was the name given by Joshua to the place chosen for this ceremony. Another possibility is that this is not a proper name but only a phrase describing the aftermath of the ceremony: where Joshua circumcised the Israelites, there was a hill of foreskins.

■ 4-5 In vv 4-8, we find the reason for this ceremony. Woudstra describes their purpose as hortatory (1981, 101). In the original, these verses proceed slowly and deliberately, as when an adult explains something very important to a child. The author may have wanted to emphasize that circumcision had not been enough to preserve the older generation from God's anger. Though marked with the sign of the covenant, they had died in the wilderness because they had failed to maintain their covenant trust. Each new generation of Israelites would need to trust and obey.

■ 6-7 The author may also have wanted to emphasize God's grace. We saw this in the timing of the crossing of the Jordan (→ v 2). This new generation did not just replace their parents, God raised them up in their place (v 7a): "But in place of these he set their sons" (NJB). One sees God's grace in the double use of **sworn** (*nišba'*) in v 6, rendered the first time as **sworn** and the second as **promised**. The first generation had failed to believe God's promise of the land, in spite of having heard his oath and seen for themselves evidence of Canaan's abundance (Num 13:26-33). Because of their rebellion, Yahweh swore they would not see the land he had sworn to give them. As God had kept his promise of judgment, he would keep his promise of blessing.

And what a blessed land this was! After forty years of wandering in the wilderness, any land would be an improvement, so long as it was theirs. This land was not just any land, however, but was **flowing with milk and honey** (v 6). This is the only time we meet this familiar phrase (see Exod 3:8, 17; 13:5; 33:3; Lev 20:24; Num 13:27; 14:8; 16:13, 14; Deut 6:3; 11:9; 26:9, 15; 27:3; 31:20; Jer 11:5; 32:22; Ezek 20:6, 15). The land flowed with milk because of its plentiful pasturage for goats. Bee honey was known among the ancients (see Judg 14:8), but **honey** could also refer to date syrup. If the latter is in view, a land flowing with honey speaks to abundant date palms. Some believe that when *The Tale of Sinuhe*, an Egyptian story from the nineteenth century B.C., speaks of the "good land, called Iaa," it is referring to Canaan. If so, this Egyptian traveler noted as well Canaan's fertility: "Figs were in it and grapes, and its wine was more abundant than its water. Plentiful was its honey, many were its olives; all manner of fruits were upon its trees. Wheat was in it and spelt, and limitless cattle of all kinds" (*Tale of Sinuhe* 1997, 31).

■ **8** Those who had been circumcised **remained where they were in camp until they were healed**. The Hebrew word rendered **where they were** could instead be translated *instead of them* (see v 7; Deut 2:23; 1 Kgs 14:27), **under them** (Job 26:8), or "where they stand" (Job 40:12). Most translations, like the NIV, prefer the last interpretation. This may be the best rendering, but we ought not to miss the point: by using the same Hebrew word in Josh 5:7 and v 8, the author points out that those who had replaced the earlier generation were the same ones who had just been properly circumcised.

The author makes another subtle point by describing the circumcised as remaining in the camp **until they were healed**. The verb for **healed** is usually translated *to live*. Perhaps the author is making the point that those recovering from circumcision may have felt like they were coming back to life after a death-like experience. More likely, as Butler notes, by undergoing this ordeal this "new generation receives new life" in the promised land (1983, 59). Looked at through the lens of the NT, the choice of verb becomes even more significant. The apostles and early church leaders considered baptism as the true form of circumcision. Those baptized experience abundant life both now and for all eternity.

■ **9** After the circumcisions, God informed Joshua that he had **rolled away the reproach of Egypt**. Not all commentators agree on what is meant by this phrase. Keil and Delitzsch (1978, 59) take it to refer to the Egyptian mockery of the Israelites, as in Exod 32:12: "Why should the Egyptians say, 'It was with evil intent that he brought them out, to kill them in the mountains and to wipe them off the face of the earth'? Turn from your fierce anger; relent and do not bring disaster on your people." Woudstra considers the reproach to refer to the shame Israel endured by having been slaves in Egypt: "Israel's bondage, which at the Exodus had been broken in principle, was finally and definitively removed now that the people were safely on Canaan's side, no longer subject to the words of shame which Num. 14:13-16; Deut. 9:28 speak hypothetically" (1981, 102). A third interpretation sees the **reproach of Egypt** as the Israelites' failure to be circumcised when they left Egypt. This fits the context that concerns their circumcision but appears to contradict the report that all who left Egypt were circumcised (Josh 5:5). One can avoid this apparent contradiction by following the LXX translation, which asserts that those who came out of Egypt were uncircumcised (Nelson 1997, 76). A fourth explanation interprets the **reproach of Egypt** as the shameful disobedience of the older generation who disobeyed in the wilderness by not circumcising their sons (Hess 1996a, 122) or at least not circumcising them properly.

Whatever the proper understanding of this phrase, two points are clear enough. First, miraculously entering Canaan was not sufficient to remove their past shame and disobedience. Not until they had accepted the covenant sign of circumcision would their **reproach** be **rolled away**. Second, the removal of this reproach marked the end of the exodus and wilderness experience. Hall correctly hears "the narrative sigh of relief at the end of a period of extended waiting and wondering" (2010, 71). The author makes a very similar point in v 12 when describing the end of the manna.

God provides, in Israel's experience, a marvelous picture of our own. Baptism marks the transition from slavery to freedom, from shame to victory. As Paul wrote to the Corinthians, "Anyone who belongs to Christ has become a new person. The old life is gone; a new life has begun!" (2 Cor 5:17 NLT). The Israelites experienced the blessing of hearing God say that their reproach had been rolled away; we too have that blessing in the witness of the Spirit (see Rom 8:16). Just as the stone memorial reminded the Israelites of the miraculous crossing, the name of their camp—Gilgal, similar to the Hebrew verb for "roll" (*gālal*)—commemorated the rolling way of their reproach through circumcision.

C. Passover (5:10-12)

■ **10** Having been purified through circumcision, the Israelites were now able to celebrate a proper Passover for the first time in nearly forty years. Moses had commanded them to observe this festival when they arrived in the land (Exod 12:25-27), using this occasion to tell their children how God had delivered them from Egypt. The Israelites may have been tempted to postpone this celebration until the following year. After all, they had crossed the Jordan only days before and were now in enemy territory, not far from the city of Jericho. Those who had been circumcised were still quite sore. Whatever their temptation, they did not hesitate to obey Moses' instructions.

Other biblical accounts of Passover describe how the festival was held as had been commanded, or they focus on the grandeur of the festival (see

Num 9:5; 2 Kgs 23:22; 2 Chr 35:18). Instead this account highlights Israel's obedience to the date and time of day of the sacrifice (**the evening of the fourteenth day**; see Exod 12:6, 18; Lev 23:5; Num 28:16). Even more, it connects the observance of Passover with the cessation of the manna and the beginning of Israel's eating from the produce of Canaan (Josh 5:11-12). Some hold the manna ceased on the day after the Passover, that is, the fifteenth of the month (see NIV mg., NLT), while others contend it was on the sixteenth day (NIV). Since the Hebrew is somewhat ambiguous, the *crux interpretum* lies in how strictly the law concerning firstfruits (especially Lev 23:14) would have been enforced (see Keil and Delitzsch 1978, 60). Butler correctly observes that the author's interest "is not the Passover as such, but the transition in life style" (1983, 60).

■ **11-12** Israel should not have been surprised by the cessation of the manna since they had been warned earlier (see Exod 16:35). From this point on they were to eat from the produce of the land. Specific mention is made of **unleavened bread and roasted grain**, likely gathered from nearby fields of standing barley. Unleavened bread is closely connected with the Israelites' hasty departure from Egypt (Exod 12:17-20, 34). Roasted grain is what David's father gave him to take to his brothers (1 Sam 17:17), what Abigail prepared to take to David (1 Sam 25:18), and what Boaz served to Ruth at the harvest (Ruth 2:14). There is no surprise finding these on Israel's menu, since both foods would be easily prepared and transported.

No mention is made here of the Israelites observing the Festival of Unleavened Bread, which was to begin immediately following Passover. Moses had commanded the Israelites to observe not only the Passover when they reached Canaan (see Exod 12:25-27) but also the Festival of Unleavened Bread (Exod 13:5-7). Howard suggests they observed the seven-day Festival of Unleavened Bread while marching around Jericho (1998a, 153 n. 277). Perhaps we are to understand the reference to **unleavened bread** as an indication that the Israelites observed this festival as prescribed.

While the cessation of manna marked their arrival in Canaan, it did not mark the end of God's provision. He would continue to meet their needs, but in a different way. To obtain God's provision, however, they must now settle in the land. Manna had been food for a traveling people who inhabited the wilderness. Now that they are living in **Canaan**, they must either obediently press forward to conquer the land or starve. This is the first time in this book that the land is called **Canaan**. We meet the term again in 14:1 and 21:2, then four times in the story of the altar built by the Transjordan tribes (22:9, 10, 11, 32), and finally in 24:3 (see Boling and Wright 1982, 191).

As the crossing of the Jordan and subsequent circumcision ceremony point toward the sacrament of baptism, so the celebration of Passover anticipates the Eucharist. Jesus made this connection explicit at the Last Supper, identifying the Passover bread and wine as fulfilled in himself. We have seen that for the Israelites, their entry into Canaan and the events of their first few days in the country marked the transition from one epoch to another, from death to life, from slavery and wandering to rest. They memorialized this moment so they would never forget. They also knew, however, that this was the beginning of a new chapter, another step closer to the fulfillment of their covenant purpose: to be that nation through whom all nations will one day be blessed.

In Jesus, the true Passover Lamb, the day they anticipated finally arrived. Christ's gospel went out to bless all nations with the good news that sin's power has been broken. Those who welcome this good news gather as the church, entering through baptism and gathering to celebrate deliverance around the Lord's Table. Like the Israelites, we too look ahead to the rest that follows the battle, when we will sit down at the wedding supper of the Lamb.

D. Encounter with Commander of Yahweh's Army (5:13-15)

■ 13 After the circumcision and Passover festivities, Joshua appears to have left camp at Gilgal and begun to reconnoiter the territory around Jericho. The Hebrew describes him as being *in* Jericho, but this seems highly unlikely. Getting in would have been very dangerous and nearly impossible since the city was on high alert even before the Israelites had crossed the Jordan (see Josh 2:2). Possibly Joshua is inside the city "in thought" (Keil and Delitzsch 1978, 62) or is having a visionary experience (Woudstra 1981, 104). It seems more likely, however, that Joshua is in the territory controlled by Jericho (Nelson 1997, 80).

While investigating, Joshua looked up to see a man standing in front of him. The Hebrew contains the word *hinnēh*, often rendered **behold** (as in KJV; left untranslated in the NIV). As Howard notes, this word often marks a change in viewpoint or an expansion of insight. He suggests we might paraphrase it as "what do you know" (1998a, 156, see also 156 n. 284). Joshua looks up and he sees a man in a threatening posture, with his **sword** drawn as if ready to fight. There are two other times in the OT when we encounter a similar scene, the angel confronting Balaam (Num 22:23, 31) and the angel whose unsheathed sword stood poised to punish Jerusalem in David's day (1 Chr 21:16). Unlike those two passages, however, here the being is described as **a man**, not an angel (or messenger). If he was just a man, why did Joshua fall prostrate in reverence before him and why was the ground on which the man stood described as holy? The only locations described in the OT by this term are the burning bush (Exod 3) and the sanctuary (Hall 2010, 87).

■ 14 These clues seem to suggest this **man** is at least an angel, if not a theophany. They point out that the being with whom Jacob wrestled was also described as a "man" (Gen 32:25), yet Jacob considered he had seen the face of

God, or at least a divine being (Gen 32:30). They also note that angels are often found on divine missions (see Exod 23:20; 32:34; 33:2; Judg 13; Dan 8) and that the man identified himself as **commander of the army of the Lord** (v 14). Granted, **commander** can refer to earthly generals, such as Sisera, general of Jabin's army (Judg 4:7); Abner, commander of Saul's army (2 Sam 2:8); Shobach, commander of Hadadezer's army (2 Sam 10:16); and Naaman, commander of the army of the king of Aram (2 Kgs 5:1). **Army** could refer to Israel's army (see Exod 12:41; Num 1:3-46) or could describe an angelic army (see 1 Kgs 22:19; Pss 103:21; 148:2). The same word here rendered **army** (sg.) is translated elsewhere as **hosts** (pl.) as in **Lord of Hosts** (see 1 Sam 1:3; 1 Kgs 22:19; Pss 103:21; 148:2) or "Lord of Heaven's Armies" (NLT). It seems likely that the being who encountered Joshua was more than human.

Joshua's question is what we would expect him to ask on the threshold of battle: Are you on our side or theirs? What we do not expect is the man's answer: No. The surprising nature of his answer is evident in the variety of alternative translations. The NIV's **Neither** is appropriate, though it requires a little more interpretation than the simple negative. The LXX assumes the man answered "to him," a homonym to the negative particle translated ***no*** or ***not***. Soggin's "indeed" (1972, 77) seems even more of a stretch.

Actually, the man did not answer Joshua's question; he rejected it. Joshua asked if the man was on Israel's side; the man responded by asking if Israel was on God's side. By reframing the question, the man portrayed the issue as more than a struggle between nations, but a contest between Yahweh and those who oppose him. Further, the man emphasized that victory would come, not by Joshua's leadership, Israel's military strength, or anything Israel does. It would come because Yahweh directs (8:1-2) and fights for (10:14) his people. The **now** in **I have now come** connects this story with the preceding events of the book. Now that Israel has entered Canaan and prepared itself through circumcision and commemoration of God's covenant, God has arrived, ready to fight on Israel's behalf.

Now that Joshua understands *who* stands before him (or at least *who* is represented by the one who stands before him), his tone changes from challenge to submission. Note that he submits to the commander, even though the man has refused to take his side. Joshua demonstrated his submission by prostrating himself and by changing his question. He no longer asks about the man's loyalties, but only asks for his orders.

■ **15** Those orders are simple: **Take off your sandals, for the place where you are standing is holy**. One cannot help but think back to the burning bush when God gave Moses a similar command (Exod 3:5). Though only five chapters into the book, we have seen numerous connections between Moses and

Joshua, principally to demonstrate the continuity of God-chosen leadership for the covenant community.

Is this all the man said? Perhaps he said more but the additional material has been lost. Perhaps it was not lost but appears in 6:2-5. Chapter divisions are not original to the text and sometimes interrupt the story (Hall 2010, 79 ff.). If this is the case here, the directions regarding the conquest of Jericho were delivered by the **commander of the Lord's army** after the brief and parenthetical comment of 6:1. A third possibility is that the man said nothing more. No further instructions were needed to make this encounter significant. The command to remove his sandals presented Joshua with another chance to demonstrate his loyalty. By doing so, Joshua made himself vulnerable and demonstrated his trust in God. To be shoeless in enemy territory is not unlike being recently circumcised in enemy territory. He did so immediately, thereby demonstrating his total commitment. Further, while bowing before a man with a drawn sword could be only an act of self-preservation, taking off one's sandals acknowledges that this man, or the One he represents, is able to make wherever he stands into a holy place.

This would be true, regardless of what **place** is actually being described as **holy**. The man might have meant that all Canaan was holy ground, although it would be strange that Israel had been in the land for several days and this is the first time anyone was commanded to remove footwear. Perhaps it was specifically the land around Jericho that was being described as holy. Jericho, after all, was to be completely devoted to Yahweh, its contents considered sacred (6:17-19). On the other hand, no mention is made of Israel's army engaging the battle of Jericho unshod. Perhaps it is best to see the particular spot where the man stood as holy. Although Yahweh had revealed himself to Joshua more than once, and although his presence has been symbolized by the ark, he has "now come" (v 14) in physical form.

Whichever view is correct, Joshua grew in his understanding of who stood before him. At their first surprise encounter, Joshua sees "a man" (v 13). When he learns this is the "commander of the army of the Lord" (v 14), he acknowledges this man as his "Lord" (v 14), a term that could refer to a human or a heavenly leader. By the end of the encounter, however, Joshua understands that the one who stands before him is God's representative or the holy God himself. Joshua has also grown in his understanding of himself. He may have left his tent that day as Israel's commanding general, but he returned with the recognition that he was, in fact, only second in command.

Joshua also grew in his knowledge of God's work. In this brief conversation he learned that Yahweh's army had arrived; therefore the battle must soon commence. He also learned that even though Israel had reaffirmed their covenant relationship with Yahweh, Israel's victory was not assured until God showed up. Victory comes not by obedience to the Law, but by Yahweh's presence. Joshua may have thought that victory would have to do with questions of strategy and strength of arms—if we can judge from his scouting expedition to Jericho and his initial question of the man—but in this encounter he discovered that if one is on God's side, one is always a majority.

Chapter 5 ends as it began, in fear. The opening verse described the fear of the Canaanites while the chapter closes with Joshua's reverent fear in the presence of the commander of the heavenly host. The Canaanites were too frightened to face the Israelites while Joshua was too devout to face the heavenly commander. God will accomplish his plan of redemption. Let his enemies cower in fear; God's people will be prostrate in obedient submission.

FROM THE TEXT

The lessons Joshua learned are important for each believer. God's Spirit transforms any place from ordinary to holy—a realization that will change the way we worship and the way we work. We may keep our shoes on, but our minds will know we are in God's presence. We may imagine that success or failure depends entirely on us, hinging mostly on how well we have obeyed. This may leave us feeling vulnerable when we realize our obedience is less than ideal, or it may leave us feeling overconfident as if our obedience has obligated God to respond. May we learn Joshua's lesson: God is not hamstrung by our humanity nor held hostage to our holiness.

Yet Joshua could not have survived this encounter with God had he not been obedient. It was only after he trusted God to work a miracle at the Jordan, only after he circumcised his soldiers in enemy territory, only after he observed Passover, that Joshua was prepared to meet the "commander of the army of the Lord." As we noted, obedience alone cannot bring victory, but victory will not come without it.

As certainly as he accomplished the liberation of his people from Egypt and the conquest of Canaan, God will accomplish his plan of redemption, foreshadowed in the crossing of the Jordan, the circumcision at Gilgal, the Passover, and Joshua's encounter with God. We may consider the challenges too great, the world too far gone, the church too weak, and the forces of the enemy too strong, but as this chapter reveals, victory depends not on our obedience or on our resources, but upon God's presence.

VI. JOSHUA 6

6:1-27

BEHIND THE TEXT

The defeat of Jericho occupies a significant place in the account of Canaan's conquest. Chapter 2 described the spying out of the city and Joshua's encounter with the commander of Yahweh's army occurred nearby (5:13-15). The entirety of ch 6 is devoted to Jericho's conquest while the shadow of that battle darkens ch 7 as well. On at least three other occasions the author refers back to this moment (see 8:1-2; 10:28, 30; 24:8-13). No other battle takes up so much space in this book.

The significance of this victory is measured, not only by the number of verses, but also by how the conquest occurs. Priests in procession, the blowing of rams' horns, the ark at the center with armed guards before and behind, encircling the town, the perfect number seven repeated again and again—all these elements portray this event as one of deep cultic significance. It is heavy with symbolism and ritual, more like an act of worship than a battle.

The town's significance was not based on its size. Nowhere in the passage or elsewhere are we told Jericho was a major city. Even reference to its king does not presuppose a kingdom, since in those days the title could be applied to what we might now call a mayor. Hess argues that Jericho was a small military outpost with its "king" actually its commander (see Hess 2008, 37, 41). This chapter dwells more on the divine source of victory than the strength of the city (Hess 1996a, 138). Jericho was significant because of its location, standing as it did on the threshold of the promised land. The defeat of Jericho marked the firstfruits of the fulfillment of God's promise to give this land to Israel. It also provided a textbook example of how victory was to be obtained: through obedience to Yahweh, and how Gentiles could be included in the people of God.

As we have seen several times already in this book, the author begins by detailing God's instructions to Joshua (vv 1-5), which Joshua then relates with further detail to others, in this case, priests and people (vv 6-7). The events of the first day are recounted in detail (vv 8-11), followed by a summary of what took place on days two through six (vv 12-14). The author emphasized the importance of day seven by dwelling on the details (vv 15-21). Verses 22-27 describe what followed Jericho's defeat, including Rahab's rescue, the disposal of the city, Joshua's curse on anyone who rebuilds Jericho, and the effect of Jericho's defeat on the rest of the Canaanites.

IN THE TEXT

A. God's Instructions to Joshua (6:1-5)

■ 1 As noted earlier, commentators disagree on whether this conversation between God and Joshua is part of the encounter described in 5:13-15. Those who regard them as parts of the same conversation point out how the commander's brief words in 5:13-15 serve as a fitting introduction to the speech in ch 6. Joshua 6:1 would then be a parenthetical comment preparing the reader to understand the significance of God's promise in v 2. The gates of Jericho are said to be **securely barred**, allowing no one to leave or enter the town. Since no mention has been made up to this point about Israel besieging Jericho, this phrase instead appears to describe the townspeople's attempt at self-defense. But it is more than a defensive maneuver. It exposes the mind-set of the king and the town's inhabitants who refuse to peacefully acknowledge the supremacy of Israel's God, as had Rahab, nor will they accept Israel's implicit right to the land of Canaan (Hess 1996a, 128).

■ 2 In the face of these closed gates and closed hearts, Israel might have become discouraged had God not provided this gracious promise: **See, I have delivered Jericho into your hands.** To call this a promise is not entirely accurate, since God does not promise anything; it is more of an announcement of what has happened, even though it had not yet happened. God points to the circumstances of the tightly closed-up town (**See**) and invites Joshua to draw the opposite of the logical conclusion: **I have delivered**. This phrase offers a powerful lesson for God's people: the future rests in God, not in the circumstances. Yahweh specifically mentions the king and soldiers of Jericho, though the author says nothing about them when the actual battle begins (but see 24:11). God brings such deliverance that those expected to fiercely resist are no-shows.

■ **3-4** God follows his "promise" with specific instructions for the Israelites about a seven-day siege (vv 3-5). In the ANE it was customary to describe sieges (Fleming 1999, 226) or campaigns (ibid., 212-13) or the time it takes to march to one's destination in terms of seven days. Some ANE accounts even describe what happens each day through the week until something significant occurs on the seventh day (Cassuto 1975a, 32). Seven-day periods are connected with warfare because both are associated with divine activity. Citing ANE examples, Fleming observes that "seven-day intervals belong to the sacred time of a military campaign undertaken by divine command" (1999, 212-13). Describing the campaign for Jericho as lasting seven days with a sevenfold circumnavigation on the seventh day was the author's way of emphasizing that this battle was God's doing.

Although we are not told when, the Sabbath must have occurred at some point during this seven-day period. Pitkänen suggests the walls fell on the Sabbath, though he points out how unusual it would be for Israel to fight on the Sabbath (2010, 158). Whenever it occurred, God's instructions to march on the Sabbath emphasize the holy nature of this battle. The seven-day siege also provides a parallel to the seven days of creation, making the conquest of Canaan a type of new creation. To see the destruction of Jericho in this light helps one understand the use of *ḥerem*, understood to reflect cosmic contact (→ Introduction). As rest is associated with creation, Jericho's defeat would mark the beginning of Israel's true rest (Stern 1991, 141).

If the events of ch 6 followed immediately after those of ch 5, there is yet another implication of this being a seven-day period. The Israelites had just observed the Passover (5:10), which, according to Jewish law, was to be immediately followed by the seven-day Feast of Unleavened Bread (Hess 1996a, 130). Connecting this feast with the siege of Jericho emphasizes the sacred nature of the siege. The conquest of Canaan was the true culmination of the exodus. Then the Israelites hastily departed Egypt; here they leisurely march around Jericho. The seventh day of the Feast of Unleavened Bread was to be celebrated with a festival to Yahweh; this time it was celebrated with the collapse of Jericho's walls.

Joshua and the armed men were accompanied by priests blowing shofars, trumpets made not with metal but from rams' horns. Shofars were associated with God's presence (see Exod 19:16), with battle (see Judg 3:27), and with Israel's worship (see Lev 25:9). Joshua, the army, and the priests were to march around the town once each day and seven times on the seventh day. Although the strategy of marching around the city once a day for six days then seven times on the seventh day may seem odd to us, God had his reasons. First, by circumnavigating the town, they simulated a siege where attackers surround a city and attempt to breach its walls. This, however, would be no ordinary siege, for none of the ordinary means—mounds of dirt heaped up against the walls, tools to weaken the walls, wooden towers to lob projectiles—were employed. Instead, there was only a slow and silent procession around the circumference.

Second, this circumambulation demonstrated to the inhabitants of Jericho that no escape was possible; surrender was the only option. God may have been delivering an even more significant message to those in Jericho, one employing symbolism they could easily understand. Apparently, the ancient Amorites had a multi-day ritual that represented the entry of a deity into a city or town. A Hittite version of this ritual describes the symbol of the deity being taken on a sevenfold circuit before entering the sanctuary. Assuming we have properly understood the details of that ritual, God may have been directly addressing those in Jericho, insisting on his right to enter their city as the true God (Pardee 2002, 69-72).

Third, by surrounding the town, the Israelites were symbolically seeking voluntary admission and revealing Jericho's stubborn refusal to admit the all-powerful Yahweh (Hess 1996a, 130). "On each day for seven days," notes Hess,

> the Israelites prepare to enter if the leader will allow it. The sevenfold refusal, a number of perfection and completion in the West Semitic world, indicates to everyone that they will never find a peaceful settlement because the leader of Jericho remains adamant. (2008, 43)

Fourth, this curious military strategy would remind the Israelites they were participants in an attack that would largely be undertaken by Yahweh. Central in this procession was the ark of the covenant, symbolizing God's presence. As with chs 3 and 4, the ark goes by several names in ch 6: the ark (vv 4, 9), the **ark of the covenant** (v 6), the ark of Yahweh (vv 6, 7, 11, 12, 13 [twice]), the **ark of the covenant of Yahweh** (v 8), and once simply as Yahweh (v 8). The abundance of references suggests the significance of the ark, while the variety of names reveals different aspects of this important object.

■ **5** On the seventh day, when the people hear "long-drawn notes" (Keil and Delitzsch 1978, 64) from the shofar, they are to shout loudly. This shout would terrify the inhabitants of Jericho and embolden the attacking Israelites. God promises that at this moment, the wall around the town would **collapse**. The

Hebrew suggests it would "fall flat, not outward or inward, but downward" (Woudstra 1981, 111). The collapsed wall was the signal for the Israelites to attack, each man going **up** and **straight in**. With many cities and towns in the ancient world built on mounds, one would have to ascend to enter.

B. Joshua Delivers Instructions to Priests and People (6:6-7)

■ **6** The author adds **son of Nun** (see 2:1), perhaps to emphasize Joshua's significance even as he conveys the divine message to the priests. The priests will accompany the symbol of God's presence, so they are addressed even before those who will precede them in march (ibid., 111). The ark is referred to twice, first as the **ark of the covenant** and then as *the ark of Yahweh*. The latter phrase is applied to it again in v 7. In v 8 the ark is again mentioned twice, the first time simply called Yahweh and the second a combination of these titles: *the ark of the covenant of Yahweh*. The effect of this variety is to emphasize how the ark symbolizes both Yahweh and Yahweh's covenant relationship with Israel. Clearly, this battle was being fought by Yahweh himself in fulfillment of his covenant promise.

■ **7** Joshua next instructs the people, either directly or through the priests. The latter is more likely since the Hebrew form of the verb, **ordered**, is masculine plural. Joshua often speaks to the people through the leaders (see 1:10-11; 3:2-3) (Keil and Delitzsch 1978, 65). The people are told to **advance**, literally, *cross over*. This verb, used three times in 6:7 and 8, is used twenty-two times in the account of the crossing of the Jordan (chs 3—4). The siege of Jericho represents the crossing of a boundary, as surely as the earlier crossing of the Jordan (Hess 1996a, 132). Some believe the forward guard was composed of soldiers from the Transjordan tribes with the rear guard made up of fighting men from the other tribes (Keil and Delitzsch 1978, 65, citing Rabbi Kimchi and Rabbi Rashi), although this is not specified in the text.

C. Day One (6:8-11)

■ **8-10** The Israelites willingly obey, immediately doing just as God and Joshua had commanded (vv 8-9). Joshua now issues further instructions (v 10). Since it would have been very difficult for him to speak these words at this point with the people moving and the trumpets blowing, he likely delivered them earlier, perhaps back at v 7 (this is why the NIV translates **had commanded** [v 10]). Why is the command placed here if it was given earlier? As noted earlier, the primary concern for Hebrew narrators "is not chronology but theological reflection" (Howard 1998a, 118). Perhaps the author wanted to emphasize that while the people are marching, they must remain completely silent, not shouting, not letting their voice be heard, not letting a word out of their mouths.

Absolute silence would have intimidated those in Jericho and would have instructed the Israelites that this battle belonged completely to God; not only were they limited to six days of parade formation, but they were not even allowed to employ the weapon of their words. Fleming refers to a seven-day siege of Udm by King Keret, which also required six days of silence, after which the king of Udm was reduced to a nervous wreck (1999, 221-23).

■ 11 Joshua **had the ark of the LORD carried around the city** (see ESV, NASB). Other translations treat the ark, not Joshua, as the subject of the sentence (see "So the ark of the LORD went around the city" [NRSV]). The verb could be translated either way, though the emphasis is clearly on the ark, or better, on Yahweh as represented by the ark. The term for camp appears twice in this verse: "So he caused the ark of the LORD to circle the city, going about it once. And they came into the camp and spent the night in the camp" (ESV). Perhaps the author repeated the term to show how the Israelites had the easy job in this battle plan.

D. Days Two through Six (6:12-14)

■ 12-14 We are told that Joshua rose early on the morning of the second day, perhaps indicating his eagerness to carry out God's will, or perhaps to make clear that what was now being described was the second day (Butler 1983, 71). By crafting the events of day two (v 13) to closely resemble day one (v 9), and by describing days three to six in only half a verse, the author demonstrates how the Israelites carefully obeyed God's direction.

E. Day Seven (6:15-21)

■ 15 That day seven is the battle's highlight is obvious from the opening word, *wayĕhî*, **and it was**. This word is often used to highlight the start of a new episode (Howard 1998a, 172); the KJV captures this with its rendering, "And it came to pass." On the second day, "Joshua rose early in the morning" (v 12 NASB) but on the seventh day, the people "rose early at the dawning of the day" (v 15 NASB), that is, extra emphasis is placed on everyone waking early. And well they should, for they would need plenty of time to march around the town **seven times**, then defeat and destroy Jericho. The author again repeats that only on the seventh day did the Israelites march around **seven times**, highlighting Israel's obedience.

■ 16 Verse 16 provides the climax of this story. At the sounding of the trumpets, Joshua commanded the people to **shout**. In between his command and the resultant shout, the author inserts instructions likely delivered earlier. The delay increases the suspense (Woudstra 1981, 112), but there is likely another reason: to highlight Joshua's specific command not to steal any of the devoted items.

■ **17-19** The Hebrew inserts an additional clause at the beginning, rendered "as for you" (NASB, NRSV), making clear that the same destruction about to be inflicted on Jericho would fall on Israel if they were to violate Joshua's clear command. That not all listened to this warning is tragically illustrated in the following episode with Achan (ch 7).

The Hebrew term lying behind the concept of **devoted** (v 18), *ḥerem*, refers to the designation of an object or a person as belonging to God. This is a more extreme form of dedication than to sanctify. Most of the uses of *ḥerem* refer to objects or people that belong to someone else and are usually taken as war spoils. Objects such as **silver and gold and the articles of bronze and iron** (v 19) were placed in the sanctuary treasury; people were killed.

Israel was not alone in practicing the *ḥerem* or ban. An ancient Moabite royal inscription mentions a city devoted (*ḥerem*) to the god Chemosh. Once an object or person was devoted, it could not be employed for personal use, for anything it contacted would become devoted. Joshua's warning was meant to protect Israel from bringing deadly contamination on its camp and all its inhabitants.

■ **20-21** The climactic moment includes the blaring trumpet, the deafening shouts, the sudden collapse of the wall, the invasion. As the author portrays this moment, his language becomes almost poetic, emphasizing God's power and Israel's obedience. We cringe when we read of the death of men, women, children, elderly, even animals. Although no words can remove our discomfort, it may be helpful to consider that the author is very likely employing hyperbole. The categories may describe, not those actually killed, but the kinds of people who would have been killed had they been encountered (Hess 1996a, 133).

F. Aftermath (6:22-27)

■ **22-23** While the events of v 21 were taking place, the spies go to rescue Rahab and her family from her house on the wall. How her house survived when it adjoined an upper portion of the wall (2:15) is not clear. Perhaps this section of the wall remained standing, or the wall may have been of casemate construction, two parallel walls divided into smaller rooms. If this was the type of wall used in Jericho, the upper portion may have collapsed while Rahab and her family took shelter on the ground floor.

Joshua 2:13 spoke of sisters as well as brothers but no sisters are mentioned here. Perhaps **brothers** (v 23) is meant to refer to siblings of both genders, hence the NIV reading. Rahab and her family were placed outside the Israelite camp where they could undergo any necessary rituals, such as circumcision, to fit them for life among the Israelites. How long they remained there before joining the Israelite camp (v 25), we are not told.

■ **24** The Israelites did everything they had been commanded (though in the next chapter we will hear of Achan's infractions). The precious metals were deposited in **the treasury of the Lord's house**. This designation for the sanctuary usually refers to the temple, but it can also be used to describe the tabernacle (see 1 Sam 1:7).

■ **25** Israel also obeyed the command to spare Rahab, who remained **among the Israelites** (v 25) for the rest of her life. The author informs us that she was there **to this day**. This could mean the book of Joshua was written close to the events it describes, during Rahab's lifetime. The Hebrew verb for **lives** is third person feminine singular—**she lives** (Pitkänen 2010, 160). Another possibility is that Rahab was still alive when this story began to be told but died before the compilation of the book of Joshua as we now have it. Most likely, this means that Rahab's descendants remained in Israel for a long time. Long after King David had died, Hos 3:5 could speak of people seeking David when they really sought someone from the Davidic dynasty.

■ **26** Over the smoldering ashes of Jericho, Joshua pronounced a curse on anyone who rebuilt this town. Apparently, he sought to insure that this site, in spite of its strategic location, would remain a perpetual monument to the firstfruits of God's victory over the Canaanites. To treat this as an ordinary place would have been an act of hubris; perhaps this is why he spoke of a curse against the one who "rises up and rebuilds this city" (ESV), rising up implying arrogance. Joshua involved the Israelites in pronouncing this curse, as the NASB makes clear: "Then Joshua made them take an oath at that time." He spoke the curse and the Israelites were to answer, "Amen," in this way taking upon themselves the responsibility to retain this site as a memorial.

Joshua may have intended a complete prohibition on anyone living here, but it seems more likely that his curse only referred to the rebuilding of walls and gates. That a village would be allowed to remain would explain how Jericho was allotted to the tribe of Benjamin (18:21) and why archaeologists have found evidence of later occupation at this site (Judg 3:13; 2 Sam 10:5). Hiel of Bethel experienced Joshua's curse, for in King Ahab's day, Hiel laid Jericho's "foundations at the cost of his firstborn son Abiram, and he set up its gates at the cost of his youngest son Segub, in accordance with the word of the Lord spoken by Joshua son of Nun" (1 Kgs 16:34).

■ **27** Joshua's victory over Jericho meant that his fame spread throughout the land. Hess rightly explains that, in the ANE success in one's first battle was considered very important (1996a, 136). No doubt, Israel's loyalty to Joshua throughout the rest of the conquest, and the resultant success in occupying the land, had a great deal to do with what they saw in Joshua during this week. The impotence of Jericho's king, mentioned once and then upstaged by the town prostitute, stands in stark contrast to the authority of Joshua.

Most important for Joshua and the Israelites, however, was the lesson that victory results from absolute obedience to Yahweh. The only reason ch 6 can end with Joshua's fame is because ch 5 had ended with Joshua on his face before the true commander of the heavenly armies (5:14-15). Because of Israel's obedience, walls that at the opening of the chapter had been tightly closed now lay in ruins.

FROM THE TEXT

Absolute obedience to Yahweh is essential, for God's directions do not always make perfect sense. The battle plan for attacking Jericho is one example, sparing Rahab and her family is another, but the cross of Christ is probably the most surprising. God's people must listen carefully to know how best to carry out his plan, and must obey, no matter how it appears to others.

The battle for Jericho also provides a window into the problems created by sin. Here was a city well-acquainted with Yahweh's superiority over their gods. When Rahab heard what God had done, she submitted to his authority and became his follower, at great personal risk. What a different story would now be told if the king and elders of the town had followed her example. What if, instead of closing the town gates, they had opened them in submission to Yahweh? The God who received a Canaanite woman and her family would surely have welcomed the rest of the town. But sin has such a blinding effect, preventing us from seeing how alienated we are from the true God, and submitting to that truth.

Sin alienates humans not only from God but also from each other. The gates of Jericho were "securely barred" (v 1), symbolizing the alienation that exists between those inside and those outside. Jericho's devastation portrays the consequences of such alienation, and the pages of history are replete with many more bloody examples. Yet out of the rubble and destruction stepped Rahab and her family, literally experiencing the promise God had made to Abram so many years earlier: "I will bless those who bless you, and whoever curses you I will curse; and all peoples on earth will be blessed through you" (Gen 12:3). It would take many more years before the fullness of this promise was realized in Christ, but God's intent had always been that Israel would be a source of blessing to all the nations. It is no coincidence that Rahab the Canaanite was part of the lineage of Jesus (Matt 1:5).

The battle for Jericho not only illustrates the problem of sin but also provides a compelling example of how sin will one day be completely destroyed. The second Joshua, through faithful obedience to his heavenly Father, defeated the power of the enemy by an unusual strategy. At the center of Israel's attack on Jericho was the ark of the covenant, symbolizing God's presence. The final victory over sin came about through Immanuel, God with us, reconciling the world to himself in Christ. This reconciliation will continue until "every knee" bows and "every tongue" confesses "that Jesus Christ is Lord, to the glory of God the Father" (Phil 2:10-11). Keil and Delitzsch express it well: "Thus the fall of Jericho became the symbol and type of the overthrow of every worldly power before the Lord, when He should come to lead His people into Canaan and establish His kingdom upon earth" (1978, 70).

Excursus on Jericho

The ancient site of Jericho, located north of the Dead Sea between the Jordan River and the mountains of Judah, was inhabited as early as 9000 B.C. Early in the twentieth century, archaeologists discovered that the city was violently destroyed by a fire. John Garstang proposed that this destruction occurred during the Late Bronze Age (1550-1200 B.C.), which fits the biblical picture well. Later excavators, notably Kathleen Kenyon, challenged Garstang's dating of the evidence and asserted that the fiery destruction occurred in the Middle Bronze Age (1950-1550 B.C.), too early for the Israelites to have been responsible. Many now associate the fire with the expulsion of the Hyksos from Egypt, with conflict among the towns and cities of Canaan, or as the result of the Canaanite population being decimated by a plague (Bienkowski 1986, 128).

According to the latest scholarly consensus, the town of Jericho was only sparsely inhabited and lacked walls or fortifications at the time when Israel is thought to have arrived (ibid., 124-25). The town and surrounding region grew weaker and smaller, eventually being completely abandoned around 1275 B.C. with no reoccupation until the eleventh century (ibid., 137, 155).

Reconciling the biblical picture with the one provided by archaeologists is difficult, but not impossible. Some, like Bryant Wood (1990, 45-49, 68), challenge the dating of Kenyon in favor of Garstang, though Wood's challenge does not seem to be getting much traction among scholars (Howard 1998a, 178). Other challenges to the present consensus focus on the fact that there has been considerable erosion on the site, making any final determination impossible. Hess contends the site was only a small military outpost, possibly only with mud-brick walls. If so, "It may be that the remnants of the fallen mud-brick perimeter wall were eroded away during the three to five centuries of occupational gap between the Jericho of Joshua and the Jericho that was rebuilt by Hiel in the 9th century (1 Kgs 16:34)" (2008, 37-38).

Kenyon herself contends that Jericho was destroyed in the latter part of the Late Bronze Age, destruction truly remembered in the book of Joshua, although she does not believe archaeology can provide the proof. The subsequent break in occupation that is proved by archaeology is, however, in accord with the biblical story. There was a period of abandonment, during which erosion removed most of the remains of the Late Bronze Age town and much of the earlier ones (1993, 2:680).

VII. JOSHUA 7

BEHIND THE TEXT

The opening words of Josh 7 shatter the euphoria of ch 6: "But the Israelites were unfaithful in regard to the devoted things" (7:1). Not only had the Israelites disobeyed, but they had violated the *ḥerem*, contaminating themselves and becoming liable to destruction as Jericho had been. Disaster threatened and Israel's status as God's covenant people hung in the balance. God would not keep his promise to give Israel the land unless Israel obeyed.

IN THE TEXT

A. Sin and Its Consequences (7:1-5)

1. Achan's Sin (7:1)

■ 1 The very first word of Josh 7 is the verb ***acted unfaithfully***. This verb provides a jarring contrast to the events of ch 6 and a fitting opening to the traumatic events of ch 7. The key question of Josh 7 is whether or not Israel will be faithful to its covenant with Yahweh.

The opening verse also introduces Achan, including his family tree. Since this same information is provided later in the chapter, its inclusion here is likely meant to contrast Achan, an Israelite from a long line of Israelites and part of the great tribe of Judah, with the Canaanite woman mentioned only a few verses earlier: Rahab the prostitute (6:25). This contrast will appear throughout this chapter. By contrasting the insider who acts like an outsider and is punished as an outsider, with the outsider who acts like an insider and becomes an insider, the author offers a lesson in true obedience.

Achan's actions make God furious, not only at Achan, but at all Israel. What was threatened in Josh 6:18 has taken place; disobedience regarding the devoted things has put the whole camp in jeopardy.

2. First Attack on Ai (7:2-5)

■ **2-5** If archaeologists have correctly located Ai, this town stood just over ten miles north-northwest of Jericho (Longman 2013, 41). The commonly accepted location, et-Tell, however, presents considerable problems for the historicity of the passage. As Butler notes, this site "has no signs of occupation during any period which can realistically be set forward as a conquest date" (1983, xxxviii). Joseph A. Callaway, who dug at et-Tell, believes "the new evidence from archeological research on the conquest of Ai supports the essential historicity of the conquest, although it seems to have been a less glorious enterprise than the traditioners have made it" (1968, 320; 1993, 39-45).

Some scholars treat this as further evidence that the book of Joshua lacks historical credibility. Others propose the actual site of Ai lies elsewhere, perhaps at a site not yet excavated. Bryant Wood suggests Khirbet el-Maqatir, just west of et-Tell (2000a, 123-30; 2000b, 249-54; 2001, 246-52; 2008, 205-40). Using rabbinic sources, Ben-Zion Luria (1989, 153-58) locates Ai only about three miles west of Jericho.

If the traditional site is correct and was uninhabited when the Israelites arrived, the defenders may have come from Bethel, less than three miles away (Kelso 1993, 192-94). Joshua 8:17 connects Ai with Bethel in this battle when it says that attackers came out from both cities. It would have been at the remains of (by then) ancient Ai that those from Bethel took their stand against the Israelite attackers (Hess 1996a, 158). The author of the book of Joshua felt it necessary to provide additional information about the town's location (**which is near Beth Aven to the east of Bethel** [7:2]), suggesting the site may have been obscure even in his day. This would make the defeat of Ai essentially the defeat of Bethel at Ai and would explain why Bethel's defeat is assumed in the book of Joshua (see 12:16) but is nowhere described.

Throughout this chapter the author connects the stories of Achan and Rahab so as to set these two figures in contrast. In 7:2 we see the first such connection: sending spies. We need not assume Joshua was wrong to send the spies on this occasion, although there is a big difference between the report of the spies on this occasion from the report given at the end of Josh 2. Both reports predicted victory, but those who went to Jericho based their prediction on the fear that gripped the hearts of the enemy (2:24), while those who went to Ai took confidence in Israel's military superiority. We are meant to hear a hint of overconfidence among the Israelites.

These spies miscalculated. They got the numbers right but failed to account for Israel's spiritual contamination. Joshua was extra cautious, sending the larger number they suggested (three thousand rather than two thousand, or three military units rather than two, depending on how one renders *'eleph*), but even he failed to take note of Israel's handicap. The outcome was disastrous: even this run-down town sent Israel scrambling and killed thirty-six Israelite soldiers. The reason for mentioning the specific number is unclear, though it sharply contrasts to previously mentioned Israelite casualties—none.

The Israelites were chased as far as *hašebāarîm* (7:5). The NIV and other translations render this as **the stone quarries** while others treat the word as referring to a place, Shebarim (see NIV mg., Vulgate). Neither option is without difficulties. If the author considered Ai's location so obscure as to require additional clarifying phrases (v 2), it seems unlikely he would mention a location less well-known, like stone quarries located near Ai, or an otherwise unknown town. Perhaps the *šebāarîm* refers to the outer extent of the remaining ruins of then ancient Ai (see Ps 60:2; Isa 15:5; 30:13). Woudstra, following the LXX, suggests this term, which can mean breach or breaking, refers to the scattering of the Israelites (1981, 123 n. 21). Clearly the defeat so terrorized Israel that their hearts melted in fear. The Israelites respond to the Canaanites from Ai just as the Canaanites from Jericho had responded to the Israelites (Josh 2:11; 5:1), yet one more contrast between the stories of Rahab and Achan.

B. Removal of Sin (7:6-26)

1. Israel's Response to Military Defeat (7:6-9)

■ **6** Joshua and the Israelite elders respond with intense mourning. The NIV implies that only the **elders**, not Joshua, **sprinkled dust on their heads**, but the Hebrew makes clear that these actions were done by all the mourners, including Joshua. They **tore** their **clothes and fell facedown to the ground before the ark, sprinkled dust on their heads**, and remained in this condition for the rest of that day (v 6). This is the first time we hear of the ark since the previous chapter, highlighting Israel's failure to seek God's direction prior to this battle. This is also the first time in the book of Joshua that we meet the elders. We meet them several more times in the book (see 8:10 [NIV, "leaders"], 33; 23:2; 24:1, 31). The elders represent all Israel just as Achan will represent his whole family (7:24).

■ **7** The intensity of Israel's mourning arose not only from the loss of three dozen soldiers, as tragic as that was, but also from the significance of the defeat. Joshua correctly observes that once the word gets out, Israel would have lost one of her chief advantages—the aura of invincibility. Without this, her enemies would be emboldened to attack. Further, Joshua correctly understood that Yahweh had a hand in this defeat. He knew God was sovereign, so defeat had not resulted from any failure on God's part. Joshua also knew it was God who had given Israel victory at Jericho.

Since God remained sovereign and had led Israel into Canaan, he must have done so to destroy them now. Hence his complaint: **If only we had been content to stay on the other side of the Jordan!**; that is, if only we had seen what God intended and not gotten our hopes up with the thought of being anything special, we could have saved ourselves the trouble of trying. Beyond the loss of soldiers and the fear of annihilation was the assumption they had been deluded; this explains the deeply felt and involuntary ejaculation of despair, **Alas**.

■ **8-9** A lesser man may have given up, but not Joshua. He still believed God was fair enough to reconsider. **What can I say?** (v 8) introduces his appeal: If Israel's **name** (v 9*a*) is wiped out, and everyone is aware that Yahweh has led Israel thus far, will not Yahweh's **great name** (v 9*b*) be sullied? The OT believers often appealed to God's reputation (see Num 14:13-16; Ps 79:9-10) because they knew this mattered to him. God cared about his reputation, not from vanity, but because knowing the truth about God is essential to human happiness.

2. God's Explanation and Instructions (7:10-15)

■ **10** Joshua's appeal fails because he has misunderstood the problem. He assumed Israel's obedience and blamed the problem on God. He thought God had been unfaithful to Israel when, in fact, Israel had been unfaithful to God (v 1). God makes this clear in no uncertain terms: **Stand up!** Joshua and the elders were prostrate, but Joshua was commanded to rise. Something needs to be done about this problem and Joshua was the one to do it, but he could not do so while lying on his face.

■ **11** God puts his finger on the problem—Israel's sin—and proceeds to dissect and expose that sin in all its ugly detail. The ASV's more literal translation of v 11 brings out the emphasis: "Israel hath sinned; yea, they have *even* transgressed my covenant which I commanded them: yea, they have *even* taken of the devoted thing, and have *also* stolen, and dissembled *also*; and they have *even* put it among their own stuff." I have italicized the words that translate the Hebrew particle (*gam*), which the author inserted multiple times for emphasis.

■ **12** In consequence of this offense, Israel would be unable to stand up to her enemies but would be defeated by them in battle. The Hebrew term for their enemies appears twice in v 12 for emphasis (though it is only translated once in the NIV). Emphasis is also placed on the word translated **backs**, indicating this is all the Canaanites will see of Israel. All Jericho had been declared *herem*—devoted to the Lord for destruction (see 6:17); now all Israel had become devoted to destruction as well (7:12), just as God had promised (see 6:18). The NIV renders the phrase in 7:12 and 6:18 as **liable to destruction**, which suggests Israel would become contaminated unless she acts immediately. Actually the contamination had already occurred. The NRSV expresses this well: "They have become a thing devoted for destruction themselves." Some hope remained, however, should Israel act immediately and resolutely to rid their camp of these devoted things. Otherwise, God would no longer be with them (**with you,** pl.).

■ **13** God not only provided them another chance but also told them how to make things right (see vv 13-15). As will become clear, God even played an active role in helping Israel find the spiritual contamination so they could remove it. In addition to this indication of grace, God calls himself **the God of Israel** (v 13); in spite of Israel's sin, he remained their God.

The restoration process was to begin with self-consecration, as they had done before crossing the Jordan (3:5). This consecration was not just to remove sin from the camp but to prepare the people for God to come among them. Much of the language is singular: ***among you*** [sg.], ***you*** [sg.] ***cannot stand, your*** [sg.] ***enemies***; each Israelite was to take personal responsibility for this problem. The language then shifts to the plural, ***you*** [pl.] **remove the devoted things from your** [pl.] ***midst***—reminding the Israelites that they succeed or fail together.

■ **14** God instructed Joshua to initiate a slow process of discovery, likely by casting lots (see 1 Sam 10:20-21; 14:41-42)—perhaps the Urim and Thummim—and likely close to the tabernacle (Keil and Delitzsch 1978, 79). The process involved God singling out the tribe, then the clan, then the household, then the family, and finally the guilty man. The process could have been quick, even immediate; God could have identified Achan from the outset, as he used Nathan to implicate King David (2 Sam 12:7). Perhaps God prolonged this investigation and held it adjacent to the holiest spot in the camp to prod Achan into confessing. God did something similar when he allowed Jericho time to repent while Israel circumambulated the city for seven days (Josh 6).

■ **15** God also instructed Joshua what should be done with the guilty man and all that belongs to him. Just as "devoted" Jericho had been "stoned" (i.e., the collapse of its walls) and then burned, so must Achan and the stolen items—now *herem*—be stoned and burned. Why? **He has violated the covenant of the Lord and has done an outrageous thing in Israel!** The first phrase—**violated the covenant of the Lord**—emphasizes the treacherous disloyalty with which the chapter began (v 1); the second phrase—**done an outrageous thing in Israel**—emphasizes that Achan's sin not only broke Israel's treaty with God but represented a crime "irreconcilable with the honour of Israel as the people of God" (ibid., 80). Although Israel had itself become *ḥerem* (v 12), God was graciously allowing a restoration not only of the covenant but also of Israel's honor.

3. Israel Follows God's Instructions (7:16-26)

■ **16-18** The phrase **early the next morning** (v 16) implies Joshua's prompt obedience. Verses 16-18 then clarify how Joshua carefully executed God's directions and how God kept his promise to identify the culprit. As in ch 3, no mention is made of Israel having consecrated itself, though God's willingness to come among them implies they had. The order in 7:15 was tribe, clan, household, family, man; in vv 16-18 it is tribe, clan, men, household, man, although the reason for the difference is unclear. There is also some question whether Achan's ancestor was Zabdi (MT), Zambri (LXX), or Zimri (vv 17-18). The NIV opts for the last, apparently to bring these verses into agreement with the genealogy of 1 Chr 2:6.

■ **19** Joshua charges Achan to tell the truth: **My son, give glory to the LORD, the God of Israel, and honor him. Tell me what you have done; do not hide it from me**. This seems a roundabout way of arriving at a confession (although perhaps no less than our practice of swearing in a witness). More than a mere formality, however, Joshua's charge perfectly frames the moment. It reminds Achan that he stands in a subservient role to Joshua, as a son to a father. Achan's primary responsibility is not to save his own skin, but to do what most honors Yahweh, the God to whom he owes gratitude, yet whose covenant he has broken. Yahweh is God of Israel, the nation placed in jeopardy by Achan's sin. Achan's obligations to Joshua, Yahweh, and Israel have been clearly delineated, and he is now charged to reveal his crime and hide nothing.

■ **20-21** It took him being singled out of all Israel by God himself, but Achan finally provides a full confession. He demonstrates his sincerity by beginning with **It is true** (v 20*a*) and putting extra emphasis on the pronoun I in **I have sinned** (v 20*b*). He repeats the same names for God used by Joshua in v 19—Yahweh and **God of Israel**, and expresses his confession slowly and deliberately (*according to this and according to this I did*). He also adds detailed information that proves he was the one who took the material: a garment of good quality from Babylon, about six pounds of silver, and a wedge, literally a *tongue* of gold, weighing just over one pound. As Hess points out, all this contraband could be easily concealed (1996a, 152-53). These objects lay buried in the floor of his tent, with the silver beneath them, an added detail that further implicates Achan in their burial.

■ **22-23** Messengers were immediately dispatched to confirm this information. They ran to fulfill their mission but also to prevent the objects being moved. The messengers found everything just as Achan had said; the language of the messengers in v 22 is very similar to Achan's words in v 21. They brought the stolen items to the tabernacle and **spread them out** or "laid them down" (ESV) or "displayed them" (NJPS) before Yahweh (v 23). Translated most literally, the messengers "poured them out" (NASB), suggesting the contraband was emptied out of a container onto the ground.

■ **24** Having discovered the culprit, heard his confession, and proven his guilt beyond doubt, there was nothing to do but carry out the punishment God commanded. Achan was removed from the tabernacle to the place of execution. Along with Achan was brought the contraband, Achan's family (no mention is made of his wife, though if alive she would presumably have been brought) and all his other possessions. Mention of the contraband before his family and possessions emphasizes the cause of this disaster, covetousness. That his goods, livestock, and tent are destroyed makes clear he was not being killed for material gain. Achan is taken to Achor—the wordplay is clear and likely meant to make the association memorable (see v 26).

■ **25** Joshua's words of condemnation leave no doubt that Achan brought this trouble on himself and all Israel. These words also make clear that the punishment was at God's insistence. In the Hebrew of v 25*b*, the act of stoning with stones is mentioned twice, using different verbs. The NIV suggests there were two stonings: first, Achan was stoned and then the rest of his household, his animals, and his objects. The NLT reduces the double stoning to one: "And all the Israelites stoned Achan and his family and burned their bodies." The LXX of v 25 also mentions only one stoning but omits any mention of burning. In the NRSV, the second mention of stones is treated as referring to the erection of a cairn over the corpses.

It is probably best to see the double reference of stones as indicating a single stoning of Achan and all the rest, repeated by the author for emphasis: "And Joshua said, 'Why did you bring trouble on us? The LORD brings trouble on you today.' And all Israel stoned him with stones. They burned them with fire and stoned them with stones" (ESV; see ASV, KJV).

Many readers struggle with why Achan's family had to be killed along with Achan. Holding sons and daughters responsible for their father's actions seems unfair, even prohibited by the OT itself. God had told Ezekiel, "The one who sins is the one who will die" (Ezek 18:4). At this stage of Israel's existence, although individual actions were not insignificant, God generally held the group responsible for the behavior of its members. In time, God began to shift responsibility more to the individual and less to the group, as illustrated by the Ezekiel passage cited above.

Holding a group responsible for the actions of an individual was the norm in the ANE. Passages in the Amarna letters, written from Canaan around this time, speak of the disobedience of an individual leading to the destruction of his whole family. "Whoever has disobeyed has no family, has nothing alive," reads one letter (Moran 1992, 240, EA 153 lines 12-20). Another, written from Pharaoh to the governor of Amurru reads, "But if you perform your service for the king, your lord, what is there that the king will not do for you? If for any reason whatsoever you prefer to do evil, and if you plot evil, treacherous things, then you, together with your entire family, shall die by the axe of the king" (ibid., 249, EA 162 lines 33-38).

Holding a group responsible for the actions of an individual does not mean the group is considered equally guilty. Even our highly individualistic culture recognizes that no sin affects only the sinner. Consequences arrive unbidden on your doorstep because of someone else's choice. Adultery and its effects spread throughout the family and down the generations. Gossip not only harms the subject of the rumors but also poisons the gossiper and all who listen. One person's sinful act immediately places a moral obligation on others who must now respond, either by correction or complicity, with more consequences flowing from that response. Achan put all Israel in jeopardy by creating a scenario where the nation must obey God or themselves be punished. Nowhere does it say that the thirty-six soldiers who died in the first battle at Ai (Josh 7:5) or even Achan's family were punished for their sin. They died as a result of forces set in motion by Achan.

Some explain that Achan's family was killed because they were culpable in the crime. How could their father hide something under the floor of the tent without their knowing about it? Although the family may have known about the crime and been guilty of not making it known, they were probably not killed for this reason. More likely, they were killed because their father had contaminated them with the deadly contraband. This would explain why the animals and tent, which could not be considered culpable, were also destroyed.

■ **26** After the people and animals were killed by stoning, they and all their possessions, including the contraband, were burned. Stones were piled over the ashes, the cairn remaining up to the time of the author. Various purposes have been proposed for the cairn. It may have been a grave on which those who pass by would cast stones (Gray, as cited by Berman 2004, 32 n. 2). Some have thought it served a magical function, disempowering those who had been executed (Abarbanel, as cited in ibid.). Most likely it was a marker to warn others against opposing Israel (Gersonides, as cited in ibid.) or violating God's commands. Since another cairn described similarly will be built in Josh 8, and since such structures are not commonly mentioned elsewhere, perhaps a clearer understanding of the stones will have to wait until after we consider the defeat of Ai.

Whatever the purpose for this cairn, its construction prompted God to turn **from his fierce anger**. We do not know what this valley was called prior to this event or where it was located. **Therefore** suggests it was because of the presence of the stones—a visible reminder of Achan's disobedience and the consequences that followed—that the valley became known from that day on as **Achor**, *Trouble*.

FROM THE TEXT

The God we meet in Josh 7 appears harsh, perhaps as harsh as anywhere in the Bible. He designates certain property as toxic, then exposes his people to this property as they invade Jericho. When Achan's God-given appreciation for beauty overwhelms his better judgment, God becomes enraged. Although only one man out of thousands has committed the offense, God allows the consequences to spill over to all Israel, leading to the death of three dozen soldiers and eventually a whole family. Yahweh does not kill Achan and his family, but makes the Israelites carry out the execution. Only the erection of a permanent monument to these events assuages his fierce anger. No wonder one commentator proposed the purpose of this monument is a reminder of God's cruelty (Dieterle 1998, 41-54).

Although our modern sensibilities recoil from such harshness, we must not miss the evidence of God's grace. Designating Jericho's booty as ḥerem and enforcing this ban was not arbitrary, but an intentional part of the curriculum by which God would teach the Israelites that he was a holy God and they were holy people. Jericho represented the firstfruits of victory, and its spoils belonged to God and were rightfully devoted to him. If he did not enforce absolute obedience at this point, he would have misrepresented who he is, who the Israelites are, and what the relationship must be between them. For Israel to enjoy God's best, they must understand that God was their holy sovereign and they were to be his loyal subjects. God graciously makes this clear to them through these events.

We also see his grace in how he refrained from immediately destroying Israel once their camp had been contaminated. He allowed them the opportunity to experience his displeasure; though it cost thirty-six lives, the consequences would have been much worse if God had not restrained his hand. When Joshua and Israel did seek an explanation, God provided one, both identifying the problem and proposing a solution. Even more graciously, God came among Israel and actively involved himself in the process of discovery. Do not miss the fact that without God's assistance, identifying the source of the contamination would have been much more difficult and time-consuming, each moment making it more likely that Israel's enemies would join to oppose them. Israel needed this sobering scenario to reinforce the cost of disobedience and the importance of remaining a holy people. They had been called to be a source of blessing to the other nations and could only fulfill this calling if they were holy.

Although they struggled with being holy, even enduring a period of exile in Babylon, the nation of Israel did retain its identity as God's chosen and holy people. From this nation, God was able to bring his solution to the sin that had prompted Achan and others to disobey God. The incarnation offers many parallels to what happens in ch 7. In both we see God's wrath displayed alongside his mercy. In both, God's holiness led to a hatred for sin that could only be assuaged by sacrifice. It was because of God's wrath that Jesus was sent as our atoning sacrifice. In both ch 7 and the incarnation, the initiative and solution were God's. In ch 7, one family died to spare the whole nation; in Jesus, one man died to spare the whole world. While hanging on the cross, bearing the sins of the whole world, Jesus felt himself forsaken by God, the victim of God's wrath. Both deaths were marked by a memorial, one a pile of stones, the other a wooden cross and a stone rolled away to reveal an empty tomb.

The contrasts between these scenarios are equally striking. Death was required in both instances, death of the guilty in Josh 7 and death of the innocent on the cross. The former saw the death of the guilty for the innocent; the latter saw the death of the innocent for the guilty. Both required a sacrifice, but in the first the sacrifice was demanded by God while in the second the ultimate sacrifice was given by God. The death of Achan and his family made possible Israel's success in warfare against the nations; the death of Christ meant eternal peace for all nations, first for the Jews, then for the Gentiles. Achan's death occurred in Achor, known thenceforth as the valley of Trouble. Christ's death took place on Golgotha, place of the skull, which became the hill of hope. Isaiah and Hosea anticipated that day when they spoke of the valley of Achor becoming "a resting place for herds" (Isa 65:10) and "a door of hope" (Hos 2:15).

It is also instructive to read this account in light of the early church. Note, for example, the similarities between this story and the account of Ananias and Sapphira in Acts 5 (Combet-Gallard 2005, 43-61). Like Achan, this couple stole what belonged to God and lied about it. The same Greek verb, rendered "kept back" (Acts 5:2) and "kept for yourself" (v 3) is used by the LXX to describe theft of sacred objects in 2 Macc 4:32 and in Josh 7:1. Both instances threatened the community, although this is only implied in Acts. Achan's death occurred at the hands of the Israelites while the deaths of Ananias and Sapphira were at God's hand. In both cases, however, God identified the guilty. Like Joshua, Peter speaks for God and the community in calling for the truth and in announcing divine judgment. Both episodes produced greater reverence for God and both emphasize the importance of God's people modeling and insisting on holiness within the community.

VIII. JOSHUA 8

BEHIND THE TEXT

Israel had just experienced a close call, placating God's wrath by purging the evil from their midst. Joshua 8 describes how they reengaged in battle with Ai, defeated that city, and recommitted themselves to Yahweh. The chapter divides unevenly between these events, with the focus on the battle in vv 1-29, and the covenant renewal ceremony at Mount Ebal described in vv 30-35.

IN THE TEXT

A. Second Battle with Ai (8:1-29)

1. Preparations for the Battle (8:1-13)

■ 1-2 The division of the narrative between ch 7 and ch 8 is unfortunate, since it obscures the remarkable demonstration of God's grace. God not only turns from his "fierce anger" (7:26) but also speaks to Joshua (8:1-2). The disasters of ch 7 made embarking on a second campaign all the more risky. How could they be sure no new sin had been committed since Achan's death? If one defeat jeopardized their safety, what disaster would befall a second defeat?

In this moment of fear, God spoke words of comfort to Joshua. The disasters described in ch 7 would have undermined Israel's confidence in Joshua's leadership, and perhaps Joshua's confidence in himself. What he needed was a reaffirmation as strong as the one given at the opening of the book. That may explain why 8:1 sounds so much like 1:6 and 1:9. It also helps explain why Joshua occupies such a prominent place in this chapter. He is the subject of thirty-two verbs in ch 8, and his name appears nineteen times, more than in any chapter previous. As Hall puts it, "The encouragement in 8:1 therefore functions, after the setbacks associated with Achan's sin, to indicate that Yahweh's powerful presence with Israel has been restored" (2010, 129; for her discussion, see 129-31). The phrase **do not be discouraged** occurs rarely elsewhere (see Deut 1:21; 31:8; 1 Chr 22:13; 28:20). Hess points out that all the passages where the phrase occurs describe the execution of a significant but difficult task assigned by God (1996a, 159).

God directed Joshua to take the entire army and attack Ai. The phrase **whole army** (*all the people of war*) is found only in the book of Joshua (8:1, 3, 11; 10:7; 11:7) and indicates Israel's unity as they engaged in battle (Howard 1998a, 203). It does not necessarily mean that every soldier was involved (Keil and Delitzsch 1978, 84), as seen in passages such as 1:14-15 and 3:12-13 (Woudstra 1981, 134), though it still suggests a sizable force.

A large force was not required for victory, but served at least four other purposes. First, it was a means to deceive Ai, making it look like Israel was trying the same frontal attack only with a much larger force than the first time. Second, a larger group would be necessary since the army would be divided into the main force and the ambush. Third, since this victory would result in the defeat of **the king of Ai, his people, his city and his land**, a larger army would be needed to carry off the spoils (v 2). Fourth, as Calvin pointed out, the larger number was a concession to Israel's fears (as cited by Keil and Delitzsch 1978, 84).

As the One directing the campaign for the conquest of Canaan (see 5:13-15), God provides the strategy for the battle. Joshua was to divide the army into larger and smaller contingents and set the smaller as an ambush **behind the city**. Hess offers an example of a similar strategy used by an Assyrian king, "While I remained in front of (the city of) Parsindi I set the cavalry (and) pioneers in ambush (behind the city). I killed fifty troops, the fighting men of Ameka, in the open country" (1996a, 160-61). Why did God choose this strategy? He could have destroyed Ai in any number of ways. Whatever God's reasons, he had Israel employ a strategy that exposed fewer soldiers to mortal danger, while still requiring Israel's involvement.

Here and in 8:27, God specifies that Israel was entitled to Ai's **plunder and livestock**, unlike the situation after the fall of Jericho. The phrase **and livestock** seems unnecessary, since plunder would include anything and everything. We meet similar phrases in Deuteronomy. The additional phrase may be intended to emphasize that although God had ceased to provide his people with manna, he was continuing to provide them with food (see Hess 1996a, 170).

■ **3-13** Verses 3-13 portray Joshua instructing the Israelite army and Israel carrying out these instructions. What is commanded is somewhat unclear.

Do two nights elapse or just one? Where does Joshua spend this night/these nights? Does he set one ambush or two? Part of the problem is that the author has described the battle plans, but not in chronological order. On the first morning, Joshua mustered the troops. From these troops he appointed an ambush of **five thousand** (v 12), that is, about thirty fighting units (see Hess 1996a, 162). Then Joshua and the rest of the soldiers marched the approximately fifteen miles from Gilgal to Ai (Keil and Delitzsch 1978, 85) and set up camp north of the city, across the valley (vv 10-11, 13). That first night, the ambush took up its position west of Ai under cover of darkness (vv 3-9*a*, 12, 13) while Joshua camped with the main force (vv 9*b*, 13*b*). His presence there reinforced the deception that Israel was attempting another frontal assault. The next morning, the people of Ai woke to see the larger force and set out to engage them in battle (v 14). If this summary is correct, vv 3-9 describe preparations, v 10 signals the commencement of the battle the next morning, and vv 11-13 present a flashback that expands on vv 3-9 (Howard 1998a, 200).

By describing the ambush first and from two different perspectives, the author heightens its importance to the story. Those in ambush should watch the battle closely, for the retreat of the main Israelite force will be their signal to attack the city. They are to **take** possession of Ai, a phrase used elsewhere for taking possession of the land of Canaan. Though they are said to take the city, it will actually be Yahweh who will **give it into** their hands (v 7). The combination of **take** and **give** would serve to remind the Israelites of the required divine–human synergy for success, of who was their true Commander, and to encourage them in the face of their earlier defeat. To warn them against further disobedience, Joshua instructed them to **do what the LORD has commanded** (v 8). This is the first of two occurrences of the phrase *kidbar YHWH*, **according to the word of the LORD,** in this chapter and in the OT (Hall 2010, 136).

Verse 9 specifies that the ambush lay hidden to the west of Ai, between that city and nearby Bethel. Since the army of Bethel joined in the pursuit of the Israelites prior to the springing of the trap (v 17), they must have passed close to the hidden Israelite troops, alerting the Israelites to the vulnerability of both cities.

Joshua spent that night **with the people** (v 9; see ESV, KJV, NASB, NIV, NJB) or better, with "the troops" (NJPS; "in the camp" [NRSV]; "among the people in the camp" [NLT]). Verse 13 tells us he slept in **the valley**. Apparently, Joshua stayed with the main part of his army rather than going with the ambush (v 9), but the specific location where he slept was in the valley (v 13), at the very front of his army. His presence there would encourage his own troops while making the temptation to attack even more enticing for the king of Ai.

The Hebrew does not mention the **next** morning (v 10), only that Joshua arose early. As noted in connection with 3:1-5, rising early can refer to prompt obedience rather than the time of day. Verses 10-13 of ch 8 describe the march from Gilgal to Ai with the author piling up verbs—*went up . . . went up . . . approached . . . came*—to vivify their advance. Verse 19 is correct to see only one ambush, not two. It would make little sense to send another five thousand troops to the same place at this point in the march when a large contingent of thirty thousand already lay hidden there. Some explain the two numbers—five thousand and thirty thousand—as a copyist's error (Howard 1998a, 204 n. 112), others that the smaller number refers to the ambush, while the larger refers to the total force (Hess 1996a, 162). Another possibility is that thirty thousand should actually refer to thirty units while five thousand was the actual number involved in the ambush. Verse 13 summarizes the situation on the night before the battle.

2. The Battle (8:14-23)

■ 14 Ordinarily, the author of Joshua shows us things through the eyes of Israel, not the eyes of the Canaanites. Berman suggests this "'objectification' of our perception of the Canaanites denies them humanity, and contributes to our perception of the process of annihilation across the narrative of the Book of Joshua" (2004, 48). In this passage, however, we are shown what is happening through the eyes of the king of Ai. He saw the Israelites encamped across the valley and arose early to engage them in battle. The people of Ai probably saw the Israelites arriving the day or evening prior and prepared to attack. Messages were sent to Bethel to elicit their help. The next day the king of Ai marched out of the city at the head of a combined army to meet Israel **at a certain place** (v 14).

Perhaps the author chose this unusual perspective—through the eyes of the enemy—to emphasize the deception involved. The king of Ai thought he saw the Israelites amassed for a second frontal assault, but he failed to see the ambush behind him. He marched out to **a certain place**, that is, either to an ideal spot for battle or "at a time appointed" (KJV), an ideal time for battle, but never suspected that this perfect place or time was actually a trap. From what he saw, he thought it would be best to engage them to the east, never suspecting there was an ambush waiting in the west.

■ 15-17 Because we know Joshua only appeared to be beaten, translators add words like **let themselves be** or "pretended to be" (ESV), but the Hebrew actually describes this as a defeat, likely continuing to present this from the Aite point of view (Kasten 2000, 1-13). On the verge of another rout, the king of Ai rallied all his troops and those of Bethel (vv 16-17) to pursue and annihilate the Israelites once and for all. In so doing, they exposed both cities to the ambush.

■ 18-19 At this point, Joshua received orders from the Commander to spring the trap, sending the signal by raising his **javelin**. Perhaps Joshua's raised weapon triggered a series of signals that quickly reached those lying hidden west of the city. How the ambush could see this signal is less important to the author than the image of Joshua standing with raised weapon. Hall considers the **javelin** to have been a sickle sword, a curved weapon with "symbolic significance during the second millennium B.C.E., as a sign of dominion" (2010, 135). She describes reliefs of Pharaoh receiving the sickle sword from the gods and wielding it over the heads of his enemies. In Mari, the javelin was a metaphor for "revolt, attack, or simply force" (ibid.). By describing him this way, the author makes clear both Joshua's military leadership and the source of the victory through Yahweh.

This image of Joshua standing with weapon raised brings to mind another Israelite leader in a similar posture. Whether we picture Moses with his arm and rod extended over the waters of Egypt (Exod 8:5, 17), over the Reed Sea (Exod 14:16), or over Israel's battle with the Amalekites (Exod 17:11), we cannot help but associate Israel's first great leader with her second. According to Howard, even the wording in Josh 8:18 is the same unusual construction as we find in reference to Moses in Exod 8:5, 17 (Heb 8:1, 13) (1998a, 208 n. 122).

We also hear a play on words in God's instruction to Joshua: "Stretch out the javelin that is in your hand toward Ai, for I will give it into your hand" (v 18 ESV). The double use of **quickly** (v 19) emphasizes Joshua's prompt obedience and that of the soldiers who had been waiting for this signal, and connects that obedience with what appears to be the almost instantaneous defeat of Ai.

■ **20** As he did in v 14, the author once again allows us to "see" this battle from the Aite point of view. Berman contends that the author's purpose is "to draw attention to the blind hubris of the king of Ha-Ai and to receive the 'confession' of error, as it were, by subjectifying them, precisely at the moment of full realization in v. 20" (2004, 48). Berman rightly connects this episode with that of Achan in ch 7: "Just as the king of Ha-Ai was led to a skewed vision, blinded by his desire to conquer and despoil Israel, so too Achan was blinded by his desire for the spoils, and led by a skewed vision" (ibid., 50).

■ **21-23** Having been given the Aite point of view in v 20, the author provides the Israelite view in v 21. The larger contingent turned back from their feigned retreat and the ambushers, having torched Ai, attacked from the other side, trapping those from Ai and Bethel in the middle **with Israelites on both sides** (*these from this and these from this*) (v 22). The description of the king of Ai being taken alive and brought to Joshua (v 23) sounds similar to other ANE battle accounts, as when the victorious Moabites dragged the leader of Gad before their god, Chemosh (Stern 1991, 31).

3. Destruction of Ai (8:24-29)

■ **24-27** The author makes a point of describing the complete and total annihilation of Ai; more is made of Ai's destruction than Jericho's. We are even given the number of dead—twelve thousand—the only time in Joshua a specific number is given (Howard 1998a, 209). Mention of all Ai's inhabitants being killed likely refers only to the soldiers and those who remained in the city after it was set ablaze. No doubt those who could took advantage of the temporary departure of Israel's soldiers (v 22) and ran for their lives. The city itself, like Jericho, was designated as *ḥerem* (**he had destroyed** [v 26] uses the verb form of this Hebrew word; see 6:15-21; 7:6-26). This time, however, God permitted the Israelites to remove the booty (8:27), thereby reinforcing the principle of retribution: obedience brings blessing while disobedience brings disaster.

■ **28-29** After destroying Jericho, Joshua pronounced a curse on anyone who would rebuild it. Here we have no curse, although Joshua's actions in v 28 imply something similar. Stern suggests the verb rendered **made** might be better translated "designated," which suggests "a symbolic or ritual act such as the Hittites practiced by sowing the weeds on the tell or by sowing it with salt" (1991, 74). Another aspect of this ritual was the humiliation and burial of the king of Ai (v 29). It is unclear whether Joshua killed the king by hanging or killed the king in some other way and then hung his corpse; his practice in 10:26 suggests the latter. Hanging, likely impalement rather than lynching, was a well-known wartime practice of the ANE (Howard 1998a, 211, citing Younger 222-23 n. 88).

Israelite law prohibits displaying an impaled corpse overnight since it defiles the land (Deut 21:22-23), so they took down the king's body, threw it into the city gate, and piled stones upon it. This may be another aspect of the ritual, but the author is almost certainly reminding us of an earlier pile of stones in the valley of Achor (Josh 7:26). The language describing the building of the two cairns here and in 7:26 is virtually identical (Berman 2004, 32). According to Berman, the pile of stones over Achan and the pile over the king of Ai symbolize "that Israel has two enemies, one internal and one external" (ibid., 34).

Although Ai's defeat and plunder is described in these verses, nothing is said of the fate of Bethel. According to 8:17, Bethel's soldiers joined with those of Ai in pursuit of the Israelites, but no mention is made of Bethel's defeat. It may be that v 17 refers, not to the city of Bethel, but to Ai's temple, since Bethel can also be translated "house of god." Bethel's defeat occurs at some point since her king is listed among those who had been killed in the conquest of Canaan (see 12:16).

Although it is not specifically mentioned in Joshua and although it might have come later, it seems more likely that Bethel was destroyed at this time (Butler 1983, 87). After all, since Bethel's soldiers passed by the Israelite ambush, the Israelites knew the city was undefended and would likely have taken this opportunity to destroy it, as they did Ai.

B. Covenant Renewal at Mount Ebal (8:30-35)

■ **30** When did this covenant renewal ceremony take place? Its placement in the book of Joshua suggests this took place just after the defeat of Ai. Moses had commanded the Israelites to hold this ceremony (see v 31; Deut 11:26-32; 27:1-26) on the day they crossed the Jordan. This is when the ceremony takes place, according to the copies of Joshua found among the Dead Sea Scrolls (Noort 1998, 127-44). The LXX places it after Josh 9:2, just before the Gibeonite deception. Josephus describes it occurring between the conquest and the apportioning of the land (Josephus 1979, 5.69-70; 4.305-8). Rabbi Yishmael (*Yerushalmi Sotah* 7:3, 21c) argued that this ceremony took place after all the land had been allocated (Angel 2008, 6).

This ceremony seems disconnected geographically from the preceding material. It would require Israel to return from Ai to Gilgal, break camp, then travel more than twenty miles to Ebal through Canaanite territory, stopping near the city of Shechem, a Canaanite city. Howard recognizes these logistical difficulties though he believes the events occurred in this order (1998a, 212). If the ceremony did occur at this point, it provides yet another example of how Israel engaged in faith-building behavior and how a significant event was followed by a religious ceremony (see Josh 5:2-10). If it did not occur in this order, the author may have placed it here to show how Israel reaffirmed the covenant they had violated through Achan's sin (Butler 1983, 91).

■ **31-35** Whenever this ceremony did occur, it took place at a site chosen long before by **Moses the servant of the LORD** (8:31, 33; see 1:1-2). He had commanded the Israelites to gather at Mount Gerizim and Mount Ebal and reaffirm the covenant (see Deut 11:26-32; 27:1-26). The author makes it clear that Joshua fulfills Moses' instructions to the letter, even to the kind of altar he builds—one made of fieldstones rather than stones worked with a tool (see Exod 20:25; Deut 27:5-6). This is the first altar built by Israel in Canaan (Butler 1983, 91).

Also according to Moses' instructions, the people offered **burnt offerings** and **fellowship offerings** (Deut 27:6-7). The former would atone for sin and express Israel's full commitment to God. The latter gave Israel the opportunity to thank God for all he had done and celebrate their relationship with him. As Moses commanded, Joshua wrote the Law on plastered stones (Deut 27:2-4, 8) and read it publicly (Josh 8:34-35; see Deut 27:12-26). Five times (Josh 8:31*a*, 31*b*, 33, 34, 35) the author points out Joshua's strict adherence to the commands of Moses.

The Law written on plastered stones served two purposes. It provided the script to be recited at this ceremony ("the blessings and the curses" [v 34]) and served along with the altar as yet another memorial for Israel. The

Hebrew of v 32 is somewhat ambiguous, leaving open the possibility that the plastered stones were those of the altar (**stones**). Those reading this account would have known Deut 27 well enough to remember there were clearly two sets of stones. The author may have intentionally blurred the distinction between the altar stones and those on which the Law was written to emphasize the connection between the sacrifices and God's word.

The area where the Israelites gathered opened up like a large amphitheater, with Mount Ebal to the north and Mount Gerizim to the south. According to Howard, almost the entirety of Canaan could be seen from these heights (1998a, 215 n. 137). All Israel gathered there; the author specifically mentions Israel's **elders, officials and judges**, perhaps to emphasize the embrace of God's covenant by all Israel. On the slopes of Mount Gerizim were the tribes of Simeon, Levi, Judah, Issachar, Joseph (i.e., Ephraim and Manasseh), and Benjamin. Opposite on the slopes of Mount Ebal were the tribes of Reuben, Gad, Asher, Zebulun, Dan, and Naphtali (see Deut 27:12-13).

Also present are **foreigners** (vv 33, 35), those who joined up with Israel since they left Egypt. Many may have come from nearby Shechem, a center for patriarchal activity. Hess suggests the Shechemites may have joined with Israel, since there is no mention anywhere in the book of their defeat or of the death of their king (1996a, 173).

The focal point of the ceremony was the ark, flanked by the Levitical priests. This is the first we have heard of the ark since Jericho. Its appearance is even more surprising since it was not required by Moses' instructions. Wherever the ark has gone, God's power has been displayed and God's will accomplished. For this reason, Joshua may have been communicating that the God to whom they were recommitting themselves is a promise-keeping God.

Excavations on Mount Ebal have identified what many believe to be a cultic site from this period, "either an altar or a paved bama [i.e. high place]" (Hawkins 2012, 226). Although the archaeologist who excavated the site refuses to conclusively connect this site and the biblical evidence, he does note "this is the only transitional Late Bronze Age/Iron Age site existing on the mountain. It correlates with the biblical tradition and general character of the site. It is well connected with the new society of the settling Israelites" (Zertal 1986, 158). Block does not believe these remains should be identified with the events of Josh 8, in part because the cult site is on the slope, not at the top of the hill where the passage implies it was located. Hence, Block writes, "The altar would not even have been visible to the participants in the ritual" (2013, 95).

Joshua 8:30-35 emphasizes how carefully Israel obeyed Moses' instructions, but one also sees some modifications. As noted above, nowhere had Moses commanded that the ark of the covenant be the focus of this ceremony. Also, Moses had instructed the Levites to recite the blessings and curses over the people (see Deut 27:12-26), with only the curses described (vv 15-26). In the account in Joshua, it is the blessings that are emphasized, not the curses (Josh 8:33). This fits the optimism of the moment, with all Israel joined in covenant loyalty.

Joshua reads the Law, not the Levites. Joshua receives the credit as the one who instructed the Levites, in order to demonstrate his role as Israel's leader. The focus is clearly on Joshua, but also on **the whole assembly of Israel, including the women and children, and the foreigners who lived among them** (v 35), yet another example of how the author has emphasized "all Israel" (see 1:16-18; 3:6-8, 12, 17; 4:1, 2, 3, 4, 5, 8, 9, 11, 14; 7:1, 25; 8:3, 11).

At least one scholar has designated this covenant ceremony as the point when Israel actually became a nation (Cohen 2003, 260-62). Hamlin considers this covenant ceremony as the "centerpiece" of the entire book, looking back to the first mention of God's teaching (1:7-8), the celebration of the Passover (5:11), and the sin of Achan (7:11), and looking ahead to the Levitical towns (ch 21) and final summaries (23:6-11; 24:14, 23). He points out the Mosaic law is also restated at the covenant ceremony at Shechem (24:25), and that the book contains a symmetry of festivals at beginning (5:11), middle (8:30-35), and end (24:1-18) (1983, xv-xvi).

FROM THE TEXT

Joshua 8 describes the God of the second chance. Israel significantly stumbled in the previous chapter, but took the necessary though difficult steps to restoration. God had responded to their repentance and painful obedience by giving them a second chance, fully reengaging with them in the conquest of Ai. He appeared to Joshua and even directed the campaign.

God is so eager and willing to grant forgiveness, it becomes easy to take that forgiveness for granted: Israel did what they needed to do so God must do what God must do. But God did not need to forgive them, then or ever. He voluntarily joined himself to Israel in a covenant relationship and voluntarily maintained his covenant loyalty after Israel reneged on the arrangement. Rather than responding to God's reengagement with Israel in 8:1 with a yawn, we should read it with delight and relief.

Israel learned several important lessons about God and being God's people from the events of Josh 8. For one thing, they saw that God was willing to give them a second chance. Though he did not need to do so, nor could he be presumed upon, he illustrated here what he said about himself at Sinai, that he is far more willing to be gracious than to punish (see Exod 34:6-7). The events of this chapter also showed them that obedience was better than disobedience. Disobedience had cost them dearly, but obedience led to victory in battle and the plunder they would need, now that the manna had ceased.

Whether or not the events of Josh 8:30-35 occurred at this point in Israel's advance, placement here reinforces a recurring theme in the book of Joshua: the importance of Israel's response to God's action. They responded to the crossing of the Jordan by building a memorial, circumcising their males, and celebrating Passover. Was it only coincidental that they did not commemorate Jericho's defeat and the next battle went poorly? When they eventually conquered Ai, they immediately reaffirm the covenant.

Worship, simply defined, is responding to God's actions. Whether gathered with other believers or alone with God, our worship is ultimately in response to what he has already done for us. Remembering as we worship that we are only in God's presence because of what he has already done for us, puts the focus where it belongs. It also helps us avoid a pathological form of self-reliance.

The worship that took place on Mount Ebal was rich with significance. Its focal point was the ark, symbolizing God's powerful presence among his people. The Israelites could recall what they had heard from their parents about how God had delivered Israel from Egypt, but they could also reflect on their own experience of how the Jordan had ceased flowing and the walls of Jericho had crumbled in the presence of the ark. When we worship, we respond both to God's past actions of redemption and to the powerful ways he delivers today.

God's word occupied a central role in this ceremony, reminding his people of their past and holding before them the promise of the future. They recalled Moses, God's servant, and how God had used him to take Israel from Egypt through the exodus. They remembered too how God had "taken Egypt from Israel"—removing Egyptian influences and the self-identity of slavery—by giving the Law. They also looked forward to God's plan being worked out among them. Now that they were residing in God's promised land, they could experience blessings if they obeyed or curses if they disobeyed. The Bible should be at the center of our worship, recalling for us God's character and redemptive work and pointing toward the hope that lies before us.

This ceremony marked a significant moment for Israel, allowing them to tangibly experience the restoration of their relationship with God after Achan's sin. Through the burnt offerings, Israel enjoyed reconciliation with God. As they held this ceremony in the midst of a land surrounded by their enemies, they enjoyed freedom from fear, an indication they had been reconciled with themselves. As they presented their fellowship offerings and enjoyed the feast that followed, they celebrated the harmony they experienced with one another. That they were joined by foreigners anticipates their calling to be a source of blessing to all nations (Gen 12:3).

IX. JOSHUA 9

BEHIND THE TEXT

9:1-27

Joshua 9 marks a change in the account of the conquest of Canaan. Until now, Israel targeted those cities standing in the way of its advance. With ch 9, Israel itself is targeted, with the events of chs 10—12 following in consequence (Hess 1996a, 175). David Dorsey suggests a helpful way of seeing the design of these chapters (1999, 92):

a all the kings of Canaan oppose Joshua <u>as one</u> (9:1-2)
  b mercy for a believing remnant: Israel makes peace with Gibeonites (9:3-27)
    c defeat of southern coalition, led by king of Jerusalem (10:1-15)
      d CENTER: ritual ceremony at Makkedah (10:16-43)
    c' defeat of northern coalition, led by king of Hazor (11:1-15)
  b' no mercy for hardened Canaanites (11:16-23)
a' all the kings of Canaan whom Joshua conquered are listed <u>one by one</u> (12:1-24)

Dorsey's outline helps us see more clearly several of the purposes served by Josh 9. First, the chapter introduces the southern and northern campaigns. Second, it offers an example of how the Gibeonites are delivered by their belief in God's power, in contrast to those lacking in faith (11:16-23). Third, the chapter explains how the Gibeonites managed to continue to live among the Israelites in a way that other Canaanites did not. Fourth, it provides yet another illustration of how God gave this land to his people in fulfillment of his promise.

The chapter divides into two parts. Verses 1-15 describe Gibeon's response to Israel's victories. Unlike the military response of the other kings (vv 1-2), Gibeon employs cunning (vv 3-15). The second part (vv 16-27) describes Israel's response to Gibeon (vv 16-23) and Gibeon's submission to their vassal role (vv 24-27).

IN THE TEXT

A. Gibeon's Response to Israel's Victories (9:1-15)

1. Coalition of Kings Responds to Ai (9:1-2)

■ **1-2** The opening verses of this chapter sound very much like what we find in 5:1, yet with marked differences. Both allude to Israel's experiences, but while ch 5 specifically mentions the parting of the Red (Reed) Sea and the defeat of Sihon and Og, ch 9 leaves matters undefined: **these things** (v 1). Both chapters refer to Canaanite kings, but 9:1 offers a more detailed description, including the **hill country, western foothills** (the Shephelah), and **Great Sea**. The nations involved are the **Hittites, Amorites, Canaanites, Perizzites, Hivites and Jebusites**, constituting an enormous army. This list contains six of the seven nations mentioned in 3:10, minus the Girgashites. Although we cannot be sure why they go unmentioned, the list is identical to the one found in Deut 20:17 (Howard 1998a, 221). It is also identical to the list in Josh 12:8, supporting Dorsey's chiastic outline that connects chs 9 and 12.

Perhaps the author of Joshua wanted to remind us of the context of the list in Deuteronomy, a context that describes how to treat enemies outside Canaan and how to treat those within Canaan. The most striking contrast between the two passages is the kings' reaction. In 5:1, they tremble with fear, but in 9:2, they form a unified coalition (***with one accord,*** omitted in NIV) to war against Joshua and Israel. The change in response may be due to the Israelites' initial defeat at Ai or could reflect an increasing sense of desperation in the face of Israel's advance.

2. Gibeonites' Response (9:3-15)

■ **3-5** Gibeon chooses another strategy, that of deception. Gibeon, part of a coalition of cities located five to ten miles northwest of Jerusalem (Howard 1998a, 228), is usually associated with el-Jib, although the identification is not certain. No Late Bronze Age "important city" (10:2) has been discovered at this site, and the early church historian Eusebius identified a different location for Gibeon (Woudstra 1981, 154). Wherever the city was actually located, the tabernacle was eventually brought here (1 Kgs 3:4; 1 Chr 16:39; 21:29) after it had been erected first at Shiloh (Josh 18:1). It was in Gibeon that God appeared to Solomon and promised him wisdom (1 Kgs 3:4-5; 2 Chr 1:3-13).

Reference to the "elders" (Josh 9:11) of the Gibeonites rather than a king could suggest that the coalition of towns that included Gibeon was under the jurisdiction of the king of Jerusalem (see 10:1 ff.). Another possibility is that Gibeon was a town of Hittite origin where elders provide leadership (Hess 1996a, 179).

While we cannot be sure what the kings heard (9:1-2), we are told that the Gibeonites heard what Joshua had done to Jericho and Ai (v 3). In the Hebrew, v 4 begins *they did, also they.* The added words contrast those in Gibeon with the coalition of vv 1-2. Or perhaps the author, having offered examples of Joshua's trickery (e.g., infiltrating Jericho with spies, setting an ambush on Ai), is offering an example of deception by the enemy. Translators differ on whether v 4 describes how the Gibeonites **went as a delegation** (NIV; see ASV, KJV, NASB, NLT), or how they "made ready provisions" (ESV; see NABRE, NJB). The latter rendering, also found in the LXX, makes a little more sense in the flow of thought and requires only a slight emendation to the Hebrew (Woudstra 1981, 155 n. 8). The Gibeonites managed their ruse carefully, giving every appearance of having traveled a long distance. Even their bread was dried out and crumbly (ESV, NABRE, NASB, NJB, NJPS) or **moldy** (ASV, KJV, NIV, NLT, NRSV) (v 5). Howard considers the former option more likely, since mold requires moisture (1998a, 223 n. 156) while Nelson opts for the latter, pointing out that this verb is used for speckled animals (Gen 30:32) and beaded or studded jewelry (Song 1:11) (1997, 122 n. b).

■ **6** The meeting between the Israelites and Gibeonites was located at Gilgal. This could be the same Gilgal where the Israelites camped after crossing the Jordan. If so, the events at Mount Ebal (8:30-35) are out of chronological order since it is most unlikely that Israel would have traveled more than twenty miles through enemy territory to Shechem, then travel back to their camp by the Jordan. More likely, this is a different Gilgal, perhaps north of Bethel in the hill country (2 Kgs 2:1) or possibly between Jerusalem and Jericho (Josh 15:7) or yet another site near Mounts Ebal and Gerizim (Deut 11:29-30); Howard prefers the last option (1998a, 224).

■ **7** Israel initially suspected the Gibeonites' request. Perhaps it all seemed too perfect. They may have remembered Moses' repeated warnings about treaties. Treaties were permissible for those who lived outside Canaan (see Deut 20:11) but prohibited for those who lived in the land (Exod 23:32; 34:12; Num 33:55; Deut 7:2). The author inserted a subtle clue of the imminent disaster by referring to the Gibeonites as Hivites. The Hivites were among those nations repeatedly mentioned in the lists of those to be defeated. They were also mentioned in Josh 9:1-2 as part of the anti-Israelite coalition. If Israel knew these were Hivites, they had all the more reason to suspect them; if they did not know these were Hivites, the reader now does and fears the worst.

■ **8** The Gibeonites respond to Joshua's initial question by acknowledging themselves to be Israel's servants. This could simply be oriental politeness, as in Gen 50:18 (Woudstra 1981, 158), or an invitation to Israel to test the veracity of their claims or even be an offer to become subject to Israel as a vassal (Halpern 1975, 303). Joshua responds by asking two questions: **Who are you and where do you come from?**—both of which pertain to Israel's concerns but neither of which the Gibeonites answer.

■ **9-13** The Gibeonites reply that they came from **a very distant** land (Josh 9:9) because of Yahweh's great reputation, though they do not say which land. Howard claims they mean to suggest they are just passing by (1998a, 225), but this seems unlikely. If so, why do the Gibeonites mention Yahweh's reputation as the reason they have come all this way. Specifically, they refer to his great deeds in **Egypt** and victories over **Sihon** and **Og** (v 10). They mention nothing about the crossing of the Jordan or victories in Jericho and Ai, since these events happened more recently. To know about them would belie their claim to have come from afar. They also suggest that theirs was a culture ruled by elders, perhaps to strengthen rapport with the Israelites, another culture governed by elders (see vv 15, 18, 19). Twice more in their reply (vv 9, 11) the Gibeonites refer to themselves as Israel's servants and also ask for a covenant (v 11). This time it appears to be more than oriental politeness but instead indicates their desire to be Israel's vassals.

■ **14** Because of their suspicions and the serious dangers involved, the Israelites investigated the claims of the Gibeonites ("the Israelites examined their food" [NLT]), the likely meaning of ***they took from their provisions***. It seems less likely that the Israelites actually tasted the moldy bread (as suggested by **sampled their provisions**). One does not need to taste moldy bread to know it is moldy. It is even more unlikely that the phrase refers to a treaty meal using the moldy bread (as suggested by Fensham [1964, 98] and others). If there was a meal, Israel would have provided the food and there would have been no need to use the Gibeonites' provisions. Further, Hall points out that ***took*** (*lāqaḥ*) is not usually used for eating food (2010, 153).

In spite of their cautious investigation, the Israelites neglected the one thing needful, asking Yahweh. They should have employed the Urim and Thummim. These sacred lots were kept in the high priest's ephod and used to provide answers to God's people at times such as these. Their neglect at this moment suggests the elders did not feel such direction was needed; the priests either agreed with the leaders or their protests were ignored. The elders trusted the evidence of their own eyes, rather than listening to the *mouth* of God. While Joshua shares the blame for this mistake, it was the elders whom the Israelites held responsible (v 18).

■ **15** Joshua "made peace with them" when he "made [cut] a covenant with them . . . and the leaders of the congregation swore to them" (ESV) an oath of confirmation. Once made, the treaty could not be unmade. By adding the phrase *for their lives* (to let them live), the author moves beyond the treaty itself. There was no point in promising in the treaty that the Gibeonites would not be killed, since killing a distant people was not a legal option for the Israelites. Instead, the phrase anticipates the confrontation that would arise later in the chapter when the Gibeonite ruse became known. Because the treaty had been sworn, the lives of the Gibeonites would be spared (vv 18-21).

B. Punishment of Gibeonites for Their Deceit (9:16-27)

1. Israel's Response (9:16-23)

■ **16-18a** The ruse was discovered three days later. Three days after that, the Israelites are marching on Gibeon. Either or both references to three days (vv 16, 17) could be intended to express a period of seventy-two hours, or more generally, shortly after the signing of the treaty (see 1:11; 2:16, 22; 3:2). The author does not describe how Israel found out, but he does emphasize that this came to light *after they had cut a covenant with them* (9:16). Also emphasized with double mention (v 16) is the fact that the Gibeonites dwell in Canaan (**neighbors, living near them**). Israel's investigations confirmed the deception, but their hands were tied since the elders had sworn a solemn oath in Yahweh's name (v 18a). This point is made even more strongly in v 19 where the we in **we have given them our oath** is emphatic. Israel's choice was now either to break their oath and obey God's command to kill the Canaanites, or to honor that oath—and the God in whose name the oath was made—and disobey God's command. Neither option was without its negative consequences: keeping their oath would allow Canaanites to remain among them as a possible corrupting influence; breaking their oath would remove that threat but would dishonor God's reputation. To be impaled on the horns of this dilemma is the punishment for their carelessness. They made the choice to honor their oath and God's reputation, thereby escaping his wrath. Having already experienced that wrath in the episode with Achan, they had no desire to experience it again (see 22:20) (Hess 1996a, 183). Saul would later choose the other option, violating Israel's oath with the Gibeonites, leaving his own descendants to suffer God's wrath (see 2 Sam 21:1).

■ **18b-20** The Israelites' reaction was to grumble against their elders. Ironically, we have heard Israelite grumbling before, with the same verb employed (Exod 15:24; 16:2, 7-8; 17:3; Num 14:2, 27, 29, 36; 16:11, 41; 17:5). Then it was an example of their unfaithfulness, here it is an example of Israel's faithfulness (contra Howard 1998a, 229). It might be more accurate to say that their grumbling resulted from their desire to be faithful being stymied by their rash treaty.

■ **21** The elders then decide that though the Gibeonites could not be killed, they could be assigned the tasks of woodcutters and water carriers for the Israelites. This is in line with Deut 20:10-15, which specifies that those who surrender to Israel were to become their servants, although that passage only allowed for surrender for those outside Canaan. There are other instances of the Israelites forcing Canaanites into servitude (Josh 16:10; 17:13; Judg 1:28). Cutting wood and hauling water were tasks done by the lowest members of society (see Deut 29:11) (see Keil and Delitzsch 1978, 102).

The NIV (also KJV, NJB) treats v 21 as direct speech (i.e., what the leaders actually said) except for the opening (**They continued**) and the final sentence (**So the leaders' promise to them was kept**). It may be best to render only the first phrase as direct speech and the rest of the verse as its result, as in the NLT: "'Let them live.' So they made them woodcutters and water carriers for the entire community, as the Israelite leaders directed" (see ASV, ESV, NASB, NJPS, and NRSV).

■ **22-23** Joshua reappears to summon the Gibeonites and convey to them the elders' decision. By calling them cursed (v 23), he may simply be reminding them that they are now Israel's servants. This seems unlikely, however, since **curse** is a strong word to describe what they had requested (vv 8, 9, 11). Instead Joshua may be observing how this turn of events fulfills Noah's prediction (Gen 9:25) that Canaan would be cursed (Keil and Delitzsch 1978, 102). The Gibeonites had succeeded in sparing their own lives by *cutting a covenant* (vv 6, 15) with Israel. Because of their deception, however, they would never be *cut off* (v 23) from being Israel's servants.

Although the elders had determined that the Gibeonites would be servants for "the whole assembly" (v 21), Joshua assigned them the more specific task of serving at the sanctuary (v 23). Perhaps this was what the elders meant, or perhaps Joshua tweaked the punishment for Israel's benefit. The danger of allowing the Gibeonites to live was that they would divert Israelites from worshiping Yahweh. Assigning them to serve the community by working in the sanctuary insured both that they would be where they could be closely observed, and also that they would themselves come to learn about Yahweh (Hall 2010, 161). Joshua may have provided the priests with additional servants in order to compensate them for Israel's failure to "inquire of the LORD" (v 14).

2. Gibeonites' Submission (9:24-25)

■ **24-25** At this point, the Gibeonites had little choice but to accept the decision of Joshua and the elders. They were likely no match for Israel on their own and had forfeited their right to assistance from the other Canaanites. Yet one does not hear bitterness in their response, only resignation to the inevitable. They had been convinced (**clearly told**) that their land had been given by Yahweh to Israel. They knew that those who opposed Israel would be annihilated (v 24). This passage echoes what we find in Deut 7:1 and 20:16-17. The Gibeonites' faith in God's word led them to fear the Israelites, which led to their ruse and then to their willing submission to live as Israel's servants.

3. Summary (9:26-27)

■ **26** One could render the opening phrase of v 26, *And this is just what happened*. The Hebrew closely connects the Gibeonites' closing words in v 25 with Joshua's actions in v 26. The ESV translation captures this well: "'And now, behold, we are in your hand. Whatever seems good and right in your sight to do to us, do it.' So he did this to them."

■ **27** Once again their sentence is repeated: to be **woodcutters and water carriers** for the community and the sanctuary, here referred to as **the altar of the LORD**.

This altar was likely the bronze altar in the tabernacle courtyard rather than the gold incense altar inside the holy place, off limits to all but priests. The tabernacle was **the place** where **the LORD would choose**. This phrase appears frequently in Deuteronomy (12:5, 11, 14, 18, 21, 26; 14:23; 16:2, 6, 7, 11, 15, 16), but when used in Joshua it anticipates the establishment of God's tabernacle at Shiloh (Josh 18:1-10). Reference to the bronze altar is striking since it is only mentioned three times in Joshua: here, in 22:19 and 29. By contrast, the ark of the covenant is mentioned thirty times in Joshua, though never after ch 8.

The author concludes this account by pointing out that the Gibeonites remain servants at the tabernacle until his own time (**to this day**). The tabernacle, including the bronze altar and presumably the other furniture except the ark of the covenant, appears to have been moved to Gibeon sometime after the defeat of the Israelites by the Philistines (see 1 Sam 4:2-11) and the slaughter of the priests at Nob by King Saul (1 Sam 21). As to the ark, after it was returned by the Philistines (see 1 Sam 6:1—7:2), it moved from Beth Shemesh to Kiriath Jearim, and eventually to Jerusalem. Apparently, it was never restored to the tabernacle. Meanwhile, the altar at Gibeon continued to be used by Israel to offer burnt offerings to Yahweh. Solomon went there after his coronation and it was there God appeared to him (see 1 Kgs 3:4-5).

FROM THE TEXT

Joshua and the Israelites failed to consult God regarding the Gibeonites, but God used this failure to accomplish his plan to give this land to Israel. This tells us a great deal about God's character. We see, first, that God is willing and able to provide his people with direction, if they will seek it. His people had been given the means to ask, most notably through the Urim and Thummim, and the priests had been entrusted with this responsibility. Clearly, God wants his people to seek his direction. Although we do not have the Urim and Thummim or Levitical priests to employ it, God remains willing to direct us and has provided other resources to that end. He guides through prayer, godly counsel, and circumstances. He has revealed his general will through his word, anchored it to the True North of his character, and placed the administration of that will in the hands of his Holy Spirit who resides within each believer and within the believing community. Can there be any question that he remains willing and able to guide?

Some contend that we need God's direction for every decision, however large or small. Others believe we can decide most things, especially as we mature in the faith, but should seek God's direction for the big decisions. It may be best to see God's guidance as part of a more subtle process of continual listening. We cannot know which decisions are big and which are small; only eternity will reveal that. By walking in step with God's Spirit we can be sensitive to the gentlest nudge and respond accordingly. But nudges do not always come, even when we ask for them. We sometimes face major life decisions without any handwriting on the wall. Here is where we must trust our ability to listen to God. We should ask, and then wait; if we receive no clear answer, God may be trusting us to use what we have already been given to make the best decision. The key is to walk close enough to hear him, to always be tuned to his frequency. In this way, you can employ your gifts while maintaining a healthy self-suspicion. The Israelites erred, not because they tested the claims of the Gibeonites, but because they assumed that such testing was sufficient.

This chapter also reveals the high importance God places on the sanctity of his name. Because the Israelite elders had sworn the oath in God's name, it could not be broken, even if keeping the oath meant compromising God's clear command to annihilate the Canaanites, even if keeping the oath meant putting themselves at risk. Their failure to inquire of God placed them in the predicament of having to choose between honoring God's name and obeying God's word. When we listen to God, we avoid this conundrum and are able to both honor and obey him. This passage reveals, however, how important it is to glorify God through our lives. He must be exalted, even if that means we are not. We must keep our promises, even those not made with solemn oaths in God's name. Because we bear his name, what we do reflects on him, whether for good or ill.

This chapter demonstrates that God may allow his people to fail when they deviate from his plan. Just because Israel had been promised this land and had experienced success did not insure they would always make good choices. Nor did their recommitment at Mount Ebal eliminate their need to trust God. Humility and daily dependence on God's grace will always be essential for living the Christian life. Anything less than dependence increases the possibility of unhealthy independence, which produces negative consequences. We see a clear example with Achan's sin, which not only led to the death of thirty-six Israelites but apparently also emboldened the Canaanites to form the coalition described in 9:1-2. This coalition prompted the Gibeonites to attempt their ruse, which the Israelites were unprepared to discover, perhaps *because of* undue trust in their recent successes and recommitments. There is no substitute for daily dependence on God to avoid self-inflicted disasters.

This leads to a fourth, very welcome insight into God's character: his ability to use even our failures to accomplish his purposes. For example, Achan's sin led to initial defeat that may have prompted this coalition, which contributed to the Israelites' unwise treaty with the Gibeonites. Yet the treaty with the Gibeonites reduced the strength of the coalition (10:1-5) and perhaps divided up the larger campaign into several more manageable ones (i.e., central, southern, and northern). With God's help, Israel could have defeated the large coalition of 9:1-2, but smaller bites were certainly easier for Israel to swallow.

Another example of how God turned failures to his purposes can be seen with the Gibeonites. Instead of leading Israel away from the worship of Yahweh, the Gibeonites actually enriched that worship through their service at the sanctuary. God remains willing and able to turn our failures into sources of strength. Many have seen their sordid past not only forgiven but transformed into the motivation and insight that fuels a present and future ministry. Challenging marriages have produced strong saints. Wrong turns have been turned to right destinations. God's ability to redeem our failures can delight but need not surprise. After all, he was able to redeem the greatest human failure, the murder of his own sinless Son, and make it the means whereby all is redeemed.

X. JOSHUA 10

BEHIND THE TEXT

Having bound themselves by solemn covenant to the Gibeonites in ch 9, the Israelites found themselves drawn into battle with a coalition of kings from central and southern Canaan. Although this battle was not of Israel's choosing and came about because of Israel's failure to consult God, God was at work through it, accomplishing his purposes. Chapter 10 provides a clear demonstration of divine-human synergy, granting victory in tandem with Israel's faithfulness.

The chapter describes two campaigns, the first opposing a coalition of kings that had marched on Gibeon, Israel's new ally (vv 1-28). The opening section describes the coalition (vv 1-5) followed by Israel's counterattack and the subsequent battle (vv 6-15). Another scene of the battle follows, with the focus on a ceremony marking Israel's conquest (vv 16-28). The second campaign, presented as flowing organically from the first, is launched against towns in the southern part of Canaan (vv 29-39). A summary of both campaigns concludes the chapter (vv 40-43). Chapter 10 provides a good illustration of how ancient historians did not always present their material in straightforward chronological order and how several different battles could be telescoped into a single campaign, in accordance with ANE historiographic techniques (Younger 1995, 261-62). The victory against the initial coalition is summarized in vv 7-10, then described in greater detail in vv 11-15 and 16-27. Twice the Israelites are said to return to Gilgal (vv 15, 43), when only one trip is feasible. Hess describes the chapter as composed of panels or pictures "that overlap in time but focus on different aspects of the victory" (1996a, 193).

Although this chapter emphasizes the divine source of victory, there were less supernatural factors working in Israel's favor. Malamat points out that the Canaanites were disunified and militarily depleted due to a prolonged period of Egyptian attacks and subjugation (1982, 29). The Israelites employed a variety of effective military strategies, such as espionage (Num 13; 21; Josh 2; 7; Judg 1; 18), deception (Josh 8:4), night maneuvers (Josh 8:3; 10:9; Judg 9:34; 1 Sam 11:11; 30:17), and the element of surprise (Josh 10:9) (ibid., 31-34).

IN THE TEXT

A. Central Campaign (10:1-27)

1. Coalition against Gibeon (10:1-5)

■ **1-2** Word of Joshua's victory over Ai and Israel's treaty with Gibeon reached the ears of **Adoni-Zedek**, king of Jerusalem (v 1). Although Jerusalem figures prominently in the Amarna letters, this is the first time the city is called by this name in the OT. We met it earlier as Salem, capital of King Melchizedek (Gen 14:18-20). Keil and Delitzsch consider Adoni-Zedek and Melchizedek to be the throne names of the kings of this city (1978, 103). The reason Jerusalem became **very much alarmed** (v 2) is left unstated. Mention of Israel's practice of *ḥerem* (v 1) suggests they understood that Israel's purpose for invading was not to join the current inhabitants but to completely remove them.

Gibeon alone was a formidable foe, but their treaty with Israel meant the two peoples were now "integrated" (Soggin 1972, 116), that is, regarded as one. The phrase "living near them" (9:16), literally ***they were in their midst***, implies shared loyalty, not shared proximity. The NIV describes Gibeon as **important** and **larger than Ai** (10:2), though both terms translate the same Hebrew word. Some translations, such as the NLT, treat both instances as referring to physical size: "Gibeon was a large town—as large as the royal cities and larger than Ai" (see NABRE, NASB, NJPS, NRSV). It may be best to regard both terms as describing importance: "Gibeon *was* a great city, like one of the royal cities, and because it was greater than Ai" (NASB, emphasis added; see ESV). Reference to Gibeon being **like one of the royal cities** (v 2) implies it was important enough to have a king, although it was ruled by elders (see Josh 9).

Perhaps Jerusalem's fear also arose from the unknown: if an important city like Gibeon surrendered, what do they know about the Israelites that we don't? If Gibeon had been under Jerusalem's control, their attack could have been in retaliation for rebellion. Perhaps most frightening of all: an Israelite-Gibeon coalition meant Jerusalem's enemies controlled a strategic region in Canaan, putting Jerusalem in particular peril (Hess 1996a, 187-88).

■3 Adoni-Zedek's fear prompted him to invite four nearby cities to join in the attack on Gibeon. Hebron, Jarmuth, Lachish, and Eglon shared Jerusalem's vulnerability and were key cities for controlling trade routes and defense (ibid., 189-90). Hebron was located almost twenty miles south of Jerusalem and controlled the road south to Beersheba and access to the Mediterranean Sea (Butler 1983, 114).

About fifteen miles to the southwest of Jerusalem was the city of Jarmuth, an important site in Early Bronze Age Canaan (Miroschedji 2008, 5:1796). It appears to have been continuously occupied from Late Bronze Age II to the Early Byzantine period (Miroschedji 1993, 2:661-65), although by the time the Israelites arrived, Jarmuth appears to be a very small settlement on the far side of the acropolis or perhaps at another site nearby (Miroschedji 2008, 5:1797).

Lachish was another twelve miles as the crow flies, in the same direction, located alongside a route that passes from the coastal plain to the Hebron hills (Ussishkin 1993, 3:897-911). This is the first mention of Lachish in the OT (Butler 1983, 114). It had been a major Canaanite city in the Middle Bronze Age but had been destroyed (Ussishkin 1993, 3:898-99). After being rebuilt, it "reached its zenith toward the end of the Late Bronze Age" and "may have been the largest city in Canaan after Hazor was destroyed" (ibid., 3:899) by sudden destruction and fire, perhaps by the Sea Peoples or by the Israelites around 1200 B.C. (ibid., 3:904). Archaeologists have found no evidence that Lachish was resettled by the Israelites prior to the monarchy (ibid.).

The location of Eglon is uncertain, some placing it seven miles west-southwest of Lachish at Tel el-Hesi. More likely it is seven miles southeast of Lachish at Tel 'Aitun (Butler 1983, 115). Verse 3 is the only time in the OT where Debir is used as a person's name; elsewhere it refers to a place. Some take this to be the mistake of a later redactor (Barr 1990, 55-68), though this is not a necessary conclusion.

■ **4-5** The coalition's attack is directed against Gibeon, not Israel. Pitkänen suggests the allies thought they could attack quickly and then withdraw, sending a warning to others who considered aligning with the invaders (2010, 228). Presumably they hoped to avoid engaging Israel directly and might have succeeded if not for Joshua's skill and faith.

2. Israel's Defense of Gibeon (10:6-15)

■ **6** The previous chapter ended with the Gibeonites as Israel's vassals; here one sees the benefits gained from vassalage. Fensham offers examples of Hittite treaties that promise protection against enemies:

> In a treaty between Suppiluliuma and Niqmadu, king of Ugarit in Akkadian a promise of Niqmadu to Suppiluliuma is inserted in the style of the short formula:
>
> "To the enemy of my lord I am hostile
>
> (and) with the friend of my lord (I am) friendly." (1963, 136-37)
>
> In another treaty:
>
> The one who is your enemy,
>
> is also the enemy of the sun.
>
> The one who is the enemy of the sun,
>
> should also be your enemy. (Ibid., 140)

Perhaps expecting a similar kind of protection from their new benefactors, the Gibeonites appealed to Joshua, "Do not relax your hand from your servants. Come up to us quickly and save us and help us, for all the kings of the Amorites who dwell in the hill country are gathered against us" (ESV). They employ wordplay in their appeal, since **Joshua** and **save** are based on the same Hebrew word. The Gibeonites refer to all the Amorite kings of the hill country coming against them, but we are told of only five. Perhaps they exaggerated to increase the likelihood of Israel's support (Butler 1983, 115), or perhaps the coalition was larger than the five cities we are told about. If the latter is correct, it may explain why the Israelites later attack cities not mentioned in v 3 (see vv 29-30, 38-39).

■ **7** Joshua responded by immediately mustering the troops and marching all night from Gilgal to Gibeon. If this is the Gilgal near the Jordan, the distance between these sites is about eighteen miles (ibid.; → 8:30-35 for an alternative view). Malamat argues for a twenty-mile march including a climb of over three thousand feet (1982, 34). In 10:7 and 9 we see not only Joshua's skills as a general but also his eagerness to live up to the terms of the treaty (Hall 2010, 166); he even took Israel's **best fighting men** (v 7). The strategy of surprising the enemy after an all-night march was employed by others in the ANE, such as this Hittite king who reports:

> I marched the whole night through, and daybreak found me on the outskirts of Sapidduwa. And as soon as the sun rose I advanced to battle against him; and those 9,000 men whom Pitaggatalli had brought with him joined in battle with me, and I fought with them. And the gods stood by me; . . . And I destroyed the enemy. (From Muršili's *Comprehensive Annals*, as cited in Younger 1990, 207)

■ **8** As before at significant moments in the conquest, God spoke words of encouragement to Joshua (see 1:1-10; 3:7; 5:9; 6:2; 8:1, 18; 11:6), words Joshua would later pass on to the Israelites (10:25). God here speaks of the coming battle as if already won: **I have given them into your hand** (v 8).

■ **9-10** Verses 9-14 describe the battle that followed. Joshua and the soldiers marched all night and surprised the enemy, but it was actually Yahweh who brought about the victory (v 10). He threw the enemy into such tremendous **confusion** that they did not retreat south toward their cities, but north and west along the road going from upper Beth Horon down to Azekah and Makkedah (v 10).

There is some question whether God or Israel is doing the action in v 10*b*, since the Hebrew only says *he*. Some translations, such as the NASB, make God the actor: "And the LORD confounded them before Israel, and He slew them with a great slaughter at Gibeon, and pursued them by the way of the ascent of Beth-horon and struck them as far as Azekah and Makkedah" (see KJV, NJB). The NIV and others explicitly or implicitly describe Israel (or Joshua) as the subject of the verb: **The LORD threw them into confusion before Israel, so Joshua and the Israelites defeated them completely at Gibeon. Israel pursued them along the road going up to Beth Horon and cut them down all the way to Azekah and Makkedah** (see ESV, NABRE, NJPS, NLT, NRSV). The ASV preserves the ambiguity of the Hebrew: "And Jehovah discomfited them before Israel, and he slew them with a great slaughter at Gibeon, and chased them by the way of the ascent of Beth-horon, and smote them to Azekah, and unto Makkedah."

■ **11** Hail is not unknown in this region, but its arrival at precisely this time and to this scale is remarkable. According to Liverani, the ancients would understand such a "natural but unexpected event" as indicative of divine activity (1990, 155). They would also consider *stones from heaven* as one of the weapons in the divine arsenal (Younger 1990, 211). The Hittite storm god hurled a meteor at a city opposed to King Muršili (from *Ten Year Annals* of Muršili as cited in ibid., 208). Sargon describes a victory over his enemies as when his god Adad "uttered his loud cry against them; and with the flood cloud and hailstones (lit. 'the stone of heaven' [NA, AN-e]), he totally annihilated the remainder" (from Sargon's *Letter to the God* as cited by Younger

1990, 210). The author makes clear that God not only fought for Israel but also inflicted more damage than did the Israelites.

■ **12-15** Commentators have devoted great attention to vv 12-15 for several reasons. It fits somewhat awkwardly into the rest of the battle account, contains a quotation from another ancient Israelite document, does not specify who speaks the words of vv 12-13, describes a remarkable event, and claims that this event is a once-in-eternity moment.

It seems very unlikely that Joshua would lead Israel back to camp at Gilgal (v 15) at this point. After all, he is pressing the battle, eager to prevent those retreating to get back to their cities (v 19). Most agree that v 15, repeated verbatim in v 43, is out of chronological sequence, appearing here for reasons other than chronological. The author may have included it to signify that a second battle scene is being introduced (vv 1-15, 16-43) or because v 15 was part of the quotation from the Book of Jashar (Howard 1998a, 239). Either explanation makes more sense than assuming such an egregious copying error.

We meet the Book of Jashar only one other time in the Bible (2 Sam 1:18). Commentators disagree on how much of Josh 10:12-15 is a quotation from this book, whether all of it (Keil and Delitzsch 1978, 107-8), only a portion (Butler 1983, 117), or none (Howard 1998a, 239-40). Nor does everyone agree on who speaks the words of vv 12-13. Miller and others suggest it was Yahweh who spoke to the sun and moon, rather than Joshua (1973, 127). This alleviates the awkwardness of Joshua praying to the heavenly bodies (Howard 1998a, 240). As Butler explains, "Such language could easily be interpreted as worship of and prayer to the heavenly deities. The biblical writer carefully avoids this. Joshua speaks to Yahweh through such language (v 12a)" (1983, 117). This explanation, however, does not explain what is meant by the phrase **when the LORD listened to a human being** (v 14).

Opinions vary widely as to what is meant by the sun and moon standing still. A literal understanding of this phenomenon is out of the question, since we know that the earth is in motion, not the sun and moon. Many have taken this to refer to a period of time when the earth ceased to rotate, thus allowing for a day lasting longer than twenty-four hours. This seems to be the way Hab 3:11 (and possibly Isa 28:21) treat this event. Ecclesiasticus 46:4, written about two hundred years before Christ, also understands the miracle this way: "Was not the sun held back by his hand, and one day drawn out into two?" (NJB). So too does the first-century Jewish historian Josephus (*Antiquities of the Jews* 5.1.17). According to Walton, this is also the view of the translators of the LXX, Augustine (*City of God* 21.8), Jerome (*Against Jovinianus* 2.15), the Vulgate, and Calvin (Walton 1994, 181). Others are willing to grant that the miracle involved a lengthened period of light, but attribute that light to something other than a prolonged day, something like a meteor shower or the refraction of light (Howard 1998a, 243; see Kruger 2000, 137-52).

Since Joshua prayed when the sun was over Gibeon in the east and the moon over the valley of Aijalon in the west (Josh 10:12), he must have been praying in the morning. Some argue it would be unlikely that Joshua would have known in the morning that more light would have been needed to finish the job and therefore prayed not for a longer day but for something else (Hess 1996a, 197; Walton 1994, 182). Perhaps he was praying for darkness, not light, that is, for something like a solar eclipse (Sawyer 1972, 139-46). Beitzel considers this unlikely since we know when observable solar eclipses occurred in central Palestine, and none correspond to the time of Joshua (1985, 97). Scott proposes the darkness was from the storm that produced the hailstones, suggesting that **stand** (v 12) suggests either silence or darkness (1952, 19-20). Some have seen this as a prayer for continued darkness to provide time for Israel's ambush to succeed (Callaway 1999, 67), but this seems unlikely since the sun and moon were already in the sky when Joshua prayed (see Hall 2010, 170). More likely, if darkness were the goal, it would have been intended to strike fear into the enemy or lower the air temperature so that the Israelites could complete the conquest in spite of the heat (Walton 1994, 181).

Some see Joshua praying for a celestial omen to encourage Israel and discourage the Canaanites. Ancient astrologers knew that the sun and moon would be in opposition on the fourteenth day of month. According to an ANE omen,

10:12-15

> When the moon and the sun are seen with one another on the 14th, there will be silence, the land will be satisfied; the gods intend Akkad for happiness. Joy in the hearts of the people. The cattle of Akkad will lie down securely in the pasture-places. (Thompson, *Reports of the Magicians*, 124:6-9, as cited by Walton 1984, 183)

To have this opposition of sun and moon occur on a day other than the fourteenth would be seen as a highly unfavorable sign (Hess 1996a, 198; Holladay 1968, 166-78). Joshua would not have needed to actually believe in such omens, only that the enemy believed in them, and may have at that moment been looking for a good sign from their gods. To receive this bad omen would then have been doubly demoralizing (Walton 1994, 188; Younger 1990, 215). This view still requires a miracle, however, since the ordinary movements of the moon would need to be altered. Nor does it match the implications of v 13, that the sun remained in the sky longer than usual.

Other explanations treat the description of the phenomenon as symbolic rather than literal. For Kruger, the passage pictures Yahweh as Israel's sun and moon, emphasizing his intervention on behalf of his people (2000, 137-52). Heller treats the passage as a demotion of the sun and moon from their status as deities (as the Canaanites would have understood them) to mere markers of time (1966, 73-78). Heller considers vv 12*b*-13*a* as original material, which a later editor misunderstood to be describing astronomical phenomenon. Similarly, Nelson sees the passage originally describing a personified sun and moon standing still in amazement, which a later redactor converted to a statement of the miraculous (1997, 144-45; see Nelson 1995, 3-10). Israel had experience in demythologizing, as when they demoted Mot, the Canaanite god of death, to the noun *māwet*, meaning death.

Other commentators point out how the events of this chapter echo events of the exodus, including the presence of hail (v 11; see Exod 9:13-35), control over the sunlight (Josh 10:12-13; see Exod 10:21-29), Yahweh fighting for Israel (Josh 10:14, 42; Exod 14:14, 25), and the confusion and flight of the enemy (Josh 10:10; see Exod 14:24, 27). There is even the similarity that in both instances, no one spoke a word against them (Exod 11:7; Josh 10:21) (Hall 2010, 181-82; see Hawk 2000, 151-54).

Miller considers the passage "probably an ancient piece of epic poetry that tells how the celestial bodies participated in the battles which Yahweh fought for Israel," similar to Judg 5:20 (1973, 123, 126). Another symbolic explanation sees the all-night march picturesquely described as the moon standing still and the all-day battle symbolized by the sun standing still (J. Sailhamer, as cited in Howard 1998a, 245). For Keil and Delitzsch, the day only appeared to be longer, enabling Israel to accomplish in one day a victory that ordinarily would have taken two. A symbolic explanation works best, they argue, given that these verses are poetic material and that Israel would hardly have been paying much attention to the time, given their total preoccupation with the battle (1978, 110-11). The medieval Jewish commentator Maimonides offers a similar explanation (Book II, ch 35, 1964, 368-69).

What actually happened? An abundance of explanations suggests caution might be more appropriate than a dogmatic conclusion. God could have suspended the movement of sun and moon; the One who created and set them in motion could certainly have pushed the pause button. The question is not what God *could* do but what the passage says God did. Since he worked miracles before through natural means, such as parting the Red Sea with a strong east wind (Exod 14:21) and stopping the Jordan apparently with a landslide (Josh 3:16-17), we cannot rule out a natural cause in this case. Inspired biblical writers sometimes used symbolic language to describe God's intervention (e.g., Judg 5:20), so that could be the case here as well.

Most impressive to the inspired author is not *how* but *that* God fought on Israel's behalf. Never before or since, we are told, had God listened to a human (Josh 10:14). Since we know from other passages that God answered human prayers, it may be preferable to take this claim to mean that this occasion was the only time a human took the initiative to propose how God would intervene (Hall 2010, 175). As Walton notes,

> The text . . . points out that the human initiation of the petition for God's intervention is the unique element. Never before had a person presumed to state what sort of supernatural strategy he wanted God to perpetrate on behalf of Israel. God granted Joshua the privilege of taking the initiative in devising the strategy. (1994, 183)

For Howard, the key is that this time Yahweh *obeyed* a human, a description only found three times in the OT: Num 21:3; 1 Kgs 17:22; and here. Not even Moses persuaded God to obey him (Howard 1998a, 250). Hall's explanation seems best. She points out two additional passages (beyond Howard's three) where God (not just Yahweh) obeyed a human, Gen 30:6 and Judg 13:9. She then notes that

> unlike the other four instances in which Israel's God listens to . . . human voices, Joshua's petition is both public (unlike Gen 30:6; Judg 13:9; 1 Kgs 17:22) and a request for something specifically miraculous (unlike Gen 30:6; Num 21:3). Perhaps it is the public, dramatic nature of Yahweh's action for Joshua that sets it apart. (2010, 174)

3. Ceremony at Makkedah (10:16-27)

■ **16-20** As the first campaign began to wind down, Israel held a ceremony to symbolize its current and future triumph. As Dorsey's outline makes clear (→ ch 9), this ceremony marks the centerpiece of chs 9—12.

Joshua was told that the five kings had taken refuge in a cave near Makkedah, west of Hebron. Some locate Makkedah at Khirbet el-Qom, while Dorsey connects that city with nearby Khirbet Beit Maqdum (1980, 185-93). The latter site, which preserves the ancient name, is located about one-half mile or less from Khirbet el-Qom, which is the Iron Age site (Dorsey, email correspondence, 3/26/13). Joshua ordered that the kings be held there while the Israelites continue to pursue the fleeing enemy. Joshua chose to complete the more important task, eradicating opposition, even though this meant forestalling the moment of triumph. Note the parallel between the moon standing still (10:13) while the Israelites were not to stand still (v 19); the same Hebrew verb is used. Similarly, although the sun delayed **going down** (v 13*b*), Israel was to hurry so that the enemy could not go down to their cities (v 19); once again, the identical Hebrew word is used. This wordplay captures the synergy between the divine and human activity, so pervasive throughout this chapter and the entire book.

According to Younger, accounts of open battle followed by retreat and search for refuge occur frequently in the ancient Near East.

> Concerning Rusa, the king of Urartu, Sargon asserts that after he had defeated him he fled and: "like a roaming fugitive he hid in the recesses

of his mountain. Like a woman in confinement he became bedridden." Aššurbanipal states concerning the Elamite king: "Ummanaldaši, king of Elam, heard of the entrance of my army into the midst of Elam, and he abandoned Madaktu, his royal city, and fled and went up into the mountains." and [sic, original text] concerning Arabian fugitives: "None of those who had gone up and entered the mountains to find refuge escaped. Not one survivor slipped through my hands. My hands captured them in their hiding-places." (1990, 221)

Another ancient battle account describes the enemy of Egypt fleeing from the pharaoh into caves, "hiding there like jackals, for the fear of you is in their hearts" (cited by Liverani 1990, 130).

■ **21** Upon returning from the pursuit, **no one uttered a word against the Israelites** (v 21), literally, no one *sharpened his tongue* against them (Howard 1998a, 253). This curious expression has been variously rendered. Some see this as describing Israel's safe return: "Not a man of the Israelites suffered so much as a scratch on his tongue" (NEB, as cited by Howard 1998a, 253). Several consider it a statement of Israel's absolute authority in the region: No one bothered them; not so much as a dog barked at them (Keil and Delitzsch 1978, 112), or "Not a single man threatened the sons of Israel" (Butler 1983, 108) or "No one dared to attempt anything against the Israelites" (NJB). Perhaps because elsewhere it is used to describe the actions of dogs, the NJPS says, "No one so much as snarled at the Israelites." For Hess, the phrase refers to Israelite silence; where before they had grumbled against the leaders for making a covenant with Gibeon (9:18), now they have no complaint, having seen the good that resulted (1996a, 201).

■ **22-23** The actual ceremony (vv 22-27) began with the five kings brought before Joshua. We were given their names earlier (v 3), when they were a real threat; now these conquered kings go unnamed. Perhaps the emphasis on the kings throughout this passage indicates they are the primary focus, with their death representing the complete destruction of their people (see ibid., 178).

■ **24** Joshua summoned all the men of Israel, specifically the army commanders—those leading Israel into battle—to place their feet upon the necks of the conquered enemy. This action is found frequently inside and outside the Bible. According to many translations, Deut 33:29 has Israel treading on the backs of their enemies (ESV, NJB, NJPS, NLT, NRSV). First Kings 5:3 speaks of God putting David's enemies "under his feet." Enemies are under the psalmist's feet (Ps 18:39 [40]) and become the anointed one's footstool (Ps 110:1). Outside the Bible, we see this ritual action in the Annals of Tukulti-Ninurta I who boasts, "I captured Kaštiliaš, king of the Kassites (alive). I trod with my feet upon his lordly neck as though it were a footstool" (E. Weidner as cited in Younger

1990, 317 n. 86). Stern sees something similar in the actions of the Sumerian king (ca. 2110 B.C.) against his enemy (1991, 71).

■ **25** The ritual continues with Joshua's word of encouragement to the commanders, a word that closely resembles the divine encouragement he himself received (see Josh 10:8; 1:8-9). Hall points out that a pep talk like this was usually given by a priest (see Deut 20:2-4) (2010, 176). Once again we see the divine-human synergy: God will defeat those Israel was fighting.

■ **26** The enemy kings are then killed and impaled, as we saw at Ai. This treatment of the enemy is documented from the ancient Near East. We see it in the writings of Sennacherib: "Thus Sennacherib states concerning the rulers of Ekron: 'the governors (and) nobles who had sinned I put to death; and I hung their corpses on poles around the city'" (Younger 1990, 223). Reliefs from Sennacherib's palace show impaled corpses from the Judean city of Lachish. More than just an execution, killing and impalement serve as part of the ritual, proving who had been vanquished.

■ **27** The removal of the corpses at sunset symbolized fealty to God's covenant requirements while interment in the cave, the hoped-for place of refuge, symbolized the total vanquishing of the foe. Even the piling of stones to mark the site has ritual significance. Younger offers examples of heaps of stones, corpses, and skulls serving as memorials:

> In order that no one might ever forget the might of Aššur my lord, that all peoples might magnify the praises of his warriorship, in the ground where I had brought about the defeat of the king of Babylon and Ummanmenanu the king of Elam—all of their lands together with Parsuas, Anzan, Pasiru, Ellipi, (and) all of Chaldea, as much as there was, all the Arameans—(in this ground) I harvested their skulls like shriveled grain and I piled (them) up into heaps. (As cited by Younger 1990, 224)

That these stones remain to the author's day suggests the ongoing power of this ritual.

B. Southern Campaign (10:28-39)

The account of this second campaign flows naturally from the first, but at a brisker tempo. Hess notes that the acceleration seen in this section grows even faster in chs 11 and 12 (1996a, 206). The descriptions of the defeat of the cities are similar in some ways yet different in others, both to anticipate patterns found in the second half of Joshua (ibid., 186) and to highlight Yahweh's involvement and Israel's obedience (Hall 2010, 180). Note the mention of **all Israel** (v 29; see 3:7, 17; 4:14; 7:23, 24; 8:21, 24; 23:2). Parker is right, I believe, that "the monotony of Joshua's actions in vv 28-39 illustrates and emphasizes the consistency of his obedience" but wrong to see this as only "an unimaginative illustration of Deuteronomic law" (1997, 67). The description of the conquest is similar to other ANE conquest accounts, says Hawk: "By use of this form, as opposed to the narrative style of the previous accounts, the author elevates Israel's status by linking it with the great powers of the ancient world; Israel too is a mighty nation with an impressive catalogue of victories" (2000, 167).

The mention of seven conquered cities suggests this number may represent an even larger victory, or it may be meant to represent a complete victory (Howard 1998a, 256). Hall notes how the repetition with variation indicates a carefully crafted structure (2010, 179-80). For Hawk,

> The symmetry aligns and realigns the components of city, people, and king. All three appear in the first, second, sixth and seventh reports. Yet the third and fifth reports mention only the cities and their people, while the centerpiece mentions only the deaths of the king and the people. (2008, 151)

Eleven features are stated repeatedly:

1. Hostile encampment (vv 31, 34)
2. Battle (vv 29, 31, 34, 36, 38)
3. Divine involvement (vv 30, 32)
4. Capture (vv 28, 32, 35, 37, 39)
5. Striking with the sword (vv 28, 30, 32, 35, 37, 39)
6. Complete destruction of place/people (vv 28, 35, 37, 39)
7. Death of every inhabitant (vv 28, 30, 32, 35, 37, 39)
8. No survivors (vv 28, 30, 33, 37, 39)
9. Death of the city's king (vv 28, 30, 37, 39)
10. Destruction of adjacent towns (vv 37, 39)
11. Comparison between present victory and a previous one (vv 28, 30, 32, 35, 39). (Hall 2010, 179-80)

We encounter repeated use of *herem* language in this section. As Stern points out, this verb "occurs . . . ten times [10:1, 28, 35, 37, 39, 40; 11:11, 12, 20, 21] in these two chapters, or nearly a quarter of the total attestations of the verb" (1991, 157). It will not appear again until Josh 19:38. The practice of *herem* may explain why there is no mention of spoils, such as we find in other conquest accounts.

Statements in 10:28-39 about Joshua leaving no survivors and subjugating the whole region in one campaign should probably be read as literary exaggeration. As we have noted before, ANE battle accounts usually contain hyperbole, such as in the words of Thutmose III on the Gebel Barkal Stele:

> The great army of Mitanni,
> it is overthrown in the twinkling of an eye.
> It has perished completely,
> as though they had never existed.
> Like the ashes of a fire.

Or the claim of Pharaoh Merenptah: "Yanoam made nonexistent; Israel is wasted, his seed is not" (as cited in Younger 1990, 227-28). The evidence from Joshua itself suggests the conquest took some time and some Canaanites remained. This would explain how in 10:37 and 39 everyone in Hebron and Debir were killed, while according to 15:13-16, Caleb still has enemies there to contend with (Younger 1995, 261-62).

■ **28-30** Although not part of the original coalition as identified in 10:3, Joshua conquered Makkedah. He may have suspected them of attempting to shield the five escaping kings. Possibly this had now become an offensive, rather than a defensive campaign. Attacks were launched at other cities not part of the coalition of five kings, such as Libnah and Debir. Jarmuth and Jerusalem were among the original five, but no mention is made here of an attack on these cities. It may be that the five cities listed at the opening of the chapter were not all who joined the coalition. We cannot be certain of Libnah's location, but it appears to be north of Makkedah.

■ **31-32** The army then turned south to Lachish. Evidence of destruction and depopulation in the mid-twelfth century may be the result of these events (Ussishkin 1983, 97-185).

■ **33** At this point, Horam king of Gezer, located about twenty-five miles north, came to the aid of Lachish, but to no avail (v 33). Gezer was located at Tell Jezer or Tell el-Jazari, "situated on the last of the foothills in the Judean Range, where it slopes down to meet the northern Shephelah" (Dever 1993, 3:496). According to Dever, "Gezer guards one of the most important crossroads in the country, where the trunk road leading to Jerusalem and sites in the hills branches off from the Via Maris at the approach to the Ayalon Valley" (ibid.).

■ **34-39** Eglon appears to have been located about five miles southeast of Lachish (vv 34-35), with Hebron less than fifteen miles to the northeast (vv 36-37). Hebron's king was killed at Makkedah. The death mentioned in v 37 may refer to this incident or to the killing of a newly appointed sovereign (Woudstra 1981, 182-83). Debir is located eleven miles southwest of Hebron, requiring the Israelites to interrupt their arc of attack; this explains the NIV's **turned around** (v 38).

C. Summary of Both Campaigns (10:40-43)

■ **40-43** The chapter concludes with a summation of both campaigns, first by identifying the regions conquered (v 40), then the extent of the conquest (v 41), then the length of time it took (v 42) (Hess 1996a, 205). The **hill country** (v 40) refers to the central highlands, the backbone of Palestine, while the **Negev** (v 40) was the wilderness area to the south. The **western foothills** (v 40) refer to the Shephelah, the rolling hills located between the central highlands and the coastal plain. Also mentioned are the **mountain slopes** (v 40). Woudstra suggests this refers either to the slopes descending from the hill country to the Shephelah or the slopes going down from the southern hill country to the Dead Sea in the east (1981, 184), while Howard proposes the "stream beds or ravines in one of these areas" (1998a, 261). Not mentioned at all in this passage is the coastal plain (Clarke 2010, 92).

This summary emphasizes several aspects of the campaigns. God is clearly responsible for the victory, having both commanded the campaigns (v 40) and brought success (v 42), so that all opposition was removed (v 40). After God, Joshua is the focal point, the subject of five verbs in three verses (vv 40-42) (Hall 2010, 181).

The text indicates that the team of God and Joshua brought about a sweeping victory in **one campaign** (v 42), although 11:18 suggests that victory may have taken a bit longer than what this implies. Niehaus suggests this phrase should be rendered as "once," rather than "all at one time" (1980, 238). Another possibility is to treat the phrase as literary hyperbole (Younger 1990, 216).

Fleming provides several examples of a similar phrase from Assyrian literature, such as when Šamši-Adad V defeated Mesai and Sargon II defeated Dur Atḫara and the king of Babylon, each battle said to last only a single day. Fleming also points out how, in the Babylonian Chronicles, Raḫilu was defeated in one day (1999, 224). According to the Mesha Stele, Israel was defeated in a battle that lasted only "from the break of dawn until noon" (Younger 1990, 228). It is best to read the battle descriptions in Joshua as divinely inspired examples of ANE hyperbole.

FROM THE TEXT

Who brought about this great victory? Clearly Yahweh, but it is also clear that God worked through the actions of Joshua and the Israelites. He could have brought about the victory all by himself, as at Sodom and Gomorrah. What the psalmist asserts—"Some trust in chariots and some in horses, but we trust in the name of the LORD our God" (Ps 20:7 [8])—is echoed by God himself through the prophet Zechariah: "'Not by might nor by power, but by my Spirit,' says the LORD Almighty" (Zech 4:6). God can do it all by himself. Nevertheless, he chooses to employ humans to assist him in his work.

What he says to Joshua in Josh 10:8 captures this divine/human synergy: "Do not be afraid of them; I have given them into your hand. Not one of them will be able to withstand you." The enemy is given into Joshua's hands and no one will be able to resist him, but only because God would bring this about. Had Israel not marched all night to Gibeon, fought the coalition, and pursued them as they retreated, it seems unlikely that any hailstones would have fallen or that any victory would have been gained.

That we see this synergy at work should not surprise us, since this appears to be God's modus operandi. Apart from the act of creation, God's other works among humans throughout the Bible have almost always included humans. God may have chosen to work this way in order for his people to learn essential lessons such as obedience and trust. Joshua and the Israelites had a front row seat in this classroom, witnessing the consequences of their disobedience when they covenanted with Gibeon without first consulting God. They also saw firsthand how God could work through this disobedience. Partnering with God allowed their trust in him to grow. How else could Joshua have found the confidence to appeal to God as he did in vv 12-14? The heroes of Heb 11 learned faith the same way, by partnering with God in his great redemptive plan.

By working with us, God allows us to do our part to help others. God helped Israel so Israel could help Gibeon. God's words to Joshua (v 8) became Joshua's words to his commanders (v 25). Just so, our victories, our lessons, even the experience of God's faithfulness in our tragedies and failures, can become a source of trust and obedience for others (see 2 Cor 1:3-4).

Yet another reason for divine/human synergy may be to demonstrate even more clearly that God deserves our praise. A golfer who wins using only garden tools instead of high-end clubs demonstrates his abilities, not the qualities of the tools. Let's face it: you and I are only rakes and shovels, but in God's hands we can do great things. We cannot say definitively why God chooses to use humans. We only know that he does and that we must be faithful to do whatever he calls us to do.

XI. JOSHUA 11

BEHIND THE TEXT

At first glance it might appear from chs 10 and 11 that Joshua and the Israelites are engaging in a systematic campaign to eliminate the enemy, first in the central and southern regions, then in the north. Those enemies are eliminated, but the campaign is more God's work than Israel's. Israel is surreptitiously drawn into a covenant with Gibeon (ch 9), and then must defend Gibeon. While defending Gibeon, they have the opportunity to defeat their enemy in the central and southern parts of Canaan, a victory the author explicitly attributes to God (10:10-12, 14). With the northern coalition, Israel once again acts only in self-defense. Once again they are victorious, but the victory here, too, is explicitly credited to God (11:6, 8, 20). These chapters are less about Joshua's military genius and more about how God conquered the land.

There are a number of similarities between chs 10 and 11. Both begin exactly the same way in the Hebrew (Howard 1998a, 264). Both proceed along the same pattern: the coalition gathers under a single named ruler (10:1-5; 11:1-5), followed by the battle (10:6-15; 11:6-9) with a surprise attack (10:9; 11:7), and then the mopping up (10:16-27; 11:10-15) (Howard 1998a, 263-64; Hess 1996a, 207; for a thorough study of the macrostructures within these chapters, see Younger 2008, 3-32).

But these chapters are more than carbon copies. Nothing in Josh 11 matches the important ceremony found in 10:16-43. The pace that accelerates in the latter part of ch 10 continues to speed up in ch 11 (Hess 1996a, 207). The opposition faced in ch 10 is more fearsome in ch 11, where it is described first in terms of kings and cities (v 1), then regions (v 2), then ethnic groups (v 3) (Hall 2010, 185). Here, for the first time, Israel encounters chariots, the cutting-edge of ANE weaponry. Chapter 11 not only describes the northern campaign but also summarizes the whole conquest. As Hall points out, this chapter

> designates the regions and boundaries of the conquered territory in both the north and the south (vv. 16-17), gives a sense of the temporal scope of the conquest (v. 18), provides a theological explanation for the hostility of the Canaanites (vv. 19-20), addresses the Israelites' oldest and greatest fears about the land (vv. 21-22), and characterizes the conquest as a fulfillment of Yahweh's promise (or, perhaps, command) to Moses (v. 23). (2010, 192-93)

Attending too closely to the similarities between chs 10 and 11 also obscures the similarities between chs 9 and 11. Both begin similarly, with the puzzling Hebrew verb for *to hear* without an object (i.e., no mention of what is heard). Both chapters open with lists of the same six people groups (9:1; 11:3-4), and both describe the opposition using similar vocabulary (9:2; 11:5) (ibid., 184). Hall concludes that "Joshua 11:1-5 is quite possibly intended to resume the narrative thread introduced in 9:1-2." What Jabin heard was what Israel had done to Jericho and Ai (see 9:1-2) (ibid., 185).

It appears that Josh 11 forms part of a still larger section, chs 9—12, which describe how God gave the land to Israel. Dorsey's chiastic outline of these chapters captures the point well (1999, 92):

a all the kings of Canaan oppose Joshua <u>as one</u> (9:1-2)
  b **mercy for a believing remnant: Israel makes peace with Gibeonites** (9:3-27)
    c **defeat of southern coalition, led by king of Jerusalem** (10:1-15)
      d CENTER: ritual ceremony at Makkedah (10:16-43)
    c' **defeat of northern coalition, led by king of Hazor** (11:1-15)
  b' **no mercy for hardened Canaanites** (11:16-23)
a' all the kings of Canaan whom Joshua conquered are listed <u>one by one</u> (12:1-24)

Within this larger section, Josh 11 describes the northern conquest (vv 1-15) and then summarizes the taking of the entire land (vv 16-23). Victory is clearly Yahweh's doing, though Israel is permitted to participate and does so with perfect obedience.

IN THE TEXT

A. Northern Campaign (11:1-15)

1. Very Large Coalition against Israel (11:1-5)

■ 1 If Hall is correct, Jabin heard what the Israelites did to Jericho and Ai and to its kings and reacts by forming a coalition. Jabin would be the king one would expect to take the lead, ruling as he did over Hazor, the most significant city of that region. Hazor sat at a junction of the Great Trunk Road (Petrovich 2008, 490). From here one could travel north to Haran, northeast to Damascus, or south into Canaan and Egypt. According to one scholar, "Hazor is like a fat spider in a wide strung web. The strategic importance of this geographic position can hardly be overestimated" (Schäfer-Lichtenberger 2001, 111). Little wonder this was among the largest and best fortified of all the Canaanite cities (Hess 1996a, 213). The walls of the Late Bronze Age palace were between ten and thirteen feet thick (Ben-Tor 2008, 5:1770), and the city may have had a population in the second millennium of around twenty thousand (http://unixware.mscc.huji.ac.il/~hatsor/).

Jabin is also referred to in Judg 4 as a Canaanite king who ruled in Hazor. For this reason, some have questioned the essential historicity of the account in Josh 11, though such questions seem unnecessary. Jabin was likely the dynastic name for Hazor's kings (as Pharaoh was for Egyptian kings). A letter dating to the eighteenth century B.C. and found in the archives at the city of Mari refers to a king of Hazor named Ibni-Adad (an Akkadian name meaning "the god Adad has created") (Malamat 1960, 17). According to Hess, "Recent excavations at Hazor have yielded Old Babylonian cuneiform texts with an example of a name beginning with the same root, also in a prefixed form, *ib-ni*" (1996b, 207). Crown proposes this scenario to explain the evidence about Jabin found in Josh 11 and Judg 4: although the king of Hazor was killed by Joshua, a member of the royal family took refuge in the same region. Later, during the time of the Judges, this king or his successor hired a *ḥabiru* chieftan, Sisera, to challenge the Israelites, though he was unsuccessful (Crown 1973, 29-32).

As Adoni-Zedek was presented as the leading king of the southern coalition in the preceding chapter, Jabin fills this role for the northern coalition. Hence we have two kings west of the Jordan to balance Sihon and Og on the eastern side. Joshua will allude to this balance in his farewell speech when he refers to the defeat of "two Amorite kings" (24:12), which could refer to either pair or to both pairs.

Jabin **sent** a written message to several other kings. Cassuto points out that the verb *sh-l-ḥ* without the addition of "saying," "and he said," or a similar expression, means "to convey in writing" or "to write in a letter" (Cassuto 1975b, 231). In this message Jabin invited these kings to participate with him in a defense of Canaan against the intruding Israelites. He sent the message to **Jobab king of Madon**, Madon being associated by some with the Horns of Hattin just west of the Sea of Galilee (Woudstra 1981, 188; Hess 1996a, 209), and by others with Maron, a city known from Egyptian sources and located several miles west of Hazor (Howard 1998a, 265 n. 257).

Shimron may be Khirbet Sammuniya, located five miles west of Nazareth (Hess 1996a, 208-9) and about ten miles north-northeast of Megiddo. The location of **Akshaph** is also unclear, although it is mentioned in several ancient documents outside the Bible, such as the Amarna letters and Egyptian Papyrus Anastasi I from the thirteenth century B.C. (Woudstra 1981, 188 n. 10). Akshaph may be associated with Tell Keisan, further northwest of Shimron (Hess 1996a, 209) or with Tell Regev, further northeast, both sites in the Plain of Acco (Cleave 1999, 63; Lawrence 2006, 47).

■ **2** Jabin also contacted **the northern kings** in various regions, suggesting this coalition included the "totality of the northern region" (Hess 1996a, 210). The **mountains** may refer to the central highlands, the mountains around the Jezreel valley, or the mountains west of Hazor. Also mentioned was the **Arabah south of Kinnereth**, likely a reference to the Jordan valley as it empties out of the Sea of Galilee (known as Kinnereth in the OT) and extends to the Dead Sea and beyond. Finkelstein argues that **western foothills** or Shephelah refers neither to the southern foothills of 10:40 nor to the low hills between the Samarian hill country and Mount Carmel. He locates the northern Shephelah in the region between Tyre and the hills of Western Galilee (1981, 84-94). **Naphoth Dor** refers to the city of Dor, located west of Mount Carmel on the Mediterranean coast. The term **Naphoth** ordinarily indicates heights but this does not fit **Dor,** which is located on a plain. Some have proposed the term here means region or dunes (Howard 1998a, 266 n. 260).

■ **3** The author expands the scope of the invitation by identifying several people groups: **Canaanites** to both east and west, **Amorites, Hittites, Perizzites and Jebusites** in the central mountain region, and **Hivites** to the north near Mount **Hermon**. Hess believes **Mizpah** refers to the eastern part of the Litani River that flows west to Tyre (1996a, 211).

■ **4** As if the preceding description was not threatening enough, v 4 adds two more details: the armies assembling were as vast as **the sand on the seashore**; and they had **chariots** and **horses**. These would not have been useful in the central and southern campaigns because of the hilly terrain. The north offered plenty of wide open plains to allow ample room for the horses and chariots to do their deadly best. Israel did not panic, perhaps because God had already warned them what to do if their enemy had horses and chariots (see Deut 20:1).

■ **5** The enemy forces assembled at the **Waters of Merom**, although we cannot be certain where these waters are located. Hess places them at Wadi el-Hamam, north of the Horns of Hattin (1996a, 211) while others locate them further north at or near modern Meron (Boling and Wright 1982, 307) or at nearby Tell el-Khureibeh (Liid 1992, 4:705).

2. Joshua's Response (11:6-15)

■ **6** The first response to this new threat came not from Joshua, but from Yahweh (v 6), who, as he has done before (see 1:1-10; 3:7; 5:9; 6:2; 8:1, 18; 10:8), provides an encouraging message of hope and promise. Joshua and the Israelites should not fear because God will provide victory (***I am giving***) and will do so quickly (**by this time tomorrow**). He also instructed Joshua to **hamstring their horses and burn their chariots**. God's command to destroy these chariots was intended for this battle only and should not be understood as prohibiting ever employing chariots in warfare (as suggested by Sensenig 2012, 73-80). Although painful, hamstringing the horses was not gratuitous cruelty, only a way of rendering them useless for combat. Hamstrung horses can still ambulate (personal conversation with Dr. Stephen D. Laudermilch, DVM, May 25, 2013; Woudstra 1981, 192 n. 24). By disabling the horses and burning the chariots, the Israelites would be unable to use them in further battles, fostering greater reliance upon God. Hall suggests v 6*a* is actually the strategy for engaging in battle: Israel was to ambush the enemy, disable their horses, and destroy their chariots (2010, 188), but this seems unlikely given how difficult it would be to disable horses and destroy chariots undetected.

■ **7** As they did in 10:9, Israel launched a surprise attack. We are not given the details, but this strategy may have caught the enemy unprepared, even in a location unsuitable for chariot use. While the Israelites had their role to play, here as elsewhere, the victory is portrayed as God's doing (v 8). Given Israel's freedom to move northward without opposition and the mention of cities like Taanach and Megiddo among the conquered (see 12:21), otherwise unknown military ventures may have taken place between the events of chs 10 and 11 (Woudstra 1981, 191).

■ **8-9** Not content with victory in battle, the Israelites pressed the attack. Some chased those who scattered to the northwest, toward **Greater Sidon**; others pursued the enemy east to **the Valley of Mizpah**, that is, the Litani River valley. The location of **Misrephoth Maim** is unclear. It may refer to Naphoth Dor (Tur-Sinai 1959, 33-35), to a location south of Tyre (Woudstra 1981, 191), or to the northeast along the Litani River (Hess 1996a, 212). Presumably the enemy did not retreat to the south because that was the direction from which the Israelites had come. Both in what they do to the horses and chariots and in how they persistently pursue their enemies, the Israelites demonstrate their obedience to God and trust in him (v 9).

■ 10 Joshua and the Israelites then **turned back** to deal with **Hazor**, the coalition ringleader. It is not clear why **Hazor** is here referred to as **the head of all these kingdoms**. Some have taken this to mean that Hazor's glory days already lay behind it when Joshua attacked. This seems to be the assumption of the NLT: "Hazor had at one time been the capital of all these kingdoms." Others, like Malamat, consider Hazor's glory days to have ended with Joshua's attack: "The pre-eminence accorded to Hazor during the Israelite conquest is probably the last vestige of the greatness of the once-mighty kingdom" (1960, 12-19). The NIV follows this latter interpretation as does the NRSV: "Before that time Hazor was the head of all those kingdoms."

■ 11 Among all the cities conquered in the north, only Hazor was said to be destroyed by fire (see vv 11, 13). Archaeologists have identified destruction levels at 1400 B.C., 1300 B.C., and 1230 B.C. Seti I of Egypt is likely responsible for the destruction in 1300 B.C., which means Israel could have been responsible for either of the others (Lewis 1985, 307; see Ben-Tor 2008, 1772-73). Not everyone agrees. Schäfer-Lichtenberger contends that Egypt, rather than Israel, is responsible for the Late Bronze Age destruction of Hazor (2001, 104-22; but see Kitchen's withering counterpoint to Schäfer-Lichtenberger [2002, 309-13]). The archaeology report confirms the distinct possibility that Israel is responsible for the destruction of the Late Bronze Age city (see http://unixware.mscc.huji.ac.il/~hatsor/). Pitkänen agrees that the archaeological evidence "fits very well with what is described in the book of Joshua" (2010, 232).

■ 12-15 As he had done in the central and southern campaigns, Joshua persisted in attacking and defeating other enemy cities in the north. In so doing he acted in obedience to Moses, **the servant of the LORD** (v 12; see 1:1, 2, 7, 13, 15; 8:31, 33; 9:24). Joshua did not burn these other cities, perhaps to provide places for the Israelites to live. The author specified that these towns were **on their mounds** (11:13) (that is, "tells," which represented layers of earlier settlements), possibly to remind the reader of the antiquity of the cities that now belong to God's people.

Verses 12-15 emphasize complete military conquest (**sword** appears in vv 11, 12, 14), *ḥerem* (vv 11, 12, 20, 21), and the defeat of kings (the noun appears eleven times in ch 11). Hall may be correct that "all this attention to the fate of Canaan's kings is perhaps a subtle statement, *à la* 1 Sam 8, that Israel is better off without one" (2010, 190), but the book as a whole seems ambivalent on this subject. Especially emphasized here is the obedience of Joshua, who "follows orders issued by both Yahweh (vv. 6, 9) and Moses (v. 12), and by Yahweh through Moses (vv. 15, 20, 23)" (2010, 191). This emphasis on obedience is highlighted by the poetic design of v 15:

A As the LORD commanded his servant Moses, so Moses commanded Joshua,

B   and Joshua did it;
  B' he left nothing undone
 A' of all that the LORD had commanded Joshua. (Hess 1996a, 216)

B. Summary of Conquest (11:16-23)

1. Conquest of Entire Land (11:16-20)

These verses were meant to summarize the entire conquest, not just what had been described in the preceding fifteen verses. The author actually provides five summaries in these verses. The first two describe the conquered territory from two different perspectives (vv 16, 17a). The third (vv 17b-18) highlights the scope of the conquest and adds a note about the time involved. The fourth summary (vv 19-20) explains how the conquest progressed, while the fifth focuses on significant opponents (e.g., Anakites) (vv 21-22). The sixth summary looks back at the conquest and still further back to Moses, then ahead to the rest that would follow the conquest (v 23).

■ **16-17a** In the first summary, the author describes the **entire land**, region by region. Most of the land mentioned in v 16 was taken in the southern campaign (described in 10:40-41): the **hill country**, or central highland region; **the Negev**, the desert region in the far south; the **whole region of Goshen**, likely referring to the border lands between the hill country and the Negev; and the **western foothills**, that is, the southern Shephelah (Butler 1983, 129). The northern campaign extended Israelite domination to other regions, including **the Arabah and the mountains of Israel with their foothills** (11:16; see v 2).

In v 17a, the author covers the same territory as in v 16, this time by pointing to a mountain in the south and one in the north. **Mount Halak, which rises toward Seir,** likely refers to a peak in the extreme southern portion of Canaan, well south of Beersheba in the Negev wilderness. **Baal Gad in the Valley of Lebanon below Mount Hermon** refers to the extreme northern reaches of the country, north of Dan and west of the towering Mount Hermon.

■ **17b-18** In the third summary, the author describes the conquest as total and complete. Such claims must be read in the context of other passages (see 11:19, 22; 13:1-7), which acknowledge that some of the enemy still remained (Clarke 2010, 89). This illustrates the ANE practice of employing hyperbole in conquest accounts. In spite of hints of a quick victory, the battle likely continued for some time, perhaps several years (see 14:12).

■ **19-20** The fourth summary mentions the Gibeonites, dampening the otherwise triumphant tone of the passage. By doing so, however, the author reminds us, primarily, that Israel did not make the same mistake twice, and also that God used this misstep to accomplish great victories. Mention of the Gibeonites also raises a question that 11:20 answers: why did no other people seek a treaty with Israel? The answer: because Yahweh **hardened their hearts.**

By referring to God hardening hearts, the author reminds the reader what God did to Pharaoh's heart. As Hall notes, "This portrays Joshua's work as the continuation of that entrusted to Moses" (2010, 189) and provides yet another link between the conquest and the exodus (see 10:11 with Exod 9:13-35; Josh 10:12-13 with Exod 10:21-29; Josh 10:14, 42 with Exod 14:14, 25; Josh 10:10 with Exod 14:24, 27; Josh 10:21 with Exod 11:7).

To say that God **hardened** the **hearts** of the Canaanites (and Pharaoh) does not mean that God made it impossible for them to do other than what they did; that would impugn God's fairness. The Canaanites remained perfectly free to choose whether to sue for peace, flee to another land, barricade themselves within their towns, or attack the Israelites. Hindsight allows us to say that any of the first three options would have been preferable to the last, which left them decimated. Instead of receiving the mercy shown the Gibeonites (9:3-27), they chose to attack. With each step in this direction they became more and more resolute, until they found themselves rushing precipitously to their own annihilation.

The kings chose the last option because of pride, stubbornly refusing to admit they could be defeated by nomadic nobodies. When consumed by stubborn pride, even intelligent people can make foolish choices. This is why God gets the credit for the kings' unwise strategy: it was God who designed humans and the laws by which humans operate.

2. Defeat of the Anakites (11:21-22)

■ **21-22** The fifth summary of the conquest focuses on the **Anakites**. Joshua 14:6-12 suggests that victory over this group of opponents may not have taken place during the northern campaign. It is included here for its symbolic significance. The Anakites, who came to Canaan as "'pre-Philistine' Sea Peoples" (Boling and Wright 1982, 388), were the inhabitants of the land who most frightened the twelve spies sent out by Moses (see Num 13:32-33). As Moses prepared the new generation of Israelites to take up the challenge their frightened fathers had neglected, he specifically mentioned the Anakites (see Deut 9:1-3). How appropriate that this summary of Canaan's conquest should mention that the enemy that had once struck fear into the Israelites had now been dispatched. Specifically, the Anakites were removed from **Hebron, Debir and Anab**, but remained in coastal cities soon settled by the Philistines.

Anab is located three miles west of Debir (Benjamin 1992, 1:219) and fifteen miles southwest of Hebron (Simons as cited by Howard 1998a, 275 n. 283; for the location of Hebron and Debir, → chs 10 and 12). When and by whom Hebron and Debir were conquered is uncertain, since it is said to occur here and in 10:36-39 at the hands of Joshua, but is still anticipated in 14:6-15 and then credited to Caleb in 15:14. Fittingly, this is the first time in the book that Canaan is called *the land of the Israelites* (Israelite territory) (v 22).

3. Summary of Conquest and Rest from War (11:23)

■ **23** The sixth and final summary of ch 11 is found in v 23. Here the author looks back to Moses who had received Yahweh's instructions and transmitted them to Joshua and the Israelites. Israel obeyed these instructions and had been victorious. The author also anticipates the allotment of the land, the next step of obedience and the next stage in God's redemptive plan. This is the first of about fifty times the term **inheritance** will occur in Joshua (Hall 2010, 193). The chapter ends with the powerful observation that **the land had rest from war**, a phrase used in Joshua and Judges to mark the end of a significant period in the life of God's people (14:15; Judg 3:11, 30; 5:31; 8:28) (Hall 2010, 193).

FROM THE TEXT

Joshua 11 makes it very clear that God has accomplished a complete victory, just as he promised, and that it came about through Israel's faithful obedience. By emphasizing the comprehensive nature of the conquest, the author is not suggesting that every Canaanite has been expelled; in fact, he makes it clear this is not the case (see v 22). Nevertheless, God has been faithful to his promise and has given Israel control of the "entire land" (v 16).

God provided this victory in many different ways. The strategies that defeated Jericho and Ai were not employed again. With Gibeon and the subsequent campaigns, God's power was able to turn human error into divine victory. The southern coalition was defeated by supernatural intervention, but no miracles are mentioned in the victory over the northern coalition.

The theme of obedience sounds repeatedly in ch 11. Israel followed God's instructions for how to treat the horses and chariots (v 9) and carefully did what God had commanded through Moses (vv 12, 14-15, 20, 23). This obedience required a significant step of faith. Disabling the horses and burning the chariots made this technology unavailable to the Israelites for further battles in the conquest of Canaan. As when they obeyed God's command to be circumcised while camped on the Canaanite side of the Jordan, their obedience placed them entirely in God's protective keeping. Israel was called to trust and obey God in reverential fear, but God assures them that fearing him meant they need fear no others. After all, even the dreaded Anakites were easily swept aside (vv 21-22).

In return for their faithful obedience, God kept his promise and granted them the land of Canaan where they and the land could experience rest (v 23), that is, tranquility and the absence of struggle. Challenges remained, but this phase of constant battle had been graciously brought to an end. This phase of God's redemptive plan—the establishment of his nation in its own homeland—had been implemented. After further twists and turns, God's plan would culminate in the incarnation of Christ, God himself coming to this very spot on the map.

We come to participate in this plan, as did the Israelites, through God's grace, to which we must respond in faithful obedience. The writer of Hebrews speaks of Israel's coming into the land to experience rest, using the same Greek term used by the LXX to translate the Hebrew word for "rest" in Josh 11:23. The writer of Hebrews says that "the promise of entering his rest still stands" (4:1) and can be experienced by those who claim it by faithful obedience. "Yield yourself in everything to obey," wrote Andrew Murray. "This will strengthen you to trust for everything He has promised to do" (1984, 158). God's plan promises not only rest for our souls but rest for the land, sky, seas, their inhabitants, even the whole universe. All creation longs for this rest (Rom 8:22), which will follow the return of the second Joshua. Until then, God calls his church to live lives of faithful obedience, of rest. In the words of Peter, "You ought to live holy and godly lives as you look forward to the day of God and speed its coming" (2 Pet 3:11*b*-12).

XII. JOSHUA 12

BEHIND THE TEXT

With ch 12, the account of the conquest of Canaan comes to a stately, decisive, and God-glorifying conclusion. Hall considers it "a sort of factual appendix to the conquest narratives" (2010, 193), although Dorsey's chiastic outline does the chapter greater justice (1999, 92):

    a all the kings of Canaan oppose Joshua <u>as one</u> (9:1-2)
        b mercy for a believing remnant: Israel makes peace with Gibeonites (9:3-27)
            c defeat of southern coalition, led by king of Jerusalem (10:1-15)
                d CENTER: ritual ceremony at Makkedah (10:16-43)
            c' defeat of northern coalition, led by king of Hazor (11:1-15)
        b' no mercy for hardened Canaanites (11:16-23)
    a' all the kings of Canaan whom Joshua conquered are listed <u>one by one</u> (12:1-24)

Note how, according to Dorsey's structure, ch 12 balances the opening verses of ch 9, which speak of all the kings of Canaan opposing Joshua "as one" (9:1-2). "One" is left untranslated in the NIV, but the NLT preserves it: "These kings combined their armies to fight as one against Joshua and the Israelites" (v 2). The same Hebrew term (*'eḥād*) appears in Josh 12 thirty-one times, one for each of the kings mentioned in vv 9-24. The author seems to be saying that the enemy came united against Israel but was scattered, with each and every enemy king experiencing ignominious defeat.

The chapter divides into two parts, the first summarizing the conquest of the Transjordan, and the second describing the conquest of Cisjordan, better known as Canaan (vv 7-24).

IN THE TEXT

A. Conquest of the Transjordan (12:1-6)

These opening verses focus on the kings who were defeated; the chapter will return to this theme at its conclusion. These verses also reach back to the wilderness wanderings to describe how Israel gained control of the land east of the Jordan, the territory given to the tribes of Reuben, Gad, and half of Manasseh. By mentioning these earlier conquests, the author of Joshua offers more than a description of the settlement of Canaan; he stresses the unity of the nation, as he has done earlier (3:12, 17; 4:1, 2, 3, 4, 5, 8, 9, 11, 14, 20; 8:1, 3, 11; 10:7; 11:7; see Woudstra 1981, 200) and will again before the book is finished (ch 22).

The author also takes another opportunity to strengthen the connection between Moses and Joshua (see 1:5 and many other passages; see Woudstra 1981, 200). As well, mention of the earlier victories allows the author to connect the events of chs 1—11 with the wilderness wanderings, as he elsewhere connects events in Joshua to those of the exodus (→ chs 4, 10). Providing this comprehensive picture further portrays the glory of this promise-keeping God.

1. Introduction (12:1)

■ 1 Here we see the western (Jordan River), southern, and northern boundaries of Canaan; it was understood that the desert formed the eastern boundary. The **Arnon Gorge** intersects the Dead Sea at about the midway point on the eastern shore, while **Mount Hermon** marks the northern boundary. **The Arabah** refers to the rift valley, which contains the Sea of Galilee, the Jordan River, the Dead Sea, and still further south. Woudstra points out that the northern boundary does not extend to the Euphrates, as promised (see 1:4), which may imply that the earlier boundary was intended as the ideal, or that Israel's work of conquest remained undone (1981, 201).

2. King Sihon of the Amorites and King Og of the Bashanites (12:2-5)

■ **2-3** Now the author mentions the two kingdoms whose defeat provided the territory mentioned in v 1: King **Sihon** (vv 2-3) and King Og (vv 4-5). Since these victories are described several times in the Pentateuch and Joshua (see Num 21:21-35; Deut 1:4; 2:24—3:22; 29:7; 31:4; Josh 2:10; 9:10; see also Judg 11:19-21; Neh 9:22; Pss 135:11; 136:19; see Woudstra 1981, 201 n. 7), the author did not need to provide details here, only describe the territory obtained.

Sihon ruled from **Heshbon**, usually associated with Tell Ḥesbân, located about sixteen miles east of the Jordan and twelve miles south of Amman (Geraty 1993, 2:626). There is evidence that this site was inhabited from about 1200 B.C. forward (Longman 2013, 777), although this seems too late for Moses' day. Horn proposes Heshbon may be located elsewhere, such as nearby Jalul (1962, 410) while others argue the site may have been too small to leave a trace (Pitkänen 2010, 240).

The southern border of Sihon's territory began at **the rim of the Arnon Gorge** at **Aroer**, not a town but a fortress guarding the King's Highway (Olávarri-Goicoechea 1993, 1:92-93). The border extended along high tableland about fifty miles north to the Jabbok River. **Sihon** also controlled territory on the eastern edge of the rift valley between the Sea of Kinnereth (Galilee) and the northern part of the Dead Sea.

■ **4-5** Og is always referred to as king of a place (**Bashan**), while Sihon is often referred to as king of a people, the Amorites (Num 21:21, 26, 29, 34; 32:33; Deut 1:4; 3:2; 4:46; Josh 12:2; 13:10, 21; Judg 11:19; 1 Kgs 4:19; Pss 135:11; 136:19). A few passages describe both Sihon and Og as kings of the Amorites (Deut 31:4; Josh 2:10; 9:10), and sometimes Sihon is called the king of Heshbon (a place) (Deut 2:24, 26, 30; 3:6; 29:7; Josh 9:10; 12:5; 13:27; Neh 9:22). Several other passages simply refer to Sihon by name (Num 21:23, 27, 28; Deut 2:31, 32; Judg 11:20, 21; Jer 48:45).

We also learn here that Og was **one of the last of the Rephaites**, a group, ancient even then, who lived in the Transjordan (Gen 14:5; 15:20). They possessed a reputation for great power and stature (Deut 2:10-11, 20-21). Og is said to have had a bed of iron (at that time a precious metal) that was six feet wide and thirteen feet long (Deut 3:11) (A standard king-size bed today is a little over six feet wide by about six and a half feet long). Old Testament writers eventually came to use Rephaim as a synonym for the dead (see Job 26:5; Ps 88:10; Prov 2:18; 9:18; 21:16; Isa 14:9; 26:14, 19). By connecting Og with the Rephaites, the author heightens the marvel of his defeat.

3. Moses Conquered and Gave to Transjordan Tribes (12:6)

■ **6** After God enabled the accomplishment of this great feat—not an absolute defeat, but rather a subjugation of the region's inhabitants, as Josh 13:13 makes clear—Moses gave this land to the two and a half tribes at their request. Twice in this verse Moses is described as the **servant of the LORD**, perhaps to emphasize that it was really Yahweh, not Moses who gave this land, further legitimating Israel's rights to possess it (Woudstra 1981, 203). By mentioning that Moses allotted the land, the author anticipates the coming allotment of Canaan (chs 13—21).

B. Conquest of Canaan (12:7-24)

1. Introduction (12:7-8)

■ **7** Having identified the defeated kings and the land to the east, the author does the same with the **west side of the Jordan**. Even the opening phrase, **Here is a list of the kings of the land,** is identical in Hebrew to the opening phrase of 12:1. Once again, the focus is on the kings, though that term may be misleading. These kings are more "kinglets," ruling only a small town or village, or occasionally over a larger city, like Hazor. While the focus is on the kings, the author once again anticipates the tribal allotment (**according to their tribal divisions**) (see 11:23).

The two mountains, mentioned in 11:17 as the southern and northern boundaries of Canaan, appear here, though in reverse order. As we saw in 11:16, the author described the conquered territory by its various regions, though the list differs from what we saw there. Goshen is mentioned in 11:16 but omitted here.

■ **8** Both lists (11:16; 12:8) include the **hill country** and **western foothills**, referring to the central highlands and southern Shephelah, respectively. Also appearing in both lists are the **Arabah** and **Negev**, the former referring to the rift valley from the Sea of Galilee to below the Dead Sea, the latter to the desert region at the southernmost part of Canaan. The **mountain slopes** are mentioned in 10:40 among the conquered regions; the **wilderness** likely refers to the Judean wilderness west of the Dead Sea (see 1:4; 15:61).

The author also summarized the conquest by describing the subjugated nations: **Hittites, Amorites, Canaanites, Perizzites, Hivites and Jebusites**. The same six were mentioned in the same order in 9:1 and in a different order in 11:3. The lists in 3:10 and 24:11 include these six nations, but add a seventh, the Girgashites. The differences between this list and the one in Gen 15:19-21, however, are considerable. The Hivites appear in Josh 12 but not in Gen

15. No mention is made in Josh 12 of the Kenites, Kenizzites, Kadmonites, Rephaites (except in Josh 12:4), and Girgashites.

2. List of Kings (12:9-24)

■ **9-24** We may not find the list of kings in vv 9-24 interesting reading, but to the ancient Israelite it would have been "a song of praise to the Lord's honor" (Woudstra 1981, 200). The genre itself—a list of conquered kings—is known in the ancient world. Younger specifically cites the Zakkur inscription dating to around 800 B.C. in which Zakkur, king of Hamath, enumerates a coalition of eighteen kings and armies gathered against him (Younger 1990, 230-32). Yitskhak Ring also points to a similar list from around this time in Greece (1977, 141-44).

It is not altogether clear why the author mentions thirty-one kings. Many other cities were allotted to the Israelites than those mentioned here, suggesting that this list is more than a summary of Josh 1—11. Boling and Wright offer other examples, such as when Ben-Hadad formed a coalition of thirty-two (1 Kgs 20:1) and Ashurbanipal thirty-three kings (1982, 329). Nelson considers the number (he counts thirty rather than thirty-one) to be "conventional" (1997, 159). Perhaps the number was chosen to represent a considerable victory, thirty-one names being thirty-one examples of how Yahweh kept his promise to give this land to Israel.

The list roughly follows the order of conquest, although it mentions more cities from the central and northern regions (Woudstra 1981, 205). The list does not presume the complete conquest of each of the towns listed, but the victories make possible eventual conquest. This may explain the repetition of the numeral one: one by one the victories accumulated.

The list was also meant, in Butler's words, to "impress the readers with the greatness of the feat of God in working for Israel and of the greatness of the leadership of Joshua in following the example of Moses and completing the task first given to Moses" (1983, 139; Hess 1996a, 229). That certain regions are passed over in haste (e.g., the Ephraimite highlands and territory north of Hazor) suggests the author may be preparing the reader for "the description of the land not yet conquered" (Hess 1996a, 229).

The author begins where the conquest began, with the cities of **Jericho** and **Ai** (v 9). The next four verses (vv 10-13) focus on the southern campaign, starting with the campaign's instigator, **Jerusalem** (v 10*a*; see 10:1, 3, 5, 23; 12:10; 15:8, 63; 18:28).

Hebron (v 10*b*; see 10:3, 5, 23, 36-39; 11:21; 12:10; 14:13-15; 15:13, 54; 20:7; 21:11, 13; Judg 1:10, 20; 16:3) is mentioned next, although the conquest of this city is variously attributed, first to Joshua and Israel (Josh 10:36-39; 11:21), then to Caleb (14:13-15), then to the tribe of Judah (Judg 1:10). No contradiction need be assumed; various attributions serve various purposes, and sequential chronology is not a given when it comes to Hebrew narrative. There is also the possibility that each attack brought the expulsion of the native population who, in time, returned to the city, making another conquest necessary.

Although Hebron played a role in the lives of the patriarchs (see Gen 13:18; 23:2, 19; 35:27), archaeological remains do not suggest a large settlement here when the Israelites would have arrived (Ofer 1993, 2:606-9). It became a city of refuge (Josh 21:13) and figured prominently in the life of David as his first capital (2 Sam 2:11).

Jarmuth (Josh 12:11*a*; see 10:3, 5, 23; 15:35; 21:29) was located in the central Shephelah about fifteen miles southwest of Jerusalem. No mention is made of its destruction in ch 10, only the death of its king. **Lachish** (12:11*b*; see 10:3, 5, 23, 31-35; 15:39) was destroyed around the time of the Israelites' invasion, but then resettled during the monarchy when it became a key city protecting Jerusalem from armies attacking from the west.

The king of **Eglon** (12:12*a*; see 10:3, 5, 23, 34, 36, 37; 15:39) is mentioned, as is King Horam of **Gezer** (12:12*b*; see 10:33; 16:3, 10; 21:21), who came to the defense of Lachish when the latter was under attack by the Israelites. According to Josh 16:10, the Israelites "did not dislodge the Canaanites living in Gezer" but only subjected them to servitude (see Judg 1:28-29). Its Philistine inhabitants were eventually conquered by the pharaoh who gave it as a wedding gift to his daughter, Solomon's wife (1 Kgs 9:16).

Debir (Josh 12:13*a*; see 13:26; 15:7, 49; 21:15) was not only the name of the king of Eglon (10:3), but a city located about eleven miles southwest of Hebron (10:38-39). Once called Kiriath Sepher (15:15; Judg 1:11), it along with Hebron and Anab (Josh 11:21) was home to the Anakites.

The location of **Geder**, mentioned only in 12:13*b*, is unclear. Some believe it refers to Gerar, what Aharoni calls "the most important Canaanite city in the western Negeb" (as cited in Butler 1983, 137). Other possibilities include Beth Gader (1 Chr 2:51), Gederah (Josh 15:36), or Gedor (Josh 15:58), located in the hills about seven miles north of Hebron (see Howard 1998a, 281; Ben-Arieh 1993, 2:468). There does appear to have been a location known as Geder, since one of Solomon's officials is called a Gederite (see 1 Chr 27:28) (Woudstra 1981, 206 n. 4).

Hormah (Josh 12:14*a*), located near Beersheba (ibid., 205), appears for the first time in Joshua, although we learned of it earlier when their king blocked the approach of the Israelites (see Num 14:45; 21:3; Deut 1:44). We meet this city again in the distribution of the land to Judah and Simeon (Josh 15:30; 19:4), with its conquest described in Judg 1:17.

Also located in the extreme southern portion of Canaan, about eighteen and a half miles east-northeast of Beersheba, was **Arad** (Josh 12:14*b*) (Aharoni 1993, 1:75), mentioned only here in Joshua. In the Early Bronze Age, Arad was "the economic and cultural center of a dense network of small communities in the vicinity" due to trade and the nearby copper industry (Amiran 1993, 1:75-82). This site was abandoned around 2650 B.C. and not reoccupied (ibid., 82) until the beginning of the Iron Age (late twelfth, early eleventh century B.C.) (Aharoni 1993, 1:82-87). It is mentioned again as being near the site where the Kenites relocated after leaving Jericho (Judg 1:16). The absence of any archaeological evidence for a settlement here during the time of the conquest is problematic, though perhaps the site shifted to another location.

The defeat of **Libnah** (Josh 12:15a) is described in 10:29-30, its allotment to the tribe of Judah in 15:42, and its designation as one of the cities of refuge in 21:13.

Adullam 12:15b; see 15:35) is likely Khirbet esh-Sheikh Madhkûr, located midway between Jerusalem and Lachish. David would later hide here from Saul's pursuit (1 Sam 22:1; 2 Sam 23:13) (Woudstra 1981, 206; Butler 1983, 137).

Makkedah (Josh 12:16a; see 10:10, 28) was where the five kings of the northern coalition had sought to hide, and where Joshua encouraged his generals (10:16-27). It too became part of the tribal allotment for Judah (15:41).

Bethel (12:16b; see 12:9; 16:1, 2; 18:13, 22; Judg 1:22, 23) is usually identified with Beitin, ten and a half miles north of Jerusalem (although Wood identifies Beitin with Beth Aven and Bethel with el-Bira [2008, 239]). Its importance lay in part in its location at the intersection of several major highways, one leading through the central highlands and another from Jericho to the coastal plain (Kelso 1993, 1:192).

Bethel was associated with the travels of the patriarchs, especially Jacob (Gen 12:8; 13:3; 28:19; 35:1-16). The city is briefly mentioned in connection with the attack on Ai (Josh 7:2; 8:9, 12); its army even participated in Ai's defense (8:17), but nothing was explicitly said there or anywhere else in Joshua about its defeat. Though initially included in the allotment for the tribes of Joseph (16:1, 2), it was then reassigned to the Benjamites (18:13, 22).

Archaeological evidence tells the story of an initial Israelite occupation, followed by Canaanite recapture, then another Israelite victory, perhaps described in Judg 1:22-26 (Kelso 1993, 1:194). Deborah held court in this vicinity (Judg 4:5), and it was one of the cities on Samuel's circuit (1 Sam 7:16). Bethel was considered a holy site in the time of the Judges (see Judg 20:18, 26, 31; 21:2) and a site of wicked apostasy, thanks to King Jeroboam I (see 1 Kgs 12:29, 32, 33; 13:1, 4, 10, 11, 32).

Tappuah (Josh 12:17a) was located in the central mountains between Bethel and Shechem on an east-west road that traversed the mountains and headed to the coastal plain. We are not told of its defeat, only of its allotment first to the tribe of Judah (15:53) then the tribe of Ephraim (16:8; 17:7-8).

Hepher (12:17*b*) may refer to a site about two and a half miles from the Mediterranean coast. This location, part of the tribal allotment for Manasseh, was "strategically located on one of the coastal routes and at the farthest inland point navigable for river traffic" (Paley 1993, 2:609). This location, in addition to its rich soil and abundant springs, allowed it to become "one of the largest and most important sites in the central Sharon Plain" (ibid.). Archaeological evidence indicates it was destroyed by fire around 1200 B.C., perhaps by Egyptians, Sea Peoples, a local catastrophe, or the Israelites, as implied in Joshua (ibid., 612).

Located south of **Hepher** in the Sharon valley lies **Aphek** (v 18*a*), associated with Tell Ras el-'Ain. Aphek sits on the intersection of a major east-west route and one of the main north-south routes through Canaan, near the modern city of Tel Aviv (Eitan 1993, 1:62). Archaeological evidence from the Late Bronze Age suggests this settlement was defeated in battle and destroyed in flames although the Israelites do not appear to have taken up residence until the second half of the tenth century (Beck 1993, 1:68-69). This land was given to Asher (19:30), but the original inhabitants were not removed (13:4; Judg 1:31).

Lasharon (Josh 12:18*b*) appears only in the Bible, prompting some to suggest it should be "To Sharon" (as in direction) or "belonging to Sharon," that is, not as a location but as a qualifier to Aphek; the LXX supports the latter (Woudstra 1981, 206). This would not explain, however, why Lasharon is designated as having a king. Egyptian inscriptions dated to the sixteenth to thirteenth centuries suggest that Lasharon refers to an actual site (Gorg 1975, 98-99).

As noted earlier, **Madon** (v 19*a*; see 11:1, 12) could refer to the Horns of Hattin, west of the Sea of Galilee, or **Madon** might be a corruption of Maron located west of Hazor. If the former is correct, the king in 12:19 is Jobab (→ 11:1).

The destruction of **Hazor** (12:19*b*) is detailed in 11:1, 10-13 and documented in archaeological remains, which also indicate a gap between the end of occupation in the Late Bronze Age and the beginning of the Iron Age (Ben-Tor 2008, 5:1773).

The king of **Shimron Meron** (12:20*a*; see 11:1, 12) and the king of **Akshaph** (12:20*b*; see 11:1, 12) were among those summoned by Jabin, king of Hazor, as part of the northern coalition. Shimron Meron was located north of Megiddo in what would be the territory of Zebulun (19:15) and may be identified with Samsimuruna in the inscriptions of the Assyrian king Assurbanipal (Tur-Sinai 1959, 33-35). Akshaph was located on the opposite side of the Jezreel valley and was allotted to the tribe of Asher (19:25).

We are not told when the king of **Taanach** (12:21*a*) was defeated. The city was also located on the edge of the Jezreel valley, southeast of Megiddo. It had been destroyed by the Egyptians ca. 1468 B.C., then reoccupied on a more modest scale (Glock 1993, 4:1432). The king was defeated and his city allotted to the tribe of Manasseh and then to the Levites, but the Israelites were unable to dislodge the inhabitants of Taanach (17:11; Judg 1:27). There is evidence of destruction around 1125 B.C. (Glock 1993, 4:1432), which Boling believes may be due to the Israelites (1975, 116). By the time of Deborah, however, the city appears to be under Israelite control (Judg 5:19).

Like Taanach, we are not told when the king of **Megiddo** (Josh 12:21*b*) was defeated. After the main coastal route turns inland to avoid Mount Carmel, it passes through the Wadi 'Iron, then enters the Jezreel valley. Here sits the city of Megiddo, occupying one of the most strategic locations in the country. From ancient times to the modern era, armies have traveled this route, giving Megiddo a front row seat on history (Aharoni 1993, 3:1003). Also like Taanach, Megiddo was allotted to the Israelites but not occupied until later (17:11; Judg 1:27; 5:19). According to Shiloh and others, the archaeological evidence does not contradict the biblical account (1993, 3:1012-24; Ussishkin 1995, 241-67; Finkelstein 2008, 5:1944-50).

This is the first mention of **Kedesh** in Joshua (12:22*a*). We cannot be sure if it refers here to a site in upper Galilee, six miles northwest of Hazor, in the territory of the tribe of Naphtali (19:37; 20:7; 21:32; Judg 4:6; 1 Chr 6:76) (Aharoni 1993, 3:855-56), or to Tel Kedesh (in the Jezreel valley), midway between Taanach and Megiddo (see Judg 4:9, 11; 1 Chr 6:72) (Stern 1993b, 3:860). Joshua 15:23 appears to refer to a third Kedesh, located in the Negev. Since the preceding four sites and the one following are located in the Jezreel valley, it may be best to identify this with Tel Kedesh.

Jokneam in Carmel (12:22*b*; see 19:11; 21:34) refers to Tel Yoqne'am, located between Megiddo and Akshaph on the western edge of the Jezreel valley near Mount Carmel. The Late Bronze Age city "was destroyed in a conflagration that left debris more than 1 m deep" with a gap in time before it was reoccupied in the Iron Age (Ben-Tor 1993, 3:809).

The destruction of **Dor (in Naphoth Dor)** (12:23*a*; see 11:2) is recounted in 11:12, although the city continued to be controlled by non-Israelites (see 17:11-12; Judg 1:27). This agrees with what we learn from the Egyptian work, "The Report of Wenamun," dated around 1100 B.C., which describes Dor as controlled by the Sea Peoples (Lichtheim 2006, 2:224-30; Stern 1993, 1:357; Stern 2008, 5:1695-1703).

Woudstra suggests that **Goyim in Gilgal** (Josh 12:23*b*) may better be rendered Goyim in Galilee, as in the LXX and similar to what is found in Isa 9:1. He also suggests this might be another way of referring to Harosheth Haggoyim (Judg 4:2) (1981, 206).

With **Tirzah** (Josh 12:24*a*), the author relocates us from the northern part of the land to the hill country, just northeast of Shechem. According to Hess, this "signals completion of the list and a return of the people to their heartland" for it is from this region that the tribal allotment would take place (1996a, 228-29). According to the archaeological evidence, the Late Bronze Age city experienced destruction "which can be regarded as the result of the Israelite conquest" (de Vaux 1993, 2:433). Allotted to the tribe of Manasseh, it became the first capital of the northern kingdom of Israel (see 1 Kgs 14:17; 15:33). The author concludes his list with a total that exudes his gratitude, **thirty-one kings in all** (Josh 12:24*b*).

FROM THE TEXT

Howard astutely expressed the message of Josh 12: "He [God] would fulfill his promises, right down to every last village or town and every last border, passing atop this hill over here and descending through that valley over there" (1998a, 278). The specific detail in this and subsequent chapters underlines the point.

Yet a second point is just as important to the author: these remarkable events came about through the obedience of God's people. "Moses, as servant of the Lord, and Joshua, as obedient to all that Moses said, are obedient to God," writes Hess. "The covenanted blessings of inheritance become Israel's (chs. 13-19) because of their faithfulness to God through all the battles and because of the faithfulness of Moses and Joshua" (1996a, 221).

We have seen this synergistic pattern before, God graciously committing himself to his covenant people in words of promise on condition of their faithful obedience. We will see it again throughout the rest of Scripture. He always takes the initiative; we can do nothing except as he creates the possibility. Yet having graced us to the point where we can respond—having made us "response-able," God requires our response, that is, makes us responsible. The result is his blessing, "pressed down, shaken together and running over" (Luke 6:38). When he keeps a promise, it is kept down to the last detail—even to details invisible except in hindsight.

The gift of salvation is the perfect example. As promised, in this salvation he has reconciled us to himself in Christ. Through Christ he has also reconciled us to each other, breaking down every dividing wall of hostility. He has reconciled us to ourselves, providing the peace of Christ that passes understanding (see Phil 4:7). In a similar way, we are beginning to experience the reconciliation he has accomplished between ourselves and the natural world, a reconciliation to be culminated in the new heaven and the new earth. His salvation has permeated every square inch of our lives and of this world, "passing atop this hill over here and descending through that valley over there" (Howard 1998a, 278).

Excursus on Geographical Lists in Joshua 13—21

The geographical lists in Josh 13—21 have aroused considerable scholarly attention. Some believe these lists come from later sources, perhaps as late as the postexilic period. If the book is a largely fictionalized account of the "conquest" of Canaan, these lists serve as a reminder that "Israel, even Israel in exile, can occupy the land, if they follow the leadership examples of Joshua and Caleb" (Butler 1983, 141). Others believe the lists arose during the monarchy and reflect matters that would only become important after Israel had become a kingdom.

The evidence suggests, however, that these lists arose closer to the time of the actual conquest. Hess points out that they must be earlier than the writing of the book of Judges, since Judg 1 "presumes their existence" (1994a, 192). The boundary descriptions in these lists corresponds, says Hess, most closely to "the Late Bronze Age world of the Amarna correspondence" (ibid., 197). He points to "boundary descriptions resembling those in Joshua 13-19 in the international relations of the Hittites and the Syrian city-states of Carchemish and Ugarit" (ibid., 203).

An important theme of Josh 13—24 is the sanctuary at Shiloh (see 18:1-10), the first place in this new land where Yahweh chose to establish his name (see 9:27). If this material originated during the monarchy or later, it would be surprising since it emphasizes Shiloh, which was abandoned during the days of Samuel, while essentially ignoring Jerusalem, the most politically and theologically significant city during the monarchic and postexilic periods.

Some argue for a later origin of this material because they describe Joshua allotting cities he just destroyed (i.e., Jericho and Hazor). Even with these cities in ruins, however, the territory could still be allotted to tribes. As well, there seems little reason for a later author to assign Levitical cities to the territory of Dan (21:23-24), when even within the period of the conquest Dan left that territory to occupy another (19:47).

12:1-24

Kaufmann contends that "the boundary-lines in Josh have no *political* or *administrative* significance whatsoever. Political and administrative boundaries must be clear and unambiguous, which the boundaries of Josh are not" (1953, 14-15; emphasis original). Hess points out that lists that assign the same cities to different tribes would be of little value as official documents (1994a, 193).

The lists are not easy to follow. Some provide boundaries and towns (e.g., 18:11-28), others only list boundaries (e.g., chs 16, 17), still others give only towns (e.g., 19:1-8, 40-48), and others mix boundaries with towns (e.g., 19:10-16, 17-23, 24-31). While this variety could have arisen from the use of multiple official documents, it is better explained by the nature of the situation immediately after the conquest. With Israelite occupation and even knowledge of the land only spotty, preparing a complete account may have been impossible (Keil and Delitzsch 1978, 132). Each tribe receives an inheritance however the author may have chosen to describe it (Howard 1998a, 317).

These geographical lists were not given to bring Israel's history into line with its monarchic present or to give hope to its postexilic future. They served both a practical and an ideological purpose for the recently triumphant Israelites.

Hess points out that, practically speaking, such lists would have "discouraged competition between various groups by appealing to divinely ordained divisions" (1994a, 205). They provide the "legal data" that would support the tribes' claims to their territories and validate "God's faithfulness to them" (Howard 1998a, 322). As Hess points out, they provided each Israelite with "two types of identity: an affiliation with one tribe and an affiliation with a unity of various tribes" (1994a, 205).

These lists also served a deeper purpose, serving as an "ideological map" (Nelson 1997, 12), an early, yet idealistic portrayal of the ultimate goal, Israel's occupation of the promised land. Throughout, these chapters present the land as a "divine gift" (Hess 1996a, 47), mapping how Yahweh had kept his promise.

XIII. JOSHUA 13

BEHIND THE TEXT

Joshua 13 begins the second half of the book. Having conquered the land, Joshua now apportions it to the twelve tribes. The author presents this apportionment in two unequal halves, first describing the allotment that has already taken place, east of the Jordan, and then an extended description of the apportionment of land west of the Jordan. Many commentators have noted a sophisticated arrangement of this material. Howard (1998a, 294) supports the following chiastic arrangement:

  A 13:8-22   Transjordan for two and one-half tribes
    B 14:1-5   The principles of the division
      C 14:6-15   Beginning: Caleb's inheritance
        D 15:1—17:18   The lot for Judah and Joseph
          E 18:1-10   The Tent of Meeting taken to Shiloh and the apportioning of the land
        D' 18:11—19:48   The lot for the seven remaining tribes
      C' 19:49-51   Ending: Joshua's inheritance
    B' 20:1-6   God's fourth initiative: designating cities of refuge
  A' 20:7—21:42   Cities of refuge and levitical cities

This outline is at its most convincing in the center, where it reveals how the author balanced Caleb's inheritance with Joshua's (C with C'), the allotment for Judah and Joseph balanced by what is given to the seven remaining tribes, and the focus on Shiloh (D with D'). The outer sections (A, B, A', B') are less convincing.

Dorsey provides a better alternative, for he not only captures the balanced sections mentioned above but also points out other examples of symmetry:

a introduction (13:1-7)
- Yahweh's challenge to Joshua, when he is old, to divide the land
- theme: <u>the land that remains</u>—whose inhabitants Yahweh will drive out

b Transjordanian tribes (13:8-33)
- their allotments outside of Canaan

c Levites (14:1-5)
- They will have no territory, only towns in other tribes

d personal allotment for <u>hero of Kadesh</u>: Caleb (14:6-15)

e non-Rachel tribal allotment: <u>Judah</u> (15:1-63)

f Rachel tribal allotment: <u>Joseph</u> (16:1—17:18)

g CENTER: allotment at Shiloh: seven tribes receive land by Yahweh's lot (18:1-10)

f' Rachel tribal allotment: Benjamin—next to <u>Joseph</u> (18:11-28)

e' non-Rachel tribal allotments: Simeon (inside <u>Judah</u>) and others (19:1-48)

d' personal allotment for <u>hero of Kadesh</u>: Joshua (19:49-50)
- conclusion of Shiloh allotments (19:51-52)

c' Levites (20:1—21:45)
- their towns in other tribes and their cities of refuge

b' Transjordanian tribes (22:1-34)
- their return to their allotments outside of Canaan, and their memorial altar to commemorate their share with the tribes in Canaan

a' conclusion (23:1—24:22)
- Joshua's closing challenge to Israel, when he is old
- theme: <u>the land that remains</u>—whose inhabitants Yahweh will drive out. (1999, 94-95)

According to Dorsey, this structure emphasizes the need to complete the conquest, the unity of all Israel (by emphasizing the inclusion of the Transjordan tribes), and "the central role played by Yahweh in the allotment of the land to the tribes" at Shiloh (ibid.).

Chapter 13 divides unequally into two parts, the first seven verses introducing the entire second half of the book and vv 8-33 providing details on the allotment of the land east of the Jordan.

IN THE TEXT

A. Introduction to Land Remaining (13:1-7)

■ I The chapter opens with a reference to Joshua's advanced age. Nelson treats the appearance of an identical reference in 23:1 as evidence for later editing. "Joshua's age is an appropriate motive for his final words of chapter 23," he writes, "but less germane to the context of land division" (1997, 164). A more likely explanation sees the author intentionally repeating Joshua's advanced age at the beginning and end of this section because the detail is appropriate in both places. Here it allows the reader to understand that while time is running out for Joshua, work remains to be done, namely, the allotment of the land. It also explains a change in strategy. When Joshua was younger, he led the troops to conquer. Now that the initial victories have been won, a new strategy begins, one that does not involve the aging Joshua as commander but that entrusts the occupation of the land to each individual tribe. This they accomplish with varying degrees of success throughout Judges, then as a nation under their kings. Butler correctly observes the "theological tension" in this book, "namely life in the Land of Promise *shared* with the inhabitants of the land" (1983, 147, emphasis original).

We cannot say how old Joshua was at this time. The same Hebrew expression is used of Abraham when he was well over one hundred (Gen 24:1) and of David when he was not yet seventy (1 Kgs 1:1). According to the rabbis, Joshua was eighty-three when he assumed the leadership of Israel and ruled for twenty-eight years (see Schatz 2013, 32-34). Schatz argues instead that Joshua was nineteen at the time of the exodus, and fifty-nine when he began to rule. According to Hess, Joshua was nearing one hundred and ten at this juncture in the conquest, the age at which he died (24:29) (1996a, 229).

God's command to Joshua at the beginning of the second half of the book is reminiscent of the command at the book's opening (see 1:2-9). There is still territory to be taken, but given Joshua's age, the former strategy must give way to a new one. The command begins in 13:1 and concludes in v 7, with vv 2-6 forming an extended parenthesis that defines more fully the last clause of v 1, the land still to be possessed (Keil and Delitzsch 1978, 133). This extended parenthesis is composed of four sections, the first describing the southern and northern extent of the land (v 2), the second referring to the territory in the south (vv 3-4*a*), the third to the Canaanite region (v 4*b*), and the fourth to the northern region (v 5).

■ **2** This land extended from the land of the **Philistines** along the coast in the southern part of the country to the extreme northeast, the land of the **Geshurites** (see v 13) (Hess 1996a, 230). Placing the Geshurites in the northeast makes the most sense given their mention in v 13. Several commentators locate them instead in southern Palestine, some citing 1 Sam 27:8. Presumably these commentators see the author moving in Josh 14:2-5 in a south to north direction (Woudstra 1981, 210; Howard 1998a, 298; Butler 1983, 148; Keil and Delitzsch 1978, 135; Pitkänen 2010, 269; Nelson 1997, 166).

■ **3** The **Shihor River on the east of Egypt** is unknown. While **Shihor** describes the Nile in Isa 23:3 and Jer 2:18, here it refers to a river east of, not in Egypt (Howard 1998a, 298). It could refer to a northeastern branch of the Nile Delta or to the Brook of Egypt, south of Gaza (Betz 1992, 5:1212; the latter identification is the conclusion of Na'aman 1980, 95-109).

Also unconquered are the five cities of the Philistines, **Gaza, Ashdod, Ashkelon, Gath and Ekron**. The Philistines arrived in Canaan around 1200 B.C., part of the influx of Sea Peoples from Crete and elsewhere. Each city was governed by a ruler known as a *seren*, rather than elders or a king; this is the first use of this distinctive word in the OT (Hess 1996a, 230). The Philistines occupied territory that had belonged to the **Avvites**, mentioned elsewhere as having been destroyed by the Caphtorites (Deut 2:23). Some identify the Avvites as Canaanites (Woudstra 1981, 210), others as either Hivites or Hyksos (McGarry 1992, 1:531-32).

Although **on the south** is included in v 4, it seems to fit better with the content of v 3, which describes territory in the southern part of the country. The NJB translates vv 3*b*-4 this way:

> The five rulers of the Philistines have their seats at Gaza, Ashdod, Ashkelon, Gath and Ekron, respectively; the Avvites are in the south. The entire territory of the Canaanites, and Mearah which belongs to the Sidonians, as far as Aphekah and as far as the frontier of the Amorites.

■ **4** With v 4 we move northward up the coast to describe **the land of the Canaanites**, including the territory of Sidon and beyond. The land of the **Sidonians** was the "entire coastal region that borders Philistia at Aphek in the south and extends north to the border of the Gebalites" (Hess 1996a, 231). Whether we translate the Hebrew phrase **from Arah** or "and Mearah" (NASB, NRSV), we know of no cities by either name. Keil and Delitzsch translate this term as "cave" and suggest it refers to the cave of Jezzon east of Sidon (1978, 137-38).

Amorites usually refers to Canaanite people in general, but this does not seem to fit here. Hess conjectures that **Amorites** refers to the kingdom of Amurru, which existed only in the Late Bronze Age (1550-1200 B.C.) north of Sidon near Byblos (1996a, 231).

■ **5** **Byblos** refers to the ancient city by that name, twenty miles north of modern Beirut. Pitkänen (2010, 270) believes Byblos is where the Egyptian story of Wenamun takes place.

The description of unoccupied territory continues east, including **all Lebanon to the east, from Baal Gad below Mount Hermon to Lebo Hamath**, essentially a broad swath of land in what is now Lebanon and Syria.

■ **6-7** God promised that he himself (emphatic in the Hebrew) would give this land to Israel. By implication, he will drive out *all* Israel's enemies, not just those in the north. Neither Joshua's advanced age nor any other obstacle can prevent it. The important thing is that this land should be apportioned to the nine and a half tribes, those who have not yet received their allotment. The NIV obscures the author's emphasis by making it seem that the land to be apportioned is what has been specifically mentioned in v 6; the Hebrew contains a strong term at the beginning of v 7, highlighting what follows. This interpretation is captured well by the NJB:

> All who live in the highlands from the Lebanon to Misrephoth in the west—all the Sidonians—I myself shall dispossess before the Israelites. All you have to do is to distribute the territory as a heritage for the Israelites as I have ordered you. The time has come to divide this territory as a heritage between the nine tribes and the half-tribe of Manasseh: from the Jordan as far as the Great Sea in the west, you must give it them; the Great Sea will be their limit.

13:5-7

B. Land Remaining East of Jordan (13:8-33)

1. Boundaries (13:8-14)

Although we are led to expect that the apportionment for the nine and a half tribes will begin immediately, the author turns next to the allotment for the two and a half tribes in the Transjordan. This detour not only builds the reader's sense of anticipation but also serves at least six other purposes: first, it provides the greatest detail to date of the Transjordan boundaries; and second, these verses signal Israel's unity, a theme emphasized repeatedly in the book. Third, these verses demonstrate Joshua's leadership. He not only shows obedience by following Moses' instruction but also acts as Moses' successor.

A fourth purpose for these verses is to anticipate the "landless" state of the Levites (see vv 14, 33); and fifth, they warn that all is not as it should be (Howard 1998a, 307). Sixth, these verses provide the model for what should follow: as the Transjordan tribes "took their inheritance," that is, took possession of it, the western tribes should do the same (ibid., 308). Although the NIV translates, "had received the inheritance" (v 8), Howard points out, "Not once is it said that any of the tribes west of the Jordan took (*lqḥ*) their lands. The focus in the later chapters is on God's and Joshua's *giving* of the land and their *possessing* it—and, sometimes, on the fact that the tribes did *not* dispossess the land's inhabitants" (ibid., emphasis original).

■ **8** Although v 8 clearly begins a new section, it is closely tied to what precedes, beginning (literally) ***with it****. It* here refers to the half-tribe of Manasseh west of the Jordan; the awkwardness may intentionally emphasize the unity of this tribe, in spite of its being split into two parts. This seems more likely than Butler's suggestion of a "long history of textual corruption" (1983, 155). Moses is referred to by name twice; once he is described as **servant of the Lord**. The repetition of Moses by name (rendered only once in the NIV and NLT) and using this description connects these verses to the earlier passages in the Pentateuch that describe this allotment. They also connect this chapter with Josh 1 where Moses is described the same way (1:1, 2, 7, 13, 15) and where the Transjordan tribes also come into focus (1:12-18). This strengthens the argument that ch 13 begins part two of Joshua.

■ **9-14** The Transjordan allotment begins with a general description, somewhat similar to 12:2-5, including the perspective from south to north. Note that this survey initially includes **the territory of the people of Geshur and Maakah** (v 11), but then specifies that these people were not driven out (v 13). After the general description comes the first of two statements about Levites (v 14). Here it specifies that they would not receive an allotment of land because, as promised, God would provide for them through **the food offerings presented to the Lord** (v 14), literally, ***fires of Yahweh***. God would provide for the Levites, but indirectly, through the other tribes, as they faithfully brought offerings to the sanctuary from what God had given them.

2. Inheritance of Reubenites (13:15-23)

■ **15-23** This general description is followed by specific tribal allotments (vv 15-31), beginning with the Reubenites (vv 15-23). Reuben was Jacob's firstborn, the son of Leah. He lost his preeminence because he slept with his father's concubine, Bilhah (see Gen 35:22; 49:3-4). The reader notes Reuben's declining importance in Jacob's blessing and Judah's increase (Gen 49:8-12), including the fact that Judah, rather than Reuben, leads the march when the Israelites travel through the wilderness (Num 2:3). Reuben's fortunes continue to decline. By the ninth century, no mention is made of Reuben in the Mesha inscription, the account of Moab's victory over the territory in the Transjordan the Reubenites once occupied (Woudstra 1981, 218).

In the original, the phrase ***clan by clan*** appears in Josh 13:23 and in the introductory statement for each tribe's allotment on both sides of the Jordan. Howard rightly notes that this shows careful attention to obey each detail of the Mosaic law (1998a, 320). Reuben's allotment is essentially the southern portion of the territory, which had been controlled by Sihon, king of the Amorites. Although v 21 speaks of the Reubenites possessing **the entire realm** of Sihon, Gad's territory included **the rest of the realm of Sihon** (v 27). One could postulate that Gad's territory was inside Reuben's, or that the author contradicts himself. It seems most likely that the "all" (**entire**) in v 21 should be understood as all the rest.

Verse 21 speaks of the Midianite chiefs whom the Israelites defeated along with Sihon. Only here and in Num 31:8 do we learn their names. Numbers 31 also speaks of the Israelites killing Balaam, although Balaam is not described there as one **who practiced divination** (v 22). Balaam's involvement with Israel is described in Num 22—24, with additional references in Deut 23:4-5; Josh 24:9-10; Neh 13:2; and Mic 6:5. He is mentioned here for more than historical reasons, but likely to warn against divination (see Woudstra 1981, 220) and encourage the Israelites, who faced a variety of temptations while living among the nations.

3. Inheritance of the Gadites (13:24-28)

■ **24-28** Verses 24-28 describe the inheritance of the Gadites, those descended from Jacob's seventh son, born to him from Zilpah, maidservant to Leah (Gen 30:10-11). Gad inherited the rest of Sihon's former territory to the north of Reuben's land and below the half-tribe of Manasseh. Some scholars believe that at least a portion of Gad's territory was located within Reuben's, based on the appearance of **Aroer** (Josh 13:25), a town also mentioned in v 16 as belonging to Reuben. The Aroer in v 16, however, seems to be a different town, since the one mentioned in v 25 is identified as being near Rabbah. Apparently, three different towns were named Aroer in the OT: one in Reuben's territory (see 12:2; 13:9, 16), one in Gad's (see 13:25; Judg 11:33), and one in Judah's allotment (see 1 Sam 30:28) (Woudstra 1981, 216 n. 4).

According to Josh 13:25, Gad received a portion of Ammonite territory, while v 10 makes Ammonite land the border for God's people. Butler explains that the Jabbok River was the boundary between Ammon and Israel, although the Ammonites controlled their capital city of Rabbah, which was west of the Jabbok. Only in David's day was Rabbah finally captured (2 Sam 12:26) (1983, 165). Gadite territory extended north to the southern end of **the Sea of Galilee** (Josh 13:27). The Hebrew of v 27*b* (enclosed by parentheses in the NIV) is less than clear, but the NABRE seems to capture it well: "with the bank of the Jordan to the southeastern tip of the Sea of Chinnereth."

4. Inheritance of the Half-tribe of Manasseh (13:29-31)

■ **29-31** Next comes the allotment to the half-tribe of Manasseh, described in greater brevity than the two allotments preceding. Pitkänen suggests something has dropped out (2010, 274), but this seems unlikely, given that the same basic pattern of introduction (v 29), territory (vv 30-31*a*), and summary (v 31*b*) are present. Manasseh was the eldest son of Joseph, Jacob's son through

Rachel (Gen 41:50-51). Jacob adopted both of Joseph's sons, Ephraim and Manasseh, as his own (Gen 48).

Half of the tribe of Manasseh inherited on the east of the Jordan and half inherited on the west. The land on the east bank corresponded to the former territory of Og, king of Bashan. Jair was an important clan in the tribe of Manasseh and had already established sixty settlements there.

This summary does differ from the others in one respect: instead of the phrase, "These towns and their villages were the inheritance of . . ." (Josh 13:23, 28), it speaks of **the descendants of Makir son of Manasseh** (v 31). Although Makir was a clan within the tribe of Manasseh, here Makir refers to the whole tribe, as in 17:3 and Judg 5:14.

5. Summary of Transjordan Allotment (13:32-33)

■ **32-33** The Transjordan allotment is summarized in Josh 13:32-33, once again indicating the primary role of Moses (see v 8) and the lack of an allotment for the Levites (see v 14). This time, however, it is **Yahweh** who is the Levites' portion (v 33), rather than the *fires of Yahweh* (v 14).

FROM THE TEXT

God did not implement his redemptive plan all at once, but gradually, a truth clearly demonstrated in Josh 13. The conquest and allotment of the land took decades, from the battles with Sihon and Og, to the conquest of the land on the west. The conquest begun by Moses and advanced by Joshua would reach its fullest extent under David and Solomon. When the Israelites crossed the Jordan, the noncombatants of the Transjordan tribes remained behind while their soldiers accompanied their brothers, remaining until the fighting ended. Only then would they learn the actual boundaries of their land and only then could they return to possess it.

We see this gradual approach in the opening verse of this chapter. Joshua's job was first to fight and conquer the enemy; then, when he was too old to fight, Joshua was instructed to begin his other job, that of allotting the land. Through this allotment, the conquest would continue and reach its culmination.

God's gradual approach can also be seen in his dealings with the Levites. Unlike the other tribes, they would not be given their own territory but would have to depend upon God. He would not supply them directly; their livelihood would come from the righteousness of the Israelites. Faithful tithing and regular sacrifices from the other Israelites put food on Levitical tables. God appears to be teaching his people of their need for interdependence (2 Cor 8:14-15).

We see plenty of examples of God's gradual work. He called a seventy-five-year-old Abram but waited a quarter century before giving him the promised son. He did not rescue the Israelites from Egypt immediately but allowed them to languish in captivity for centuries. Nor did he liberate them with one decisive blow, but through a succession of celestial smackdowns with Pharaoh and the Egyptian gods.

He first allowed people to relate to him through the Mosaic law, later clarifying that this Law pointed to something ahead. He did not reveal the Messiah all at once, but only in the "fullness of time." Hebrews 11 is replete with examples of those who participated in God's gradual approach, those who lived by faith until Jesus came.

The kingdom of God itself did not arrive all at once. Promised in the OT and consummated in Jesus, it awaits its ultimate fulfillment at Christ's return. We all experience the gradual nature of God's redemptive plan, with our spiritual formation happening progressively through grace. Although delivered at once from the penalty of sin, deliverance from the power of sin usually comes gradually. God has allotted our "territory"—freedom from the power of sin, setting this before us as an attainable goal.

One reason God chooses to work gradually is because of those with whom he works. While created in his image, humans are also significantly affected by sin's curse. As the psalmist observed, "He remembers that we are dust" (Ps 103:14). Yet God is able to accomplish great things through our weakness. In fact, in our weakness, he manifests his strength (see 2 Cor 12:9). After Joshua grew aged, God found other ways to use him to bring about the conquest, inspiring the tribes to continue by allotting land not yet controlled by Israel and eventually, by giving them a leader like David.

Another reason God may employ this gradual strategy is his desire to remind us how much we depend upon him. Living in this "in-between" time is not easy, but it does make clear our weakness and teaches us to trust in him. So much of what God does among us is meant to strengthen our faith, for he knows that without faith we cannot have a relationship with him. How else could we follow such a promise-making God? Calvin captures this well when he summarizes God's command:

> Only do what is thy duty in the distribution of the land; nor let that which the enemy still hold [sic] securely be exempted from the lot; for it will be my care to fulfil what I have promised. Hence let us learn in undertaking any business, so to depend on the lips of God as that no doubt can delay us. It is not ours, indeed, to fabricate vain hopes for ourselves; but when our confidence is founded on the Lord, let us only obey his commands, and there is no reason to fear that the event will disappoint us. (Calvin n.d., *Joshua*, 168)

We must walk by faith if we are to experience the ultimate reconciliation God has in mind. His gradual work will eventuate in the ultimate fulfillment of his plan. Joshua 13 provides a reminder that while we are engaged in taking the territory allotted to us, we look forward to the day when all the "land" is under his control.

XIV. JOSHUA 14

BEHIND THE TEXT

Joshua 14 follows naturally after ch 11. The intervening chapters provide summaries, but little new action. With ch 14, however, we take up the allotment in earnest. This is how the chapter begins (vv 1-5), although we soon pause again to settle some unfinished business between Caleb and Joshua, the only two survivors from the exodus generation (vv 6-15). This conversation is more than a pause, however, but illustrates a main theme of the book: God's faithfulness to keep his promises to those who live by faith. Joshua 14 introduces the allotment of the western land, beginning with how God kept his promise to faithful Caleb.

IN THE TEXT

A. Introduction to the Division of the Land West of the Jordan (14:1-5)

1. Introduction (14:1)

■ 1 According to Num 34:16-29, God instructed Moses how to allot the land west of the Jordan. We are even told there the names of the tribal leaders; Caleb is mentioned first as a leader of the tribe of Judah. Although the names are not provided here, Josh 14:1-5 essentially mirrors the instructions in Num 34. Numbers refers to these tribal leaders as princes, while Joshua calls them *the heads of the fathers of the tribes of the sons of Israel* (see Howard 1998a, 324 n. 71). As required in the Numbers passage, Eleazar the priest was present at the allotment of the land. The son and successor of Aaron, Eleazar was present at Joshua's commissioning (Num 27:18-23) and was to guide Joshua using the sacred lots, the Urim and Thummim (vv 19-22). This is the first time we meet Eleazar in Joshua. Aaron had other sons; two were killed because they offered "strange fire" (Lev 10:1 KJV, NASB) and a fourth, Ithamar, is only mentioned in Exodus and Numbers and not again until 1 Chr 24:3-5. That Eleazar is to be present at the allotment indicates the allotment is more than a political act, but one of profound religious significance. His mention prior to Joshua accentuates this point (Howard 1998a, 324; Woudstra 1981, 225).

Joshua is referred to as the **son of Nun**, perhaps because he is referred to this way in Num 34:17, but possibly to highlight the significance of this occasion (Howard 1998a, 324). This is the first of four times the phrase **land of Canaan** appears in Joshua (21:2; 22:9, 10), each time referring to land on the western side of Jordan. It has this meaning in Num 34:29 and again in Num 35:14, where it is specifically distinguished from the land east of the Jordan. The term **Canaan** is mentioned elsewhere in Joshua (5:12; 22:32) with this extensive meaning but also with a more limited scope (see 13:3-4) (Butler 1983, 171).

A key word in this chapter is the Hebrew term *n-ḥ-l*, rendered in its verbal form as **received as an inheritance** and **allotted**. As a noun it is translated as **inheritance** (twice in 14:3, 9, 13, 14 [KJV, NASB]) or **inheritances** (v 2). According to Butler, the noun is the "key term which holds the final half of the book of Joshua together" (1983, 171). Howard points out that this root, implying a lasting claim to property, is used more times in Joshua than in any other OT book, and most of those uses are found from ch 12 on. He contends the primary referent is the possession of the tribes, whether those east of the Jordan (13:8, 23, 28) or west (13:7; 14:2), whether Judah (15:20), Ephraim and Manasseh (16:5, 8, 9; 17:14), or the remaining seven tribes (referred to nineteen times in chs 18—19).

Howard points out that Hebrew has another term for "inherit," *y-r-š*, but this focuses more on the act of taking possession while *n-ḥ-l* "focuses somewhat more on the measuring and demarcating of the boundaries of the inheritance" (1998a, 302-4). The psalmist sang about the inheritance of the land: "The boundary lines have fallen for me in pleasant places; surely I have a delightful inheritance [*n-ḥ-l*]" (Ps 16:6) (see Boling and Wright 1982, 353).

2. Assignment by Lot to Nine and a Half Tribes (14:2)

■ **2** The land was **assigned by lot** to the nine and a half tribes west of the Jordan as Yahweh had **commanded by the hand of Moses.** This is the first mention of the lot in the book of Joshua, although its use is implied in the Achan affair (7:14-18). It appears repeatedly from this point on (see 15:1; 16:1; 17:1, 14, 17; 18:6, 8, 10, 11 [twice]; 19:1, 10, 17, 24, 32, 40, 51; 21:4 [twice], 5, 6, 8, 10, 20, 40).

One way for Israel to determine God's will was through the use of the sacred dice contained within the ephod worn by the high priest. Given the nature of the allotment, matching tribe with territory, some suggest the lot involved two containers, one containing the name of the tribe, the other a description of the territory (Keil and Delitzsch 1978, 147). Allotment by divination was understood to mean that the land was apportioned by Yahweh himself. To be divided by Joshua's decision or democratic vote might signal it was Israel's land or at least Israel's decision how to apportion it. Apportionment by sacred lot made clear this was God's land divided by God's hand, as he had promised beforehand. This is also the implication of the presence at the allotment ceremony of the high priest, Eleazar.

The land appears to be apportioned to the nine and a half tribes on this occasion at Gilgal, although Josh 18 describes the tribes receiving their land at Shiloh. Various attempts have been proposed to reconcile these passages. Perhaps all that took place at Gilgal was the granting of Caleb's request, with the full tribal allotment taking place at Shiloh (see Pitkänen 2010, 277, 279). This does not explain, however, why ch 18 opens with the tribes of Judah, Ephraim, and Manasseh having already received their land. If they did not get it at Gilgal, but have it by Shiloh, when did their apportionment occur? It seems most likely that the land was distributed among the nine and a half tribes at Gilgal, but only the tribes of Judah, Ephraim, and Manasseh actually took possession. Chapters 18 and 19 then describe a subsequent distribution to those tribes that had failed to act.

3. Previous Allotment to Two and a Half Tribes and Explanation of How There Came to Be Twelve Tribes (14:3-4)

■ **3-4** Verses 3-4 review information provided earlier: the Transjordan tribes had already been given their land (v 3*a*); the Levites did not receive their own allotment (v 3*b*); and Joseph's two sons each received territory (v 4*a*). Reminding the reader of these facts serves several purposes. First, it allays any concerns that the Levites will unfairly benefit from Eleazar's superintendence of the process. Second, the additional explanation heightens the solemnity of the allotment and accentuates Israel's obedience to Yahweh and Moses. Third, and most important, this information celebrates the unity of God's people, a theme mentioned several times throughout this book (see 3:7, 17; 4:14; 7:23, 24, 25; 8:21, 24; 10:29; 23:2).

The Levites would not be forgotten, for in addition to receiving the sacred offerings (13:14), they would also be given towns and pastureland (14:4*b*; see ch 21). The Hebrew of 14:4*b* literally reads **they did not give,** but who are **they?** Some suggest **they** are the tribes of Joseph, mentioned in v 4*a*, as implied in the NASB: "For the sons of Joseph were two tribes, Manasseh and Ephraim, and they did not give a portion to the Levites in the land." Others treat the verb as passive: "For the people of Joseph were two tribes, Manasseh and Ephraim. And no portion was given to the Levites in the land" (ESV). It seems more likely that the pronoun (**they**) refers to Eleazar, Joshua, and the tribal leaders of v 1.

4. Allotment of Land as Commanded to Moses (14:5)

■ **5** This summary concludes by reasserting an important truth: Israel had conducted this allotment in obedience to Yahweh, **just as the LORD had commanded Moses.**

B. Hebron Given to Caleb (14:6-15)

1. Caleb Requests Land from Joshua (14:6-12)

It appears that Judah is about to be given its land. We are not surprised to see Judah go first. Although not the firstborn, Judah had by this time become the largest and among the most significant of the twelve tribes. The narrative abruptly turns, however, from the whole tribe of Judah to one man within the tribe, Caleb. This episode may have taken place earlier, during the activity of the first twelve chapters. Note its location at Gilgal (an early headquarters for Israel), as well as Caleb's approach to Joshua, rather than Eleazar, Joshua, and the tribal elders (see v 1). If it did occur earlier, the author may have mentioned it here to balance the personal allotment to Joshua (→ Behind the Text for ch 13 for Dorsey's chiastic outline; see 19:49-50). The author may have had another reason for interrupting his account of the allotment with this story, to show how God keeps his promises to individuals as well as to the nation. Caleb is almost certainly being held up here as an example for how all Israel should take possession of the land they would soon receive.

There are four accounts of the taking of Hebron and its environs: 10:36, where it is attributed to Joshua; here, where it is assumed that Caleb removes the Anakim; in 15:13-19, where Caleb is explicitly described as doing so; and Judg 1:9-15, where Caleb does this along with the men of Judah. These accounts are not necessarily contradictory but may be four ways of describing the same conquest. Another possibility is that the region actually had to be taken more than once, since the inhabitants may have fled an initial assault (perhaps the one described in 10:36), then returned after the Israelites had turned to conquer other territory.

Nelson has identified five episodes in chs 14—21 where someone requests and is given a specific plot of land as an inheritance. He calls these land grant narratives, stories told about special apportionments in order to "solve problems and disputes" (1997, 189). This is the first of the five, followed by Aksah (15:18-19), the daughters of Zelophehad (17:3-6), Joseph (17:14-18), and the Levites (21:1-3). As Pitkänen notes, some of this land had been promised earlier (e.g., Caleb, the daughters of Zelophehad, the Levites), while others represent a new request (e.g., Aksah) (2010, 277). These accounts usually contain a confrontation that establishes the setting and characters (e.g., 14:6a), followed by the presentation of the suppliant's case and request (14:6b-12). This case may contain a flashback to Moses (e.g., 14:6-9; 17:4). The land is then granted (e.g., 14:13), sometimes with a reference to a command from Yahweh (missing from this story but see 17:4b; 21:3), followed by a summary of the resolution (e.g., 14:14-15) (see Nelson 1997, 177-78, and helpful summaries by Howard 1998a, 327, and Pitkänen 2010, 277).

■ **6** Caleb is described here as the **son of Jephunneh the Kenizzite**. All the Bible tells us about Jephunneh is that he is Caleb's father and a Kenizzite. We are not sure whether this means he was always an Israelite or whether he or his ancestors originally had been part of a non-Israelite group (see Gen 15:19). For Pitkänen, "It clearly seems that we have the assimilation of a non-Israelite into the tribe of Judah" (2010, 280). Caleb's name means dog, a name found in other cultures (Crawford 2004, 20-27), but not among Israelites. If there was assimilation of a foreign group, it would likely have happened prior to Caleb, since Caleb is already a leader in the tribe of Judah just after the Israelites leave Egypt (see Num 13:6). Others believe that **Kenizzite** in Josh 14:6 refers to descendants of a certain Kenaz from the tribe of Judah. Howard points out that Caleb's brother, Othniel, is described as the "son of Kenaz" (15:17) (1998a, 327). As well, Caleb's grandson was named Kenaz (see 1 Chr 4:15).

Caleb's forcefulness is seen in the first words he speaks on this occasion. The pronoun **you** in **You know** is emphatic in the Hebrew. He reminds Joshua what the two of them know—the two of them alone among all those present on this occasion—that God had promised this land to Caleb. He also bases his claim on the authority of Moses, whom he describes as **the man of God** (v 6*b*) and "the servant of the LORD" (v 7). Caleb was referring to the events surrounding the report of the twelve spies (see Num 13—14), events that occurred at Kadesh Barnea in the second year after the exodus, forty-five years earlier (see Josh 14:7, 10).

There were two faithful spies that day, Caleb and Joshua, a point briefly touched on in Caleb's speech (**you and me**). Caleb focused on his own role, for it was this role that gained him the divine promise of land.

■ **7** On that occasion he reported *just as it was in my heart*. This may refer to his honesty (see NJB, NLT, NRSV, Butler 1983, 168), but given the bravado of the rest of this speech, more likely refers to his courage (**according to my convictions** [v 7]; "forthright" [NJPS]; "exactly what I thought" [Boling and Wright 1982, 351]; "frank" [NABRE]).

■ **8** Caleb contrasts the fortitude that prompted his report to the fear fostered by the reports of the ten spies, a report that **made the hearts of the people melt in fear**. Caleb claims to have **followed the LORD my God wholeheartedly**, literally, *but I myself, I completely filled myself after Yahweh my God*. This idiom, which beautifully illustrates the entire consecration that is to be the lived experience of each Christian, occurs numerous times within the OT, many of them referring to Caleb (see Num 14:24; 32:11-12; Deut 1:36; Josh 14:8, 9, 14; 1 Kgs 11:6).

■ **9** In consequence of Caleb's courageous faith, Moses swore an oath to give this land to Caleb and his descendants **forever** (Josh 14:9). No such oath is recorded in Num 14:24, although much of Josh 14:9 echoes Deut 1:36.

■ **10** His actual request, which starts in Josh 14:10, begins with an attention-getting Hebrew word, *'attâ*, often translated **now,** followed by another attention-grabber, **behold** (*hinnēh*). A second *'attâ* occurs later in the same verse. Caleb has a point and is not afraid to make it. God kept him alive for a long time so that Moses' promise could be fulfilled. Caleb will bring that promise to fulfillment, if Joshua will give him the chance.

■ **11** Although he is eighty-five, he sets aside the obstacle of age by claiming to be just as strong as ever. The Hebrew phrase, rendered by the NIV as **to go out to battle**, is literally, *for battle, to go out, and to come in.* Some translations, such as the NIV, treat the whole phrase as referring to warfare. The phrase *to go out and to come in* is used in 1 Sam 29:6 when Achish tells David how pleased he would be "to have you serve with me in the army." This interpretation also fits the combat context of battle with the Anakites. On the other hand, the phrase could refer to "goings and comings" (see ASV, ESV, NASB, NJB, NRSV), "activity" (NJPS), or "travel" (NLT). Butler notes this phrase is used for daily activities in 2 Kgs 11:8; 19:27 (1983, 168). Either Caleb has pronounced himself fit for battle, or fit for any activity, including battle.

■ **12** Verse 12 begins with yet another *'attâ*—**now**. This feisty octogenarian requests **this hill country**, then refers to its current inhabitants, **the Anakites**. According to Boling and Wright, the Anakites are "'pre-Philistine' Sea Peoples" (1982, 388). Calling the territory **this hill country** does not mean Joshua and Caleb are currently in that location (contra Nelson 1997, 178). Joshua 1:4 refers to "this Lebanon," though the speaker was far from Lebanon (→ 1:4). The use of the demonstrative pronoun **this** is likely intended to emphasize this as the land that had been promised to Caleb. **You yourself heard**, says Caleb to Joshua, **that the Anakites were** living **there** in **large and fortified** cities.

Mentioning giants may not seem the most promising strategy to convince someone to give you land, especially if you are eighty-five years old. Caleb may have been pointing out that **the Anakites** pose a very real threat to the Israelites, one requiring immediate attention, which he was prepared to provide. Or he may have been making clear that he is fully aware of the dangers ahead but still wants to proceed. Most likely, Caleb was reminding Joshua that, from the beginning, defeating the Anakites symbolized the conquest of the entire land (→ 11:21-22).

The author intends Caleb to illustrate how Israel should possess the land, while Caleb's opponents illustrate all of Canaan's inhabitants. Caleb knows he will not win this battle on his own strength, but requires the help of Yahweh. The NIV captures the meaning of the Hebrew expression—**but, the LORD helping me, I will drive them out**—implying hope in the face of difficulty (see Gen 16:2; Num 22:6, 11; 23:3; 1 Sam 6:5; Jer 20:11; see Keil and Delitzsch 1978, 150). As Boling and Wright express it, "This was the one completely uncontrollable, yet trustworthy variable. Everything turns upon Yahweh's faithfulness, justice, and compassion toward his covenant-partners" (1982, 357).

2. Joshua Grants Caleb's Request (14:13-15)

■ **13** Joshua granted Caleb's request but not before blessing him (Josh 14:13). This is only the second instance of blessing in the book (8:33-34) and the first time blessing is directed to an individual. Joshua no doubt blessed Caleb's efforts, but also affirmed Caleb's intent. Joshua **blessed Caleb** for the faith and courage that motivated his request. In this blessing, Joshua affirmed that this same faith and courage should characterize all of God's people as they take the land. Some have seen in 14:13 a constraint being imposed by Joshua on Caleb's aspirations. The latter claimed to have been promised all the land he walked on (v 9) and requested the "hill country" (v 12), but was only given **Hebron** (v 13) (Nelson 1997, 179). Such a reading contradicts the tone of the passage, which celebrates Caleb's aspirations. More likely, this is an example of particularization: Caleb was given the whole territory, of which **Hebron** was the chief city (Keil and Delitzsch 1978, 150). The other passages that describe Caleb's conquest (15:13-19; Judg 1:9-15) also extend his victory outside Hebron.

■ 14 Hebron belonged to Caleb's family **ever since**, literally, *until this day*, a phrase used sixteen times in Joshua. Caleb gained this territory, the author reminds us, because **he followed the LORD, the God of Israel, wholeheartedly**, using the same idiom as earlier (see vv 8, 9). Its threefold mention in this chapter points to one of the story's main themes: wholehearted obedience.

■ 15 The former name of Hebron is included, perhaps to highlight its capture from the ferocious and feared former inhabitants. The final sentence in the chapter is, literally understood, untrue, since the book describes further battles (see 19:47). It may be better taken either as a reference to the fact that the major battles were over or to mark the end of a significant period in the life of God's people (Hall 2010, 193; see Josh 11:23; 14:15; Judg 3:11, 30; 5:31; 8:28-29). The sentence may also have been added to reinforce that the enemies remaining in the land were not able to stop the distribution of the territory (Keil and Delitzsch 1978, 150-51). It also continues an earlier theme of the chapter: the need for faith and courage to conquer, qualities seen in ample supply in Caleb. After he defeated the Anakites, who represented the entirety of Israel's enemies, **the land had rest from war**.

FROM THE TEXT

Caleb is not mentioned in Hebrews 11's Hall of Heroes of Faith, but we can assume he is among those about whom the author did not have "time to tell" (Heb 11:32). In the face of significant obstacles, he courageously persevered in pursuit of God's promise until that promise was granted. As we noted above, the author likely included Caleb's request here as an example to the Israelites for how to take the remaining land of Canaan. He has illustrated faith, courage, obedience, and perseverance ever since.

When he was forty years old and a leader in his tribe, Caleb was put to the test: would he doubt God's promise and side with the other spies in discouraging the Israelites from entering Canaan, or would he remain true to his convictions, jeopardizing his leadership role and perhaps even his life (see Num 14:10)? Because he chose faithfulness, God promised that Caleb would live to inherit a portion of this land. That promise was a long time in coming. Thirty-eight more years of wandering and seven years of fighting later, Caleb finally got the chance to stake his claim.

His faith endured the long delay, but several obstacles still remained between him and a home in Hebron. There was Joshua, once his partner in the minority report, but now his superior, the one who would have to grant this request. Caleb had to humble himself and ask for what had already been promised by Yahweh through Moses. Then there were the Anakites, that formidable foe who dwelt in "large and fortified" cities (v 12). They were an obstacle forty-five years earlier; at eighty-five, Caleb hardly seems up to the challenge. He appears to be aware of this; why else assert his strength (v 11)?

Although those over eighty are the fastest-growing demographic in our society today, Dickerson and Watkins contend they are generally overlooked by church leaders (2003, 201-13). Caleb refused to be overlooked. He did not let his age rob him of his confidence that God would keep his promise, no matter how many years had passed or how much of his strength had decreased. He had too much confidence in God to lack confidence in himself. Too many Christians labor under the delusion that God wants them to downplay their abilities as an act of humility. In fact, we should celebrate our abilities as tools to be employed in God's service. Our limitations should be minimized, not maximized; after all, they place no limit on God working through us. Here again, Caleb provides the example, for he speaks of his physical strength being equal to the task, "the LORD helping me" (v 12).

Because Caleb trusted God to keep his promise, and because he persevered in that trust in spite of the obstacles, Joshua blessed him and granted his request. As Caleb illustrates the courage and faithfulness of the believer, Joshua illustrates the Lord Christ, who will one day welcome the faithful believer: "Well done, good and faithful servant! . . . Come and share your master's happiness!" (Matt 25:21).

XV. JOSHUA 15

BEHIND THE TEXT

In Josh 13:6-7 God commanded Joshua to allocate the land west of the Jordan to the remaining nine and a half tribes. The remainder of ch 13 describes the territories of the Transjordan tribes. The opening verses of ch 14 merely state that the allotment occurred, then describe the fulfillment of God's promise to Caleb. What had been commanded in ch 13 and stated as accomplished in ch 14 is now described in detail in ch 15. This chapter presents the allotment for the tribe of Judah, even while encouraging Israel to complete the conquest.

The opening allotment falls to the tribe of Judah and is presented in greater detail than the others. Some have used this to support the argument that the book comes from a much later period when Judah was the most prominent tribe in the monarchy. The boundary and town lists, they propose, represent or arise from official documents used by the monarchy for taxation and other purposes. This is certainly not impossible, but a later date fails to do justice to the many elements in the book and in these lists that suggest an early date. Furthermore, the imprecision of the lists, such as towns assigned to two different tribes, argues against their usefulness for the centralized government of the monarchy (→ From the Text for ch 12, Excursus on Geographical Lists in Joshua 13—21).

There are better reasons why the allotment began with Judah. It was likely the largest of the tribes and had become increasingly important within the confederation (see Gen 49:9-12; Num 2:3-4), even first among equals (see Judg 1:2). The decision as to which tribe came first, however, was not made by Israel but by God, through the casting of lots. It appears likely that God chose to begin with Judah to signal that tribe's significant role in the future of Israel and beyond. All Israel is important—this is a major theme of Joshua—but the detail surrounding Judah's apportionment represents its coming significance. David would be from Judah, and his tribe would form the bulk of the southern kingdom. The kingdom of Judah would house God's temple in Jerusalem, and the tribe of Judah would produce David's most honored descendant, the incarnate Son of God.

The allotment to Judah is described in three ways, by tracing the boundaries of the territory (Josh 15:1-12), then by providing a lengthy list of cities (vv 20-63); in between we are given another vignette featuring Caleb (vv 13-19; see 14:6-15). Hess is correct that "the division of the land was idealistic at the time of the allotment" (1996a, 232). Land is allotted that is clearly not yet possessed (e.g., 15:45-47). This juxtaposition of promise fulfilled yet not fully realized continues a theme from previous chapters (→ ch 14). The boundary list describes first the southern, then the eastern, northern, and western boundaries of the tribal allotment. "Boundary" (*gebûl*) is an important term in Joshua but particularly in this chapter. Fully one-fourth of the book's use of the term occurs in ch 15. Howard points out the term occurs twenty-one times in this chapter and eighty-four times in the book (1998a, 334). Most of these are in the first twelve verses.

The town list is organized into four regions, the Negev, foothills, hill country, and eastern desert; these four regions are further divided into eleven (or twelve) districts. Use of the term "districts" is meant to imply a semiofficial function of the list during the premonarchic period. Organization into regions and districts would make it easier to recruit soldiers (e.g., Judg 4:6, 10) and to ascertain census data (e.g., Judg 6:15). As Nelson points out, boundary lists would help in arbitrating tribal claims, that is, whether disputed land is part of one tribe or another: "They are intended to foster good relations and reduce tensions" (1997, 185). Town lists, on the other hand, are more useful for purposes like conscription into the army (ibid.). Although many of the places mentioned in the lists are unknown to us, the main point still comes through: God has kept his promise to give this listed land to Israel.

IN THE TEXT

A. Boundaries around Judah (15:1-12)

1. Introduction and Southern Boundary (15:1-4)

■ 1-4 The description of Judah's allotment begins in the southern desert and moves counterclockwise (Hess 1996a, 242). The southern boundary begins at the southeast, at **the bay at the southern end of the Dead Sea** (v 2). **Bay** translates the Hebrew word for "tongue," leading some to see this as a reference to the peninsula that juts from the eastern bank of the Dead Sea. In this instance, **bay** is likely preferred since it describes something on the western, not the eastern bank, and since the same noun is used in v 5 where **bay** makes more sense. The southern boundary proceeds westward from the Dead Sea to the Mediterranean by way of the **Wadi of Egypt** (v 4), likely the same as the Brook of Egypt, or Shihor River (13:3), south of Gaza.

2. Eastern Boundary and Northern Boundary (15:5-11)

■ 5-11 The eastern boundary was the Dead Sea up to the point where the Jordan River empties into it (15:5a). At this point begins the northern boundary of Judah, which corresponds to the southern boundary of the allotments of Benjamin and Dan. In fact, Beth Arabah is here assigned to Judah (vv 6, 61) and later to Benjamin (18:22). This could mean that the line passed through the town (Pitkänen 2010, 287), or more likely, the town changed hands. The boundary passed by **the Stone of Bohan** (15:6), a landmark recognizable then but unknown today. That it is associated with Bohan, an (unknown) son of Reuben is also perplexing, since the Reubenites' territory lay across the Jordan. This identification with Reuben may have something to do with unknown events in the patriarchal period or during the conquest. The northern boundary continued past the valley of Achor, the site of Achan's execution (see 7:24, 26).

The boundary ran close to Jerusalem, still at this time occupied by Jebusites, and then past **the spring of the waters of Nephtoah** (15:9). This spring is thought by many to be the Wells of Merenptah referred to in Egyptian records (Woudstra 1981, 238 n. 22; Pitkänen 2010, 288). The **Mount Seir** of v 10 is not the better-known mountain by the same name in Edom, but a mountain southwest of Kiriath Jearim. **Timnah** (v 10) may refer to the site now identified as Tel Batash (Mazar 1980, 89-97), or it could be a common noun meaning south (Butler 1983, 180, citing some Hebrew manuscripts and the LXX).

3. Western Boundary (15:12)

■ **12** The boundary is said to extend to the Mediterranean, although the Israelites were not able to occupy the coastal plain (13:1-3).

B. Caleb's Inheritance (15:13-20)

1. Expulsion of Anakites from Vicinity of Hebron (15:13-17)

■ **13-17** These verses essentially continue the story begun in 14:6-15. They appear to be placed here because they conclude "the account of Judah's borders, just as the earlier Caleb story stood at its beginning" (Woudstra 1981, 240). This episode also provides an account of how Caleb's family acquired Debir. This material is quite similar to what we read in Judg 1:12-15. Perhaps the author of Joshua used the material in Judges or vice versa, or it may be that both authors drew their material from a common source (Keil and Delitzsch 1978, 156).

This passage repeats the allotment of this land to Caleb from ch 14, although here it is described as according to Yahweh's command to Joshua (v 13), rather than to Moses. It may be that an additional command came directly to Joshua on the matter of Caleb's allotment; more likely, the author is describing the command earlier given to Moses as equally binding on Moses' successor. We met the Anakim earlier in Joshua (see 11:21-22; 14:12), including the name of their legendary patriarch Arba (14:15). Here we are told that Caleb defeated **Sheshai, Ahiman and Talmai** (15:14), names we first learned in Num 13:22 and that may refer to individuals or to clans.

Since we already learned of the conquest of Debir in 10:38-39, 15:15-17 may describe the same events in more detail, or a subsequent victory over **Debir (formerly called Kiriath Sepher)** (v 15). Hess points out that it is not unusual to provide the older name for a site in "early accounts of the capture of noteworthy places" in order to reflect a mixed population and focus attention on an important site (1996a, 244-45). As promised for conquering Debir, Othniel received Caleb's daughter, Aksah as a "trophy wife" (Pitkänen 2010, 289). Othniel may have been Caleb's nephew or his brother, depending on how we render the Hebrew. Most translations assume the former, though Keil and Delitzsch argue for the latter, citing the MT (1978, 157). Othniel went on to become Israel's first judge (see Judg 3:9-11).

2. Land Grant Narrative for Aksah (15:18-19)

■ **18-19** According to Nelson, this section provides another example of a land grant narrative (also found in 14:6-15; 17:3-6, 14-18; 21:1-3) (1997, 188-89). Among the standard elements of this type of narrative, we have the confrontation (15:18), the case and request (v 19*a*), and the granting of the request (v 19*b*). Sometimes also found, though missing here, is a flashback to Moses (see 14:6-9; 17:4), a direct command from Yahweh (see 17:4*b*; 21:3), and a summary of the resolution (see 14:14-15). As Nelson points out, these stories demonstrate that "even in the foundational period, Yahweh's gift of the land was to some degree provisional and required a continuing struggle on the part of the people to realize it completely (v. 16; 17:18)" (1997, 189).

The story itself raises plenty of questions: Why did Aksah ask Othniel to appeal to Caleb, but then go herself (15:18)? The verb translated **urged** (v 18) usually has a negative connotation, such as "lead astray, seduce, incite" (Holladay 1971, 255); how does this meaning fit here? Why did she initially request a field, but then ask for a spring (v 18)? How should we render the verb that the NIV translates **got off** (v 18)? Mosca suggests a resolution to the first two problems by proposing that Aksah did not appeal to her husband but went directly to her father and tricked him into giving her the upper and lower springs (1984, 18-22). This suggestion fits neither the Hebrew nor the spirit of the passage.

It would appear that Aksah approached Othniel for permission to appeal to her father, which he granted (Butler 1983, 180). When she arrived, she did not trick her father, but persuaded him to give her the spring. Although **urged** usually has a negative connotation, it can also mean to stir up or motivate, as in 1 Sam 26:19 where it is attributed to Yahweh himself:

> But now let my lord the king listen to his servant. If the LORD has stirred you up against me, then let him accept my offering. But if this is simply a human scheme, then may those involved be cursed by the LORD. For they have driven me from my home, so I can no longer live among the LORD's people, and they have said, "Go, worship pagan gods." (NLT)

It could be that her request was for "arable land" (Josh 15:18 NJB), which Caleb answered by giving her the springs as a way to irrigate the land. Another possibility is that she was requesting "some property" (NJPS) as a dowry, which her father apparently had not initially provided. The Tanakh renders v 19*a* as "you have given me away as Negeb-land." Without a dowry she lacked what she needed as a wife, as the Negev region lacked water. Others have suggested that the **field** (v 18) was her dowry. What she now requested was a **special favor** (v 19), a water source to make the field usable (see Fleishman 2006, 354-73; Hess 1996a, 245 n. 2). Woudstra considers the **special favor** to be a "marriage gift" (1981, 241), while Boling and Wright see it as a "technical term for the groom's gift to the bride ... distinct from the bride price, which the groom here rather eccentrically supplied on the basis of his military success" (1982, 375). The Hebrew term behind **special favor** can also be translated "blessing," the noun form of the verb used in the previous chapter to describe what Joshua did to Caleb (14:13). Back-to-back blessings strengthen the case for seeing Caleb—and now Aksah—as the author's models of the kind of dogged perseverance needed for the Israelites to occupy the land God had promised.

Interesting proposals have circulated about the meaning of the Hebrew verb behind **got off** (15:18), and the discussion continues (see Nicholson 1997, 259-65). Most believe it describes a downward movement (see Judg 4:21); in the case of someone riding a donkey it would mean to dismount. Keil and Delitzsch propose the more active "sprang down" (1978, 158). Whether she was intending to demonstrate her eagerness or respect (Nelson 1997, 189, citing Gen 24:64; 1 Sam 25:23), Aksah's action clearly suggested to her father that she had come to request something, which is why he asked what he could do for her (Josh 15:18).

3. Summary (15:20)

■20 Many translations and commentators consider this verse to introduce the next section (see Hess 1996a, 246; Pitkänen 2010, 290). Nelson believes it connects Judah "to a web of similar formulas for the other tribes: 13:23, 28; 16:8; 18:20, 28; 19:8, 16, 23, 31, 39, 48. A similar set of headings and a summary encompasses the land division for the whole people: 13:32; 14:1; 19:51" (1997, 189). It is better seen as a summary of the preceding verses. Howard points out that wording very similar to this verse appears twelve times in Joshua, "always and only as a summarizing statement" (1998a, 338; see Josh 13:23, 28; 15:20; 16:8; 18:20, 28; 19:8, 16, 23, 31, 39, 48). Woudstra also considers it a summary that "helps the reader to see the Caleb-Othniel episode as a concrete instance of how Judah received its inheritance according to its families" (1981, 242; see Butler 1983, 183; Keil and Delitzsch 1978, 158).

C. Towns within Judah (15:21-63)

1. Negev Region (15:21-32)

The town names in vv 21-63 are arranged according to four regions, each with eleven or twelve districts. The lists begin in the Negev (or south land) with one group (vv 21-32), then move from west to east, starting at the Shephelah with three groups (vv 33-44) and a pocket of Philistine cities (vv 45-47), to the hill country with five or six groups (vv 48-60), and finishing in the Arabah with one group (vv 61-62). In addition to the names of the towns, the author provided a running total of the towns in each district.

■ **21-32** As with the boundary list, the list of towns begins in the south in the Negev region (vv 21-32). The locations of most of these towns are unknown to us today. **Eder** (v 21) could be a copyist's error for Arad, and **Kedesh** (v 23) could refer to Kadesh Barnea (Pitkänen 2010, 290). **Hazor** (vv 23, 25) refers here not to the better-known city in the north, but as a common noun describing an enclosure, like a sheep pen. **Telem** (v 24) could refer to Tell Malhata, east of Beersheba (Na'aman 1980, 95-109). **Ziklag** (v 31), where David and his men stayed when on the run from Saul (1 Sam 27:6-7), may be located at Tell es-Sharia (Pitkänen 2010, 291; see Oren 1982, 155-66).

The total number of towns listed in the NIV is thirty-six, while Josh 15:32 gives the total number as **twenty-nine towns and their villages**. Some have attributed this discrepancy to "corruption (and/or editing) during transmission" (Pitkänen 2010, 292). Others have suggested that some of the locations listed "represent localities too small to be counted as cities" while others have given up on a "completely convincing explanation" (see Woudstra 1981, 246). Nelson lists thirty-three but suggests removing the four compound toponyms identified as Hazor/Hazar ("enclosure of . . .") to arrive at twenty-nine (1997, 184). The compound toponyms are *Hazor-ithnan* (v 23), *Hazor-hadattah* (v 25), *Hazar-gaddah* (v 27), and *Hazar-shual* (v 28).

2. Western Foothills (15:33-47)

■ **33-47** The next list focuses on the Shephelah or **western foothills** (v 33) region with its three districts (vv 33-44), each district divided by a major valley running east-west. The first district (vv 33-36, no. 2 on the map below) is the northernmost of the three. It contains fourteen towns, two of which—**Eshtaol** and **Zorah** (v 33) were also allotted to Dan (see 19:41). These could have been originally Judah's but were then given to Dan, just as Simeon's territory came from what had been originally given to Judah (see 19:9). Another possibility is that the towns were allotted to Dan but, after Dan's migration (19:47), were granted to Judah (Pitkänen 2010, 292). **Gederah** or some variation appears several times in the town lists (15:36, 41, 58; see 12:13), not surprisingly since it means "sheepfold" (Boling and Wright 1982, 385). **Shaaraim** (15:36) may be Khirbet Qeiyafa, located on a main road from the coastal plain to the hill country. Its name, meaning "two gates," matches the discovery at this site of two gates, an unusual feature for a town. Archaeological evidence, however, dates occupancy of Khirbet Qeiyafa only to the tenth century (Garfinkel and Ganor 2008, electronic).

The next district in the Shephelah (vv 37-41, no. 3) lies farthest south, spreading east to west from the coastal plain to the hill country (Rainey 1980, 194-202; Rainey 1983, 1-22). Rainey calls it the district of Lachish, named for the major city by this name, which he locates at Tell ed-Duweir (1983, 6). As noted in the commentary on 10:16-28, Dorsey locates Makkedah at Khirbet Beit Maqdum, very close to Khirbet el-Qom (1980, 185-93).

The third of the districts of the Shephelah (15:42-44, no. 4), which Rainey refers to as the Libnah district, lies between the first and second, not east of the Lachish district (vv 37-41) as Howard claims (1998a, 341). Key to this identification is the location of Libnah at Tell Bornât, near the western boundary of the district (Rainey 1983, 11; Hess 1996a, 253).

The author next includes a list of Philistine cities (vv 45-47). This list differs from the others in that it provides a fuller description but no total. By including these Philistine cities in a list of Judah's towns, the author appears to be saying that they fall within Judah's boundaries. By varying his presentation, the author may be implying that territorial allotment does not imply total occupation.

3. Hill Country (15:48-60)

■ **48-60** The next region to be considered is the hill country (vv 48-60), which is presented in a general south-to-north listing (Howard 1998a, 342) with five or possibly six districts. The first district (vv 48-51, no. 5) includes **Debir** (v 49), mentioned in the Caleb vignette (vv 13-19), but here described as **Kiriath Sannah** (v 49). We have already been told that Debir used to be known as Kiriath Sepher (v 15), so perhaps we should consider **Sannah** as the result of textual corruption precipitated by the preceding name, Dannah (Nelson 1997, 184). The NIV and most translations retain the translation **Kiriath Sannah**, but NJB renders it "Kiriath-Sepher." The next district (vv 52-54, no. 6), located just north, includes **Hebron**, described by both its newer and older names (v 54). Some suggest **Dumah** (v 52) should instead be Rumah (as LXX) (Elitzur 1994, 123-28).

The third district in the hill country (vv 55-57, no. 7) contains ten towns, several of which have names of other cities in Canaan (**Jezreel** in v 56 and 19:18; **Gibeah** in 15:57, 18:28, and 24:33). North of the preceding two districts and extending from the Shephelah in the west to the Arabah in the east is the district described in 15:58-59 (no. 8), with its six towns and villages.

An additional district of the hill region has been preserved in the Septuagint (between vv 59 and 60) but left out of the MT. It is located north of the eighth district and contains eleven additional cities: "Tekoa, Ephrathah, now Bethlehem, Peor, Etam, Kulon, Tatam, Sores, Carem, Gallim, Bether and Manach: eleven towns with their villages" (NJB). Its omission from the town list leaves a big geographical gap in Judah's territory. Several scholars suggest it may have dropped out due to a scribal error where "in Hebrew a copyist had jumped from 'towns and their enclosures' at the end of v. 58 to the same words at the end of the restored unit" (Boling and Wright 1982, 390).

The final district in the hill country (v 60, no. 10) contains two towns with their villages. **Rabbah** is not to be confused with the Ammonite capital of the same name. Aharoni suggests that a seal reading "(Belonging) to Zeryahu the Rabbat(ite) may refer to an inhabitant of this town" (1974, 157-58). He also suggests this same Rabbah, which he considers to be Khirbet Bîr el-Hilû, may be mentioned in Egyptian sources (there called Rubute), located on the road between Gezer and Jerusalem, near Kiriath Jearim. Aharoni points out that "its importance as the nearest and most convenient approach to Jerusalem explains its organization as a special district with only two major cities" (1969, 137-45).

4. Desert (15:61-62)

■ **61-62** These verses contain a listing of the towns in the fourth region, **the wilderness** (v 61). This region along the western coast of the Dead Sea is elsewhere known as the Judean Wilderness. En Gedi refers to the oasis located halfway down the Dead Sea coast (Howard 1998a, 343). Some believe the **City of Salt** (v 62) may refer to Khirbet Qumran, where the Dead Sea Scrolls were discovered (Boling and Wright 1982, 392), while others associate Qumran with **Sekakah** (v 61) (Hess 1996a, 255) and the **City of Salt** with Masad Gozal (Eshel 1995, 37-40). From ancient times until today, this region was valued for its salt (Greenhut 1993, 32-43). As the lowest spot on earth, the Dead Sea serves as a large drying pan where a variety of chemicals are left behind after evaporation. I once stood in a large circular cave in this region, its walls towering perhaps a hundred feet in the air and opening to the blue sky. The chamber had been created by a thick coating of chemicals on the rock wall that had been eroded by wind and water over the millennia.

5. Unable to Dislodge the Jebusites (15:63)

■ **63** The chapter closes on a somber note, pointing out that Judah was not able to dislodge the Jebusites in Jerusalem, what Howard calls the first "Conquest Lacuna" (1998a, 343). Jerusalem was part of Benjamin, not Judah (see v 8; 18:28), so it seems strange to mention that Judah failed to conquer it. The inclusion of this negative picture of Judah speaks more to a premonarchic date for Joshua than one during the monarchy.

FROM THE TEXT

Although largely a list of places, this chapter conveys several important theological truths. Caleb's reappearance reminds us of his role as a positive example for all God's people, from his day until our own. In Josh 14, we noted his faith, courage, and perseverance. This chapter demonstrates how those same qualities persisted in his son-in-law and daughter. Not dissuaded by Debir's inhabitants, Othniel bravely took up the challenge to conquer Kiriath Sephir (15:16-17). He proved himself worthy of Caleb's daughter by demonstrating the same courage Caleb had shown in expelling the sons of Anak from Hebron. Aksah's example is also noteworthy, especially in a culture that paid scant attention to women. She asked Othniel's permission to appeal to her father (v 18), but with a boldness worthy of her father. Again, she showed herself respectful by dismounting, but bold in her request. The author chose a strong word to describe that request, not to connote impertinence or deception, but to convey Aksah's resolute determination. She had the faith and perseverance to ask for a blessing from her father, the same qualities shown by her father when he received his blessing from Joshua (14:13). Do not miss the point of her request: she plans to make a life in this land, regardless of its challenges, whether enemies or hot dry climate. The author's point in inserting this story appears to be to provide another example for God's people, showing them the kind of perseverance needed to obtain their share of God's promise. Aksah remains an example for us today.

There is a second theological lesson, this one gained not from the vignette between the lists but from the lists themselves. There seems no reason to doubt that the author is relying on semiofficial documents that provide the boundaries and towns of Judah. Prepared originally to serve the administrative functions of the tribal confederation, the author here turns these documents toward a deeper, more lasting purpose. As Butler has noted, "What might appear to be simply political bases of power are interpreted by the biblical writer as parts of the divine domain given by God to his people" (1983, 189). Ordinary records become concrete evidence for a promise-keeping God.

In doing so, the author of Joshua has revealed an important and abiding truth: human authority is not the final word, even when that authority—as the tribal confederation—acts on God's behalf. "Above, beyond, and behind all political activity and authority stands the ultimate authority of God" (ibid.). Governments are not evil, but they are not ultimate. All human effort and all expressions of human authority remain at God's disposal, to be transformed, as were these official documents, into demonstrations of God's glory.

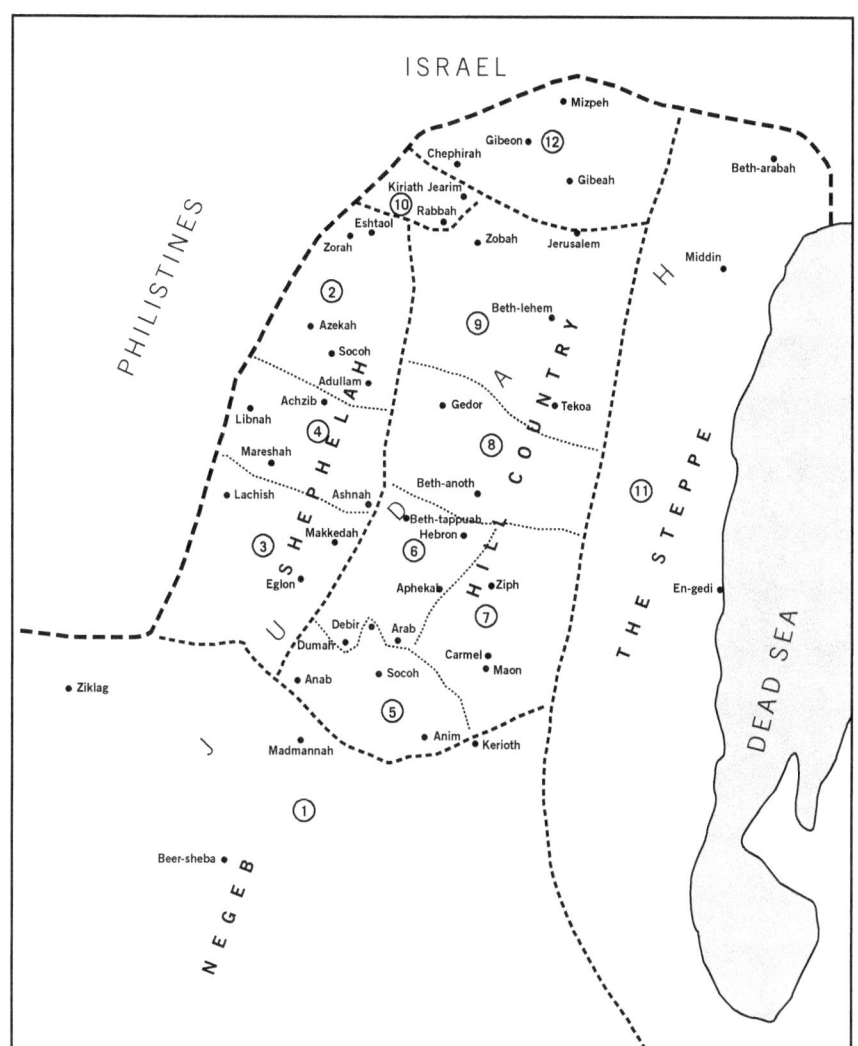

Fig. 15.1. Regions, districts, and towns within Judah

XVI. JOSHUA 16—17

BEHIND THE TEXT

Chapters 16 and 17 appear to be intended as a single unit treating the tribal allotment of the Josephite tribes (→ ch 13 and Dorsey's chiastic outline). The author opens and closes this section with material that speaks of the two tribes as one (see "allotment for Joseph" [16:1] and "the people of Joseph" [17:14]). Butler points out that 17:18 signals a natural break since we have a geographical change in 18:1 and since each subsection in chs 15—17 concludes by describing ongoing conflict with the Canaanites (1983, 183). It is less clear why the Josephite tribes should be treated next after Judah. Dorsey offers the possibility that the allotment was based on whether the ancestral matriarch was Rachel or another of Jacob's wives (1990, 94-95).

These two chapters are challenging to interpret. They lack so much information (e.g., town lists) compared with the tribal allotment to Judah (ch 15), and the boundary descriptions are no less obtuse. While these difficulties present a challenge, they also increase the likelihood we are dealing with very early sources. If these were official documents from the monarchy, one expects they would be easier to understand. What is clear enough is that the tribes of Ephraim and Manasseh were given their portion directly north of what would then be given to the tribes of Dan and Benjamin, and south of the Jezreel valley (Hess 1996a, 256). These chapters provide parallel information. Both begin by treating the Josephite tribes together (16:1-4; 17:14-18). Then come the border descriptions with exceptions (16:5-9; 17:7-11) and boundary lacunae (16:10; 17:12-13), concluding with land grant narratives (17:3-6; 17:14-18) (see Nelson 1997, 195, with slight modifications). These chapters were included to describe the allotment for the Josephite tribes west of the Jordan, and to encourage all tribes in the continuing conquest of Canaan.

IN THE TEXT

A. Overview of Allotment for Cisjordan Josephite Tribes (16:1-4)

When the lot *came out*—perhaps out of the container in which the die were kept—the Josephite tribes west of the Jordan (i.e., Cisjordan) were treated as a single entity. It is unclear why they only drew one lot, rather than one for the tribe of Ephraim and one for the tribe of Manasseh. Based on their complaint in 17:14, they had hoped for something different. No explanation is given, although they do receive a very large allotment of land, paralleling that given to Judah. Whatever the reason for only one lot, Joshua's answer at the end of ch 17 makes clear that this arrangement left them at no disadvantage compared to the rest of Israel.

1. Southern Boundary (16:1-3)

These verses describe only the southern boundary for the Josephite territory on the western side of the Jordan. The Jordan River bordered their territories on the east and the Mediterranean Sea on the west; the northern boundary would be added in the description of Manasseh's allotment. Given what we are told here, it would seem that the southern boundary of the Josephites, the second group receiving its allotment, would be the northern boundary of the first group, that of the tribe of Judah. As it will turn out, Josephite land will not border Judah since the territory for Benjamin (18:11-27) and Dan (19:40-48) will be placed between them.

■ 1 The *Jordan of Jericho*, that is, the Jordan River, flows east of the city of Jericho and the **springs of Jericho**. According to Howard, the latter phrase "undoubtedly refers to the perennial spring east of the city" (1998a, 346 n. 134; see Pitkänen 2010, 299; Nelson 1997, 196). From there the border heads west, climbing in elevation into the hills near Bethel.

■ **2** The Hebrew makes it appear as if **Bethel** and **Luz** are two separate places. This is reflected in the NASB: "it went from Bethel to Luz." Other translations, such as the NLT and NIV, treat the two as one: **from Bethel (that is, Luz)**, perhaps influenced by Gen 28:19, which identifies Bethel as the name Jacob gave to Luz (see Gen 35:6; 48:3; Josh 18:13; Judg 1:23).

The **Arkites** may have been a clan within Benjamin (Cohen 1962, 209) or a non-Israelite group located southwest of Bethel that eventually became part of Benjamin (Johnson 1992, 1:369, citing Josh 16:2). This may be the same ancient group referred to in Gen 10:17, but the spelling of the name is very different. Whatever the ethnic makeup of the **Arkites**, they provided King David with a very wise counselor in Hushai (see 2 Sam 15:32, 37; 16:16-18; 17:5-7, 14-15; 1 Kgs 4:16; 1 Chr 27:33).

■ **3** Less is known about the **Japhletites**. Some have suggested, based on 1 Chr 7:30-40, that this was a clan of the tribe of Asher. While it is not out of the question that an Asherite clan would have already become established so far south of the rest of their tribe, it may be best to see the Japhletites as another non-Israelite group inhabiting Canaan.

The boundary description grows progressively more vague as it approached the Mediterranean Sea, likely because this territory was controlled by non-Israelites (see Josh 13:1-3). Howard speculates that the Josephite boundary

> would appear to move now to the sea in a sharply northwestern direction, on the basis of the Danite city list in 19:40-48, particularly the cities of Joppa, on the coast, and Gath Rimmon, near the Mediterranean and just south of the Yarkon River. (1998a, 346)

This is possible, since the southern boundary left room for Dan. It seems more likely, however, that Dan's cities were either carved out of the Josephite territory or that these boundaries presume Dan's move north (see Josh 19:47).

2. Summary (16:4)

■ **4** The introduction concludes with a summary of the Josephite inheritance. Manasseh's name is mentioned first, perhaps because he was the firstborn, but the first allotment goes to Ephraim (vv 5-10), echoing Jacob's prophecy that Ephraim would have preeminence, in spite of birth order (Gen 48:12-20).

B. Allotment for Ephraim (16:5-10)

1. Boundary for Ephraim's Territory (16:5-9)

■ **5-9** The boundary description begins by briefly summarizing the southern boundary (vv 5*b*-6*a*). It then starts at a point roughly central to the northern boundary and proceeds east to the Jordan River (vv 6b-7). Returning to near the same central point, the description then proceeds westward through the Wadi Kanah to the Mediterranean Sea (v 8a). Knobel considers this spot to be "a central point near the watershed" (as cited by Keil and Delitzsch 1978, 177). While it is somewhat unusual to identify a boundary by starting at the center, moving in one direction, returning to the center, and moving in the other direction, we find something similar in 1 Chr 7:28 (Nelson 1997, 196, who misidentifies this verse as 7:29). Keil and Delitzsch note a similar format in 19:10-12 (1978, 192).

The town name, **Ataroth**, appears several times in Josh 16 (vv 2, 5, 7). While clearly different from the town with the same name on the east side of the Jordan (Num 32:3), it is unclear whether Josh 16:2, 5, and 7 all refer to the same town west of the Jordan. Since the Hebrew word means "crowns," it may be an appropriate name for any town sitting atop a hill. Aharoni has identified **Ataroth Addar** (v 5) with Khirbet Raddana, southwest of Bethel (1971, 130-35). **Mikmethath** (v 6) could refer to the name of a town identified with various sites near Shechem (Dyck 1992, 4:815). Others suggest it refers to a geographical feature, like a mountain or a valley, since it is written with a definite article (Howard 1998a, 347 n. 140).

After a brief summary statement (v 8b), we learn that the **Ephraimites** also possessed towns in the territory belonging to Manasseh. Keil and Delitzsch speculate this may have been the result of realignment that took place after the formal allotment when "it was found that Ephraim had received too small a possession" (1978, 179 n. 1). It is also possible that members of one tribe may have settled in an area that was later allotted to a different tribe (→ 16:3 in reference to the Japhletites).

As noted earlier, the Ephraimite allotment contains no town list like the one for Judah and like the ones found later with other tribes. Some commentators speculate that a town list may once have stood at this point in the text but has since dropped out (Pitkänen 2010, 299, 301). Others speculate that the list was excised by a later redactor (Kaufmann 1953, 34). Kaufmann believes the Judahite editor of the book of Joshua

> was not interested in the detailed city lists of Ephraim and Manasseh. He left the boundary demarcations, but excised the lists of cities, and in some places the scars remain clearly recognizable. . . . His motive was neither political nor religious, but, if one may say so, publisher-scribe's convenience. (Ibid., 36)

2. Boundary Lacunae (16:10)

■ **10** This chapter ends as did Josh 15, with the recognition that **the Canaanites** were not entirely removed. Specifically we learn that **the Canaanites** in **Gezer** remained. Unlike those in Jebus (see 15:63), however, these were subjected either to tribute or to forced labor up to the author's day. Since the city was fully conquered by Pharaoh in Solomon's day and presented to him as a wedding present, **this day** is not likely later than the tenth century B.C. The LXX rendering of this verse specifically refers to Pharaoh's defeat of the city.

C. Allotment for Manasseh (17:1-13)

1. Introduction (17:1-2)

■ **1** The tribal allotment for the half-tribe of **Manasseh** that settled west of the Jordan begins with a brief refresher on the tribal history of the clans descended from Ephraim's older brother. Manasseh was Joseph's firstborn but was placed second after Ephraim, as predicted by his grandfather (Gen 48:12-20). **Makir** was Manasseh's only son (Gen 50:23). He and his descendants, notable for their military prowess, obtained land east of the Jordan (**Gilead and Bashan**), where half of Manasseh had already begun to settle. **Makir** was the father of his son, Gilead (Num 26:29), and Makir's descendants possessed the land of **Gilead**, named after that son (Howard 1998a, 350 n. 147). As Keil and Delitzsch point out, **Gilead**, when used with an article (as here), refers to the territory (Josh 13:11, 31; 17:5; Num 32:40; Deut 3:10) rather than the son (1978, 179).

■ **2** The clans of Manasseh that had not received land across the Jordan were **Abiezer** (referred to in Num 26:30 as Iezer), **Helek, Asriel, Shechem, Hepher and Shemida**. To be more precise, these were the clans descended from the **male descendants of Manasseh**. Hepher's son, Zelophehad, fathered only five daughters, leaving that clan at risk of losing its territory should those daughters marry outside the clan. This issue was raised with Moses (Num 27:1-11; 36:1-12) who, at Yahweh's command, declared the rule that, "No inheritance in Israel is to pass from one tribe to another" (Num 36:7). The daughters of Zelophehad were to marry within their own clan but would inherit their property just as would the male descendants.

2. Daughters of Zelophehad (17:3-6)

■ **3-6** These verses describe the fulfillment of Moses' command. An example of a similar legal practice has been found among the Nuzi tablets, an archive that documents events in the Hurrian Empire in the mid-second millennium B.C. In one tablet (IM 6818), a father adopts his only daughter as a son, then identifies her as heir to his property (Ben-Barak 1978, 116-23).

The daughters came (**They** is feminine plural [v 4]) to state their claim before the same trio of authorities found in 14:1. As there, Eleazar is mentioned first and is described as **the priest**, Joshua is called **son of Nun**, and they are accompanied by the **leaders** (17:4). In 14:1, this group was referred to as **heads of the fathers of the tribes of the sons of Israel,** while here they are described using the same term found in Num 27:2 and 36:1, ***princes,*** or "chieftains" (NJPS).

Nelson points out that this is another example of the literary subgenre known as land grant narratives. It begins by establishing the setting and characters (Josh 17:3), followed by the case being made for the land, based on the divine command to Moses (v 4*a*). The land is granted (v 4*b*) followed by a summative statement indicating resolution (vv 5-6) (1997, 177, 201-2). Five of Manasseh's six male descendants each received a tract of land, while the sixth, Hepher, received five, one for each of the daughters of Zelophehad (**ten tracts of land** [v 5]). This does not count the two tracts given to those from Manasseh who settled east of the Jordan River in Gilead and Bashan.

Some have suggested that there *is* in fact a town list for the tribe of Manasseh, and we can find it in in vv 2-3. An archive of pottery shards containing writing, or ostraca, was found in Samaria. These administrative records dated around the eighth century B.C. provide a picture of life, specifically in the region assigned to Manasseh (Kaufman 1992, 5:921). Many of the town names from the ostraca are the names of the clans in vv 2-3 (see map in Boling and Wright 1982, 408).

3. Boundary for Manasseh's Territory (17:7-10)

■ **7-8** Verses 7-10 contain the boundary allotment for Manasseh. There is some question whether **Asher** refers to the tribal allotment of Asher or to a now unknown site. Keil and Delitzsch defend the latter option, based on a list of town names dating to the late third or early fourth century A.D., which identifies Asher as a town about fifteen Roman miles from Neapolis (near Shechem) on the road between that city and Scythopolis (ancient Beth Shan) (1978, 180). On the other hand, v 10 specifically identifies Asher's land as the northern border of Manasseh.

Mikmethath appears again (see 16:6), this time as the south-central boundary marker for Manasseh. Here the town is identified as east of **Shechem**, the first direct reference in Joshua to Shechem as a location (Boling and Wright 1982, 412). South of Mikmethath was **En Tappuah**, or the spring of Tappuah, which belonged to Manasseh, Tappuah itself being part of Ephraim (v 8).

■ **9-10** The boundary continued south to the Wadi **Kanah** (see 16:8). The Hebrew of 17:9 is difficult, suggesting both that the **ravine**, which runs east to west, provided the boundary between Manasseh and Ephraim (echoed in v 10*a*), but also that some cities of Ephraim were in the territory of Manasseh. Nelson suggests that the boundary may have cut across the ravine so that some territory south of it belonged to Manasseh, then the boundary turned north and ran along the north rim to the sea (1997, 203; see Keil and Delitzsch 1978, 181). The tribal land of Asher provided the northern border and that of Issachar the eastern border (v 10*b*). No mention is made of Zebulun, another northern neighbor. Nor is it clear why Issachar is placed on the east. It lies to the northeast, but the Jordan River is, more precisely, Manasseh's eastern boundary. Keil and Delitzsch explain these anomalies as characteristic of boundaries being still in flux (1978, 181).

4. Manasseh's Cities within Other Tribes (17:11)

■ 11 Fluid boundaries would also explain how cities occupied by those from one tribe might be located in the allotment of another tribe. Verse 11 identifies six such cities: **Beth Shan, Ibleam and the people of Dor, Endor, Taanach and Megiddo**, although Boling and Wright locate these towns not in but "near" Issachar and Asher (1982, 407). **Beth Shan** (or Beth Shean) stands at the junction where the Jezreel valley intersects the Jordan River valley. This made the site very important throughout its history, dating back into the Chalcolithic period. There is a strong Egyptian presence up to and beyond the time of Israelite occupation, until the town was finally brought into the Israelite orbit, at least by Solomon's day (1 Kgs 9:15) (McGovern 1992, 693-96).

Ibleam also sat at a strategic location, a pass leading from the hills of Ephraim into the Jezreel valley. The site is known from Egyptian records and later Israelite history (see 2 Kgs 9:27) (Hunt 1992, 3:355). The author specifies that **the people** in the next four towns belonged to Manasseh. It is tempting to assume that this has something to do with the continuing Canaanite presence in these towns (see Keil and Delitzsch 1978, 182), although the Canaanites remained in Beth Shan and Ibleam as well (Josh 17:12; Judg 1:27).

If **Dor** is the same as Naphoth Dor, its defeat was mentioned in Josh 12:23. The king of Dor is listed among the conquered monarchs (→ 12:23). **Endor** is located north of Jezreel and close to the site of Gideon's battle with the Midianites (Judg 7) as well as the home of the medium consulted by Saul (1 Sam 28). (For more on **Taanach and Megiddo**, → Josh 12:21.)

There is no consensus among translators on what is meant by the last phrase in 17:11, **the three of Naphoth.** Some translate Naphoth as a reference to a country (KJV) or region ("these constituted three regions" [NJPS]). Others take Naphoth as a common noun meaning "heights," such as the ASV's "the three heights," the NJB's "the Three of the Slopes," or the suggestion of Keil and Delitzsch, "the three-hill-country" (1978, 182). Woudstra acknowledges that taking the term as a noun meaning "heights" "does correspond accurately to the geographical situation of the last three cities mentioned, each of which was situated near a mountain ridge" (1981, 266).

Another approach treats Naphoth as a proper noun. The NIV treats this phrase as a parenthetical addition, clarifying that the third town mentioned, Dor, is the same as Naphoth. The NABRE makes this even more explicit ("the third is Naphath-dor"), the NLT even more so. That translation inserts, immediately after Dor, "that is, Naphoth-dor." Boling and Wright propose treating this phrase as a question written in the margin of the manuscript by a later scribe, wondering about "the third [Dor]. Is it Napheth?" (1982, 407). It seems most likely the additional phrase was added by the author specifically to clarify that he was referring to two towns, Dor, also known as Naphoth Dor (see 11:2) on the coast, and Endor in the valley.

5. Boundary Lacunae (17:12-13)

■ 12 While Manasseh inherited these six towns, they were not able to **occupy** them because the Canaanites **were determined to live in that region**. **Were determined** suggests a stubborn resolve on the part of the Canaanites. The same verb is used to describe Israel's insistence on worshiping idols (Hos 5:11), and Abraham's resolve to speak up, even to Yahweh, on behalf of the righteous (Gen 18:27, 31). Joshua himself uses this term after the disaster at Ai. In his grief, he wishes Israel had resolved to remain east of the Jordan and had never entered this land, assuming God was no longer supporting them (Josh 7:7). The phrase indicates that the Canaanites living in these towns were determined not to leave.

■ 13 Here as with Ephraim (16:10), the tribe of Manasseh eventually either **subjected the Canaanites to forced labor** or "imposed tribute" (NJPS) on them.

D. Josephite Desire for More Land (17:14-18)

1. Appeal (17:14)

■ 14 Once again we meet the tribes of Ephraim and Manasseh in one group, as **the people of Joseph**. Their appeal is actually delivered in the first person singular: "Why have you given me but one lot and one portion as an inheritance, although I am a numerous people, since all along the LORD has blessed me?" [ESV]). Their reference to being **blessed** by Yahweh is the third use of "blessed" in a land grant narrative (see 14:13; 15:19). In the first, Yahweh's blessing was given to Caleb by Joshua for his courage in seeking to take enemy-occupied land. In the second, a blessing of additional land was sought by Aksah from her father. Here it was Yahweh's blessing that made necessary additional land beyond what had been allotted to them.

Nelson considers 17:14-18 another example of a land grant narrative (1997, 177; see 14:6-15; 15:18-19; 17:3-6). The confrontation and appeal comes in v 14*a* with the specific request and allusion to a divine promise in v 14*b*. The grant itself comes in vv 17-18*a* with the summary of results in v 18*b*. Although it is the same literary subgenre, the tone of these verses differs markedly from the tone of the previous land grant narratives. There the appeal was made in a courageous spirit; here the tone is one of fear.

Howard sees their request in a very negative light. He contends that by challenging the lot, they were actually challenging Yahweh (1998a, 356).

We need not see their words so negatively. Granted, they were not the largest tribe; a literal reading of the census numbers put them at 58,000 to 59,000, not as strong as Judah (76,500), Dan (64,400), or Issachar (64,300) (Keil and Delitzsch 1978, 183). Their request, however, was based not on their being the largest tribe but on the fact that their territory was not large enough for their population. This probably had something to do with how much of their land was wooded and therefore less suitable for farming and grazing.

2. Joshua's Response (17:15)

■ **15** Joshua encouraged them to clear the forested portion at the higher elevations of their current territory (Nelson 1997, 204), even though this was occupied by the Perizzites and Rephaites. The Perizzites have been mentioned earlier among the inhabitants of Canaan (see 3:10; 9:1; 11:3; 12:8). The Rephaites are usually associated with Bashan, on the eastern shore of the Jordan River (Deut 3:11, 13; Josh 12:4; 13:12). Here the term probably refers to a valley of Rephaim near Jerusalem (15:8; 18:16), implying their presence on the western side of the Jordan as well (Howard 1998a, 356).

3. Further Protest (17:16)

■ **16** Joshua's proposal is a nonstarter, they say, since there is not enough room in the **hill country**; nor can they spread out onto the plain, since that is occupied by **Canaanites**. These enemies—they specifically mention **those in Beth Shan and its settlements and those in the Valley of Jezreel**—live in the plain, the terrain dominated by those with **chariots fitted with iron** (i.e., wooden chariots plated or otherwise equipped with pieces of iron).

4. Joshua's Second Response (17:17-18)

■ **17-18** Their fears are without warrant, responds Joshua, for there is plenty of land for the taking. Not only will they possess the hill country they were allotted, both what is tillable and what is now forested, but they can also control the plain, home of the dreaded Canaanites. The allotted land was just the beginning of what the tribes could possess; more land could be theirs, if they have the courage.

The Josephites had used their large population as cause for complaint instead of seeing it as reason for confidence. This strength will make it possible "to clear the forests and even conquer the Canaanites in the lowlands" (Pitkänen 2010, 308). It will even allow them to possess the ***outgoings of it***. Keil and Delitzsch consider this phrase to mean the "fields and plains bordering upon the forest" (1978, 185) but most, like the NIV, see it referring to the land's **farthest limits** (v 18).

Joshua has more confidence in them than they have in themselves. With words both solemn and emphatic (Woudstra 1981, 269), Joshua challenges them to trust in Yahweh, whose blessing was manifest in their sizable population. As Butler points out, Joshua's answer is at once consoling and challenging: "He accepts the fact that they are a great and thus blessed people. He emphasizes their great power, thus their great potentiality" (1983, 192).

FROM THE TEXT

Joshua's words to the Josephite tribes conveyed an important truth to ancient Israel: the land remains to be taken, and no enemy, however powerful, can stand in the way. Caleb expressed this confidence when he sought his territory from Joshua; Aksah expressed her confidence more subtly when she sought a blessing from her father, Caleb. She sought on behalf of her family to live in the land that had been taken from the enemy. Although the Josephites did not express this confidence, Joshua expressed it for them. They could have as much territory as they needed, even if that land was occupied by the enemy. Israel did eventually take possession of the whole land in the early years of the monarchy.

In Joshua's words, we hear God's words to us. With the Apostle Paul we confess:

> Though we live in the world, we do not wage war as the world does. The weapons we fight with are not the weapons of the world. On the contrary, they have divine power to demolish strongholds. We demolish arguments and every pretension that sets itself up against the knowledge of God, and we take captive every thought to make it obedient to Christ. (2 Cor 10:3-5)

We know that whatever we face, God can make us "more than conquerors through him who loved us" (Rom 8:37). By God's sanctifying power we can experience not only the subjugation of our sins but also their total expulsion.

As with the Josephites, we may be counting as a weakness something God considers a strength. Paul was taught this through his "thorn" (2 Cor 12:7). At first he actively sought to be rid of it, but eventually he came to see that thorn as something for which to be grateful. When he discovered that God's power is "made perfect in weakness," he began to "delight in weaknesses, in insults, in hardships, in persecutions, in difficulties. For when I am weak," he wrote to the Corinthians, "then I am strong" (2 Cor 12:9, 10).

This combination of consolation and challenge that shines in God's words to Paul is present also in Joshua's words to the Josephites. What greater consolation to hear that God's grace is sufficient and that God's power is perfected in weakness? Yet few things are more challenging than embracing one's weaknesses and claiming God's grace as sufficient.

XVII. JOSHUA 18—19

BEHIND THE TEXT

If this is your first time reading through the book of Joshua, you might be surprised at what you find in chs 18 and 19. Based on what you have read thus far, you might imagine that all the land had been apportioned in 14:1-5. That chapter begins, "Now these are the areas the Israelites received as an inheritance in the land of Canaan, which Eleazar the priest, Joshua son of Nun and the heads of the tribal clans of Israel allotted to them. . . . So the Israelites divided the land, just as the Lord had commanded Moses" (14:1, 5). Yet what you find in Josh 18—19 is a very detailed picture of the land being apportioned to the remaining seven tribes.

At least three explanations are possible. These might be two versions of the same event, the author having combined (somewhat clumsily) multiple versions of the single apportionment. This seems unlikely given the care he took in crafting this (e.g., → chs 3—4). A variation on this first explanation is that 14:1-5 describes in summary fashion what is spelled out more fully in chs 18 and 19. This seems unlikely since 14:1-5 takes place in Gilgal (14:6), while the events of chs 18—19 are set in Shiloh (18:1).

The second explanation postulates two different occasions when the land was allotted to the remaining tribes. At Gilgal (ch 14), land was allotted only to Judah, Ephraim, and Manasseh, with the rest of the tribes receiving their land at Shiloh (chs 18—19). This would explain why Judah and the Josephite tribes arrive at the later allocation already in possession of their territory, but it ignores 14:1-5, which states that all the tribes, not just three, were given their land at Gilgal.

A third explanation suggests that all the tribes received their land by lot at Gilgal, as 14:1-5 describes. In the days following, only Judah and to a lesser degree Ephraim and Manasseh actually occupied their apportionment. The seven remaining tribes failed to take possession of the land they had been given, partly because their land lay in territory where Canaanites remained, mainly in the north. The initial apportionment at Gilgal had provided the ideal scenario, but reality had prevented this scenario from being realized. This precipitated a second allotment (chs 18—19), one more realistic, limited, and something of a compromise (Assis 2003, 7-8). As Assis explains, "The first apportioning is an ideological division, that includes the expansive territories of the Land of Israel, while the second primarily encompasses the area actually conquered by the Israelites" (2003, 8).

The third explanation makes the most sense of Joshua's scolding words in 18:3. One can best account for Joshua's accusation that they have been lazy, if these seven tribes had already received their land and yet failed to take possession. The scolding may continue in the name Joshua uses for Yahweh, "the God of your ancestors" (v 3). Appearing only here in Joshua, this name may have been used to remind these seven tribes that although God had promised this land to their forefathers, they had failed to possess it. "No one can blame Yahweh," as Butler notes, "if Israel does not have her land. Yahweh has given it to her" (1983, 204). God is also described by this name in Exod 3:13. By using this name, Joshua may be suggesting to the seven tribes that if God could deliver Israel from the Egyptians, he can also be trusted to deliver them from the Canaanites. A few verses later, as Joshua describes their second chance for land, he names Yahweh differently, this time as "our God" (Josh 18:6).

The third explanation also accounts for why Joshua, not Eleazar, is credited with the second apportioning (18:3). As Eleazar was present and active at Gilgal (14:1), so he was at Shiloh as well (see 19:51). But Joshua, not Eleazar, stands at center stage here. In so doing, the author is distinguishing between the two allotments. This explanation also accounts for why the surveyors do not explore the entirety of the remaining land. When the seven portions are described (18:11—19:48), no mention is made of the territory in the far north, such as Lebo-Hamath (Assis 2003, 4). The only territory mentioned is the land that Israel already controls essentially, though not absolutely (see reference to Jerusalem as "the Jebusite city" in 18:28).

Postulating two allotments—the more idealistic and optimistic Plan A in ch 14 and the more realistic and limited Plan B here—also explains why the territory of Judah and the Josephites is so large compared to the land given to the other tribes. Judah, Ephraim, and Manasseh had actually occupied the land they were apportioned at the earlier ceremony. Had the other tribes done so, their portions too would have been larger. Judah and the Josephites were allowed to keep the land they had gained (18:5), while the remaining tribes had to accept their portion from what remained available.

This explanation would also account for why some tribes inherited land in the territory of another tribe. Note that such occurrences principally involve the tribes of Judah and Ephraim. Having conquered more than enough land for itself, Judah was able to give up some of its territory to others. This is what we would expect after the first apportionment, when the tribal boundaries seem to have been more fluid and based in part on what that tribe could occupy. For example, 16:9 may suggest a scenario where an ambitious clan from Ephraim actually conquered several cities in what ended up in the land of Manasseh, and were permitted to keep those cities.

Boundary lacunae appear in the allotments to the tribes of Judah (15:63), Ephraim (16:10), and Manasseh (17:12-13), but only once in the allotments to the seven remaining tribes (see 19:47). The author of Joshua may not have been aware of how much land the northern tribes failed to occupy (although this information was known to the author of Judges [see Judg 1:30-33]). More likely, our author knew of such lacunae among the seven tribes but only mentioned the most egregious example: the tribe of Dan. In this way he contrasted the faithful albeit incomplete struggle of Judah and the Josephites with the less demanding work of the last seven tribes, whose land was already in Israelite hands.

Whenever the tribes received their land, whether at Gilgal, at Shiloh, or at both places, the allotment did not proceed as one might have expected, in order of tribal size or birth order. Instead, it follows "the order which prevailed in Jacob's household" (Woudstra 1981, 276 n. 1). First came the children of Jacob's two wives, Judah, Ephraim, and Manasseh. Levi's allotment has been mentioned several times already, although more details will follow in ch 21. The other children from Jacob's wives follow: Benjamin, Simeon, Zebulun, and Issachar. Next came the children of Jacob's concubines, Asher, Naphtali, and Dan (ibid.). As Dorsey notes in his outline (1999, 94-95; see below), the allotment proceeds chiastically with a non-Rachel tribal allotment first, then an allotment to a Rachel tribe, then another Rachel tribal allotment, followed by non-Rachel tribal allotments.

a introduction (13:1-7)
  b Transjordanian tribes (13:8-33)
    c Levites (14:1-5)
      d personal allotment for hero of Kadesh: Caleb (14:6-15)
        e non-Rachel tribal allotment: Judah (15:1-63)
          f Rachel tribal allotment: Joseph (16:1—17:18)
            g CENTER: allotment at Shiloh: seven tribes receive land by Yahweh's lot (18:1-10)
          f' Rachel tribal allotment: Benjamin—next to Joseph (18:11-28)
        e' non-Rachel tribal allotments: Simeon (inside Judah) and others (19:1-48)
      d' personal allotment for hero of Kadesh: Joshua (19:49-50)
    c' Levites (20:1—21:45)
  b' Transjordanian tribes (22:1-34)
a' conclusion (23:1—24:22)

As we saw with chs 16—17, chs 18—19 were meant to be considered together. The chapters begin and end with mention of the tent of meeting (18:1; 19:51) with the remaining tribes accounted for in between (Howard 1998a, 357). Each allotment (18:11—19:48) follows a similar pattern. After an introduction comes a description of the territory, then a summary. Nelson points out the tendency for each list to move on an east/west axis (1997, 219). In at least three of the territory descriptions (i.e., Zebulun, Asher, Naphtali), the border is described by starting in a central point and moving in one direction, then returning to that starting point and proceeding in the opposite direction (ibid.).

The boundary descriptions for the six tribes of ch 19 follow a recognizable chiastic pattern.

  a 19:1-9 Allotment for Simeon: town lists only
    b 19:10-16 Allotment for Zebulun: boundary list distinct from town list
      c 19:17-23 Allotment for Issachar: mixture of town and boundary lists
      c' 19:24-31 Allotment for Asher: mixture of town and boundary list
    b' 19:32-39 Allotment for Naphtali: boundary list distinct from town list
  a' 19:40-48 Allotment for Dan: town list only

These two chapters describe the allotment of the land to the remaining seven tribes and to Joshua in order to show God's faithfulness in keeping his promise to all Israel.

IN THE TEXT

A. Survey and Allotment of the Land (18:1-10)

I. Introduction (18:1-2)

■ I Earlier God promised that when they had been given rest from their enemies and were living in safety, he would choose a place for them to worship (see Deut 12:8-12). That time has come and the place chosen was **Shiloh**, which translates aptly to Rest (Keil and Delitzsch 1978, 185). Located about fifteen miles northwest of Jericho, **Shiloh** was central to all the tribes. It was in Ephraim's territory, that is, in land already conquered. Since they would remain here until the apportionment had been completed, Shiloh became the place not only for the **tent of meeting** but also for Israel's new **camp** (v 9).

This is the first mention of the **tent of meeting** in Joshua, here used as a synonym for the tabernacle. Shiloh would remain the center of Israelite worship through the period of the judges (see Judg 21:19), until the ark of the covenant fell into Philistine hands (see 1 Sam 4). The sanctuary (*sans* ark) was then moved to Nob (1 Sam 21:2), possibly located between Gibeah and Jerusalem. After Saul massacred the priests at Nob (see 1 Sam 22:19), the sanctuary was moved to nearby Gibeon (1 Kgs 3:4), where it remained until the temple was built. Although initially chosen by God, Shiloh later provided an example of a once sacred place that was later abandoned (see Ps 78:60; Jer 7:12; 26:6).

The tabernacle was not set up in order to provide a place to allot the territory; if such a place was needed, it would have been erected earlier when Judah and the Josephites received their land (Josh 14). It was set up because Israel had now arrived at a season of safety, with the **country ... brought under their control**. This should have meant that Israel was in full possession of the land, but for more than half of the tribes this was not the case. Hence the reason for this second allotment. Also at such time as the **country [is] ... brought under their control**, the Transjordan tribes were free to return home (see Num 32:22). This they do when the gathering at Shiloh is concluded (see Josh 22). The same root verb for **brought under their control** is used to describe God's command to the first humans to subjugate the earth (Gen 1:28). This suggests what other passages in Joshua make clear (Josh 15:63; 16:10; 17:12-13): **under their control** does not necessarily imply elimination of the enemy.

■ 2 The NIV's translation, **had not yet received their inheritance,** could be misleading, since they had received it according to 14:1-5. What they had not done, however, was take possession of it; that is, they "had not divided their inheritance" (as the NASB renders the phrase at the end of 18:2). If the NIV rendering is retained, it should be understood that they had received the title deed to the land but had not yet moved in and evicted the former tenants.

2. Joshua's Instructions to All Israelites (18:3-7)

■3 Joshua's response to their neglect of duty was to scold them and then offer them another chance. He first castigates them for not having occupied the land already given. Howard points out that the use of the verb rendered **take possession** (*y-r-š* in the *qal* stem) in this book refers to "Israel's actively taking possession of the Canaanites' land" (1998a, 301). The Hebrew verb behind **will you wait** can suggest slackness or laziness that leads to destruction (see Prov 18:9), in which case Joshua warns them that their delay could make matters worse. Or the verb could convey a failure of nerve, as in Prov 24:10: "If you lose heart when things go wrong, your strength is not worth much" (NJB). According to this meaning, Joshua is criticizing their fear rather than the idleness their fear produced.

■4-5 After chastising them, Joshua proposes Plan B. They are to appoint three men from each tribe to survey the land, divide it into seven parts, and report back to him (Josh 18:4-5). We are not told if men were chosen from only the seven tribes, from the nine and a half Cisjordan tribes, or from all twelve tribes. The emphasis on "all Israel" throughout the book suggests the last option is best. Joshua may have specified three men from each tribe, rather than two, in order to allow for a tie-breaker (Assis 2003, 10) or to provide greater safety in numbers.

The meaning of the phrase **according to the inheritance of each** (v 4) is unclear. Many translations, like the NIV, render it in a fairly literal way (ASV, KJV, NASB). Others propose something less literal, such as "with a view to their inheritances" (ESV), "for purposes of acquiring their heritage" (NABRE), or "of their proposed divisions of their new homeland" (NLT). The author may have included this phrase to connect this passage with Num 26:54, which dealt with the same subject. In the earlier passage, Yahweh instructed Moses to allot the land of Canaan according to the size of the tribes, so that "each is to receive its inheritance according to the number of those listed." The phrase in Numbers is close to what we find here. Or the author may have included **according to the inheritance of each** as a shorthand way of indicating that the surveyors were to assign the land in proportion to the size of the tribes, as God had directed Moses.

■6 The written descriptions of the land likely included the surveyors' recommendations based on tribal size so that the allotments would be seen as fair and proportional. Since the surveyors' report was to be in writing, the author may have had a written source when preparing the material found in these chapters. As Butler notes, "It is precisely this tradition which can account for the preservation of premonarchical border lists for the tribes" (1983,

203). That Joshua would cast the lot, not Eleazar, suggests we are witnessing a second apportionment for these tribes. That this allotment is no less divinely sanctioned is clear from the emphasis on the distribution taking place **in the presence of the** LORD **our God**. Verse 6 speaks of it happening **here**, that is, where the tent of meeting is located; v 8 refers to it happening "here at Shiloh in the presence of the LORD"; according to Josh 18:10, it happens "in Shiloh in the presence of the LORD."

■ **7** Once again we are reminded that the **Levites** and the Transjordan tribes have already received their land; such reminders are included for emphasis. The author wants us to recognize the importance of "all Israel." As Boling and Wright express it, "It is impossible to be Israel without twelve tribes, whether in Canaan or elsewhere" (Boling and Wright 1982, 423). The reader is also meant to understand that the tribal allocations have all proceeded according to Yahweh's direction and with his approval.

3. Joshua's Instructions to Surveyors (18:8-9)

■ **8-9** **As the men started on their way** (v 8), Joshua reiterated his instructions. Such repetitions, which may seem extraneous to the modern reader, were employed in Hebrew narration to emphasize the importance of what the surveyors are to do (Howard 1998a, 361). The men do as they are told, writing the description **town by town** (v 9), that is, laying out the borders through the combination of boundary and town lists we find in 18:11—19:48.

4. Land Distributed (18:10)

■ **10** When the men returned, Joshua did as he promised, casting the lot for them **in Shiloh in the presence of the** LORD. We are not given details on the process, but we can surmise that the surveyors proposed not only seven parcels of land but a recommendation as to which tribe would receive which parcel. This recommendation had been arrived at consensually and proportionate to the habitable space in each territory and the size of the tribe. The lot would then have been God's affirmation of these assignments. In this way, Israel would have obeyed their instructions to allot the land by size of tribe *and* by drawing lots (see Num 26:52-56).

B. Allotment to Benjamin (18:11-28)

1. Introduction (18:11-20)

■ **11-14** Benjamin was the first of the seven tribes to receive their territory. It lay between Judah and Joseph and is given both as a description of boundaries (vv 12-20) and a town list (vv 21-28). Benjamin's boundary description is unique among all twelve tribes in that it is spelled out according to its "four quarters" (**side**) (Boling and Wright 1982, 429). The northern border is given first (vv 12-14*a*) and corresponds to Ephraim's southern border. The name

Beth Aven (v 12) is later used as a polemic against the sanctuary built by Jeroboam I at Bethel (see Hos 4:15; 5:8), because *'āwen* can mean wickedness (*'āwen* can also mean "place of refuge"). That there was a town by this name is clear from its appearance in Benjamin's territory and elsewhere (Josh 7:2; 1 Sam 13:5; 14:23) (see Knauf 1984, 251-53).

■ **15-20** After the northern boundary, we are given the western (Josh 18:14*b*), then southern boundaries. The one on the south began at Kiriath Jearim. Since we have already been given the western boundary, we are surprised to hear that the boundary line **then ran westward** (v 15). Some translations omit the seemingly extraneous phrase (ESV, NRSV), but the NIV's **on the west** or "From that western point it ran" (NLT) are preferable. According to the NIV, the southern boundary included **Beth Arabah** (v 18). The Hebrew does not treat Arabah as a town name, but the LXX does. The NIV mg. follows the Hebrew more closely ("slope facing the Arabah"), as does the NLT: "From there it passed along the north side of the slope overlooking the Jordan Valley. The border then went down into the valley." The southern boundary ended at the **northern bay of the Dead Sea** (v 19), then turned north so that the **Jordan** River formed the **eastern** boundary (v 20*a*).

2. Town List (18:21-28)

■ **21-28** Benjamin's town list contains summary totals and is divided into districts. We encountered these attributes in Judah's allotment, but not with Ephraim's and Manasseh's. District one (vv 21*b*-24) included towns in the northern and extreme eastern portions of the territory. Mention of **Jericho** (v 21) reminds us of Joshua's curse on anyone who rebuilt the walls and gates (6:26), suggesting the Jericho referred to here was a small, unwalled village.

Some consider **Avvim** (18:23) to refer to the Avvites mentioned in 13:3 while others see Avvim as an alternate name for Ai (see Boling and Wright 1982, 430-31).

District two (18:25-28*a*) included towns in the central, southern, and western portion of Benjamin's territory. The towns associated with **Gibeon**, with whom Israel struck an unwise bargain, are included in this district (**Gibeon**, **Kephirah**, **Beeroth**, **Kiriath** Jearim [vv 25-26, 28]) (see 9:17; Pitkänen 2010, 316). Benjamin received the city of **Jerusalem**, although it continued to be occupied by Jebusites (18:28).

C. Allotment for Simeon (19:1-9)

1. Introduction (19:1)

■ **1** The tribe of **Simeon** received its apportionment next, although the land they received lay entirely within the southern portion of Judah's territory. This does not contradict Joshua's instructions in 18:5, which mandated that

Judah remain in its territory. Judah did remain there, but having more land than it needed, shared some of its territory with another tribe.

2. Towns in Simeon (19:2-8a)

■ **2-8a** Simeon's territory is described only in terms of its towns (→ Behind the Text for Josh 18—19), but these towns were divided into two districts. Hess considers these districts to align east and west (1996a, 267). Howard proposes a more complicated picture, locating district one in the Negev and describing district two as containing two Negev cities and two cities in the Shephelah to the west (1998a, 367). The additional city in the **far** south (v 8) was added "to define the extent of the Simeonite cities to the south, since it is not part of the two lists preceding it" (ibid., 368). Boling and Wright point out that both of Simeon's districts are closely related to the second part of Judah's district one, which involved the northern Negev around Beersheba (see 15:26-32) (1982, 436). Zorn suggests reading **Ziklag, Beth Markaboth, Hazar Susah, Beth Lebaoth** (19:5-6a) as equivalent to the parallel passage in 15:31-32a, describing Judah's tribes. This would make Beth Markaboth another name for Madmannah, Hazar Susah the same as Sansannah, and Beth Lebaoth the same as Lebaoth (1992, 3:84).

3. Summary (19:8b-9)

■ **8b-9** Simeon's summary does more than summarize (19:8a); it also explains why that tribe's territory lay within Judah's (v 9). In addition to being sufficiently courageous to occupy more than enough territory for itself, the tribe of **Judah** was also generous and willing to allow the tribe of Simeon to take some of that territory for their own. Simeon later appears in league with Judah against common enemies (see Judg 1:4, 17) but gradually disappears as a separate tribe. This could be seen as fulfilling Jacob's curse on Simeon to "scatter them in Jacob and disperse them in Israel" (Gen 49:7). The curse was imposed because of Simeon's violence, apparently a reference to their treatment of the residents of Shechem (see Gen 34) (Keil and Delitzsch 1978, 190).

D. Allotment for Zebulun (19:10-16)

1. Introduction and Boundary List (19:10-14)

■ **10-14** Zebulun's territory, described in both boundary and town lists, was located in the western area of lower Galilee (Hess 1996a, 269), with Asher to the west and northwest and Naphtali to the north and east. On the south it was bordered by Issachar and Manasseh. The boundary description begins at **Sarid** (Josh 19:10b), about five miles southeast of Nazareth, on the southern border. From Sarid, the boundary moves first to the west as far as **the ravine near Jokneam** (vv 10b-11). It then returns to Sarid and heads off to the east toward Mount **Tabor** (v 12). We saw a similar pattern of border description in

16:6, beginning from the center and moving in one direction, then returning and moving in the other direction. Although the border goes near **Daberath** (v 12), the town itself appears to be part of Issachar rather than Zebulun (see 21:28) (Howard 1998a, 370).

2. Town List and Summary (19:15-16)

■ **15-16** A brief town list follows in v 15, although one cannot help but feel something is missing. The list speaks of twelve towns after listing only five. Pitkänen writes off the verse as textually corrupt, pointing out that the Greek version "lists only the five place names of the verse and omits the statement about the total" (2010, 320). Keil and Delitzsch speculate that the towns may have been misidentified, miscopied, or that there is a "gap in the text" (1978, 195). Perhaps the author intended us to include in the total the towns mentioned in the boundary description, as with Issachar (v 22). Even when we do, the total still does not equal twelve.

Another possibility is that the author did not intend the number twelve to refer to the total of the towns listed, but only a total of the towns allotted, a number of which have gone unmentioned. One of the towns mentioned, **Bethlehem** (v 15), refers not to the more famous Bethlehem, birthplace of David and the Messiah, but to another town known as *house of bread*.

E. Allotment for Issachar (19:17-23)

■ **17-23** Issachar is next to receive its allotment, described in the form of a town list with a brief boundary "fragment" in v 22a (Nelson 1997, 221). Issachar's territory appears to be located north of Manasseh, southeast of Zebulun, and south of Naphtali, with its eastern boundary the Jordan River. It is hard to be certain, in part because Manasseh's northern boundary is somewhat ill-defined ("Asher on the north and Issachar on the east" [17:10]) and because Issachar's southern boundary is even less clear (Hess 1996a, 270).

The total number of towns given in 19:22b tallies, if one assumes that **Tabor** (v 22) refers to the city. If it refers to Mount Tabor, one can still arrive at the number sixteen by dividing **Shahazumah** (v 22) into two names or by adding the town Beeroth, as does the LXX (ibid., 270). As noted above, however, the number may not be intended as a total of the towns listed but of the towns allotted.

F. Allotment for Asher (19:24-31)

■ **24-31 Asher** received the fifth lot, being apportioned the land that lies along the Mediterranean coast between Mount Carmel in the south and **Tyre** in the north. As with Issachar, Asher's territory is a mixture of towns and boundaries. It begins with a brief list of cities (vv 25-26a), then traces the borders on the south, beginning in the west (v 26b) and heading east before turning north (v 27). As it proceeds north, several cities are mentioned, though not precisely in order from south to north (v 28*a*). After arriving at the fortified city of **Tyre**, the border then hooks south and ends at the Mediterranean Sea (vv 28*b*-29*a*). Several cities are then mentioned: **Akzib, Ummah, Aphek and Rehob** (vv 29*b*-30); three of these four are specifically identified in Judg 1:31 as remaining under the control of the Canaanites. Once again, the total number of towns listed in vv 25-29 comes close but does not match the number given in v 30.

G. Allotment for Naphtali (19:32-39)

■**32** Naphtali's territory lies just west of Asher's and is described, like Zebulun's, as a combination of boundary and town lists. The land of **Naphtali** "received the rich, forested land in the heart of the Galilee region" (Howard 1998a, 375); this land included both upper Galilee and the eastern portion of lower Galilee (Hess 1996a, 273). It borders Zebulun and Issachar on the south and the Jordan River north of the Sea of Galilee on the east (ibid.).

■**33-34** Although it also borders the Sea of Galilee and mentions towns along the lake, no mention is made of the lake itself. The southern border is described first, beginning at **Heleph** (v 33) and going east to the **Jordan**. According to one scholar, **Adami Nekeb** may not refer to a town but to a road or path (Ziv 1985, 273). Returning to **Heleph**, the border is then described as it moves west, around Mount Tabor (**Aznoth Tabor** may be a place name or could refer to the mountain itself) (v 34*a*). **Zebulun** is described as its southern border and **Asher** as its western border (v 34*b*).

Curiously, the Hebrew describes Naphtali bordering *Judah of the Jordan* on the east (v 34*b*). Since Judah's territory ends well to the south, many see this as resulting from textual corruption and follow the LXX in omitting the phrase (Boling and Wright 1982, 457). Keil and Delitzsch propose that this reference to Judah actually refers to Jair whose sixty towns lay across the Sea of Galilee in Bashan in the Transjordan (13:30; Num 32:41). Although Jair was a Manassite on his mother's side, he is here reckoned according to his Judahite ancestry through Hezron on his father's side (see 1 Chr 2:5, 21, 22) (1978, 204). While this explanation may seem a stretch, it does have the advantage of noting that the far shore of the Sea of Galilee was also Naphtali's eastern boundary.

■**35-39** A town list follows in Josh 19:35-38, in which at least some of the cities mentioned are described as **fortified**, meaning they possessed a wall and gate. This term only appears three times in the book of Joshua, one of them being v 29, in reference to Tyre. Since the Hebrew word for Tyre and **Zer** (v 35) have identical consonants, perhaps **Ziddim** and **Zer** do not refer to two cities but represent a phrase describing the fortifications associated with Tyre (as in the LXX) (Frankel 1992, 6:1089-90).

Among the towns mentioned in these verses, several lie along the western coast of the Sea of Galilee, including **Hammath**, usually understood as referring to Hammoth Dor (see 21:32), and **Kinnereth**, known from Egyptian records. Also included in Naphtali's territory was **Hazor** (19:36), a significant opponent in the northern campaign until decimated by the Israelites (see 11:10-11). By treating "Nekeb" (19:33) as a noun describing a path and "Aznoth Tabor" as referring to Mount Tabor (v 34), and by taking the phrase **Ziddim, Zer** (v 35) as a reference to the fortifications of Tyre, the total number of cities mentioned in Naphtali's territory comes out to **nineteen** (v 38).

H. Allotment for Dan (19:40-48)

1. Introduction and Town List (19:40-46)

■ **40-46** The last lot came out for **Dan**, whose territory is given only as a town list, as with Simeon (vv 1-9). Dan's territory lay west of Benjamin's in the strip between Judah to the south and Ephraim to the north. The borders of Dan are left out because, as Kaufmann notes, "The boundaries of Dan had been *absolutely and completely fixed* by those of its three neighbors: Judah, Benjamin, Ephraim" (1953, 16, emphasis original). The towns appear to be divided between those in the east (vv 42-44) and west (vv 45-46).

2. Explanation for Relocation and Summary (19:47-48)

■ **47-48** Although the author has provided the list of Dan's towns, he seems equally interested in explaining how the Danites occupied a different territory. The story is told in greater detail in Judg 18, but Josh 19:47 provides the basic plot: the Danites had trouble displacing the Canaanites in the territory just described (vv 41-46), so they traveled to the northern portion of Naphtali's territory. There they found the city of **Leshem** (or Laish) where the opponents were less formidable. They displaced them, settled down, and renamed the town after their patriarch, Dan. This would become the northernmost point for Israel throughout much of the rest of their history, as seen in the oft-repeated expression, "from Dan to Beersheba."

This is the only boundary lacunae mentioned in the seven remaining allotments. The Danites faced a challenge so dire that they abandoned their territory, something not done by any of the other tribes. Hence, one might consider Dan the weakest of the tribes. In fact, the author may have presented Dan as a positive example, worthy of emulation. In all the other instances of recalcitrant Canaanites, the tribes endured their presence and, if possible, enforced additional obligations on them. Dan did something more, actually relocating to territory not occupied by Israelites, and possessing it. In fact, the verb *possess* (occupied [v 47]) is the key verb in this section. It opens with Joshua chastising the remaining tribes for not taking possession (18:3), but draws toward its close with the resourceful Danites having **occupied** their new land.

I. Allotment for Joshua (19:49-50)

1. Land Grant to Joshua as Yahweh Commanded (19:49-50a)

■ **49-50a** Before allotting territory to any of the tribes west of the Jordan, one of the heroic spies of Kadesh, Caleb, had received his land (14:6-15). At the conclusion of the allotment, it is appropriate that the second spy, **Joshua**, receive his territory. Once again he is referred to as **son of Nun** (19:49), underscoring the significance of the occasion. We have no record of God promising this territory to Joshua. Either this promise was made and not recorded, or it was assumed that God would approve this bequest in recognition of Joshua's faithfulness on both sides of the Jordan. Although he had earned it, he did not claim the land for himself but asked for and received it from a grateful nation.

2. Grant of Timnath Serah in Ephraim (19:50b)

■ **50b** The city he requested was **Timnath Serah**, also known as Timnath Heres (see Judg 2:9), located sixteen miles southeast of Shechem in the territory of Ephraim, Joshua's tribe (Hess 1996a, 276).

J. Summary of Final Allotment (19:51)

■ **51** The account of the allotment concludes with a summary verse that identifies the main figures: **Eleazar the priest, Joshua son of Nun and the heads of the tribal clans of Israel**. The final phrase describes the tribal chieftains almost exactly as they had been described in 14:1, further demonstrating that, as Nelson points out, Josh 19:51 "does double duty as a closing bracket for the structural segments of 14:1-19:51 (nine-and-a-half tribes) and 18:1-19:51 (seven tribes)" (1997, 226).

FROM THE TEXT

God had promised this land to his people, and these chapters represent the final apportioning of the land among the twelve tribes. What emerges from this scene is a picture of a sovereign God fulfilling his promises in spite of obstacles. The author wants to make it very clear that God is not only present but actively involved throughout this distribution. Every allotment must first obtain his express permission, through the casting of the lot, before it becomes official. Accompanying him are his ordained representatives, "Eleazar the priest, Joshua son of Nun and the heads of the tribal clans of Israel" (v 51), so it is clear to all that the land is distributed equitably and as God wills.

Yet God's presence and blessing do not preclude problems, some of which are of human origin. However one settles the question of whether there was one apportionment or two, Joshua's criticism of the remaining seven tribes (18:3) makes clear that the Israelites had, to some degree, failed in their responsibility. Here is where we see God's grace most clearly in this story. Although sovereign, he willingly allows for a second chance.

If, as we have argued, the gathering at Shiloh represents a compromise, God is allowing the tribes another opportunity to occupy their land. Although their failure in their first attempt was not God's fault, he made it possible for them to enjoy rest in the land. Even Dan's backup plan—moving far north—appears to have been done with divine sanction (Judg 18:6, 10). "Even to a disobedient, reluctant people," writes Butler, "God gives new marching orders" (1983, 205).

God did not cease to be sovereign when he allowed for Plan B. His sovereignty can achieve his purposes even through human disobedience. Perhaps the greatest example of this can be found in the first act of human disobedience: the fall. Christians have long recognized this sin of our first parents as a "felix culpa," a "happy fault." So sang the ancient Latin Easter hymn, "O happy fault which deserved to have so great and glorious a Redeemer" (as cited in Oden 1989, 115). While it has brought great suffering, the fall has also brought a capacity, as Wesley wrote, "of being more holy and happy on earth; and . . . of being more happy in heaven, than otherwise they could have been" (1984a, 232). Furthermore,

> If God had prevented the fall of man, "the Word" had never been "made flesh"; nor had we ever "seen his glory, the glory as of the only-begotten of the Father." Those mysteries never had been displayed "which the" very "angels desire to look into." Methinks this consideration swallows up all the rest, and should never be out of our thoughts. Unless "by one man judgment had come upon all men to condemnation," neither angels nor men could ever have known "the unsearchable riches of Christ." (Ibid., 239)

XVIII. JOSHUA 20

BEHIND THE TEXT

20:1-9

Now that the land has been allotted to all the tribes, the author takes the next two chapters to highlight important aspects of life in the promised land, specifically how to maintain justice and how to provide for those responsible for the care of God's house. Chapter 20 describes the setting up of the cities of refuge to which someone could flee for asylum if they accidentally killed another. Without such cities, blood would be unjustly shed, polluting the land Israel had just received (see Num 35:33-34). God had commanded Moses to designate the cities of refuge when Yahweh has "destroyed the nations whose land" he is giving Israel, and when they had "driven them out and settled in their towns and houses" (Deut 19:1). Joshua 20 describes this designation.

Chapter 21 concerns the cities prescribed for the Levites, the tribe that had received no land "because the priestly service of the LORD is their inheritance" (18:7; see 13:14, 33). Yahweh addressed Moses regarding both Levitical cities and cities of refuge in Num 35; indeed, the topics were related, since the six cities of refuge were among the forty-eight Levitical cities (Howard 1998a, 379).

IN THE TEXT

A. God's Command to Joshua (20:1-6)

1. Introduction (20:1)

■ 1 According to the book of Joshua, Yahweh spoke directly to **Joshua** almost a dozen times during the conquest, always at moments of significance: at the beginning of the invasion (1:1), at the crossing of the Jordan (3:7; 4:1-3, 15-16), at the circumcision of Israel (5:2, 9), at the attack on Jericho (6:2-5), after the debacle at Ai (7:10-15; 8:1-2), before encountering the southern (10:8) and northern coalitions (11:6), and at the beginning of the allotment of the land (13:1-7). We have not heard from God since then, which makes his direct address to Joshua all the more striking.

2. Command to Joshua (20:2)

■ 2 The Israelites had already been told about cities of refuge, having been **instructed . . . through Moses** (see Num 35; Deut 4:41-43; 19:1-14). God now instructs Joshua to tell the Israelites that the time had come to designate these cites, now that God's people were "settled in" the "towns and houses" once occupied by the enemy (Deut 19:1).

As far back as Mount Sinai, God had made provision for those seeking asylum for accidental homicide. The place of asylum, at that time, was the tabernacle, specifically the bronze altar (Exod 21:12-14). After their years of wandering had ended and they queued up in Moab on the far side of the Jordan, God again spoke to Moses about asylum (Num 35:6, 9-34). There he provided another plan, one more suited to a settled yet dispersed population.

These cities of refuge were never intended to protect murderers; "the assembly" (Num 35:24-25) must determine whether the killing was intentional or unintentional and only in the case of the latter should they shelter the one who sought asylum. In Deut 4:41-43, Moses designated the three cities of refuge in the Transjordan. Several chapters later, Moses instructed the Israelites on their responsibility to set up additional cities west of the Jordan in the land they would conquer (Deut 19:1-13). (See Butler 1983, 213, for an excellent chart comparing the five passages that discuss asylum.)

3. Purpose of Cities (20:3)

■ 3 Israel already knew the purpose for the cities of refuge—indeed, Josh 20:3 is almost identical to Num 35:11*b*-12*a*. That purpose is here reinforced: anyone who kills another **accidentally and unintentionally** may avoid being killed by the **avenger of blood**. (The close similarity between this verse and the verses in Numbers suggest a possible literary dependence.) Both adverbs, **accidentally** and **unintentionally**, are used for emphasis, since their meanings significantly overlap. More literally, the killing must be innocent of any intention to do harm. It must also be "without knowledge," that is, without knowing that a certain action would bring about another's death. Those granted asylum must not have killed in a premeditated or careless way, nor in a crime of passion.

Numbers 35:16-28 provides further clarification as to what is accidental and unintentional. If someone wielded an instrument that could cause death (e.g., an object of iron, stone, or wood), and another person died, that death is likely murder, not accidental and unintentional homicide (vv 16-19). If someone felt malice toward another and expressed that with a shove or punch, or if one threw something at another, "that person is a murderer" (vv 20-21). On the other hand, if someone killed another for whom he harbored no feelings of hostility ("that other person was not an enemy" [vv 22-23]), then this was likely done **accidentally and unintentionally** (Josh 20:3). If acquitted in a trial, that person was eligible to take refuge in one of these cities and should not be surrendered to the avenger of blood (Num 35:22-25).

Make no mistake, any killing—premeditated or not, purposeful or accidental, intentional or unintentional—any shedding of blood required atonement. As Greenberg has written, "Shedding an innocent man's blood, even unintentionally, involved bloodguilt, and no manslayer was considered clear of this guilt" (1959, 127). The killer may live, but a penalty must be paid. Part of that payment was the need to remain within the four walls of the city of refuge. Should the killer prematurely leave the city, his blood was on his own head (vv 26-28).

Within the city, the killer was safe from the **avenger of blood** (*gō'ēl haddām*) (Josh 20:3), the family member with the God-given responsibility to "restore the balance in the family relations which had been upset by the slaying of one of its members" (Woudstra 1981, 299). This he did by tracking down and putting the killer to death. His goal was not private vengeance, which God forbade, but justice.

This was just one of the responsibilities of the *gō'ēl*, or kinsman redeemer. This person might also redeem a family member from financial difficulty or even marry the widow of a kinsman to perpetuate the lineage of the deceased. As Hubbard argues, the kinsman redeemer served as God's representative, bringing about the justice God valued (1991, 11).

Pitkänen and others have noted that the ANE offers no direct parallels to the cities of refuge (2010, 334). God implements these cities as an unprecedented step, in Nelson's words, to "limit the social damage of unrestrained blood vengeance" (1997, 228). Greenberg contends that these cities allowed for "public justice to intervene between the slayer and the avenger" rather than the "prior custom of regarding homicide as a purely private matter to be settled between the families of the two parties" (1959, 125).

If God had wanted to establish public over private justice, why not just outlaw the avengers of blood? Because he wanted to make it very clear that killing of any kind—even accidental—must be punished. The avenger represented the social obligation to privately restore justice. The gates of the city of refuge represented the intervention of public justice into the process of vengeance.

Now the responsibility for justice rested, not just with the family and tribe of the deceased, but with the offender (who had to flee to this city and make his case) and the community (who had to ascertain guilt or innocence and shield the killer). Because the avenger remained under obligation to restore justice, the killer had to remain in the city, unable to return home, paying his share of the penalty for his accidental and unintentional act. He was in what Greenberg called "enforced detention" (1959, 129). He could not ransom himself by paying a bribe to the avenger as this is clearly prohibited in Num 35:32. Only at the death of the high priest was the price fully paid. The avenger's responsibility was fulfilled, as was the killer's penalty. Both became free to resume their lives. By maintaining both private and public justice, God reinforced the seriousness of taking a life.

4. Procedure (20:4-6)

■ **4-5** These verses reiterate the procedure found in Num 35, and add a few elements. We learn, for example, that the killer was to stand before the elders in the gate and plead his case. Archaeologists have found that the city gate was more than a portal through the walls. It was a complex with bench-lined rooms and courtyards that could accommodate trials such as these (Boling and Wright 1982, 474). The elders, satisfied that the killing was unintended, would give permission to enter the city (**gather him to the city and they will give to him a place**), where he would stay. Some contend that "place" is here a technical term for "sanctuary" (Boling and Wright 1982, 474). Joshua 20:4 also makes clear that should the avenger arrive, the elders must not surrender their city's new resident.

Living in a Levitical city, while not home, would offer some opportunities to the asylum seeker. Given that the Levites would be a significant presence in the town and since the priests and Levites were the resident legal experts, the one granted asylum would likely have a greater opportunity to understand the Mosaic law. Assuming the Levites were engaged in periodic travels to the sanctuary at Shiloh, the detainee would have opportunities to be of assistance while the Levites were away.

■ **6** The description in v 6 of the rest of the judicial procedure is rather truncated. Were it not for the parallel accounts in Numbers and Deuteronomy, we might have more trouble ascertaining what happens next. The asylum seeker was to face a trial **before the assembly**. While this could refer to the initial trial held at the city gate before the elders (see NABRE; Hawk 2000, 221), the repetition of **assembly** in vv 6 and 9 suggests a group other than the elders.

Numbers 35:24-25 suggests the detainee was to be returned to his hometown or the site of the killing, probably under escort. Here his trial would be held. If found guilty, he would be handed over to the avenger or executed by the townspeople. If found innocent, he would be escorted back to the city of refuge until the death of high priest (Num 35:25*b*, 28; Josh 20:6).

What is it about the death of the high priest that makes this the appropriate ending point for the ordeal? Some have suggested that the death of the high priest marked a period of general amnesty (Boling and Wright 1982, 474). Greenberg observes, however, that amnesty generally marks the beginning, not the end of an epoch (1959, 127). More likely, the death of the high priest was considered to have an atoning effect, providing a form of "expiation" (ibid.). This was the view of the rabbis (ibid., 129), and best fits the evidence.

Note that there has been no mention of a blood sacrifice in any of the accounts of the city of refuge. Mosaic law made provision for atonement for other unintentional sins (Lev 4—5; Num 15:22-29), but nothing is said about a sacrifice to atone for killing another person. This is especially noteworthy given the high value the Israelites placed on human life. Israel's "insistence of life for life, to the exclusion of monetary compensation" reflected "a severity unparalleled in ancient Near Eastern law" (ibid.). Any killing, even unintentional, required that a life must be given up, yet nowhere in these passages do we read anything about the killer having to offer a blood sacrifice in place of the deceased.

According to Greenberg, "Only another human life can expiate the guilt of accidental slaying" (ibid., 130). That human life is not the killer's or an animal in place of the killer, but the life of the high priest himself. If even the high priest's clothing could "take on . . . any guilt incurred in the holy offering that the Israelites consecrate" (Exod 28:38 NRSV), the high priest himself could be seen as an atoning sacrifice in such cases.

For reasons that are unclear, Josh 20:4-5 are missing in some ancient Greek manuscripts. The last clause of v 3 is followed by part of v 6. Boling and Wright translate the Greek: "³The killer shall not die by the agency of the blood redeemer ⁶until he has stood fair trial before the congregation" (1982, 473).

B. Designation of Cities of Refuge (20:7-9)

1. Cities in Cisjordan (20:7)

■ **7** The author does not relate Joshua's words to the people, the people's response, or the process by which the cities were chosen. He tells us only that the people obeyed. The three cities, listed north to south, were **Kedesh** in **Naphtali**, **Shechem** in **Ephraim**, and **Hebron** in **Judah**. The verb for designating these cities (*q-d-š*) means to set something or someone apart as sacred, or to consecrate. Solomon used this same verb when speaking of consecrating the temple he would build (2 Chr 2:4). All of these cities are described as being in the **hill**

country of their respective tribes, likely because most of the population lived in the hill country. In other words, the towns were placed where they would be most useful. Indeed, "No place in the land was more than a day's journey from one of these [six] cities" (Howard 1998a, 386). Deuteronomy 19:8-9 permitted them to establish additional cities should their numbers increase, but three must have seemed sufficient for the land they currently occupied.

2. Cities in Transjordan (20:8)

■ **8** The three cities **east of the Jordan (on the other side from Jericho)** had already been **designated** by Moses (Deut 4:41-43), using a different verb from *q-d-š*. While the cities on the western side of the Jordan were identified from north to south, those on the eastern side go from south to north. Auld has pointed out that Josh 20:8 is very similar to Deut 4:43 (1978, 29).

3. Purpose of Cities Summarized (20:9)

■ **9** The account of the establishment of these cities closes with a summation of their purpose. We are reminded of what we learned in Num 35:15: these cities would be not only for Israelites but also for **any foreigner residing among them**. The chapter concludes with a clear juxtaposition of private (**avenger of blood**) and public justice (**standing trial before the assembly**).

FROM THE TEXT

No sooner has God given Israel the land than he requires that some of it be used for a purpose close to his heart, maintaining justice. God cares that people are treated fairly, whether the person that has killed unintentionally or the family that is duty-bound to avenge the killing. The system God designed meets the needs of both, even in the case of non-Israelites who happen to be living in the land. Through this system, God helped his people understand the importance of life, each person's responsibility to preserve it, and the importance of the community to establish and maintain justice.

Humans are not the only ones affected by a killing; God is affected too. He is the giver of life and only he has the right to take it. The only way to atone for the taking of a life is at the cost of another life. Yet this would mean a perpetual stream of bloodshed without end. God's system brought about justice not only by insisting on atonement for the act of killing but also by mercifully providing that atonement through the high priest whose death would have expiatory effect.

For the Christian, the parallels to the work of Christ are striking. Once again, God provides the sacrifice in the person of his Son. The death of this high priest represents the atoning sacrifice that satisfies the divine judge once for all. The pollution has been removed; the guilty may now return home absolved.

XIX. JOSHUA 21

21:1-45

BEHIND THE TEXT

Having assigned the cities of refuge, the Levites now step forward to request those towns where they and their families were to live. In Num 35:1-8, Yahweh commanded that the Israelites were to designate from their tribal allotments forty-eight cities, including the six cities of refuge, where the Levites would live. Joshua 21 describes Israel's eager obedience to this command, explaining first how the allotment was undertaken (i.e., by lot) and providing a general description, then by listing in detail the assigned towns. This double mention heightens the importance of the allotment, as does the high degree of repetition and correspondence (e.g., agreement in the numbers of towns and the order in which the Levitical clans are mentioned). The allotment to the Levites marks the final step in the tribal allocation; the chapter's closing verses emphasize the fulfillment of Yahweh's promise.

The cities were not removed from the control of the other tribes and placed into the hands of the Levites. Instead, the Levites were to live within these cities, among their non-Levite brothers and sisters. They were not given farmland but were permitted to graze their livestock on the immediately adjacent pastureland. As Weinfeld has noted, these cities are never described as the Levites' inheritance, only as "towns to live in" (Josh 21:2; see Num 35:2-3) (as cited by Pitkänen 2010, 342). Some have speculated that the Levites were also given the land between their towns (see Aharoni and Avi-Yonah 1977, map 108). Not only is this not stated in the text, but it contradicts the clear statements given elsewhere that the Levites would not receive territory of their own.

The assignment of these cities appears to describe their potential rather than actual settlement. Some of their cities, such as Gezer (Josh 21:21) and Taanach (v 25), were not controlled by the Israelites at this time (see 16:10; 17:11) (Howard 1998a, 391). One might even suggest that Yahweh placed the Levites precisely where the temptation to syncretism would be greatest. This picture resembles what we noted with regard to the other tribes: they were located within territory that could only be occupied by faith. "The list of levitical cities therefore contains an element of unreality," says Woudstra,

> not because of its utopian lateness but because the Israelites, in distributing the land and allotting these cities in the land, acted in the belief and expectation that conquest would be made if the tribes only put their faith in what the Lord had promised (13:6b). (1981, 310)

The importance of the Levitical cities is apparent in their mention in 1 Chr 6:54-80 (Howard 1998a, 388). Although Auld argues that Josh 21 depends on 1 Chr 6 (1998, 25-36), most agree that the author of Chronicles relied on Josh 21 or another source like it (Butler 1983, 225). "Everything," says Butler, "points to the originality of Josh 21" (ibid.). Nelson agrees: "There are numerous indications that the Joshua format is primary to that of Chronicles" (1997, 237). Although they are very similar, the two passages differ in the order in which the material is presented and disagree on the names for several of the cities. Some of the differences reflect varied forms of the same name (e.g., Hilen for Holon [v 15; 1 Chr 6:58], Ashtaroth for Be Eshterah [Josh 21:27; 1 Chr 6:71]). In some cases, the Chronicler clarifies confusion in the MT of Joshua (e.g., Bileam for Gath Rimmon [Josh 21:25; 1 Chr 6:70]), while in many others, Chronicles preserves what appear to be erroneous readings (e.g., Kedesh for Kishion [Josh 21:28; 1 Chr 6:72]). Some of the differences can be accounted for by a town changing its name over time (e.g., Jokmeam for Kibzaim [Josh 21:22; 1 Chr 6:68], Ramoth for Jarmuth [Josh 21:29; 1 Chr 6:73], Anem for En Gannim [Josh 21:29; 1 Chr 6:73]) (Keil and Delitzsch 1978, 212 n. 1).

Those who doubt that the book of Joshua reveals what actually happened during Canaan's settlement have speculated on which later period of Israel's history gave rise to Josh 21. Butler dates the list of towns to the time of David and Solomon (1983, 226). Others postulate an eighth-century date based largely on archaeological evidence (Boling and Wright 1982, 494). For Nelson, the chapter reflects "a largely artificial construction, although erected on the foundation of an inherited source list which covered only the kingdom of Judah (vv 13-18)" (1997, 238-39).

Nothing in the chapter requires a date even as late as the united monarchy. Since the chapter focuses on the allotment, rather than the occupation of the cities, archaeological evidence cannot speak conclusively (Howard 1998a, 388). A later date cannot account for the list's "broad territorial extent" (Nelson 1997, 238), nor have scholars been able to agree on "a convincing political rationale for such a system" (ibid., 239). Had the list arisen very late, we would expect a greater correspondence to the Chronicler's version. If the list had arisen during the united monarchy, we might expect to see Jerusalem mentioned, or at least more cities close to Jerusalem (see Woudstra 1981, 309).

When Israel camped in the wilderness during their forty-year sojourn, the Levites were assigned the area immediately contiguous to the tabernacle. Centuries later, in the vision given to the prophet Ezekiel, the territory of the Levites was close to the temple. The picture described in Josh 21 is very different, for here the Levites are scattered among the twelve tribes. Although the tabernacle stood at Shiloh in the territory of Ephraim, no Levites were assigned to live there or, indeed, anywhere close to there. Gibeon, a future tabernacle location, was one of the Levitical cities (v 17), but not Jerusalem. God appears to have scattered the Levites throughout Canaan to serve as salt and light. In this way they could more effectively carry out their assigned role as teachers of the law of Moses (Deut 33:10; 2 Chr 17:7-9; 35:3; Mal 2:6-9). Thus these forty-eight cities could become centers for the "preservation and dissemination of the faith and culture of Israel" (Hess 1996a, 281).

IN THE TEXT

A. Introduction (21:1-3)

■ **1-2** The leaders of the **Levites** approached **Eleazar**, **Joshua**, and the tribal chiefs at **Shiloh in Canaan** (v 2) to press their claim for the land Yahweh had promised (Num 35:1-5). They stepped forward in the same faith that motivated Caleb, but only did so now that the cities of refuge had been allotted (Josh 20), knowing these six cities were to form part of their eventual apportionment. By mentioning that this encounter took place at Shiloh, the author connects it to the other tribal allotments described beginning in ch 18.

Referring to Joshua more formally as **son of Nun** emphasizes the significance of the occasion; adding the strictly unnecessary qualifier, **in Canaan**, implies that Israel had finally arrived at its final destination (see Num 34:29; 35:10).

As with the earlier distributions, the Levites would receive their land through the casting of lots (see 14:1-2; 15:1; 16:1; 17:1; 18:1—19:51). This detail, plus the front-loading of Yahweh for emphasis, plus the mention of Eleazar before Joshua, highlights the "divine appointment underlying the assignment" (Woudstra 1981, 305). Perhaps each tribe decided which cities to allocate, with the lot determining which branch of Levites would receive those cities (Keil and Delitzsch 1978, 211).

The Levites were to be allotted cities **with pasturelands**, a detail mentioned nearly sixty times in this chapter alone. Whatever the reason for the frequent repetition, the effect is to reinforce Israel's generosity and obedience to Yahweh's command in Num 35. Although the term **pastureland** came to refer to a town's suburbs (Barr 1984, 15-31), here it refers to the land immediately adjacent to a town where cattle, sheep, and goats could graze. Since the towns' other non-Levite inhabitants would also need a place to pasture their flocks, what is granted here appears to be grazing rights, not exclusive possession of the land. Butler points out this would not be land for planting and harvesting (1983, 226-27). For grain, wine, and oil, the Levites would depend on Israel's tithes.

■ **3** The author specifies that it was Israel, not Eleazar, Joshua, or the tribal elders that gave the land to the Levites. This emphasizes not only Israel's obedience to God's command but also Israel's unity. They collectively contributed to the needs of the Levites, those appointed by God to represent them before the altar. Although Yahweh had allowed for the allocation of cities according to population, all the tribes contributed more or less equally (Howard 1998a, 391).

B. Summary of Allocation (21:4-8)

1. Lot for the Kohathites (21:4-5)

■ **4** The lot came out first for the Kohathite clans. This is appropriate since Kohath was Levi's firstborn, but also because it was from this clan that the priests, Aaron's descendants, were taken. Although there were only three Levitical clans, special attention to the priests means the allotment was distributed among four groups. The priests were given land from the allotments to the southernmost tribes, Judah and Simeon, and from the tribe of Benjamin, just to the north. The total number of cities was thirteen, slightly more than the average of four cities per tribe.

■ **5** The Kohathites who were not from the Aaronic line were responsible for the care of the ark, table, lampstand, bronze and gold altars, curtains, and items related to these objects (Num 3:27-32). They received ten cities from the tribes of Ephraim, Dan, and the half-tribe of Manasseh that remained west of the Jordan River, that is, just north and west of the other Kohathites. Since Manasseh counted as a single tribe, half of their cities (i.e., two) came from the western branch and half from the eastern branch of the tribe. The cities of Dan are located in their original territory, not in the land further north that they eventually occupied as well.

2. Lot for the Gershonites (21:6)

■ **6** The Gershonites received thirteen cities from the tribes of Issachar, Asher, Naphtali, and the half-tribe of Manasseh that was across the Jordan to the east. These were the clans responsible to care for the fabric that made up the tabernacle and its surrounding curtains (Num 3:21-26). As will become clear in the town list that follows, half of Manasseh gave two towns, while Issachar and Asher each gave four. For some reason, Naphtali only gave three.

3. Lot for the Merarites (21:7)

■ **7** Twelve cities from the tribes of Reuben and Gad on the east side of the Jordan and Zebulun on the west were given to the Merarite clans. The reason for this combination of tribes is unclear. It does not seem to be explicable geographically and appears nowhere else in the OT. These clans were responsible for the care of the tabernacle framework, such as the crossbars, posts, and bases for the surrounding curtain (Num 3:33-37).

4. Summary (21:8)

■ **8** The brief version of the allocation concludes with a summary that bookends Josh 21:3, framing the proceedings. Both verses begin with the same phrase, ***and the sons of Israel gave to the Levites***, and both contain the phrase ***these cities and their pastureland***. Both refer to Yahweh's command, though using different Hebrew phrases. Verse 3 mentions where the cities were taken from ("their own inheritance"), while v 8 focuses on how they were apportioned ("by lot" [KJV, ESV, NASB]).

C. Towns Allotted by Clan (21:9-42)

1. Kohathites (21:9-26)

■ **9** Having provided an overview of the apportionment, the author elaborates in considerable detail. He does not introduce this section but begins the allotment from **Judah** and **Simeon** with an unusual phrase: "mentioned by name" (KJV, ESV), a phrase "completely without parallel in the rest of the book" (Boling and Wright 1982, 487). The author may have included it to provide one more way to draw attention to what God had given them. As we noted in the commentary on Josh 12, the detail in this chapter is the author's way of celebrating how God had fulfilled his promises, "right down to every last village or town and every last border, passing atop this hill over here and descending through that valley over there" (Howard 1998a, 278).

■ **10** Since the first lot fell to the subgroup of the Kohathites made up of the priests, they received towns from the tribes of Judah and Simeon. These two are mentioned as if one tribe because the territory of Simeon actually lay within that of Judah (see 19:1-9).

■ **11-12** **Hebron** is mentioned first, using its former name; as noted earlier (14:15; 15:14-15), this highlights its symbolic significance as the home of the Anakites, who terrified the spies (Num 13). It is likely mentioned first here because it is a city of refuge, and these are always mentioned in this chapter at the beginning of the lists where they appear (see Josh 21:21, 27, 32, 38). It may also be mentioned first because it was already assigned to Caleb. The attentive reader will naturally want to know how competing claims were resolved. The author takes pains to point out that while the Levites were permitted to dwell in the town and were given access to the pastureland, Caleb and his descendants retained **possession** of the fields and villages surrounding Hebron (v 12). Boling and Wright point out that this is the first occurrence of **possession** in Joshua. "It will be echoed in the summary to the chapter (v 41) and the root is a key element in the story to follow (22:4, 9, 19), in which the focus shifts rapidly" (1982, 488).

■ **13-16** Having explained the situation in Hebron, the author resumes his city list in v 13 by paraphrasing v 11. The Chronicler referred to **Holon** (v 15) as Hilen (1 Chr 6:58) and to **Ain** (Josh 21:16) as Ashan (1 Chr 6:59). The conquest of **Debir** (Josh 21:15) had won Othniel the right to marry Aksah, Caleb's daughter (see 15:15-17). Most of these towns were south of Hebron, except **Libnah** (21:13) and **Beth Shemesh** (v 16), which were to the northwest. Although the average number of towns from each tribe is four, Judah and Simeon combine to provide nine, which likely reflects Judah's sizable territory (see 19:9).

■ **17-18** Benjamin also provided cities to the priests. **Gibeon**, **Geba**, **Anathoth** and **Almon** (or Alemeth [1 Chr 6:60]) were clustered just north of Jerusalem (which is not included among the cities given to the priests). After the tabernacle was removed from Shiloh, it was set up in Gibeon, where it remained until the days of Saul. The Gibeonites had relied on trickery to earn their place among the Israelites, but they paid for their deception through service to the tabernacle (Josh 9). The prophet Jeremiah would come from Anathoth (Jer 32).

■ **19** The priestly allotment concludes with a summary statement, the elements of which can be found at the end of each of the four groups (Josh 21:19, 26, 33, 40): the name of the group (e.g., **the priests, the descendants of Aaron** [v 19]; **the rest of the Kohathite clans** [v 26]), the number of towns given, and mention of **pasturelands** (missing in v 40).

■ **20-22** The remaining Kohathites received their territory from Ephraim, Dan, and the half-tribe of Manasseh that settled west of the Jordan (vv 20-26). **Ephraim** provided **Shechem** (mentioned first, as the city of refuge), **Gezer**, **Kibzaim** (or Jokmeam [1 Chr 6:68]), and **Beth Horon**. Shechem appears to have been initially assigned to the tribe of Manasseh (Josh 17:2, 7). It must have passed early into Ephraim's hands, for it is located by 20:7 in the hill country of Ephraim.

■ **23-26** The four cities **Dan** provided were **Eltekeh**, **Gibbethon**, **Aijalon**, and **Gath Rimmon**. The Chronicler's version omits any mention of Dan and credits Ephraim for giving Aijalon and Gath Rimmon (1 Chr 6:69). The half-tribe of Manasseh located west of the Jordan provided two cities, **Taanach** (Aner [1 Chr 6:70]) and Bileam (or Ibleam). The MT identifies the second city as **Gath Rimmon**, but most scholars consider this a scribal error "occasioned by the wandering of the eye to the previous verse" (Keil and Delitzsch 1978, 213; Butler 1983, 222). Butler points out that Tanaach and Ibleam belonged to Manasseh but were located in Issachar (Josh 17:11). According to Judg 1:27, these towns remained in Canaanite hands (ibid., 230).

2. Gershonites (21:27-33)

■ **27** Whereas in the summary description (Josh 21:6), the tribes were identified as Issachar, Asher, Naphtali, and the half-tribe of Manasseh across the Jordan, here **Manasseh** is the first tribe mentioned, rather than the last. Instead of **Be Eshterah**, Chronicles has Ashteroth (1 Chr 6:71), which Pitkänen considers the preferred reading (2010, 346).

■ **28** Scholars are less enthusiastic about the Chronicler's replacement of **Kishion** (Josh 21:28) with Kedesh (1 Chr 6:72). Three of the four cities mentioned as belonging to Issachar are identified with other tribes. **Daberath** (Josh 21:28; 1 Chr 6:72) appears in Zebulun's boundary list (19:12), but Howard explains this as the result of the town being located on the common border (1998a, 390).

■ **29** The other two cities, **Jarmuth** (Remeth [19:21]; Ramoth [1 Chr 6:73]) and **En Gannim** (Anem [1 Chr 6:73]), appear in Judah's city list (Josh 15:34-35). Howard is probably right that this duplication reflects the presence among the Israelites of more than one city by the same name (1998a, 390).

■ **30-33** **Asher** provided **Mishal** (Mashal [1 Chr 6:74]), **Abdon**, **Helkath** (Hukok [1 Chr 6:75]), and **Rehob**. From **Naphtali** came **Kedesh in Galilee**, the city of refuge, as well as **Hammoth Dor** (Hammon [1 Chr 6:76]), and **Kartan** (Kiriathaim [1 Chr 6:76]). Note that Naphtali only provided three cities, rather than four. It may be that this was because its population was less than that of Issachar or Asher (see Num 26), although there were smaller tribes that gave four cities.

3. Merarites (21:34-40)

■ **34-35** As with the Gershonites, the author altered the order in which he mentions the tribes (v 7), this time beginning west of the Jordan with Zebulun and then mentioning two tribes in the Transjordan. The addition of the phrase **the rest of the Levites** (v 34), while not strictly necessary, complements the formal and comprehensive tone of the passage. **Zebulun** provided **Jokneam, Kartah,** and **Dimnah** (Rimmono [1 Chr 6:77]). Woudstra suggests Dimnah could be the same town as Rimmon (Josh 19:13) (1981, 312). The Chronicler has Tabor (1 Chr 6:77) in place of **Nahalal**.

■ **36-40** The first-mentioned of Reuben's towns, **Bezer,** was identified in Josh 20:8 as a city of refuge, although this is not specified here. **Reuben** also gave **Jahaz, Kedemoth,** and **Mephaath. Gad** provided **Ramoth in Gilead (a city of refuge for one accused of murder),** as well as **Mahanaim, Heshbon and Jazer.**

4. Summary (21:41-42)

■ **41-42** The allotment concludes with a final tally of forty-eight towns along with pastureland (v 41). In the next verse, the author repeats and repeats again that each town was accompanied by its pastureland (v 42). Repetition of this detail, as noted earlier, may have been intended to emphasize Israel's generosity and obedience.

To what is found in the Hebrew, the LXX translation of v 42 adds:

And Joshua finished dividing the land according to its borders, and the sons of Israel gave a share to Joshua according to the command of the Lord. They gave him the town which he asked for; they gave him Tamnasachar from the mountain of Ephraim. And Joshua built the town, and lived in it. Joshua also took the knives of stone with which he circumcised the sons of Israel that had been born on the way in the wilderness, and put them in Tamnasachar. (As cited in Pitkänen 2010, 340)

The first three sentences repeat what is found in 19:49b-50, while the remaining sentence preserves a detail not found elsewhere. Butler believes the Greek translators were working from an older tradition, since "it is highly unlikely that the LXX translators would invent such a story and place it here" (1983, 223). Howard grants Butler's point and agrees that the addition may have been in the Hebrew manuscript being used by the Greek translators, but questions whether this Hebrew manuscript reflects the original text of Joshua, given the duplication of 19:49-50. He concludes, "The entire addition in Greek was secondary, not original, despite its fascinating contents" (1998a, 396-97).

D. Section Summary (21:43-45)

A second summary follows in vv 43-45, this time concluding the land distribution that began at ch 13. Hawk points out that the same three elements found in Yahweh's opening speech to Joshua (1:1-6)—that Yahweh had given the land, that Israel was to enter and possess the land, and that this land had been sworn on oath to Israel's ancestors—are also present in 21:43-45 (2000, 224). Keil and Delitzsch also note the connection between these verses and 11:23 and suggest that 21:43-45 connects the two halves of the book, chs 1—12 and 13—21 (1978, 215). Woudstra draws even more explicit connections, finding in 21:43 an allusion to the distribution of the land in chs 13—21, v 44 reflecting "on the actual stories of the conquest as told in chs. 1-12," and v 45 placing "the entire book under the perspective of God's faithfulness" (1981, 314). Butler is right to claim that this "small section summarizes the theological point of the book of Joshua. The entire book is to be read in light of these three verses, particularly the last. God directs history for his disobedient people through his warning and judging word" (1983, 236).

■ **43** Yahweh had kept his oath to give the land to Israel, a promise made many times to the patriarchs, as well as to Moses and Israel (see Gen 12:1-3; 15:18-21; 22:17-18; 24:7; 26:3; 50:24; Num 11:12; 14:16, 23; Deut 1:8, 35; 6:10; see Hess 1996a, 284 n. 1). What had been promised had been granted, and what had been granted had been possessed (Josh 21:43) (see 1:11, 15; 12:1; 18:3; 19:47; 23:5; 24:4, 8; Boling and Wright 1982, 499). The Hebrew word for ***all*** appears six times in these verses, expressing, in Hawk's words, "the comprehensive scope and completion of YHWH's acts on behalf of Israel" (2000, 225).

■ **44** All Israel's enemies had been defeated, just as Yahweh had sworn. The double repetition in rapid succession of Yahweh swearing an oath (vv 43, 44) is striking. Now Israel could enjoy **rest on every side**. As we have seen, rest is a key word in Joshua. It was promised in Exod 33:14 (see Deut 3:20; 12:10; 25:19), a promise echoed by Joshua in 1:13-15. It seems likely that this rest refers to more, though not less, than military peace.

■ **45** By living peacefully in this land, Israel could increasingly experience the spiritual rest they anticipated each week in the Sabbath (see Exod 16:23; 20:11; 23:12). They had long been a nation with a law. Now able to dwell unmolested in their own land, they could better carry out that Law, living out the true purpose for which they had been chosen by Yahweh. This is what the writer of Hebrews alluded to centuries later (Heb 4). As if there could be any doubt, Josh 21:45 adds that **all** the **promises** Yahweh had made to the Israelites had now been **fulfilled**.

Anyone who has even a passing knowledge of the book of Judges or who has read Joshua carefully will recognize that the picture painted in vv 43-45 is naive at best. Israel did not possess all the land of Canaan nor had all their enemies been subdued. How can we reconcile the optimistic picture of these verses with passages that describe unconquered enemies (see Josh 13:1-5; 15:63; 16:10; 17:12-18; 19:47; 23:4-5, 7, 12-13)? Scholars who discount the historicity of Joshua and postulate a long process of compilation involving many hands use this contradictory evidence to support their hypotheses (see Nelson 1997, 242).

Others interpret the optimism of vv 43-45 as emphasizing God's faithfulness in order to heighten the disaster that followed Israel's disobedience. For example, Calvin distinguished between "the clear, unwavering, and certain fidelity of God in the fulfillment of his promises, and the weakness and indolence of the people, which caused the blessings of God to slip from their hands" (as cited by Keil and Delitzsch 1978, 216). Later scholars have pursued the same general tack by taking these verses as an example of the author being ironic. For Polzin, "Joshua is scarcely intelligible if 21:41-43 is not read in an ironic sense" (1980, 132). Although one must grant that Israel's history played out disastrously, the verses in question are not intended to cast reproach on Israel, as these approaches suggest.

A better approach treats these verses as speaking truthfully, but according to ANE conventions where hyperbole is not only permitted but expected in conquest accounts. The two pictures—one portraying Israel as totally victorious and the other picturing a land where the enemy remained entrenched—were meant to be viewed together, stereoscopically. God had certainly kept his promises, allowing Israel to expel the inhabitants of Canaan and occupy the land. Israelites could live in houses they did not build and harvest crops they did not plant without fear of significant military opposition. Enemies stubbornly remained, which is precisely what God predicted and intended so the land would not "become desolate and the wild animals too numerous" for the Israelites. Instead, he promised, "Little by little I will drive them out before you, until you have increased enough to take possession of the land" (Exod 23:29-30; see Deut 7:22). As Israel grew more powerful and sought to expel those enemies, God would "do everything necessary to bring matters to a successful completion" (Hawk 2000, 225).

FROM THE TEXT

Earlier chapters pictured God providing for his people in a variety of ways. We saw him provide directly and miraculously, such as when he toppled the walls of Jericho, stopped the sun in the middle of the sky, or pelted Israel's enemies with hailstones. What we do not see in Joshua is the miraculous provision of food, as had been the case with the manna in the wilderness. In fact, the author specifically informs us that the manna ceased when the Israelites began to eat the food they found in Canaan (5:12). God provided for the material needs of his people, but he did so indirectly, in ways that required the Israelites to take responsibility for themselves. The twelve tribes had to harvest what the Canaanites had planted, then plant and cultivate their own crops.

This chapter reveals further dimensions of God's provision. We were told earlier that the Levites would receive no territory because Yahweh, the God of Israel, would be their inheritance. Here we see more clearly that God would provide for their needs through their fellow Israelites. Not only would their inheritance be the tithes and "offerings presented to the Lord" (13:14), but they would also be given towns in which to live, towns taken from the territory of the other tribes. In turn, God provided for the Israelites through the Levites, who were to teach them the Law, maintain the tabernacle, and carry out the rituals essential to Israelite well-being.

As we can see, God is the great provider who does so in a variety of ways. One of his favorite ways is through the community of faith. The Apostle Paul understood this and compared the community to a body whose needs are met through the faithfulness of its members. While less miraculous than manna from heaven, people helping people is still an act of the God who works in the hearts of the faithful.

It was faith in God's promises that prompted the Levites (and others like Caleb, Aksah, and the daughters of Zelophehad), to ask God to meet their needs. It took faith to occupy those towns, especially those where the enemy remained. Faith is always the key that unlocks God's provision. One must believe that God is able to provide, whether miraculously or by very normal means. Those who believe find him faithful, for "not one of all the Lord's good promises to Israel failed; every one was fulfilled" (21:45).

21:1-45

22:1-34

XX. JOSHUA 22

BEHIND THE TEXT

Some have seen the three chapters that follow the conclusion of the land distribution (Josh 21) as only tying up loose ends or serving as an appendix (Soggin 1972, 207). In truth, however, these chapters mark a significant turn in the book. As Dorsey's chiastic outline shows, the chapter looks backward to "close the loop" with the Transjordan tribes whom we met near the book's opening. The chapter also looks forward to illuminate Israel's future in their new land.

- a introduction (13:1-7)
  - Yahweh's challenge to Joshua, when he is old, to divide the land
  - theme: <u>the land that remains</u>—whose inhabitants Yahweh will drive out
- b Transjordanian tribes (13:8-33)
  - their allotments outside of Canaan
- c Levites (14:1-5)
  - they will have no territory, only towns in other tribes
- d personal allotment for <u>hero of Kadesh</u>: Caleb (14:6-15)
- e non-Rachel tribal allotment: <u>Judah</u> (15:1-63)
- f Rachel tribal allotment: <u>Joseph</u> (16:1—17:18)
- g **CENTER: allotment at Shiloh:** seven tribes receive land by Yahweh's lot (18:1-10)
- f' Rachel tribal allotment: Benjamin—next to <u>Joseph</u> (18:11-28)
- e' non-Rachel tribal allotments: Simeon (inside <u>Judah</u>) and others (19:1-48)
- d' personal allotment for <u>hero of Kadesh</u>: Joshua (19:49-50)
  - conclusion of Shiloh allotments (19:51-52)
- c' Levites (20:1—21:45)
  - their towns in other tribes and their cities of refuge
- b' Transjordanian tribes (22:1-34)
  - their return to their allotments outside of Canaan, and their memorial altar to commemorate their share with the tribes in Canaan
- a' conclusion (23:1—24:33)
  - Joshua's closing challenge to Israel, when he is old
  - theme: <u>the land that remains</u>—whose inhabitants Yahweh will drive out. (1999, 94-95)

The two parties involved in the conflict described in Josh 22 reflect competing concerns. The ten tribes dwelling to the west of the Jordan River, whom the author refers to here as Israelites, were willing to engage in civil war to preserve religious orthodoxy. The Transjordan tribes—Reuben, Gad, and the half-tribe of Manasseh—were willing to skirt heterodoxy (without crossing the line), to ensure the unity of the twelve tribes. Israel struggled with these two challenges for the rest of its existence as a nation. Within a few hundred years of this encounter, unity was broken as one nation split into two and become the northern kingdom of Israel and the southern kingdom of Judah. About two centuries after that split, the northern kingdom reaped the bitter fruit of its constant heterodoxy (722 B.C.); Judah endured for another century and a half until it too succumbed to the fruit of its disobedience (586 B.C.).

All of this lies well into the future for the author of this book, but recognizing the importance of both orthodoxy and unity, he relates this story that ends with all Israel uniting on behalf of true worship of Yahweh. The story is meant to illustrate the truth the psalmist celebrates poetically: when "righteousness and peace kiss each other" (Ps 85:10 [11]).

No little attention has been given to this chapter by scholars who believe the book was compiled over centuries by various authors from a variety of theological perspectives. Some have seen in this chapter words and themes associated with the much later Priestly author, thought to have been responsible for the material in the Pentateuch related to priestly matters. Others, arguing that this chapter sounds like Deuteronomy, have used this chapter to contend for a Deuteronomic History completed in the postexilic period. These scholars disagree on how to divide the passage into its sources or even whether there is a postexilic setting that can accommodate the narrative's themes (Pitkänen 2010, 367). Among those who contend that an original story has been modified, "practically all of them disagree concerning what the original form of the story was" (ibid.).

One needs no such theories to make sense of the chapter. It falls into two uneven sections: the first (Josh 22:1-8) involves Joshua's dismissal of the Transjordan tribes with his blessing, while the second (vv 9-34) describes the conflict between orthodoxy and unity. Chapter 22 was included to show that at this point in Israel's history, God's people were determined to preserve both.

IN THE TEXT

A. Dismissal (22:1-8)

1. Joshua Dismisses the Transjordan Tribes with a Call to Remain Faithful (22:1-5)

Several earlier chapters began with groups of Israelites approaching their leaders with requests (see 14:6-12; 17:3-4; 21:1-3). Here, Joshua took the initiative and summoned the Transjordan tribes to him. From 22:9 we know that Joshua was in Shiloh. We cannot be sure how long after the events of chs 13—21 this conversation occurred, though we can see no reason why Joshua would not have dismissed these tribes promptly since their work was done (see 21:43-45).

These verses echo Joshua's words to the Transjordan tribes in 1:12-18. Both passages refer to Moses more than once as "the servant of the Lord" (1:13, 15; 22:2, 4, 5). Both speak of Moses' promise of land to these tribes (1:13, 14, 15) and his command to them to fight on behalf of their brothers (1:14; 22:3) until they experience rest from their enemies (1:15; 22:4). Both speak of those the Transjordan soldiers left behind (1:14; 22:8). Both passages speak of their obedience to Moses and Joshua, the first as a promise (1:16-18), the second as a strong statement of fact, followed by instructions to remain obedient (22:2, 5). Both clearly imply the unity of all Israel, whether east or west of the Jordan River (1:14; 22:3-4). From these echoes we can see that "the story has come full cycle" (Woudstra 1981, 316); God's promise has been fulfilled.

■ **1-3** Joshua's words make clear that the Transjordan tribes have complied fully with all that was asked of them. The **You** in **You have done** (v 2) is emphatic. Joshua goes on to speak of their obedience in **all that Moses** commanded and **everything** that he commanded, even though it had taken **a long time** (v 3). Not only had they not abandoned their brothers, they had **carried out the mission** given to them by God. In other words, their motivation was not only filial affection but also faithful obedience to Yahweh's command. **Carried out the mission** translates an unusual phrase since **carried out** and **mission** both use the same root word; it might more literally be rendered, "You have guarded the guardianship" (Boling and Wright 1982, 508). The phrase is yet another way to emphasize their obedience.

■ **4** Because of this obedience, they were free to return home, literally, ***now turn and go***. **Gave you** translates a term elsewhere rendered "possessions." It is only used seven times in Joshua, four of them in this chapter (vv 4, 9, 19 [twice]), but frequently in passages credited to the Priestly writer (→ Behind the Text for ch 22).

■ **5** While free to return home, they remain obligated to obey God. In one verse, Joshua expresses the heart of Israelite religion. They are to be very careful to obey (***keep greatly to do***) the **commandment and the law** given by Moses, which Joshua summarizes in five phrases.

First, they are to **love** Yahweh. In the ANE, to love a sovereign meant to express loyalty to that sovereign. The Amarna letters, dated prior to the conquest but written from this same region, often use love this way (Moran 1992, xxiv n. 59). Israel had been brought into covenant relationship with Yahweh, and they were to express their covenant loyalty to him. Second, they are **to walk** in all his ways. Since **to walk** is a metaphor describing a person's lifestyle, Joshua calls them to conduct themselves as befits those in a covenant relationship with Yahweh.

Third, they must obey the commands Yahweh issued through Moses (**commands** here is the same term rendered **commandments** just above), as they had from the beginning of the conquest (see v 3). Fourth, they must **hold fast**, that is, cleave to him. This implies firm resolve in the face of temptations to rebel. Finally, their obedient service must be wholehearted, nothing withheld.

2. Joshua's Blessing on the Transjordan Tribes (22:6-8)

■ **6-7** In this section, the author first summarizes the content of blessing (v 6), before providing a parenthetical note of explanation (v 7a). The explanation itself appears at first glance to be in need of explanation. We have already been told about the makeup of the tribes across the Jordan (1:13-18; 13:8-33), so why are we told this information again? And why only explain about Manasseh, not Reuben and Gad (22:7)?

As to the first question, repetition of such details is standard practice in Hebrew narrative. The reason to mention only Manasseh may concern the chief distinction between this tribe and the other two: this tribe was split, with half on the east and half on the west. Howard points out that only Manasseh was mentioned "for the purpose of stressing the unity of this tribe" (1998a, 404). The unity of this tribe, in spite of the intervening Jordan River, was meant to symbolize "the larger unity that was to characterize the entire nation" (ibid.). The blessing is only mentioned in v 6 but is now related in detail (vv 7*b*-8).

■ **8** In the original, **with your great wealth** appears at the beginning of the blessing for emphasis. The Transjordan tribes had profited from the spoils of war and were returning home with livestock, silver, gold, bronze, iron, and clothing. The term used for **wealth** is not common in the OT, appearing only here, in 2 Chr 1:11-12, and in Eccl 5:19; 6:2. Since 2 Chronicles and Ecclesiastes are generally agreed to have been written late in Israel's history, some take this as evidence that this chapter was written long after the events it describes, though this conclusion is not necessary.

Joshua instructed them to share the spoils with their **fellow Israelites**. This could refer to the Israelites west of the Jordan, but one assumes they had gathered their own loot in battle, as had the Transjordan tribes. Butler suggests Joshua is only offering general instruction or a "programmatic note for the future" and is explaining that henceforth all spoils must be evenly divided among all (1983, 245). Most likely, the **fellow Israelites** are those Israelites in the Transjordan left behind to watch over families, livestock, and property while the army was away.

B. Transjordan Tribes Build an Altar (22:9-10)

■ **9-10** Having demonstrated their obedience to the satisfaction of no less a figure than Joshua himself, and at his instructions, the eastern tribes depart. The Hebrew gives no cause to see vv 1-8 and vv 9-34 as two independent stories compiled later but reflects a smooth transition from what precedes to what follows (see Butler 1983, 241). One is struck, however, by the fact that those who remain west of the Jordan are referred to as **Israelites** (see vv 9, 11, 12, 13, 32), suggesting this term does not apply to the Transjordan tribes. Some conclude this means the story was only written after the Transjordan territory had been lost to the Israelites.

While we cannot rule out this possibility, the use of **Israelites** to describe only the western tribes is better explained as the author's way of making a point. The chapter deals with the question of whether Israel will remain united and orthodox. These are not equal values: Israel was to embrace only that unity based in orthodoxy. This was why they were not to make treaties with any of the Canaanites.

As this chapter progresses, the western tribes are seen as zealously orthodox, while the orthodoxy of the eastern tribes is questioned. Hence, only the western tribes could wear the label Israel. As Howard notes, "Beginning with v. 30," however, "there is no reference again to such all-inclusive terms as 'all Israel' or 'the whole community,' only to the more general terms, the 'the Israelites' or 'the community'" (1998a, 407).

On their way to Gilead (v 9), here probably referring generally to the land across the Jordan (see Pitkänen 2010, 357), the Transjordan tribes stop at the Jordan to build an altar (v 10). The story unfolds from this point chiastically, as seen in this outline from Hawk:

A Eastern tribes build the altar (vv 10-11)
  B Western tribes gather for war (v 12)
    C Delegation selected and sent to the eastern tribes (vv 13-15a)
      D Delegation accuses the eastern tribes (vv 15b-20)
        E Eastern tribes deny the allegations (vv 21-23)
          F Eastern tribes explain the altar (vv 24-28)
        E' Eastern tribes deny the allegations (v 29)
      D' Delegation is satisfied with the explanation (vv 30-31)
    C' Delegation returns to the other tribes (v 32)
  B' Plans for war are called off (v 33)
A' Eastern tribes name the altar (v 34). (2000, 231, modifying Jobling)

The author's main point in a chiastic outline is found at its center. The explanation by the Transjordan tribes given at the center of this outline is the key moment in this episode, since it establishes their orthodoxy, which makes unity possible.

According to the NIV, the altar was built at **Geliloth** (vv 10, 11), a town in Benjamin's allotment (see 18:17; see NLT). The LXX and Syriac versions translate this term Gilgal. Some take this to support the hypothesis that this chapter originally concerned two rival sanctuaries, one at Shiloh and the other at Gilgal (Josh 4:19—5:15; 9:6-15; 1 Sam 10:8; 11:15; 13:8-14; 15:12-15, 21; Amos 4:4-5; see Butler 1983, 243). Others translate the Hebrew word rendered **Geliloth** as region or district, its meaning in Josh 13:2 (ASV, ESV, KJV, NABRE, NASB, NJPS, NRSV, Boling and Wright 1982, 505; Pitkänen 2010, 357).

Somewhere **near the Jordan in the land of Canaan** (v 10), **on the border of Canaan** (v 11), and **on the Israelite side** (v 11), the eastern tribes built an altar. In spite of the repeated clues, we still cannot be sure whether the altar was built "on the west side or on the east side of the river" (Woudstra 1981, 321). **Canaan** (vv 10, 11) could be used to describe the river valley; that is, either side would be in Canaan (Keil and Delitzsch 1978, 218). The phrase **on the border of Canaan** (v 11), literally "in the face or in front of the land of Canaan," could refer to either bank (ibid.). **On the Israelite side** (v 11) could instead be translated "across from the Israelites" (NJPS; see NABRE).

Some believe locating the altar on the eastern bank makes more sense since the purpose of the altar was to convince those on the western bank of the Jordan that those on the eastern bank were also Israelites (see Pitkänen 2010, 359). More likely, the altar was on the western bank since it is said to be **in the land of Canaan** (v 10), and in this chapter **Canaan** refers specifically to the land west of the Jordan (vv 9, 10, 11, 32; Butler 1983, 245; Hess 1996a, 291; Keil and Delitzsch 1978, 221; Snaith 1978, 330-35; Elitzur 2004, 7-19).

The altar was constructed as a "replica" (v 28) of the altar at Shiloh to demonstrate the faithfulness of the Transjordan tribes, but built literally, *large for seeing* (v 10). This phrase is rendered variously as "conspicuously large" (Boling and Wright 1982, 511) and "visible for miles" (Butler 1983, 237). Its large size was so that it could be clearly seen from the Transjordan side of the river.

C. Israel's Reaction to the Altar (22:11-20)

1. Israelites Learn of Altar and Muster Army (22:11-12)

■ **11-12** The immediate response of the Israelites (i.e., those remaining on the western side of the Jordan River) upon learning of the altar was to return to Shiloh and prepare for war. This response does not necessarily point to "serious tribal tensions within the nation as a whole" (Hawk 2005, 565). The Israelite response arises from the righteous indignation of the western tribes.

2. Israelites Send Delegation to Inquire (22:13-20)

■ **13** Although prepared for war, the Israelites waited to attack until a delegation was sent to clarify the reason for building the altar (vv 13-14). The delegation was led by Phinehas, son of Eleazar, the high priest.

Although this is the first time we meet Phinehas in Joshua, he is well-known from the episode at Baal Peor (Num 25:1-13). At that time, the Israelites were camped at Shittim, opposite Jericho, east of the Jordan, when the men began to worship Baal. Phinehas stepped forward with a zeal that mirrored God's own to punish a particularly flagrant example of immorality. In response, God stopped the plague he had sent in punishment, and commended Phinehas. Phinehas appears again, accompanying the Israelites as they go into battle against the Midianites (Num 31:1-6). After Josh 22, we meet

Phinehas once more, interceding for Israel (Judg 20:28). His choice to lead this delegation makes sense, given his demonstrated zeal for Yahweh.

■ 14 Those chosen from each tribe were important figures in their tribes. Butler considers each the head of his extended family as well as the **chief** of his tribe (1983, 246). The makeup of the delegation indicates it represents the nation as a whole on a mission more spiritual than political or military.

■ 15-16 The delegation crossed the Jordan and confronted the two and a half Transjordan tribes in Gilead (Josh 22:13, 15, 32). Although the delegation only represents ten of twelve tribes, they speak as the **whole assembly** of Israel since they represent the orthodoxy that should characterize Israel (→ v 9). Although still only a fact-finding mission, they immediately accused their brothers of rebellion. Had they already known this was rebellion, no delegation would have been needed. Making such an accusation was a Hebrew rhetorical strategy intended to prompt the accused to avoid doing what they had been accused of (e.g., 24:14-22).

The Transjordan tribes were accused of building an alternative site for burnt offerings and sacrifices to the sanctuary at Shiloh, something specifically prohibited by Lev 17:8-9. As had been instructed in Deuteronomy, at the slightest hint that such false worship was taking place, the Israelites were to "inquire, probe and investigate it thoroughly" (Deut 13:14; see vv 12-14). If found to be true, the Israelites were to "put to the sword all who live in that town," treating them as they had treated the Canaanites (v 15).

■ 17 The delegation offered two examples from Israel's history to show how the sin of one part affected the whole. Phinehas was very familiar with the first example, the worship of Baal Peor at Shittim (see Num 25:1-13). The second was when Achan stole the devoted things and brought death and defeat on Israel (Josh 22:20; see ch 7). Repeatedly, the delegation accused the Transjordan tribes of rebellion; the root word for rebellion is used seven times in the chapter (22:16 [twice], 20 [twice], 22, 31 [twice]). This same root appears in Num 31:16, referring to the sin of Baal Peor, and twice in Josh 7:1, referring to the sin of Achan.

■ 18 As these acts of rebellion had pervasive effects on present and future generations, so the Transjordan rebellion **today** was said to threaten disaster on Israel **tomorrow**. They emphasized that not just the Transjordan tribes, but the **whole community of Israel** would suffer. Their rebellion would be principally against Yahweh, but also against the Israelites (v 19), who were duty-bound to retaliate.

Woudstra contends that the delegation's chief objection was not that an altar had been built but that it had been built without God's permission. He points out that a "plurality of sanctuaries does not seem to have been frowned upon in the OT prior to Josiah's reforms. Neither was such a plurality ruled out by the law of Deut. 12" (1981, 320). While this may be a proper interpretation of Deut 12, it does not take account of the prohibition stated in Lev 17:8-9.

The chief issue is not whether one could build additional altars but what the proper place for sacrifices is. This can be seen in the defense offered by the Transjordan tribes where they repeatedly emphasize that this altar was not built for sacrifices (see Josh 22:23, 26, 27, 28, 29). They make this strong denial in spite of the fact that the delegation had not mentioned sacrifices. Because the Transjordan tribes knew of the prohibition against offering sacrifices anywhere but at the sanctuary, says Howard, they "took care to show that this was not their intent" (1998a, 412).

■ **19-20** The delegation did not claim that the land east of the Jordan was **defiled**. Such a claim would contradict the repeated assertions in this chapter and elsewhere that the Transjordan tribes had been given that land by God. The delegation only offered this as a possible reason for why the altar had been built. They followed their assertion with a solution: move in with us. The delegation was willing to slice up their pie—the Cisjordan—into smaller pieces. They were willing to have less for themselves in order to make room for their brothers.

D. Transjordan Tribes Defend Their Actions (22:21-29)

1. Altar Not Built in Rebellion (22:21-23)

■ **21-23** The Transjordan tribes began their defense in a highly dramatic and emphatic fashion. The long buildup in v 21 is followed up by a dramatic assertion of loyalty in v 22. This verse begins with the same phrase repeated twice, the phrase being only three names for God: El, Elohim, Yahweh. It could be rendered in a variety of ways. The NIV proposes **The Mighty One, God, the LORD!** (v 22; see Ps 50:1). Woudstra suggests, "God, God the Lord," "God of gods, the Lord," or "El, God, the Lord," (1981, 327). Hess proposes, "The LORD is the greatest God" (1996a, 292), and the NRSV translates, "The LORD, God of gods." By any translation, with this repeated phrase the Transjordan tribes "affirmed as forcefully as possible their loyalty to this God" (Howard 1998a, 411).

He knows (Josh 22:22) is literally, **He is knowing**, that is, "God is fully aware of what we have done and what we are saying in our defense." They seek full disclosure, with nothing to hide and no appeal for mercy, either from the Israelites (v 22) or from Yahweh (v 23). They did not build this altar to rival the sanctuary at Shiloh as a place for sacrifices (v 23).

2. Altar Built in Fear of Future Alienation (22:24-29)

■ **24-29** Their strong denial in v 22 is followed in vv 24-29 by "an equally strong asseveration" (Woudstra 1981, 327). Their purpose for building was to ensure they would always be able to worship Yahweh as part of Israel (vv 24-25, 27). Their fear that the Jordan would one day be seen as a boundary was not without grounds. Since all the promises applied to the land west of the Jordan (see Num 34:1-12), "it was quite a possible thing that at some future time the false conclusion might be drawn from this, that only the tribes who dwelt in Canaan proper were the true people of Jehovah" (Keil and Delitzsch 1978, 221).

Their reply only mentioned the tribes of Reuben and Gad, omitting the half-tribe of Manasseh (Josh 22:25; see vv 21, 30). Woudstra suggests, "Perhaps its share in the altar building episode was not as great as that of the others" (1981, 329), while Keil and Delitzsch attribute it to "brevity" (1978, 222). Most likely, the tribes omit Manasseh because there was less danger that this tribe would be excluded from Israel, given its Cisjordan counterpart.

If inclusion in Israel was their purpose, why build an altar? The practice of building monuments to mark significant moments is well established in Joshua (4:20-24; 8:29; 10:27); there is even precedent for building an altar in 8:30. Unlike that one, this altar would replicate the one that stood in the tabernacle courtyard (22:28). The term rendered **replica** is used in Exod 25:9 to refer to "the pattern" for the tabernacle given to Moses. It is also used to describe "the plans" for the temple given to Solomon by David (1 Chr 28:11). By constructing a copy of the altar at Shiloh, they meant to demonstrate to all that they were well acquainted with the original, having often brought their sacrifices and offerings to the tabernacle.

Because their motive was honorable, they were happy to call down curses on themselves if they had rebelled. **Far be it from us** (Josh 22:29) is far too mild. Even the KJV's "God forbid that we should rebel" does not go far enough to represent their self-malediction. The suggestion of Boling and Wright comes closest: "But we are damned if it was to rebel against Yahweh" (1982, 503), so long as we take "damned" in its truest sense.

E. Israel Accepts Explanation (22:30-33)

1. Phinehas and Others Respond (22:30-31)

■ **30-31** This explanation satisfied the delegation. They announced that because the Transjordan tribes had not rebelled, Yahweh was clearly ***in our midst*** as the Unifier of his people. Transjordan faithfulness had **rescued the Israelites from the LORD's hand** (v 31). Since both groups had been in danger, perhaps the phrase **the Israelites** is meant to again refer to both groups (see discussion in vv 9-10).

2. Phinehas and Others Report Back to Israelites (22:32-33)

■ **32-33** The rest of the Israelites also responded favorably to the Transjordan explanation and **praised God** (v 33) who had allowed them to avert conflict. Perhaps they also blessed Yahweh for providing conclusive evidence that Israel remained orthodox and unified. Howard notes that the use of **devastate** is the only occurrence of this term in the book of Joshua (1998a, 415).

F. Naming of Altar (22:34)

■ **34** The Transjordan tribes named this altar, though we are not sure what they called it. The NIV considers the name to be **A Witness Between Us—that the LORD is God**. Others regard the name as simply "Witness," followed by an explanatory phrase (Woudstra 1981, 329; ASV, ESV, KJV, NASB, NJPS, NLT, NRSV). The NABRE treats the whole phrase as explanatory: "The Reubenites and the Gadites gave the altar its name as a witness among them that the LORD is God." The NJB leaves an ellipsis, implying that the name had dropped out, then adds, "'Because,' they said, 'it will be a witness between us that Yahweh is God.'" The LXX makes Joshua the subject of the verse: "And Joshua gave to the altar of Reuben, Gad, and half Manasseh a name and said: 'It is a witness between them that the Lord is their God'" (see Woudstra 1981, 327 n. 10).

FROM THE TEXT

22:32-34

Throughout the book of Joshua, the author has promoted the need for orthodoxy. Most of the time we have seen its benefits; occasionally, as with Achan, we encountered the serious consequences resulting from its absence. Throughout this book we have also seen Israel united in its common cause. As the book nears its conclusion, however, these themes collide. The western tribes risked Israel's unity for the sake of orthodoxy while the eastern tribes risked orthodoxy for the sake of Israel's unity. In the end, both emphases are celebrated. We also see that proper unity cannot be obtained except through orthodoxy.

In 22:5 we see the essence of orthodoxy, just as relevant today as it was for the Transjordan tribes. While we are now under the law of Christ rather than "the commandment and the law" of Moses, the essence of both laws is the same: love for God and neighbor. "To love the LORD your God" (v 5; Deut 6:5; Matt 22:37) implies our absolute loyalty to him, no matter what. With this as our motivation, we can avoid the Scylla of rule-keeping and the Charybdis of rule-ignoring. A Christian can aspire to nothing greater than, in John Wesley's words, "the humble, gentle, patient love of God and man ruling all the tempers, words, and actions, the whole heart and the whole life" (as cited by Collins 2007, 302).

Our love for God must be expressed by walking in all his ways. As we saw earlier, to walk was a Hebrew way of describing one's lifestyle; this phrase calls us to make loving God our second nature, what we do every day, without even having to think about it. The Israelites had just completed a great conquest. Now came the tough part: living for God in the realm of the ordinary.

Jesus reminded his disciples that if they love him, they will obey what he commands (John 14:15). We can only truly love God to the extent that we "keep his commands" (Josh 22:5). God has given us commands; we dare not treat these as suggestions. Nor should we unthinkingly treat the suggestions from ourselves or others as God's commands. How can we tell the difference? At their essence, God's commands tell us how to carry out his one command: love him and our neighbor for his sake.

We must "hold fast to him" (v 5), or cleave to him. As did the Israelites in their day, we will face challenges. But in spite of our troubles—even in spite of the times when it appears God is our trouble—we must hold fast to him by faith.

The final phrase calls upon the faithful to "serve him with all your heart and all your soul" (v 5). Wesley rightly called us to embrace the faith of a child instead of a slave. He also reminded us that our service to the Father should involve

> vigorous, universal obedience, in a zealous keeping of all the commandments, in watchfulness and painfulness, in denying ourselves, and taking up our cross daily; as well as in earnest prayer and fasting, and a close attendance on all the ordinances of God. And if any man dream of attaining it any other way, . . . he deceiveth his own soul. (1984b, 402-3)

XXI. JOSHUA 23

BEHIND THE TEXT

Joshua 23 presents the first of two farewell speeches delivered by Joshua. Some see these as two versions of the same speech (Soggin 1972, 218). This implies careless editing, which seems unlikely in a book that offers manifest examples of the author's careful craftsmanship. Others believe ch 23 was meant to conclude the book of Joshua while ch 24 was meant to conclude the Hexateuch (Genesis through Joshua) (Römer 2010, 93). Rosel considers the two speeches to correspond to the two introductions in Judges (Josh 23 with Judg 2:6 ff.; Josh 24 with Judg 1:1—2:5) (1980, 342-50).

While we cannot completely rule out these hypotheses, there seems no reason to dismiss the straightforward sense of the passage: Joshua delivered two farewell speeches, the first to a select audience of Israel's leaders, the second to all Israel. The first focuses on the days to come while the second stresses God's actions in the past. The first contains Joshua's heartfelt concerns while the second calls for the Israelites to respond by affirming the covenant (see Woudstra 1981, 332). If this seems a rather elaborate way to say good-bye, recall that Moses' farewell speech takes up the entire book of Deuteronomy.

The author relies heavily on Numbers and Deuteronomy, especially the latter (Howard 1998a, 417). Given the abundant repetition, it would appear that the author presented this material chiastically, such as the following:

A Past successes and future victories (vv 1-5)
   B Call to remain loyal to Yahweh (vv 6-8)
      C Past success should lead to future loyalty (vv 9-11)
   B' Warning against disloyalty to Yahweh (vv 12-13)
A' Past successes ensure future justice (vv 14-16)

The tone of the chapter grows increasingly dire as the author nears this book's conclusion (Howard 1998a, 418).

IN THE TEXT

A. Past Successes and Future Victories (23:1-5)

1. Introduction (23:1-2a)

■ 1 The author describes the setting of this speech only as taking place **After a long time had passed**. Scholars disagree as to when that **long time** began. Woudstra believes the clock started at the beginning of the conquest (1981, 332), while Howard starts counting at the end of the allotment (1998a, 419-20). The phrase describing Joshua as **a very old man** offers little help because this is nearly identical to the phrase used in Josh 13:1, prior to the allotment. At the end of this speech, Joshua indicated his approaching death (23:14), a death that occurred when he was 110 (24:29). Based upon Caleb's announcement during the allocation that he was eighty-five (14:10), and assuming that Caleb and Joshua are about the same age (see Schatz 2013, 32-34), one might guess that this and the next speech were delivered about twenty-five years after the allocation, which would qualify as a **long time**.

The author does not mention where this speech took place. Joshua's home was at Timnath Serah (19:49-50); the absence of another location may suggest he summoned them to his town. A more likely possibility is Shiloh, the location of the tabernacle. Verse 2 of ch 23 mentions nothing about inviting priests, a striking omission considering the nature of the speech. Either the speech was delivered only to "secular" leaders (Butler 1983, 254), or priests were already present at the location where the meeting was held, that is, Shiloh.

The meeting took place after **the LORD had given Israel rest from all their enemies around them**. We have heard of this rest several times throughout the book. It was initially spoken of as a future reality (1:13, 15), then as something attained (11:23; 14:15; 21:44), and finally as the signal that something new was about to happen (22:4; 23:1). In 22:4, rest signaled the time when the Transjordan tribes were free to return home. Here it marks a time befitting a farewell address.

■ **2a** The author first says that **all Israel** was summoned, then qualifies the invitation to Israel's **elders, leaders, judges and officials**. The mention of these specific groups likely implies leaders from the whole nation were present. The only other time we see this description of all four groups is 24:1 where the whole nation is included. Keil and Delitzsch suggest **elders** is the general term, with the other three representing subcategories (1978, 223). The **leaders** had been mentioned in keeping with the allocation of land (see 14:1; 19:51; 21:1) and the incident with the Transjordan tribes (see 22:14, 21, 30).

We read of "elders, officials, and judges" present at Shechem for the covenant renewal ceremony (see 8:33). The **judges** in the book of Joshua play a role different from those in the book of Judges (Woudstra 1981, 333). Both filled a judicial role, but the latter combined that with a military role; Joshua filled the military role in this book. We met **officials** prior to and during the crossing of the Jordan (see 1:10; 3:2), where they seem to serve as military commanders.

Earlier we mentioned that both 23:1 and 13:1 use the same phrase to refer to Joshua's age. It is possible both passages take place at the same time, but this seems very unlikely. In the former God assigns Joshua more work to do, while in the latter, Joshua's work nears its conclusion. A more promising explanation is that the author connected the two chapters to remind us to read the latter in light of the former, as we attempt to do in what follows.

2. Past Successes (23:2b-4)

■ **2b** Joshua began his recitation of Israel's successes by drawing attention to his advanced age. He may be indicating that the time had come for him to depart the scene, or he may use this language to remind them of his long experience of God's blessings.

■ **3** Not only he but they too had seen God's faithfulness. **You yourselves** preserves the Hebrew emphasis. What they had witnessed had been Yahweh, "The One Who Fights for Us." This is how Boling and Wright (1982, 519) translate the Hebrew verb that the NIV renders as **who fought for you**. The verb, also found in v 10, is a participle, meaning it could describe ongoing action (i.e., *he who has been fighting for you*) or could function as a noun, as in Boling and Wright's translation. Woudstra renders it, "the fighting one," and points out that the presence of the definite article rules out all others who might be fighting (1981, 334 n. 3). Although using different language, the author conveyed the same picture in 13:6 where Yahweh says, "I myself will drive them out."

Outside this chapter, we meet the verb form behind "will fight for you" in Deut 3:22, part of Moses' encouragement to Joshua. A very similar form of this verb appears in Exod 14:25 in the mouth of an Egyptian soldier who, in the midst of the Red (Reed) Sea disaster, concludes that Yahweh is fighting against the Egyptians. We meet this similar verb form twice in Josh 10, first in connection with the miracle of the stationary sun (v 14), then in a statement summarizing the southern campaign (v 42). Braulik considers this a stock phrase used to connect the crossing of the Red Sea to the conquest of Canaan (2011, 209-23).

■ **4** Alongside this clear indication that Yahweh does all the fighting stands Joshua's claim: **the nations I conquered**. This is a strong claim, but, as Howard points out (1998a, 421), it is anticipated in 11:23—"So Joshua took the entire land, just as the LORD had directed Moses, and he gave it as an inheritance to Israel according to their tribal divisions." These claims appear to contradict each other. Did Yahweh do all the fighting or did Joshua "cut off" all the nations? No contradiction exists, however, only an example of how things work in the divine economy. All that happens, happens by God's permission.

The biblical writers were clear on God's absolute sovereignty. Yet this must not be taken to mean that humans lack freedom in our actions, doing only what we are predetermined to do. The biblical writers were equally clear that humans remain free and responsible agents, rewarded for obedience and punished for disobedience, cooperating with God in divine/human synergy.

Joshua not only conquered the nations but also allotted their territory to the tribes of Israel. Once again this echoes ch 13 where Joshua was commanded to "allocate this land to Israel for an inheritance . . . and divide it as an inheritance among the nine tribes and half of the tribe of Manasseh" (vv 6-7). Israel was told to **Remember** that Joshua had allotted the land; that is, the conquest had come to an end and the time for possession has come.

The syntax of 23:4 is unusual, as seen in the highly literal ASV: "Behold, I have allotted unto you these nations that remain, to be an inheritance for your tribes, from the Jordan, with all the nations that I have cut off, even unto the great sea toward the going down of the sun." The author pictures the conquest as beginning at the Jordan and extending as far as the Mediterranean, as well as north and south. The nations cut off by God were located between the Jordan and the Great Sea.

Verse 4 makes clear what was stated earlier (see 13:2 ff.): not all the enemy had been extirpated (**the nations that remain**). That this acknowledgment stands alongside Joshua's claim to have conquered the nations and close to where God is said to have given Israel "rest from all their enemies around them" (23:1), illustrates the need to qualify those passages in Joshua that claim an absolute conquest. The Hebrew term rendered **nations** appears seven times in this chapter (vv 3, 4 [twice], 7, 9, 12, 13) and only six times elsewhere in Joshua (3:17; 4:1; 5:6, 8; 10:13; 12:23) (Howard 1998a, 421). Its appearance more than forty times in Deuteronomy reveals a close connection between

Joshua's speech in this chapter and Deuteronomy. It also appears in the other four books of the Pentateuch and in all but a handful of other OT books.

3. Future Victories (23:5)

■ **5** Based upon past successes—but especially on what has been revealed about Yahweh—Israel can be assured of future victories. It is **the LORD your God himself** who will **drive them out**. The use of both **drive them out** and **push them out** (see 23:9, 13) reinforces the picture of the conquest as more of an expulsion, rather than an extermination of the enemies. God's promise to expel the enemy is repeated several times in this chapter (vv 10, 14 [four times], 15 [three times]). The story of the conquest and allocation of Canaan is essentially the story of how God kept his promise.

The LXX reads quite different from the MT:

But the Lord our God will destroy them before us until they perish. And he will send wild animals against them until he will have completely destroyed them and their kings from before you, and you will inherit their land as the Lord your God said to you. (As cited by Pitkänen 2010, 381)

Boling and Wright consider this version original, as it provides an explanation of how the promise will be fulfilled (see 24:12; Exod 23:28; Deut 7:20). This version was omitted, they contend, through a copying error (1982, 523). Most translations, however, follow the MT, which "works" even without an explanation for the coming triumph.

B. Call to Remain Loyal to Yahweh (23:6-8)

■ **6** If, as v 5 promises, Yahweh himself would drive out the nations, what remained for Israel to do? Joshua now calls upon them to remain loyal to Yahweh. This loyalty looks very much like Yahweh's instructions to Joshua in ch 1. Joshua tells them to **Be very strong**, using the same word God had used to him (1:6, 7, 9). The Israelites are told to obey the law of Moses, as God had told Joshua to do (1:7, 8). They are not to turn aside from that Law either **to the right or to the left**, the same counsel given to Joshua (1:7). As with God's earlier counsel to Joshua, the path to victory is the path of obedience.

■ **7** Obedience will not be easy, given the presence of the enemy among them. The Israelites should protect themselves by limiting their contact with the enemy; they should *come not among* them. Joshua focused on the names of these gods as a rival source of power (see Exod 20:23; 23:13; Deut 6:14; 10:20; 12:3 for similar phrases; Woudstra 1981, 335).

Using the strongest form of prohibition found in Hebrew (Hess 1996a, 296), Joshua prohibited the Israelites from doing four things with the names of these gods. First, they were not to **invoke** them. This term could mean "mention" (ESV), boast, take pride, be strong, or use to take an oath (Smelik 1999, 321-32, who opts for the last). Second, they should not **swear by** these names, that is, call upon these gods to guarantee their promises (Butler 1983, 255). Third, they must not **serve** these other gods. This word can be used to indicate worship but may be better understood here as "total binding of oneself as a servant" (Butler 1983, 255). Finally, Israel was not to **bow down** or worship these gods.

■ **8** This section began with a positive command to be loyal (v 6), then moved to a prohibition against associating with other gods and thereby becoming disloyal (v 7). It concludes with another call to loyalty, this time using the striking word "cleave" (**hold fast**). As noted in the commentary on 22:5, this implies a resolute loyalty such as should characterize husband and wife (Gen 2:24). The psalmist used this term to picture loyalty to Yahweh:

My soul clings to you;

your right hand upholds me. (Ps 63:8 [9] ESV, NASB)

We meet this word twice in Deut 13, once to describe the kind of loyalty demanded by Yahweh (v 4) and again to describe the opposite (v 17). The latter was illustrated when Achan clung to contaminated items (see Josh 7). The word appears twice in ch 23 as well, here describing how the Israelites should live and, in fact, had been living. This applies to the Israelites engaged in the conquest, as distinct from the wilderness generation (Butler 1983, 255). The second use of "cleave" describes the kind of disloyalty that would bring about Yahweh's displeasure (v 12, "ally yourselves"). The author not only emphasized the need for loyalty by employing this striking term but also frontloaded the phrase, **But in Yahweh your God**.

C. Past Success Should Lead to Future Loyalty (23:9-11)

■ **9-10** The theme of loyalty continues, but this time the appeal is based on the successful conquest. The first two verses of this section are arranged chiastically:

A Yahweh had driven out a stronger enemy (v 9*a*)

B Israel had been invincible (v 9*b*)

B' Israel had been invincible (v 10*a*)

A' Because Yahweh had fought for Israel (v 10*b*)

Consistent with the overall theme of this book, the conquest had come in fulfillment of Yahweh's promise (v 10*b*; see 1:5; 21:43-45). The description of their military prowess—one routing a thousand—employs an idiom found elsewhere (see Lev 26:7-8; Deut 32:30). **Thousand** (Josh 23:10) could instead be rendered "troop" (Pitkänen 2010, 381).

■ **11** The section concludes with another call for loyalty. Perhaps the description of the conquest (vv 9-10) was meant to arouse Israel's gratitude, which would prompt their loyalty. More likely, Israel was meant to understand that the conquest had come about in response to their loyalty. Hence, they should be sure to remain loyal to God; using the Hebrew idiom, they are to **love** him). **Be very careful** is more literally, ***keep greatly to your souls.*** Woudstra notes that this phrase "strengthens the intensity of the command to love. The Israelites are to love for their life's sake" (Woudstra 1981, 337).

D. Warning against Disloyalty to Yahweh (23:12-13)

■ 12 The Israelites have been turned in the right direction, toward Yahweh (see v 8), so rebellion would involve turning away. The author emphasized the willfulness of this rebellion in the phrase **turn away**, literally, ***if turning you turn***. He also specified what this turning away would look like: political alliances with those nations that remain among them as well as intermarriage. The danger of rebellion was insidious for it not only involved significant encounters like these but could also result from everyday interactions, as suggested by the phrase, **associate with them** (*you go with them and they with you*).

■ 13 Israel's rebellion would mean the loss of Yahweh's support. The author leaves no doubt about this sorry consequence; **you may be sure** is another emphatic verb form (***knowing you will know***). A simple way to deal with these remaining enemies would be accommodation—if you can't beat them, join them. This would be disastrous, for it would cut off Israel from Yahweh's aid. Without his restraining and refining influence, the enemy would become **snares and traps**, subtly enticing Israel into fatal associations. Once trapped, Israel would experience harsh domination—the cruel whip digging into its back (or sides)—and total defeat—**thorns** tearing at its eyes (see Num 33:55). What began as simple accommodation would result in the undoing and loss of all they had obtained (see Josh 23:15-16).

E. Past Successes Ensure Future Justice (23:14-16)

■ 14 Joshua's speech now reaches its conclusion, marked by the use of *hinnēh*, **Now**, and by another reference to his old age (see v 2*b*). As loving with all one's heart and soul (Deut 13:3) means complete loyalty, and serving with all one's heart and soul (see Deut 11:13) means complete devotion, so knowing with all one's heart and soul means absolute certainty. How could there be any doubting God's faithfulness after what they had witnessed? This is the third explicit reference in this chapter to God having kept his promises (Josh 23:5, 10). It is also the most emphatic, repeating the same point three times in three different ways: **not one** of God's promises **has failed**, all have been fulfilled, and **not one has failed**.

■ **15** This is very good news for Israel, but also very bad news. God kept his promises because he is faithful, but his faithfulness is double-edged. He keeps *all* his promises, even those promises to punish disobedience. One cannot have the good news without the bad news, the **good things** (*good word*) without the **evil** (*evil word*). This is known as the principle of retribution, that obedience brings blessing while disobedience brings disaster. We meet this principle throughout the OT, especially in Deuteronomy and the historical books. This principle follows naturally from the covenant relationship between God and Israel.

■ **16** Because of God's faithfulness, Israel's disloyalty to the **covenant** would have disastrous consequences. Joshua had earlier described disloyalty as turning away (v 12*a*) and accommodation (v 12*b*); here he suggests a different image. The Hebrew term rendered **violate** is the same verb used several times in Joshua to refer to the crossing of the Jordan (Hess 1996a, 299). Its appearance here reinforces the picture of disloyalty as undoing the conquest (see v 13), as if recrossing the Jordan River, only this time from west to east, rather than as before, from east to west.

Earlier Joshua had spoken of this disloyalty as political treaties, intermarriage, and association (v 12). Here he focuses on the chief danger, the action toward which all those other actions would eventually and fatally lead, idolatrous worship. This would result in God's anger burning against Israel. The verb used here for **burn** occurs only one other time in Joshua, in 7:1. There it is in consequence of Achan's sin and is also directed at Israel. In fact, the only references to God's anger in Joshua concern his anger against Israel.

In the heat of divine fire, Israel would be **quickly** consumed. This adverb was likely meant to contrast with the lengthy conquest. Just as a forest fire consumes timber that has taken decades, even centuries to grow, so the years Israel had spent anticipating, obtaining, and possessing the land would be undone in a moment due to disobedience. The nexus between action and consequence is highlighted by the wordplay in v 16 between **serve** (*'-b-d*) and **perish** (*'-b-d*) (the only difference is between similar-sounding initial consonants; see Pitkänen 2010, 385).

FROM THE TEXT

In part one of his farewell address, Joshua warned that the greatest threats arise from within. Bad choices would produce bad consequences. Obedience had brought victory to the Israelites as they fought to possess the land of Canaan (see 23:3-5, 9-11). We see many other examples of how obedience brought God's blessing: Abram (see Gen 15:6), David (see 2 Sam 23:1-5), Hezekiah (2 Kgs 18:5-8), to name a few. The principle of retribution also means that disobedience brings disaster. Joshua warned Israel that all they had obtained could be quickly lost due to disobedience (Josh 23:12-13, 15-16).

Although Israel heeded Joshua's warning for the short term, sadly they did not remain faithful. The book of Judges illustrates the disaster that follows disobedience. So too does Israel's subsequent history, culminating in the exile of the northern kingdom of Israel in 722 B.C. and that of Judah in 586 B.C.

The principle of retribution is not a law that God must obey, for there is no law more authoritative than himself. This is a principle, how God ordinarily works as an expression of his faithfulness. He would not be true to himself if he allowed obedience to go unrewarded and evil to go unpunished. The principle of retribution expresses God's affirmation of human freedom, what Butler called the "danger of freedom": "If Israel does not do her part, then God will not do his" (1983, 256). Humans are free to operate within the universe as God designed it, reaping whatever they freely choose to sow. God remains absolutely sovereign, since he created the universe to operate this way.

Some, like Job's "comforters," misunderstand this principle, assuming one can determine the measure of righteousness by measuring blessing. Modern-day "comforters" attribute all suffering to sin. Others seek blessings more than the obedience that brings the blessings. The principle remains valid, though we often lack the perspective to see how. Only because he remained faithful throughout his trials was Job blessed again in the end (see Job 42:7-17).

Even while operating according to this principle, God retains the freedom to employ mercy. We see this with the sin of Achan, where God confronted Joshua with the facts and provided an opportunity to repent. We see it when David was confronted by God with his adultery and murder and given the opportunity to repent. Consequences remain—thirty-six innocent Israelites died because of Achan's sin, and many died, directly and indirectly, because of David's. God is able to take these consequences of disobedience and use them for good. Perhaps the disaster surrounding Achan may have helped Israel remain faithful for as they long as they did (see Josh 23:8; 24:31).

Perhaps the greatest example of this principle is the cross of Christ. Our disobedience brought disaster in the form of alienation from God, from ourselves, from each other, and from the natural world. Knowing we could not help ourselves, God sent Jesus. Although he lived a life of perfect obedience, he bore the full brunt of the disaster that originated from our disobedience. By graciously including us "in Christ," we now experience the blessings of Christ's obedience. This is what Paul meant when he wrote to the Corinthians: "God made him who had no sin to be sin for us, so that in him we might become the righteousness of God" (2 Cor 5:21).

XXII. JOSHUA 24

BEHIND THE TEXT

Based on the amount and diversity of scholarly opinion, Josh 24 may be one of the most controversial in the entire book. Disagreements abound as to "its compositional history, time of origin, or possible relationship to the history or cultic life of Israel," with "no consensus" at present (Nelson 1997, 265).

Among the less controversial conclusions is that Joshua's speech is part of a covenant renewal ceremony, a ceremony similar to what was described in Josh 8:30-35. Some scholars see these two chapters as referring to the same events (Soggin 1972, 230, 240 ff.; Boling and Wright 1982, 533).

Although the chapter is not a covenant document, it appears to have been patterned on the six-part format known from ANE covenants. Such agreements between two parties generally opened with a preamble (24:1-2*a*) followed by a historical summary of the relations between those involved (vv 2*b*-13). Considerable attention would be given to stipulations for behavior (vv 14-25). Covenant documents also contained instructions about the storage and reading of the covenant (v 26), the invoking of witnesses (vv 22, 27), as well as curses and blessings based on the measure of compliance (implied in vv 19-20) (see Howard 1998a, 427).

The previous chapter contains the speech Joshua delivered to the Israelite leaders where he focused on the need for loyalty in the days ahead. In Josh 24 he calls the Israelites to renew their covenant with the God who has proven himself faithful to his word.

IN THE TEXT

A. Joshua's Farewell Speech (24:1-15)

1. Preamble (24:1)

■ 1 Although not told explicitly, we presume Josh 23 was delivered either at Timnath Serah or, more likely, Shiloh. The author explicitly mentions the location for this gathering: **Shechem**. Why did Joshua gather the Israelites here? Shiloh would have been equally central to the tribes plus it would have allowed the meeting to be held at the site of the tabernacle (see 19:51). According to Keil and Delitzsch, Joshua chose this site for its historical and theological significance. After calling Abram to leave his homeland, God led him to Shechem, where he spoke to Abram again, promising to give this land to his offspring (Gen 12:6-7). It was at Shechem where Jacob built an altar to the mighty God of Israel (33:18-20) and later summoned his household to fidelity to Yahweh (35:1-5). Somewhere in this vicinity, the idols of Jacob's family lay buried.

> As Jacob selected Shechem for the sanctification of his house, because this place was already consecrated by Abraham as a sanctuary of God, so Joshua chose the same place for the renewal of the covenant, because this act involved a practical renunciation on the part of Israel of all idolatry. (Keil and Delitzsch 1978, 226-27)

The audiences for Joshua's two farewell speeches were not the same, although there were those who heard both. The second speech and subsequent ceremony were intended for **all the tribes of Israel**, but Joshua wanted the leaders to be present as well; the categories mentioned in Josh 24:1 are the same as those in 23:2. Joshua likely wanted these leaders to hear both speeches because they, along with the high priest, would assume the leadership of Israel after Joshua's death (see Hess 1996a, 300, 311; Keil and Delitzsch 1978, 234).

The double invitation may help to explain why the book closes with no successor appointed.

That the people and leaders **presented themselves before God (*Elohim*)** suggests the possibility that the ark had been brought to Shechem from Shiloh. Howard interprets the phrase to mean they "undoubtedly [came] before the ark." He cites the appearance of a similar phrase (before Yahweh) elsewhere in Joshua where the ark is present (4:13; 6:8; 7:23). This is the only reference to *before Elohim* in Joshua, but Howard notes that 1 Chr 13:7-8 and 16:1 use this phrase in reference to the ark (1998a, 430). Keil and Delitzsch disagree, treating the phrases "before Yahweh" and "before Elohim" as different. The latter, in their estimation, refers not to a sacred place or object but to a sacred purpose (1978, 227).

2. Historical Prologue (24:2-13)

■ **2** The account of the relationship between the two parties is told in the first person, as if Yahweh himself were speaking. He begins with Abraham's father, **Terah** who lived **beyond the Euphrates River** with his sons, **Abraham** [then called Abram] **and Nahor**, the ancestor of Rebekah and Laban. Since the focus is clearly on Abraham and his descendants, why mention Terah and Nahor? This is the first of several examples in this speech where apparently extraneous information is provided as spurs off the main rail line. These sidetracks are not extraneous, however, but highlight the distinctions God made in preserving the line of Abraham. Terah and Nahor were not chosen, although Nahor's descendants would enter the line of promise through marriage. The chief distinction between Abraham and others in his family lay in God's gracious choice of Abraham and Abraham's response of exclusive loyalty to Yahweh. By contrast, the rest of Abraham's family **worshiped other gods**. Whether Abraham's loyalty began prior to or at the point of his call in Gen 12 is not clear; what is unmistakable is his devotion to Yahweh from that point on.

■ **3** Yahweh speaks of leading **Abraham** throughout Canaan, the very land where the Israelites now stood. He speaks of how he **gave him many descendants**, including Isaac. Those who know the story of Abraham and Sarah understand the test of faith implied in that brief phrase.

■ **4** In this opening portion (Josh 24:2-4) of the historical prologue, God's role is chiefly that of leading Abraham and providing him with many descendants. **Esau** represents another spur off the main line. He was not chosen, while Jacob was (note the order of their names). Esau received property, but it was outside of Canaan: **the hill country of Seir** in Edom. The listener expects what follows to concern Jacob's experience in Canaan, but instead Joshua takes us down to **Egypt**, where the second portion of the historical prologue begins (vv 5-7).

■ **5-6** In this section, God's chief action is "deliverance from enemy peoples, beginning with Egypt" (Hess 1996a, 302) through **Moses and Aaron**. Although Aaron did play a role in the exodus, it was only minor. His mention here may be meant to imply God's gift of his presence through the tabernacle, Aaron's purview.

The phrase, **by what I did there (*just as I did in its midst*)** seems to call for another word, like "wonders" (NJB) or "signs" (Boling and Wright 1982, 527). Boling and Wright suggest the Hebrew word dropped out by a scribal error (ibid., 530). Another possibility is that the more abrupt phrase is an example of divine understatement, in which God refers to the ten plagues simply as something "I did." The speech continues as if given by God himself, although with a change. Joshua's audience is addressed in vv 2-4 in the second person as the descendants of the patriarchs (i.e., "your ancestors" [v 2]). Beginning in v 5, however, they are addressed as participants in the exodus. None actually were, excepting Joshua and Caleb. All the others who had come out of Egypt had died in the wilderness. Speaking of a later generation in solidarity with an earlier is one way the OT believer expressed the unbroken nature of God's covenant community.

■ **7** Joshua briefly reverts to distinguishing between his audience and the Israelites in Egypt when he says about the latter, **they cried to the LORD for help**. Just as quickly, however, he returns to solidarity: **and he [Yahweh] put darkness between you and the Egyptians**. Joshua seems to be saying to his audience, "That is what your ancestors did in their difficulty. What will you do in yours?"

Sinai goes unmentioned in this account, although not because the events of Mount Sinai were considered unimportant. There is no mention of the rebellion of the exodus generation or the miraculous stopping of the Jordan either, though these too were crucial moments. Hawk is likely right to base the omission of Sinai on stylistic grounds, allowing the focus to remain on Joshua as true successor to Moses (see v 29) and on Israel's current response to the covenant (2000, 268). The Law given at Sinai and recorded in a book will be mentioned later (v 26; see 23:6). Israel will shortly be called to ratify the covenant originally made at Sinai.

■ **8-10** The speech jumps ahead to the Israelites' travels in the Transjordan region (24:8-10), representing the events of Num 21—24 (Hess 1996a, 302). Here God's chief activity is one of defense. He protected Israel from the attacks of Sihon and Og, then decimated the enemy so they could cause no further harm and so that Israel could possess their land (Josh 24:8). God also protected Israel from supernatural attacks. **Balak** (v 9) initiated such a battle against the Israelites by hiring **Balaam** to curse them. Although the account in Numbers presents Balaam as obedient to Yahweh, Joshua here suggests Balaam tried to **curse** Israel. God would not **listen** to him (v 10), instead causing Balaam to produce overflowing blessings. This is likely what the Hebrew implies by its use of the emphatic form in v 10. The NIV presents this as continual blessing (**again and again**), but it could instead be rendered "emphatically blessed you" (Boling and Wright 1982, 528), or as a strong contrast: instead of cursing you, "he had to bless you" (NASB).

■ 11 The historical prologue now describes the actual conquest of Canaan, from the crossing of the Jordan to settlement in the land (vv 11-13). Here God is presented as giving victory and territory to his people. Even without mentioning the major miracles that marked the conquest—the stopping of the Jordan, the toppling of Jericho's walls, or the prolonged day—these verses echo what the rest of the book makes clear: God, not Israel, defeated the enemy.

After crossing the Jordan, the Israelites came to Jericho where they were met by the **citizens of Jericho**. **Citizens** is literally *lords*, likely the "chief leaders of the town" who make decisions for the citizens (Hess 1996a, 303 n. 4, which cites Judg 9:2; 1 Sam 23:11-12). Although this account does not contradict Josh 6, the battle for Jericho is presented here as a real fight. The rest of the conquest is summarized briefly by mentioning victory over the seven nations that occupied Canaan. The same nations appear in 3:10, although in different order (Howard 1998a, 432). In 24:8, the Amorites are those living in the Transjordan while in v 11 the term describes one group living west of the Jordan. In vv 15 and 18 it refers to the entirety of Canaan.

■ 12 Reference to a **hornet** driving out enemies (v 12) brings to mind Exod 23:28 and Deut 7:20. The first passage informs the Israelites how the hornet, a symbol of "terror" (Exod 23:27), will "drive the Hivites, Canaanites and Hittites out of your way" (v 28). This will not happen all at once, God says, but over a period of time (vv 29-30). Following a brief historical reminder of the exodus (Deut 7:18-19), Moses promised that Yahweh would send "the hornet" among the enemies so that even those who go into hiding will be rooted out and eliminated (v 20). Some have suggested that this and other such texts represent either the memory or experience of "an early form of biological warfare" (Neufeld 1980, 31, citing rabbinic sources). Garstang argues that it refers to the Egyptians (identified with the bee) who involuntarily weakened Canaan, making the Israelite conquest possible (1931, 258-60). Most likely, the hornet is used here as a metaphor for terror or panic, although the first and second explanations may have contributed to the association between hornets and terror.

The mention of the **two Amorite kings** has provoked a variety of interpretations. The two Amorite kings usually mentioned in connection with the Israelites are Sihon and Og, but the historical prologue has already described Israel crossing the Jordan. Referring to them now would have to be as a flashback. Edelman blames the phrase on textual corruption, suggesting it should read "the kings of the Amorites are swept away" (1991, 285). The LXX solves the problem by referring to twelve kings, not two. Howard rejects this suggestion since there is no list of twelve kings in Joshua (1998a, 433). Soggin contends that the number twelve was meant "to give the impression of a great number, . . . a round number, a complete number," similar to what is found in Assyrian annals (1972, 235).

Howard proposes that the **two Amorite kings** are Adoni-Zedek and Jabin, leading kings of the southern (10:1 ff.) and northern coalitions (11:1 ff.) respectively (1998a, 433). If he is right, these two kings balance the two kings (Sihon and Og) defeated in the Transjordan. Whatever is meant by **hornet** and the reference to the **kings**, the Israelites clearly did not achieve victory on their own. They did have to fight, however. Joshua states this in a most pointed way, speaking of *your* [sg.] *sword* and *your* [sg.] *bow*.

■ **13** The historical prologue concludes with a picture of the completed conquest. The Israelites came into possession of farmland already cleared of brush and stones (**land on which you did not toil**). They took up residence in houses and cities they **did not build**. They were able to harvest grapes from vines and olives from trees that they **did not plant**. Having well-established grapevines and especially olive trees was important because these take several years to produce fruit. Moses had promised this (see Deut 6:10-11), immediately after warning them not to forget Yahweh (vv 12 ff.).

3. Fear Yahweh (24:14-15)

■ **14** Having spoken in God's voice up to this point, Joshua now speaks for himself as he describes the stipulations of the covenant with a summons to **fear the Lord**. This means to **serve him with all faithfulness**, more literally, "in sincerity and in truth" (ASV, KJV). Sincerity suggests something complete or entire, as seen in the only other use of the term in Joshua where it refers to the whole day (10:13). When used to describe people, it denotes blamelessness or integrity, as in Ps 15:2,

> The one whose walk is blameless,
>
> who does what is righteous,
>
> who speaks the truth from their heart.

The two terms, "sincerity and truth," likely represent a hendiadys for "undivided loyalty" or **all faithfulness**.

Some have taken Joshua's words to imply that Israel was actively engaged in idolatry at that time. This seems unlikely given the commendation they received in Josh 23:8, nor do we see any idols surrendered as in Gen 35:1-5. Here and a few verses later, Joshua seems to put his finger on Israel's difficulty maintaining a commitment to monotheism (or at least, henotheism).

■ **15** Joshua makes a rhetorical shift: suggesting one direction to encourage the free choice of another. Although God had chosen the Israelites to be in this covenant relationship, they remained free to choose whether to live in obedience to that covenant and yield the blessings that would follow, or be disloyal and reap the disastrous consequences. Joshua has already made his choice, setting the example Israel should follow.

B. Response (24:16-24)

1. People: We Will Serve Him (24:16-18)

■ **16-18** What follows is a back-and-forth conversation between Joshua and the Israelites, likely through their leaders. Their initial response (Josh 24:16) to his challenge in vv 14-15 is quite strong, literally calling down a curse on themselves should they become disloyal (see 22:29). They also agree that Yahweh had done everything just as Joshua had described (24:17-18*a*). **Brought** (v 17) is actually a participle, describing ongoing action. In other words, the people recognized that what God had done for them in the past was part of what he was doing for them in the present. Hess points out the contrast between the **slavery** they had endured in Egypt (v 17) and the call to **serve** Yahweh (v 18), both terms translating the same Hebrew root (1996a, 305). Their commitment to Yahweh is stated emphatically (v 18*b*): *Also we, we will serve Yahweh, for he is our God.*

2. Joshua: You Are Not Able to Serve Him (24:19-20)

■ **9-20** Joshua's reply is a stunner: **You are not able** (vv 19-20). There is no need to assume this was Joshua's true feeling or that this was added later based on Israel's failures (see Butler 1983, 274). It seems best to take Joshua's response as rhetorical, intended to produce a more thoughtful and therefore stronger commitment. Joshua based his assessment on God's holiness and jealousy. This is the only reference to God's holiness in Joshua. We do not usually consider jealousy a commendable quality, but Eichrodt called it "the basic element in the whole Old Testament idea of God" (1961, 210 n. 1).

Although jealousy and holiness have different semantic ranges, in this passage they converge to describe God's absolute intolerance of any disloyalty. If the Israelites commit to serve him but then forsake him by serving **foreign gods** (v 20), they forfeit access to his forgiveness (v 19). This strong statement should be understood analogously to what the NT describes as the unpardonable sin, the sin that cannot be forgiven because no forgiveness is sought. According to Kitchen, these verses represent the curses and blessings usually found in a covenant (as cited in Howard 1998a, 427).

3. People: Yes, We Will (24:21)

■ **21** The people firmly deny Joshua's assessment: **No!** (also monosyllabic in the Hebrew). They continue this emphasis in the next sentence, *but Yahweh we will serve*.

4. Joshua: Are You Sure? (24:22*a*)

■ **22*a*** Not one to back down from a challenge, Joshua's response is also strong. He frontloads **witnesses** (***witnesses are you with yourselves***). The **you** in **you have chosen** is emphatic, and **serve** appears again (one of nearly twenty uses of this root in this chapter).

5. People: We Are Sure (24:22*b*)

■ **22*b*** This time the Israelites respond with a strong affirmation, brief even for the normally laconic Hebrew. Their answer takes only one word: ***witnesses!*** Covenants need witnesses, a role ordinarily filled in the ANE by the panoply of gods. Israel itself takes on this role, soon to be joined by a stone that stood nearby (see vv 26-27).

6. Joshua: Reject Idolatry and Serve Yahweh (24:23)

■ **23** Since they have made their commitment, Joshua once again instructs the Israelites to **throw away** their idols (see v 14). As noted above, we need not assume widespread idolatry in Israel at this point. What Joshua commanded was a rejection of their inclination to deviate from complete loyalty to Yahweh. He also instructed them to **yield** their **hearts** to the **God of Israel**. **Yield** can convey the idea of turning an object to a particular purpose, such as a pitcher to pouring (Gen 24:14), a shoulder to lifting (49:15), a hand to working (Exod 6:6), or an ear to hearing (2 Kgs 19:16). To **yield** one's heart to Yahweh means to surrender it to his control, since he is Israel's rightful God.

7. People: We Will Serve Yahweh (24:24)

■ **24** In their response, the Israelites promise to **serve** Yahweh (see v 22*a*) and to **obey him**. Their response is emphatic, with *in Yahweh our God* placed first. Hess correctly observes that the "omission of an explicit note of obedience" to the command to rid themselves of idolatry is "ominous" (1996a, 307) given what we know of Israel's future history. We need not assume, however, that the Israelites were making this promise with their fingers crossed.

C. Renewal of Covenant (24:25-28)

■ **25-28** Ancient Near East covenants generally contained instructions regarding the reading and storage of the agreement. Verses 25-29 provide the closest counterpart in this chapter. By stating that Joshua **cut** a **covenant** for the people (v 25), the author may want the reader to envision a ceremony similar to what we see in Gen 15, with animals cut in half and the Israelite leaders passing between the pieces.

In addition to this sacred action, Joshua **reaffirmed for them decrees and laws** and **recorded these things in the Book of the Law of God** (vv 25-26). By **decrees and laws**, the author may be referring to a specific command to remain committed to Yahweh alone (Howard 1998a, 440) or to the "general content of the agreement" (Boling and Wright 1982, 539). The phrase **decrees and laws** (v 25) is used in Exod 15:25 to describe something less like a formal law and more like an agreement (see Exod 15:26) based on Israel's experience at Marah. The same phrase is found in Ezra 7:10 where it looks more like a description of the formal contents of the Mosaic law. The use of this phrase in Josh 24:25 more closely resembles what we find in Exod 15:25 than anything as official as the Mosaic law. As at Marah, the Israelites are here called to recommit themselves to Yahweh; the "decree and law" (the terms are singular in the Hebrew) represents a record of this recommitment.

What then does it mean that **Joshua recorded these things in the Book of Law of God** (v 26)? It seems unlikely that he was actually revising the Torah, as Butler suggests (1983, 277), since Joshua has always been subservient to this Law (see 1:7-8; 8:31-34; 22:5; 23:6). Equally unlikely is the suggestion that the **Book** in question is another book, not the written Mosaic law (see Howard 1998a, 440; Woudstra 1981, 357). Although this is the only appearance of the phrase, **the Book of the Law of God** in the OT, the **Book of the Law** in Joshua refers to the Mosaic law (see 1:8). It would appear that Joshua wrote down the **things** that took place on that occasion, or the *words* spoken (the Hebrew term could be translated either way). He wrote these either on a document that was placed in the ark alongside the Mosaic law (Keil and Delitzsch 1978, 233) or as a marginal note on the actual Law, as one might record a significant spiritual commitment in the margin of one's Bible.

Although the people had declared themselves witnesses to their agreement, Joshua **set . . . up** a **large stone** (v 26) as a second **witness** (v 27) to what God had spoken to them. Stones played an important role in the conquest and settlement of Canaan (see 4:20-24; 8:29; 10:27) and earlier (see Gen 28:16-22; 31:43-54; Exod 24:4), marking important moments in Israel's covenant history.

Trees also marked important sites. Pagans preferred wooded sites for their idolatrous worship, likely because of the fertility represented by the tree or for its shade (Isa 1:29; 57:5; Ezek 6:13; 20:28; Hos 4:13). God sometimes chose a wooded spot for an important moment (see Gen 12:6; Judg 9:6), as did God's people (Gen 35:4, 8). So it is not insignificant that Gen 35:4, Josh 24:26, and Judg 9:6 all describe the same general area, if not the same tree near Shechem. According to Keil and Delitzsch, the **holy place of the L**ORD

> under the oak at Shechem was nothing else than the holy place under the oak, where Abraham had formerly built an altar and worshipped the Lord, and where Jacob had purified his house from the strange gods, which he buried under this oak, or rather terebinth tree (Gen. xii. 6, 7, xxxv. 2, 4). (1978, 233)

After setting up the stone, Joshua reminded the people that Yahweh had **heard** all they had promised and that the stone was the **witness**. If they ever broke their promises, the stone's silent presence would testify against them. The only other place in Joshua where the verb rendered **untrue** (v 27) appears is in reference to the deceit of Achan (7:11).

After these words, Joshua **dismissed the people** to their **inheritance** (24:28). Hess points out that on three previous occasions, Joshua has sent someone out: the spies to Jericho (2:1) and to Ai (7:2), and the messengers to discover Achan's plunder (7:22). "Having completed the covenant with God," Hess explains, "there now begins the work of living faithfully in the land" (1996a, 309).

D. Final Matters (24:29-33)

1. Death and Burial of Joshua (24:29-30)

■ **29-30** Having faithfully carried out God's purposes, Joshua died at the ripe old age of 110. He was buried in Timnath Serah (or Timnath Heres), his inherited property (v 30; 19:49-50). The location of **Mount Gaash** is unknown. Note that he is once again called by his full name, **Joshua son of Nun**, a title that appears at significant moments in this book (see 1:1; 2:1, 23; 6:6; 14:1; 17:4; 19:49, 51; 21:1). Even more significant is Joshua's designation, **the servant of the Lord** (24:29). Often used of Moses, this is the first and only time in Scripture that it is used of Joshua. As Howard notes, God had promised to exalt him (see 3:7; 4:14) and has kept this promise (1998a, 444).

Verses 28-31 are found in Judg 2:6-9, although the content of v 31 is located between the content of vv 28 and 29. The LXX of v 30 is expanded: "There they placed with him in the tomb, into which they buried him, the stone knives with which he circumcised the sons of Israel in Gilgal, when he brought them out of Egypt, just as the Lord had commanded them, and they are there to this day" (as cited by Howard 1998a, 443). As with 21:42, the additional content may be original, but this seems doubtful.

2. Israel's Obedience (24:31)

■ **31** The addition of this verse demonstrates the continuing influence of Joshua's legacy and that **of the elders who outlived him**. Somehow these men were able to keep alive the memory of what God had done for Israel. Once that story ceased to be told and embraced, Israel's resolve, here affirmed so adamantly, began to weaken.

3. Joseph's Burial (24:32)

■ **32** Prior to his death in Egypt, Joseph made his family promise to take his bones with them when they left Egypt. Well before Israel's dark days of Egyptian slavery and the exodus that brought those days to an end, Joseph believed God's promise that Canaan would be given to Israel. By mentioning Joseph's burial in Canaan, the author of Joshua once again shows how God has kept his promise and draws the great pentateuchal story to a conclusion (Howard 1998a, 444). The price paid for the land, **a hundred pieces of silver (*a hundred kesitahs*)**, refers to an "obscure monetary unit" (Harrington and Saldarini 1987, 7). Its mention here, as Woudstra notes, may be the author's way of pointing out that "no longer is there need to buy a parcel of land!" (1981, 361).

4. Eleazar's Death (24:33)

■ **33** The final word in the book records the death and burial of Eleazar. This seems like a curious way to conclude, which may explain the LXX expansion:

> On that day the Israelites took the ark of God and carried it by themselves. Phinehas held the priesthood in place of Eleazar his father until he died. He was then buried in his own tomb in Gabaath. The Israelites each returned to their own places and towns. There they worshipped Astarte and Astaroth and the gods of the surrounding nations. So the LORD gave them into the hand of Eglon, the Moabite king, who ruled them for eighteen years. (As cited by Hess 1996a, 311 n. 2)

The more original ending was likely the MT. It mentions only that **Eleazar** died and was buried, either at the town of **Gibeah,** which had been allotted to **Phinehas** (NIV, ESV, NABRE, NJB, NRSV; see 15:57; 1 Sam 13:2; 15:34), on the hill of Phinehas (ASV, KJV, NASB, NJPS) or at Geba (modern Tel el-Ful; Pitkänen 2010, 400).

FROM THE TEXT

By addressing the generation then taking possession of Canaan as if they had been present in Egypt (Josh 24:5-7), God was pointing out the unity that exists in God's people from generation to generation. That unity extends to the present, enabling us to see ourselves as part of that covenant people who left Egypt and entered the promised land. Although God relates differently to his people since Christ, the differences are less like night and day and more like dawn to noon.

God remains as holy and jealous as he was on this occasion at Shechem, but since then we have come to see these qualities more clearly. We saw his jealousy at the destruction of Jerusalem in 586 B.C. (Ezek 23:25). His jealousy has never been more clearly seen than at Bethlehem, with Jesus' birth. There we saw a God so jealous for his people he became incarnate to win them back. We now understand that not only is God too holy to tolerate sin, but he is too holy to allow any trace of sin to remain. We now know, in light of the cross, that he will stop at nothing to remove it.

Joshua challenged the Israelites to choose whom they would serve: other gods, or the One who had faithfully kept all his promises to his people. The same choice remains for us today. This holy and jealous God has kept his promises, providing reconciliation with himself and the opportunity to settle in the promised land of full salvation. We must each choose whom we will serve.

www.ingramcontent.com/pod-product-compliance
Lightning Source LLC
Chambersburg PA
CBHW070301240426
43661CB00057B/2613